NEW TESTAMENT XI

JAMES, 1-2 PETER, 1-3 JOHN, JUDE

EDITED BY

GERALD BRAY

GENERAL EDITOR

THOMAS C. ODEN

IVP Academic

An imprint of InterVarsity Press
Downers Grove, Illinois

InterVarsity Press
P.O. Box 1400, Downers Grove, IL 60515-1426
ivpress.com
email@ivpress.com

InterVarsity Press® is the book-publishing division of InterVarsity Christian Fellowship/USA®, a movement of students and faculty active on campus at hundreds of universities, colleges, and schools of nursing in the United States of America, and a member movement of the International Fellowship of Evangelical Students. For information about local and regional activities, visit intervarsity.org.

Scripture quotations, unless otherwise noted, are from the Revised Standard Version of the Bible, *copyright 1946, 1952, 1971 by the Division of Christian Education of the National Council of the Churches of Christ in the U.S.A., and are used by permission.*

Selected excerpts from Fathers of the Church: A New Translation. Copyright 1947-. Used by permission of The Catholic University of America Press.

Cover design: David Fassett
Images: gold texture background: © Katsumi Murouchi / Getty Images
       stained glass cathedral window: © elzauer / Getty Images
       gold texture: © Katsumi Murouchi / Getty Images
       abstract marble pattern: © NK08gerd / iStock / Getty Images Plus

ISBN 978-0-8308-4363-3 (paperback)
ISBN 978-0-8308-1496-1 (hardcover)
ISBN 978-0-8308-9753-7 (digital)

Printed in the United States of America ∞

InterVarsity Press is committed to ecological stewardship and to the conservation of natural resources in all our operations. This book was printed using sustainably sourced paper.

Library of Congress Cataloging-in-Publication Data
A catalog record for this book is available from the Library of Congress.

P 32 31 30 29 28 27 26 25 24 23 22 21 20 19 18 17 16 15 14 13 12 11 10 9 8 7 6 5 4 3 2 1

Y 47 46 45 44 43 42 41 40 39 38 37 36 35 34 33 32 31 30 29 28 27 26 25 24 23 22 21 20 19

Contents

Introduction to the Catholic Epistles

To help the modern reader to explore the Catholic Epistles through the eyes of the ancient Christian writers, we will examine four preliminary issues:

Who wrote the Catholic Epistles?

Why are the Catholic Epistles important?

How were the patristic quotations used here selected?

How are references presented so as to enable the reader to easily locate the original
text and examine it in its context?

Who Wrote the Catholic Epistles?

This apparently simple question conceals one of the most longstanding controversies in the history of New Testament interpretation. Even in ancient times it was by no means agreed that the seven Catholic, or General, Epistles were written by the people to whom they were attributed. On the surface and in the mainstream tradition represented by the names that these letters bear in our Bibles today, they were the work of four different authors, all of whom were closely connected with Jesus and the first generation of the church. But the authenticity of these attributions of authorship was widely disputed, even if the letters themselves were generally accepted by the majority. This is clear from what our main source of information, Eusebius of Caesarea, had to say about them. In his famous *Ecclesiastical History* he wrote: "Disputed books which are nevertheless familiar to most include the epistles known as James, Jude and 2 Peter, and those called 2 John and 3 John, the work either of the Evangelist or of someone else with the same name."[1]

From this we may conclude that the two letters that are not mentioned (1 Peter and 1 John) were generally regarded as the authentic writings of the apostles of the same name, and this conclusion is supported by what Eusebius says elsewhere. Of 1 Peter he writes: "Of Peter one epistle, known as his first, is accepted, and this the early Fathers quoted freely, as undoubtedly genuine, in their own writings."[2] And of 1 John he says: "The Gospel of John and the epistle begin in the same way and are in agreement."[3] Agreement on these two may not have been universal, but it was sufficiently wide-

---

[1]*HCCC* 3.25 (FC 19:178).
[2]*HCCC* 3.3 (FC 19:139).
[3]*HCCC* 7.25 (FC 29:135)

spread to command general assent, and this view has held its own over the centuries. There have been some scholars who have dissented from this consensus, but even those who do not accept that 1 John is the work of the Beloved Disciple must agree that it is closely connected to the Fourth Gospel and that a common authorship of the two books is plausible, if not certain.

The widespread acceptance of 1 Peter and 1 John as authentic was important in the early church. It allowed the Fathers to use them freely because virtually everyone received them as canonical Scripture. Again, Eusebius points out that this habit can be traced back to Polycarp of Smyrna (c. 69-155), who made considerable use of 1 Peter in his *Epistle to the Philippians*.[4] Presumably Polycarp would not have done this if he did not believe that 1 Peter was authentic, and since he lived only a few years after the letter was written, he was in a good position to know what its origin was.

Identification of 1 John as the work of the Beloved Disciple can be traced back as far as Origen (c. 185-c. 254), again thanks to Eusebius, who preserves a fragment from a commentary on John's Gospel that is otherwise lost. Apparently Origen was also prepared to accept that 2 and 3 John were the apostle's work, though he admitted that their authenticity was more widely questioned.[5] There is no doubt that 2 and 3 John come from a single author who identifies himself merely as the elder. This did not worry most of the Fathers, who noted that the other Johannine works were also anonymous,[6] but they at least allowed for the possibility that there may have been a John the Elder who is otherwise unknown to us. The short length of the epistles makes it difficult to say much about the circumstances in which they were written, and no early writer seems to have thought that the matter was important enough to warrant a full investigation. Broadly speaking, the same position holds the field to this day. The letters have a common author, probably somebody called John, and they are connected with the other Johannine literature. This makes it possible to argue for the Beloved Disciple's authorship without providing conclusive evidence for it, and it seems unlikely that we shall ever advance much further than that.

On the basis of this testimony we can say that the parameters of the dispute mentioned by Eusebius were in place by about A.D. 200, and possibly well before that. Of the remaining letters, James and Jude were rejected by some, and apparently this had the effect of limiting the use which was made of them, but they were nevertheless widely known in the church. Eusebius's summary of the situation may be regarded as a fair assessment. He writes: "The first of the 'General' Epistles is attributed to James. Admittedly its authenticity is doubted, since few early writers refer to it, any more than to Jude's, which is also one of the seven called General. But the fact remains that these

---

[4]HCCC 3.14 (FC 19:233). References in Polycarp's *Epistle to the Philippians* are to 1 Pet 1:8 (1.3); 1:13, 21 (2.1); 3:9 (2.2); 2:11 (5.3); 4:7 (7.2); 2:22, 24 (8.1); 2:12 (10.2).

[5]HCCC 6.25 (FC 29:49-50): "In the fifth book of his commentary on John's Gospel, Origen said that in addition to it, John left an epistle of a very few lines and possibly two more, though their authenticity is denied by some. Anyway, they do not total a hundred lines between them."

[6]Apart from Revelation, which some rejected precisely because it bore the apostle's name, something that was thought to be out of character for him.

two, like the others, have been regularly used in very many churches."[7]

In the canonical collection pride of place was normally given to James, because it was believed that his letter was the first of the seven to have been written, and this view would be widely supported by modern scholarship. The identity of James has caused some difficulty, since there were two apostles who bore that name, as did one of the brothers of Jesus, but Eusebius and the serious commentators of the early church all attributed the letter to the last of these. James the brother of Jesus was the leader of the Jerusalem church from A.D. 44 until he was martyred (at the instigation of the Jewish authorities) in 62, and his authorship of the letter is at least as plausible as any alternative suggestion.[8] If this James is the author of the letter bearing that name, then the letter ascribed to Jude could have been the work of his brother, a view that the Fathers generally accepted and that still commands considerable support. The main difficulty with Jude is that, like 2 and 3 John, it is so short that it is difficult to know what to say about its origin, and the traditional ascription remains as plausible as any, if only for want of evidence to the contrary.

Real controversy has been limited to 2 Peter, though this goes back a long way. Once again, the fairest presentation of the matter is the one given by Eusebius: "The second Petrine epistle we have been taught to regard as uncanonical, though many have thought it valuable and have honored it with a place among the other Scriptures. On the other hand, in the case of the Acts attributed to him, the Gospel that bears his name, the Preaching called his and the so-called Apocalypse, we have no reason at all to include them among the traditional Scriptures, for neither in the early days nor in our own has any church writer made use of their testimony. These then are the works attributed to Peter, of which I acknowledge only one epistle as genuine and recognized by the early Fathers."[9] From this we can see that Eusebius himself rejected 2 Peter as canonical, as did the majority of the Greek Fathers who examined the matter at all seriously. The result is that the letter is seldom quoted in their writings, though its contents are occasionally alluded to. But Eusebius is forced to admit that 2 Peter is quite different from other spurious works attributed to the apostle, and he recognizes that many people have found it valuable and regarded it as canonical, which means that they accepted that Peter was its author.

However, even those who were prepared to accept the genuineness of 2 Peter were forced to admit that it was very different from 1 Peter, and they sought different explanations for this. Perhaps, it was suggested, Peter used a different secretary or even attempted to write the letter himself. This is not an absurd suggestion, since the polished Greek of 1 Peter is very unlikely to have been the work of a Galilean fisherman, but of course there is no way of proving it. Then too, some of the

---

[7]*HCCC* 2.23 (FC 19:130).
[8]It has been defended, for example, by L. T. Johnson, *The Letter of James* (Garden City, N.Y.: Doubleday, 1995), who examines the whole question in some detail.
[9]*HCCC* 3.3 (FC 19:139-40).

differences might be accounted for by saying that Peter was deliberately adopting a humbler tone than he had used in his first letter, perhaps in response to a criticism that he had been allowing his exalted position as chief of the apostles to go to his head. Modern scholarship has tended to reject the letter's authenticity, though it still finds defenders and almost everyone would agree with Eusebius that 2 Peter is far removed from the spurious Petrine works that he names and rejects. A particular difficulty with 2 Peter is the very personal tone that its author adopts. There is no question that he wants people to believe that he is the apostle Peter, as his intimate recounting of the transfiguration of Jesus makes clear. Given that 2 Peter, like the other Catholic Epistles, is largely concerned to defend the true apostolic preaching against the counterfeit versions of various heretics, these personal details and the claims attached to them take on particular importance. If 2 Peter is pseudonymous, then it is worth nothing because its author is even more hypocritical than the heretics he is condemning. Faced with this conclusion, majority opinion in the early church swung behind the view that 2 Peter is the authentic work of the apostle, and by the time of Bede (673-735) the personal allusions in it were regularly cited as proof of this.

To summarize all this, we may say that defenders of the authenticity of the Catholic Epistles relied mainly on historical considerations, whereas those who rejected them preferred literary (stylistic) arguments. Historically speaking, there was no one in the first generation of the church who could plausibly be regarded as a second Peter or John, and so the tendency to attribute the letters bearing their names to these two apostles was thereby strengthened. James and Jude both appear in the New Testament as brothers of Jesus, which also gave the attributions of the corresponding letters greater plausibility. On the other side, differences of style (especially in the case of 1 and 2 Peter) and of presentation (particularly of 1 John, over against the other Johannine letters) argued against common authorship in those cases. Modern scholarship is much more detailed and sophisticated than anything attempted by the Fathers, but it is hard to say that it has advanced much further. Literary considerations are still the strongest arguments for those who deny the traditional ascriptions of authorship, and those who defend them still use the historical argument that there is no compelling alternative explanation that obliges us to reject the tradition. If due weight is given to these opposing arguments, it is possible, according to modern scholarship, to rank the Catholic Epistles as follows:

Probably authentic: 1 Peter, 1 John

Possibly authentic: James, 2 John, 3 John, Jude

Doubtfully authentic: 2 Peter

This was the state of affairs in the early fourth century, and broadly speaking it remains the position today. All that remains to be said is that of the possibly authentic letters James was generally more highly regarded than the rest and was included in the Antiochene canon along with 1 Peter and 1 John. In the fourth century this must have meant that these three were accepted as authentic at Antioch, though this was disputed by Isho'dad of Merv (c. 850), who has left us an interesting commentary on them. He says, "I am writing commentaries on the three catholic epistles [James, 1 Peter and 1 John]. About these three Eusebius of Caesarea and others say that they really are by the apostles, but others deny this because their style is not apostolic. Theodore of Mopsuestia does not mention them at all, although he draws illustrations from the Testament of Job, Wisdom and Ben Sira [Ecclesiasticus], which are not inspired by the Holy Spirit but written by human learning alone."[10] Isho'dad clearly did not believe that any of the letters were authentic, though how fairly he represents the position of Theodore of Mopsuestia (d. 428) is impossible to say. All that we know for certain is that long after the Greek and Latin churches had both accepted the canonicity and therefore the authenticity of all seven Catholic Epistles, there was still a voice on the edge of the Christian world that was prepared to voice the ancient skepticism, and that in its most radical form.

Why Are the Catholic Epistles Important?

The importance of the Catholic Epistles lies primarily in the fact that they offer a non-Pauline witness to the beliefs and practices of the first Christian communities. It is true that they are not the only non-Pauline voice in the New Testament, but they are the only group of letters that has never been associated in any way with the great apostle to the Gentiles. Letters, by their very nature, have an immediacy that is lacking in more formal documents, and it has long been held that in them we get a truer picture of early church life than is available to us in the Gospels or in the Acts of the Apostles. Whoever the writers were, they were responding to real needs in the early Christian communities, and by examining these problems we can reconstruct the intellectual and spiritual atmosphere that shaped the first generations of the church.

There can be no doubt that this is how the Fathers themselves regarded these letters. To them, the Catholic Epistles were all written in order to defend orthodox faith and morals against the rising challenge of the heretics who were still a major problem in their own time. This gave the Catholic Epistles a freshness and a relevance to conditions in the fourth and fifth centuries that might otherwise seem surprising, since the Jewish Christian milieu in and to which they were written had almost vanished by that time. The Fathers were not unaware of the original Jewish context that governed the composition of these letters, and they make particular reference to it when commenting on James and 1 Peter, since both authors state explicitly that they are writing to Diaspora Jews who have accepted Christ. But the letters say little or nothing about the tensions between Jews and Gentiles in the church, which figure so prominently in Romans and Galatians, and when Gentiles are mentioned, the word clearly refers to people who were pagans. This does not mean that the

---

[10]*CIM* 36.

churches had no Gentile converts in them, but any that they may have had were either ignored or (more likely) regarded as Jewish believers.

That suggests that the Catholic Epistles must date from a very early time, but the Fathers had little historical sense where heresy was concerned. They often interpreted the Catholic Epistles as anticipatory attacks on Marcion, who drew a radical distinction between the Creator (whom he identified with the God of the Old Testament) and the Father of Jesus Christ, and many thought that 1 John in particular was written in anticipation of the Arians, whom they obviously realized did not exist as such in the first century. The reason why they could think this way is simple. To them, truth was eternal, and deviations from it had existed from the beginning. The ultimate cause of heresy was the devil, who had always been a liar and who had tempted Adam and Eve away from the bliss that God had originally intended for the human race to enjoy. It did not matter to them what the precise details of individual deviations might be. Just as the authors of the letters referred to the Old Testament when attacking dissidents in their own time, whom they compared quite naturally to Cain, the Sodomites, Korah and Balaam, so the Fathers were not bothered about who John thought the antichrist was. All that mattered to them was that the apostle used the word to describe church members who had abandoned the orthodox faith and begun to teach their own versions of Christianity instead. Such people were plentiful in the fourth and fifth centuries, and they were all antichrists, whatever the precise nature of their heresy might have been. By the same token, the Fathers never questioned the assumption that their orthodoxy was identical with that of the apostles, and they had no hesitation in reading the Catholic Epistles as statements of the post-Nicene faith.

This confident assumption runs counter to the historical-critical approach of modern scholarship, but even if it can be proved that the Fathers were wrong in particular details (e.g., everyone would now admit that none of the Catholic Epistles was specifically directed against Marcion), it may legitimately be objected against the modern consensus that there is a general assumption in them of an apostolic orthodoxy doing battle against deviations that were largely the product of renegade Christians (i.e., heretics, not Jews or pagans). This in turn means that they offer important evidence for the existence of an identifiable body of acceptable beliefs in the earliest Christian congregations that had been transmitted by the apostles in the full awareness that they would be objected to and opposed by others. Even if the words *orthodoxy* and *heresy* are technically anachronistic, the phenomena that they describe can be traced to the first century and to a church that was still primarily Jewish, not Gentile, in composition.

Another way in which the Catholic Epistles are important is that they make it clear that Christian faith is a matter of practice as well as of formal belief. Peter, James and John are all agreed on the assumption that faith without works is dead. They do not mean and none of the Fathers took them to mean that it is possible to earn one's way to heaven by doing good works; indeed, such a notion was firmly resisted by almost all the ancient commentators. The works spoken of in these letters are not those of the Mosaic law but those that spring naturally from faith in Jesus Christ. The Catholic Epistles insist that actions speak louder than words and that the latter must always be backed up by deeds that correspond to them and give them meaning. What the epistles and the Fathers who interpreted them understood by "works" can be summarized in three words: self-sacrifice, generosity and humility. The former meant that Christians must be prepared to give their lives, if necessary, for their faith. The patient endurance of suffering here and now is a preparation for this supreme sacrifice, as the example of Jesus' earthly life bears witness. Generosity is seen primarily in almsgiving and in hospitality, both of which were regarded as essential marks of the true believer. In an age in which there was no form of Social Security or even a reliable network of inns for passing strangers, generosity of this kind was immediately noticed by everyone, and where it was practiced it became one of the most impressive things about the Christian community. Humility was the spiritual foundation of both self-sacrifice and generosity. Toward God, humility meant recognizing that we have done nothing to save ourselves and even as Christians remain entirely dependent on his grace. Toward other people, humility was to be seen in a kind of behavior that avoided arrogant criticism of the failings of others. Christians were expected to hold their tongues and instead to do all in their power to help each other overcome their weaknesses, on the understanding that everyone has them. Even the elders of the church were to exercise their authority in a humble way, by respecting and encouraging those under their authority. The governing principle of life in the Christian community is love, for God and for one another. The two can be distinguished but never separated, and Christians must learn that their professed love for God in heaven will be judged by their behavior toward their fellow believers here on earth.

Perhaps the most significant feature of the Catholic Epistles is the way in which they are manuals of spiritual warfare. It is a basic assumption common to all of them that we are in the midst of a cosmic struggle between good and evil. This struggle takes place in heaven (understood as the spiritual realm) and on earth, with a hierarchy of forces arrayed as in table 1.

Good	Evil
God	
Angels	Demons
Chosen people	Unbelievers

Table 1. Hierarchy of forces in spiritual warfare

The cosmic struggle is not a form of dualism, because good and evil are not equal or independent of each other. What is now evil was originally created by God and was therefore good. The evil that we see now is the result of a rebellion against God the Creator; it is not inherent in the nature of the beings who are caught up in it. The demons have a leader whom we call Satan but who is not mentioned by this name in the Catholic Epistles, which prefer to call him "the evil one" or "the devil." God does not fight him directly, because such a contest would be unequal. Instead, the fight against the devil and the demons is waged by angels, such as Michael, who disputed with him over the body of Moses.[11] At the level of belief, however, there is complete agreement in the spiritual world, where the demons know God and fear him just as much as the angels do. The struggle is therefore not one of faith but one of works, because in spite of what they know to be true about God, the demons are still in revolt against him.

At the human level things are more complicated. In principle human beings are divided into those who belong to God (the elect) and those who do not (the condemned). Although this division is fixed in the mind of God, it is not fully apparent to us. The first reason for this is that many of the elect are still trapped in the clutches of the devil and his demons, waiting for the proclamation of the gospel message which alone can set them free. The second reason is that the devil is a deceiver and has infiltrated the ranks of the elect with his own servants. These people look as if they have been saved, but in reality they are still in the devil's power and are doing their best to fool the elect into turning away from the new light and life that they have received in Christ. They are anti-Christ, but however numerous and diverse they may seem, fundamentally they are all one. To complicate matters still further, a number of people belong to the company of the elect but have not yet fully understood the implications of this. These are the people to whom the authors of the Catholic Epistles are primarily writing. They have been born again into God's family, but they still have a lot of growing up to do. Very often they have not seen the practical implications of their new faith and so do not live up to its demands. Sometimes they have not fully absorbed the right teaching, which makes them prone to fall back into idolatry and other pagan ways. In the final analysis the devil cannot subvert the elect, but as long as he can play on their weaknesses he stands a chance of dividing the church against itself and making its witness ineffective in the world. Such tactics will eventually be exposed and defeated, but believers who have allowed such things to happen must not imagine that they will escape God's judgment on their behavior.

Virtually everything in the Catholic epistles can be understood once this basic framework is grasped. In particular, the cosmic dimension of the struggle explains the interest that the writers have in the way in which this warfare is conducted in the spiritual realm. This is why we read here of things like the descent of Christ into hell[12] and the way in which angels conduct themselves under fire.[13] The Fathers had a particular interest in such matters and spent a good deal of time trying to explain their

---

[11]Jude 9.
[12]1 Pet 3:18-19.
[13]2 Pet 2:11.

meaning to the church. In this way the Catholic Epistles show us to what extent and in what way the early church appropriated the world of Jewish eschatological mysticism, which, thanks to modern discoveries and research, is now much more familiar than it has been at any time since these epistles were written. From James, Peter, John and Jude we learn that there was some truth in this mysticism, which must be understood within the wider framework of the cosmic struggle between good and evil already mentioned. This struggle takes different forms at different times, and its modern representatives may be as superficially different from the heretics of the first-century church as they were from people like Korah and Balaam. But underneath it is only one battle, which will be fought by God's people until the end of time, when Christ will come again to judge the living and the dead. That end is never far away but grows nearer with every passing day. In this sense the message of these letters is not merely valid for all time; as time itself comes to an end, their message becomes even more urgent, because the battle is reaching its climax and ultimate victory is in sight. This is the hope for which we live and the faith which we practice in that love which is God's unique blessing to those whom he has chosen, for it is nothing less than his own presence dwelling in the heart of every believer.

How Were the Patristic Quotations Used Here Selected?

Allusions to the text of the Catholic Epistles are almost all that we have to go on for the very earliest period (before A.D. 200), and so a selection of quotations from authors like Justin Martyr, Irenaeus and Tertullian has been given in order to give readers a flavor of how these letters were used before commentary writing became common. These allusions must be used with a certain degree of caution, since in almost every case the writer was making some other point and merely alluding to one of the Catholic Epistles in order to bolster his argument. For the purposes of this collection, an effort has been made to ensure that such references do have a genuine link with the relevant epistle, but even so, readers will be well advised to treat this material with discretion.

Fortunately, we possess a considerable number of commentaries on the epistles, most of which have survived more or less intact. From very early times it seems to have been the practice, at least in the Greek-speaking church, to regard the Catholic Epistles as a unit. Initially it seems that a distinction was made between the "catholic" epistles, which included all the ones that claimed apostolic authority, and the "canonical" epistles, which referred only to those that were recognized by the church as authentically apostolic. In spite of some lingering doubts about James, it can be said that by the early fourth century, if not before, there was a core canon of three letters: James, 1 Peter and 1 John. This canon was accepted by the whole church. Later on the other four letters were also recognized in the West and in most of the East, though the Antiochene tradition that later gave rise to Nestorianism resisted this trend. Nevertheless it seems that many churches recognized more than three letters as canonical from the beginning, and it is even possible that a majority recognized all seven.

The first commentator of the canonical epistles was Clement of Alexandria (b. c. 150; fl. 190-

215), who wrote on the basic three plus Jude. His commentary *Adumbrations* was a kind of interlinear gloss on the text, and it survives only in a Latin translation made by Cassiodorus in the sixth century. Unfortunately we have no way of knowing whether we possess the entire text or only those parts of it known to or liked by Cassiodorus. This does not matter very much in some ways, but it would be nice to know what Clement made of 2 Peter and of 2 and 3 John. The fact that there is no extant commentary by him on these books leads us to suppose that he rejected their authenticity, but this is an argument from silence and may not be correct.[14]

Following Clement, the next Greek-speaking commentator of importance was Didymus the Blind, also of Alexandria (c. 313-398). He definitely commented on all seven epistles, but we know from what survives that he did not accept 2 Peter as authentic. Presumably he included it because by his time it had become traditional to do so, at least at Alexandria, though he did his best to relegate it to a kind of deuterocanonical status. Didymus's commentary is fully extant only in a Latin translation that appears from the surviving Greek fragments to be a reasonably faithful rendering of the original. It is important because Didymus seems to have been the chief source for the later Greek commentary tradition, which consisted of a series of excerpts taken from different writers and pasted together to form a chain or *catena*, to use the Latin equivalent.

The first and in some ways most important catena is attributed to a seventh-century monk called Andreas, about whom we know nothing other than that he selected the relevant texts. Many of these can be identified from other sources but many cannot, and therefore we cannot say to what extent this catena contains original material. In this selection all references to Andreas must therefore be treated with some caution; they may be his, but more probably they come from some other source that is now lost. In any case, the sources that Andreas used were earlier than his own time, and so they represent a patristic opinion that may be said to have become in some sense a commonplace of biblical exposition by the time Andreas got round to passing it on. Among the identifiable sources are several selections from sermons preached by John Chrysostom that have not otherwise survived. It is also largely thanks to him that we have important selections from Ammonius of Alexandria (fifth century), Eusebius of Emesa (c. 300-c. 359), Hesychius of Jerusalem (fifth century), Severus of Antioch (c. 465-538) and even Maximus the Confessor (580-662). However, it appears that important people like Theodore of Mopsuestia avoided the Catholic Epistles, and it has to be said that the Greek tradition is not nearly as rich as it would have been had these letters been more widely accepted as canonical Scripture.

There are two later catenae, one of which is an eighth century commentary attributed to Oecumenius, a sixth-century orator and philosopher, but this identification is disputed.[15] The other is

---

[14]John Calvin, for example, has left us no commentary on 2 or 3 John, but he regarded them both as canonical.
[15]Not to be confused with Oecumenius the bishop of Tricca, fl. tenth century.

attributed to Theophylact of Ohrid, a Byzantine archbishop of Bulgaria (c. 1050-c. 1108, fl. 1070-1081). The first of these cannot be the direct work of Oecumenius, at least not in its present form, and is usually dated to the ninth century or later. However, it is at least possible that in the sixth century Oecumenius played some part in its composition and transmission.[16] The second may well be the work of Theophylact in its final form, though like both Andreas and Oecumenius, he was highly dependent on earlier compilers. Both catenae show the influence of Didymus the Blind and clearly depend on common sources. Whether Theophylact used Oecumenius is less clear because although there are many resemblances between them there are also a number of differences that make it difficult to say that his work is no more than a further recension of Oecumenius. It is also hard to tell whether or to what extent they used Andreas, once again because of the use of common source material to which Theophylact may have had independent access. It extends beyond the range of this series to seek to engage in form-critical study to discern proximately the sources of these catenae, but that is a task that invites future scholarly speculation.

In the Latin world the catena tradition did not catch on until much later. The Catholic Epistles were frequently referred to by Augustine and Jerome, and the former has left us ten essays on 1 John. There was also an Augustinian commentary on James, put together by his students, as he himself tells us: "Among my works I found *An Explanation of the Epistle of James*. During my review of it I noticed that what were no more than annotations for the exposition of certain passages in the epistle had been collected into a book, through the diligence of my brothers who did not want them to be left in the margins of the manuscript. These notes are of some help, but when I dictated them we did not have an accurate translation of the epistle from the Greek."[17] The loss of this commentary is particularly unfortunate, as it would be most interesting to read what Augustine had to say about the relationship between faith and works that James upholds so strongly. Perhaps his views on the subject would have been little different from what we find elsewhere, but it would be fascinating to see how his exegesis of such a text might have been influenced by the Pelagian controversy.

After Augustine's time there is the first full-scale Latin commentary by Hilary of Arles (401-449). It contains a great deal of fascinating information, despite a strong tendency to digress into fanciful etymologies and the like. Hilary became an important source for later writers, including Gregory the Great (d. 604). Gregory did not write a commentary on the catholic epistles as such, but what he had to say about them was collected by his secretary Paterius and circulated as a kind of catena. This was imitated and extended in the twelfth century by a French monk called Alulfus, and the two works bear eloquent witness to the popularity that Gregory enjoyed throughout the Middle Ages.

---

[16]The premise on which we include this commentary in our collection is that it draws from sources within our time frame, which ends mid eighth century. We will refer to this document as it has typically been referenced—the Catena on the Catholic Epistles—and attribute it to Oecumenius, or perhaps more modestly, Pseudo-Oecumenius.

[17]*Retractations* 58 (FC 60:186).

By far the greatest of the Latin commentaries on the Catholic Epistles is that of Bede the Venerable. His knowledge of history, geography and etymology was encyclopedic, and usually accurate, which is more than one can say of Hilary. More importantly, Bede goes beyond merely explaining difficult texts and develops what amounts to a manual of pastoral instruction, using the Catholic Epistles as his source material. He combines exegesis, theology and practical application in a way that is oddly reminiscent of the seventeenth-century Puritans and of the great Anglo-American preachers of more recent times. The latter may not be aware of it, but there does seem to be an Anglo-Saxon tradition of spiritual reading that can be traced down through the centuries and of which Bede is by no means the meanest example.

A selection referenced simply as *Catena* refers to *Catena in Epistolas Catholicas* (ed. J. A. Cramer [Oxford: Clarendon Press, 1840]). These selections were presented in their Greek and Latin original form by Cramer, untranslated into English. We have provided English translations and sought to provide, where possible, fuller references for them.

Outside the Greek and Latin worlds use of the Catholic Epistles was restricted by lingering doubts about their canonicity. The surviving ninth-century commentary of the Nestorian Isho'dad of Merv makes it clear that although he felt obliged to deal with the three core books, which the Nestorians regarded as canonical, he himself did not believe in the authenticity of any one of them. In those circumstances neither commentary writing nor practical application of the texts was likely to get very far, and so the oriental traditions, which are so rich in other ways, have contributed little to our understanding of these particular letters.

How Are References Presented?

Gaining access to writings that were produced long ago in ancient languages is never an easy matter, and translations into English do not always help us very much. A number of such translations were made in the nineteenth century, which was a great age of patristic scholarship, but the style of the English is often dated. Modern readers do not want to plow through long sentences full of subordinate clauses and polysyllabic words whose meaning is clear only to those with a classical education. It is also the case that the Fathers wrote to be read aloud, not silently, and they are therefore much more rhetorical in their style than we would be. Sometimes this is attractive, but more often than not the modern reader finds it high-blown and irritating. It can also become unnecessarily repetitive and even disjointed in places, as speech often is.

In this edition, all that has been smoothed out. Contemporary style has been preferred, even when this has meant recasting the literal wording of the original text. Because we are presenting extracts, not complete texts, it has sometimes been necessary to supply bridging material that is not explicitly in the original text, but that is either implied by it or is contained there at much greater length. Rather than quoting an entire page merely to retain a particular sentence, we have at times taken the liberty of condensing such paragraphs into a sentence or two, using ellipses so as not to detract from the essence of what the Father in question was trying to say. Existing English translations have been consulted and used to some extent, but we have felt free to alter them to fit the style and needs of the present edition, so that it is only occasionally that their wording has been preserved intact. In particular we have tried to establish some consistency in the rendering of theological terms, and whenever possible we have opted for the variants that are normally used by theologians today. All this may cause a certain amount of irritation to the professional scholar, but it should be remembered that the purpose of this commentary is to allow the Fathers to speak to the present generation, not to give people the impression that it is necessary to have a classical Greek or Latin education in order to understand them.

When selections are taken from complete commentaries organized sequentially on a verse-by-verse basis, such as those of Andreas, Hilary of Arles, Bede, Oecumenius and Theophylact, only brief forms of references are given. In many cases these commentaries are untranslated, and we have translated in this series only the portion of them relevant to our editorial premises. It is assumed that anyone wishing to consult the original will have only to look up the relevant chapter and verse of the commentary in question. Hence where the commentary references appear, the reader may proceed directly to the commentary referred to and consult the specific Scripture text under discussion. Apart from line-to-line commentaries, however, quotations are referenced according to source, either in the original language or translation. Where possible, reference is also made to the best available English translation, though the reader must be warned that what is found in this book is at most a dearchaized adaptation of that and probably not a direct quotation.

Each selection is referenced first by its title and in some cases by its book, chapter and section reference (and subsection where necessary), and then it is footnoted by an abbreviated citation (normally citing the book, volume and page number), usually in its original source and in some cases in translation. For the convenience of computer users, many of the digital database references are provided in the appendix, either to the Thesaurus Linguae Graecae or to the Latin Cetedoc. Some previous English translations have been dearchaized or amended for easier reading. We have in some cases edited out superfluous conjunctions for easier reading.

Furthermore, each group of verses is preceded by a short overview that gives the reader some idea of what the following discussion is about. Where there are notable differences of opinion among the Fathers, or where one of them has presented a particularly significant argument, this is also noted, so that readers may be alerted to the particular importance of the selection that follows. The function of the overview in a given pericope is to provide a brief appraisal of all the comments to follow and to show that there is a reasonably cohesive thread of argument among passages taken from diverse sources and generations. We concede that the overview might reasonably be stated by other perceptive interpreters in various ways using other editorial criteria.

Where a selection has no heading, the previous heading applies. In some cases there may be several selections grouped under a single heading. Or when the selection is either very short or very obvious, no heading is included. Headings were selected[18] to identify either a key phrase of the text being commented upon, a key metaphor in the comment or some core idea of the selection.

It remains only to be said that the main purpose of this volume is to edify the communion of saints so that Christians today may be encouraged to examine and appropriate what the writers of an earlier time, many of whom have been canonized by the tradition of the church and all of whom are still worth reading, had to say about some of the greatest letters ever written—the seven Catholic, or General, Epistles. May God by his grace open the hearts and minds of all who read these texts, and may we, together with them, come to that perfect peace and joy that is the inheritance of the saints in light.

Gerald Bray
Feast of St. Gregory the Great

---

[18]By the general editor.

THE EPISTLE
OF JAMES

1:1 JAMES INTRODUCES HIMSELF

¹James, a servant of God and of the Lord Jesus Christ,
To the twelve tribes in the Dispersion:
Greeting.

OVERVIEW: In his letter to the churches, James identifies himself as a servant of Christ sent to the Jews of the Diaspora. In the early church it was customary to assume that New Testament books had been written by apostles or under the close supervision of an apostle, and two of the original twelve were called James. One of these was the brother of John and son of Zebedee, and the other was the son of Alphaeus. The first of these was the associate of Peter and John and became the first head of the church at Jerusalem, where he was martyred about A.D. 44. The second disappeared from view after the resurrection of Jesus. Some of the Fathers assumed that one of these two wrote this letter, though they were not sure which one. Most Fathers, though, concluded that it was another James, the one who appears in the New Testament among the brothers of Jesus. This James was head of the Jerusalem church from A.D. 44 to 62 and is a much more plausible candidate for authorship than either of the others. The assumption then was that this James, whose authority derived from his close kinship with Jesus, was writing from the Jewish capital to those Jews who had left Palestine and were scattered across the Roman world. The fact that he refers to himself as a "servant" was regarded as a sign of his humility and as standing in sharp contrast to the usual letter-writing practice of the time. Today the authenticity of James is still questioned, but most scholars recognize that it must be one of the earliest New Testament writings. The authorship of James the brother of Jesus continues to find its defenders and must be regarded as plausible, even if it cannot be proved now any more than it could be in patristic times. To be a slave of Christ is, for the apostles, greater than having command of all the kingdoms of the world (DIDYMUS, OECUMENIUS). This is a voluntary servant-hood (HILARY OF ARLES). James wrote this letter to those suffering persecution (BEDE).

1:1 The Identity of James

THE MARTYRDOM OF JAMES. JOSEPHUS: Caesar sent Albinus to Judea as procurator when he was informed of the death of Festus. But the younger Annas, who as I said had received the high priesthood, was headstrong in character and audacious in the extreme. He belonged to the sect of the Sadducees, who in judging offenders are cruel beyond any of the Jews, as I have already made clear. Being a man of this kind, Annas thought that he had a convenient opportunity, as Festus was dead and Albinus still on the way. So he assembled a council of judges and brought it before James, the brother of Jesus, known as Christ, and several others. Annas charged them with breaking the law and handed them over to be stoned. But those who were considered the most fair-minded people in the city, and strict in their observance of the law, were most indignant at this, and sent secretly to the king, imploring him to write to Annas to stop behaving in this way. His conduct had been wrong from the first. Some of them too waylaid Albinus on the road from Alexandria and explained that it was illegal for Annas to assemble a council without his authority. Convinced by their arguments, Albinus wrote an angry letter to Annas, threatening to punish him. In consequence, King Agrippa deprived him of the high priesthood, which he had held for three months only, and appointed Jeshua son of Dammaeus. JEWISH ANTIQUITIES 20.9.1.[1]

SLAVES OF GOD. DIDYMUS THE BLIND: Those who seek worldly glory display the qualifications which they think they have in their correspondence. But the apostles boast, at the beginning of their letters, that they are slaves of God and Christ. CATENA.[2]

VOLUNTARY SERVANTHOOD. HILARY OF ARLES: Christ deigned to reveal himself to James after his passion, and eventually it

became proverbial to say: "He appeared also to James."[3] James refers to himself as a servant, but we must remember that there are two kinds of servitude, voluntary and involuntary. The involuntary servant is a slave who fears punishment, and therefore his service does not spring from love. But the voluntary servant is really no different from a son. INTRODUCTORY TRACTATE ON THE LETTER OF JAMES.[4]

TO THE PERSECUTED. BEDE: We read that when Stephen was martyred a great persecution of the church broke out at Jerusalem and that they were all scattered across the countryside of Judea and Samaria, except for the apostles. James then wrote this letter to those who had been scattered because they had suffered persecution for the sake of righteousness. And not only to them, but also, as the rest of the letter testifies, to those who had become Christians but who were still struggling to achieve perfection, as well as to those who remained outside the faith themselves and did their best to persecute and disturb believers. All of these people were exiles, though for different reasons. But we also read in the Acts of the Apostles that at the time of our Lord's death there were devout Jews "from every nation under heaven."[5] What these nations were is explained a little further on, where Luke mentions Parthians, Medes, Elamites, inhabitants of Mesopotamia, and so on.[6] James also exhorts the righteous not to lose their faith, and he rebukes sinners, warning them that they must refrain from sinning and practice virtue, so that they would not be

---

[1] Since the Jewish historian Josephus is the key source for this narrative, I quote him in this collection, which otherwise is limited to ancient Christian writers. [2] CEC 2. [3] 1 Cor 15:7. [4] PL Supp. 3:60, 62. [5] Acts 2:5. [6] Acts 2:9-10.

condemned by those who had received the sacraments of faith in an unfruitful way, even worthy of hell. He goes now to warn unbelievers to repent of the murder of the Savior and of the other crimes in which they were implicated before divine retribution overtook them secretly, or even openly for that matter. CONCERNING THE EPISTLE OF ST. JAMES.[7]

SLAVES OF CHRIST. OECUMENIUS: More than any worldly dignity, the Lord's apostles gloried in the fact that they were slaves of Christ. That is how they wanted to be known in their preaching, in their writing and in their teaching. COMMENTARY ON JAMES.[8]

TO THE TWELVE TRIBES IN DISPERSION. ISHO'DAD OF MERV: The opening resembles the titles of St. Paul's letters, and perhaps James is the author of it, whoever he may be. He was unacquainted with Paul's custom of writing to one particular nation and city, and for a particular reason. Instead, this author writes to the twelve tribes scattered among the nations because of the captivity, and not to the churches in every place, because he had no particular reason to be so specific. COMMENTARIES, PROLOGUE.[9]

---

[7]PL 93:10-11. [8]PG 119:456. [9]CIM 36.

1:2-15 TRIALS AND TEMPTATIONS

[2]*Count it all joy, my brethren, when you meet various trials, [3]for you know that the testing of your faith produces steadfastness. [4]And let steadfastness have its full effect, that you may be perfect and complete, lacking in nothing.*

[5]*If any of you lacks wisdom, let him ask God, who gives to all men generously and without reproaching, and it will be given him. [6]But let him ask in faith, with no doubting, for he who doubts is like a wave of the sea that is driven and tossed by the wind. [7,8]For that person must not suppose that a double-minded man, unstable in all his ways, will receive anything from the Lord.*

[9]*Let the lowly brother boast in his exaltation, [10]and the rich in his humiliation, because like the flower of the grass he will pass away. [11]For the sun rises with its scorching heat and withers the grass; its flower falls, and its beauty perishes. So will the rich man fade away in the midst of his pursuits.*

[12]*Blessed is the man who endures trial, for when he has stood the test he will receive the crown of life which God has promised to those who love him. [13]Let no one say when he is tempted, "I am tempted by God"; for God cannot be tempted with evil and he himself tempts*

no one; ¹⁴*but each person is tempted when he is lured and enticed by his own desire.* ¹⁵*Then desire when it has conceived gives birth to sin; and sin when it is full-grown brings forth death.*

OVERVIEW: James was writing to people who were suffering from temptations of various kinds, though there is no sign that a general persecution of Christians had as yet broken out. The Greek word *peirasmos* can be translated either as "trial" or as "temptation," and the second of these possibilities dominated the Fathers' interpretation of these verses. To them the cure for temptation was patient endurance, which was the fruit of a spiritual wisdom that could be obtained only from God. There was no problem with obtaining this, as long as believers asked God for wisdom in faith, without doubting that they would receive it. Doubt and riches appear as the greatest enemies of true faith because in their different ways, they both contributed to human pride and arrogance. Once those vices took control, it was impossible to wage war against temptation, because temptation was also the fruit of human lusts and therefore a close ally of pride. It was essential therefore to overcome this basic human weakness, since failure to do so would lead inevitably to spiritual death.

Prepare for many temptations (CHRYOSOSTOM, HILARY OF ARLES). They will be like a raging torrent that only a strong swimmer can negotiate (CYRIL OF JERUSALEM, AUGUSTINE). The joy of faith is proved through endurance (OECUMENIUS, SYMEON). No one can take away this joy (BEDE). We are tempted by adversities in order to learn the virtue of patience (BEDE) and faith (HILARY OF ARLES). We are not to be discouraged by these trials (ANDREAS). The purity of faith is made perfect by patient endurance of affliction (BEDE,

ANDREAS, OECUMENIUS), which casts out fear (HILARY OF ARLES).

We pray that the faith that justifies may increase in those who already have it and also that it may be given to those who have not yet received it (AUGUSTINE). We must ask God for the spiritual wisdom to face temptations (BEDE, OECUMENIUS, THEOPHYLACT), a wisdom that only God can give (AUGUSTINE, HILARY OF ARLES, BEDE). One who does not ask in faith is not heard (HILARY OF ARLES, BEDE). The root of doubt is pride (CYRIL OF ALEXANDRIA), which easily turns into despair (OECUMENIUS). Ask without hesitation without being double-minded (BEDE, OECUMENIUS). Do not worry inordinately about your guilt, but count on God's mercy (HERMAS). A double-minded person is one who prays to God yet fails to obtain anything because one's conscience is still accusing all the time (BEDE). Such a person is unstable (ORIGEN), like waves on the sea (OECUMENIUS). Meanwhile every good thing comes to the humble (HILARY OF ARLES, OECUMENIUS, THEOPHYLACT).

Only those who endure adversity are rewarded (BEDE). What puffs up the rich is what brings them down (OECUMENIUS). Their wealth is vulnerable (HILARY OF ARLES, BEDE, OECUMENIUS). The heavier the endured sufferings of the righteous, the more courageous are their victories (SULPICIUS SEVERUS). A crown awaits them (CHRYSOSTOM, BEDE). James encourages the hope that the present situation will be put aright (DIDYMUS). Any testing that comes from God is for good, not for evil. Not so with the devil, who tempts in order to kill and who does not know us as

God knows (CYRIL OF JERUSALEM, AUGUSTINE, BEDE, ANDREAS). God may abandon us at times to reveal our own stubborn willing (PETER CHRYSOLOGUS). To find a remedy our very nature must be healed (AUGUSTINE). Lust does not give birth unless it conceives, and it does not conceive unless it receives willing consent to commit evil (AUGUSTINE). Until we labor and give birth to our corrupt thoughts, we seem happy and joyful, but once the wicked child called sin is born we are in pain as we realize the shame to which we ourselves have given birth (CHRYSOSTOM). Lust coaxes and urges on, positively encouraging us to do something bad. If we ponder it willingly, then it will conceive and give birth (AUGUSTINE, HESYCHIUS). Suggestion, experiment and consent are the three stages of temptation (BEDE, HILARY).

1:2 Finding Joy in Suffering

COUNT IT JOY. ORIGEN: If you count it all joy when you fall into various temptations, you give birth to joy, and you offer that joy in sacrifice to God. SERMONS ON GENESIS 8.10.[1]

THE TORRENT OF THE TRIAL. CYRIL OF JERUSALEM: "Falling into temptation" may mean being overwhelmed by temptation, for temptation is like a raging torrent which engulfs the traveler. In times of temptation some people manage to cross this torrent without being overwhelmed by the rising tide, because they are good swimmers who can avoid being swept away. But if others who lack their strength try to do it, they are overcome. MYSTAGOGICAL LECTURES 5.17.[2]

PREPARE FOR TEMPTATION. CHRYSOSTOM: Suffering is a real bond, an encouragement to

greater love, and the basis of spiritual perfection and godliness. Listen to the one who says: "If you want to serve the Lord, prepare your soul for temptation."[3] And again Christ said: "In the world you will have tribulation, but take courage."[4] And again: "straight and narrow is the way."[5] Everywhere you see suffering being praised, everywhere it is accepted as necessary for us. For in the world there is no one who wins a trophy without suffering, who has not strengthened himself with labors and dieting and exercise and vigils and many other things like that. How much more is that true in this battle! CATENA.[6]

A DANGEROUS LIFE. AUGUSTINE: Because we are human, we live a most dangerous life amid the snares of temptation. LETTERS 250.[7]

THROUGH MANY TEMPTATIONS. HILARY OF ARLES: Just as the world has to pass through winter before the spring comes and the flowers bloom, so a man must go through many temptations before he can inherit the prize of eternal life. For as Paul said: "Through many tribulations we must enter the kingdom of God."[8] Temptations come in three ways, by persuasion, by attraction and by consent. Satan persuades, the flesh is attracted, and the mind consents. INTRODUCTORY TRACTATE ON THE LETTER OF JAMES.[9]

ADVERSITIES WILLINGLY BORNE. BEDE: Nobody will take the disciples' joy from them because, although they suffered persecution and torture on behalf of Christ's name, yet they willingly bore all adversities because they

---

[1]FC 71:146*. [2]FC 64:201. [3]Cf. Sir 2:1. [4]Jn 16:33. [5]Mt 7:14. [6]CEC 2. [7]FC 32:242*. [8]Acts 14:22. [9]PL Supp. 3:63.

were enkindled by hope in his resurrection and by their vision of him. Moreover, they thought it perfect joy when they encountered different kinds of temptations. HOMILY ON THE GOSPELS 2.13.[10]

HOW FAITH IS PROVED. OECUMENIUS: For those who have been tried and tested, trials and afflictions are the source of the greatest joy, for that is how their faith is proved. COMMENTARY ON JAMES.[11]

DESPISE PAIN. SYMEON THE NEW THEOLOGIAN: The Word of God . . . causes us to despise all life's painful experiences and to count as joy every trial that assails us. DISCOURSES 3.8.[12]

1:3 Patience Is the Reward of Suffering

UNWANTED TRIALS. ANDREAS: When our Lord and God taught his disciples that they must pray to be delivered from temptation,[13] he meant the kind of temptation which we readily and willingly fall into and which does not contain any kind of trial. But James is talking about the kind of trials which are unwanted and teaches that those who struggle for the truth should not be discouraged by them. CATENA.[14]

TEMPTATIONS ENDURED. HILARY OF ARLES: Temptations can be endured by spiritual knowledge and faith in the Trinity. INTRODUCTORY TRACTATE ON THE LETTER OF JAMES.[15]

LEARNING PATIENCE. BEDE: James says that we are tempted by our adversaries in order to learn the virtue of patience, and thereby to be able to show and to prove that in our hearts we

have a firm belief in a future retribution. In interpreting this verse we must bear in mind what the apostle Paul said about the same thing: "Knowing that suffering produces endurance, and endurance produces character."[16] CONCERNING THE EPISTLE OF ST. JAMES.[17]

1:4 Patience Leads to Perfection

TRIALS PRODUCE PATIENCE. ANDREAS: Why do trials produce patience? It is because patience brings those who experience it to perfection. CATENA.[18]

CASTING OUT FEAR. HILARY OF ARLES: Perfection is the love of God, which is that very same "perfect love which casts out fear,"[19] that is, the fear of being tempted. Perfection is also patience, which is the guardian of the soul as Scripture says: "By your patience you will gain your souls."[20] INTRODUCTORY TRACTATE ON THE LETTER OF JAMES.[21]

BUILDING CHARACTER. BEDE: Patience builds character, so that someone who possesses it cannot be overcome but is shown to be perfect. For this reason believers are tested in order to improve their patience, so that by it their faith may be seen to be perfect. CONCERNING THE EPISTLE OF ST. JAMES.[22]

PATIENT ENDURANCE. OECUMENIUS: Why do trials produce patience? It is because trials demonstrate the purity of faith, which is made perfect by the patient endurance of affliction. COMMENTARY ON JAMES.[23]

---

[10]HOG 2:121. [11]PG 119:456. [12]CWS 68. [13]Mt 6:13. [14]CEC 3. [15]PL Supp. 3:63. [16]Rom 5:3-4. [17]PL 93:11. [18]CEC 3. [19]1 Jn 4:18. [20]Lk 21:19. [21]PL Supp. 3:63. [22]PL 93:11. [23]PG 119:457.

1:5 *Wisdom Is God's Gift*

THE FAITH THAT JUSTIFIES. AUGUSTINE: This is the faith by which the righteous person lives. This is the faith which believes in the one who justifies the ungodly. This is the faith by which glorying is cut out [Rom 1:17]. . . . This is the faith which gains the bountiful outpouring of the Spirit. ON THE SPIRIT AND THE LETTER 56.[24]

NOT FROM OURSELVES. AUGUSTINE: What blessing will that man not possess who has asked for and received this wisdom from the Lord? This will give you an understanding of what grace is, for if this wisdom were from ourselves it would not be from above and we would not have to ask for it from the God who created us. ON GRACE AND FREE WILL 24.[25]

FAITH A GIFT. AUGUSTINE: Just because faith may be given to us before we ask for it, it does not follow that it is not a gift of God. God may well give it to us before we ask him for it, just as he also gives peace and love. This is why we pray both that faith may be increased in those who already have it and also that it may be given to those who have not yet received it. ON THE GIFT OF PERSEVERANCE 44.[26]

ONLY GOD GIVES WISDOM. HILARY OF ARLES: Why does James tell them to seek wisdom?[27] It is so that they might have God's assurance. Only God should be asked for wisdom, not philosophers or astrologers. God gives wisdom like a fountain which never runs out of water, and he fills everyone whom he enters, but the wisdom of philosophers and other human agents is not given in abundance,

and it is soon spewed out. INTRODUCTORY TRACTATE ON THE LETTER OF JAMES.[28]

WISDOM TO FACE TEMPTATION. BEDE: Saving wisdom can come only from God and cannot be found by human free will, without the help of divine grace, as the Pelagians insist. Here, however, James is speaking particularly about that wisdom which we need when we meet temptations. He says that if there are some among us who do not understand why it is that we need to be tested in this way, then we should ask God to explain to us that a father must punish his children in order to make them ready for the inheritance of eternal life. CONCERNING THE EPISTLE OF ST. JAMES.[29]

ASK GOD FOR WISDOM. OECUMENIUS: James calls wisdom the cause of perfection. He knows that faith is tried and tested in affliction. There is no need to ask God for perfect people. What we need are wise people. This is why he encourages those who want to be on top of their afflictions to ask God for wisdom. COMMENTARY ON JAMES.[30]

SPIRITUAL WISDOM. THEOPHYLACT: James is referring here to spiritual wisdom, not the human kind. Spiritual wisdom is the cause of all perfect action. This is the heavenly wisdom, and when we have been strengthened by it we can do anything perfectly. COMMENTARY ON JAMES.[31]

---

[24]LCC 8:240. [25]FC 59:308. [26]FC 86:315. [27]James asks a rhetorical question so as not to insult the people he is writing to. For if he had said that they lacked wisdom he would have stirred them to indignation. He would seem to regard them as stupid and he alone as wise. [28]PL Supp. 3:64. [29]PL 93:11. [30]PG 119:457. [31]PG 125:1137.

1:6 *Have Faith and Do Not Doubt*

The Doubter. Cyril of Alexandria: The doubter is really full of pride. For if you have not believed that God will hear your request, you have not acted in such a way as to avoid being condemned already by the one who tests everything. The doubter has become double-minded even without wanting to be. It is therefore necessary to condemn a plague as dreadful as this. Catena.[32]

Wisdom Grounded in Faith. Hilary of Arles: James shows that the basis of human wisdom is faith. Here he may be contending against Simon Magus, who asked the apostles to give him the Holy Spirit but did not ask in faith. Introductory Tractate on the Letter of James.[33]

Worthiness to Be Heard. Bede: The believer must present himself to God, by his exemplary life, in such a way as to appear to be worthy of being heard by him. For whoever knows that he has not kept the Lord's commandments will quite rightly have no hope of being heard by him. As Scripture says: "If one turns away his ear from hearing the law, even his prayer is an abomination."[34] Concerning the Epistle of St. James.[35]

Pride Turns to Despair. Oecumenius: If a person is confident, let him ask. But if he doubts he should not ask, because he will not receive what he is not sure about. Such a person soon retreats from the faith which he does have and then backslides. This happens to him because of his pride, because he quickly despairs of ever getting something which he asks for if it does not turn up immediately. In any case, it is no bad thing if someone who thinks too highly of himself has his prayer requests turned down. Commentary on James.[36]

1:7 *The Doubter Does Not Receive God's Gifts*

Gifts Unmerited. Augustine: Purely human merits are evil, and God does not crown them. Any good merit is a gift of God. On Grace and Free Will 6.[37]

Windblown by Doubt. Bede: The person who, because of his biting conscience, doubts that he will receive any of the heavenly gifts will easily abandon his faith when he is tempted and be carried away into various sins as easily as if he were blown about by the wind. Concerning the Epistle of St. James.[38]

Ask Without Hesitation. Oecumenius: This refers to the person who asks in a spirit of haughtiness and contempt. Take away all double-mindedness, and above all, when you ask God for something, do not hesitate, saying to yourself: "How can I ask God for something, seeing that I have sinned so greatly against him?" Commentary on James.[39]

1:8 *The Double-Minded Person*

Counting on God's Mercy. Hermas: Put away doubting and do not hesitate to ask of the Lord. Do not say to yourself: "How can I ask of the Lord and receive from him, seeing that I have sinned so much against him?" Do

---

[32]CEC 3. [33]PL Supp. 3:64. [34]Prov 28:9. [35]PL 93:12. [36]PG 119:457. [37]FC 59:267. [38]PL 93:12. [39]PG 119:457-60; cf. Hermas *Shepherd* 2.9.

not reason with yourself like this, but turn to the Lord with all your heart and ask of him without doubting, and you will know the multitude of his tender mercies, that he will never leave you but fulfill the request of your soul. SHEPHERD 2.9.[40]

THE UNSTABLE. ORIGEN: We who do not follow our Lord with complete and perfect faith but yet have withdrawn from foreign gods dwell in a no-man's land. We are cut down by the foreign gods as deserters, but because we are unstable and unreliable, we are not defended by our Lord. SERMONS ON EXODUS 8.4.[41]

PRAYING WITH AN ACCUSING CONSCIENCE. BEDE: A double-minded man is one who on the one hand prays to God and on the other hand fails to obtain anything from him because inside his conscience is accusing him all the time. A man is double-minded when he wants to have fun in this world but also reign with God in heaven. Likewise, a man is double-minded when he seeks the approval of others for his good deeds rather than spiritual rewards from God. CONCERNING THE EPISTLE OF ST. JAMES.[42]

TOSSED LIKE WAVES. OECUMENIUS: A double-minded person is someone who is unstable and unreliable. Such a person has no clear vision of the future and no sure grasp of the present but rather drifts about here and there, grasping at whatever he can. He may be compared with the waves of the sea which are tossed to and fro, or to a flower of the field which is here today and gone tomorrow. COMMENTARY ON JAMES.[43]

1:9 The Lowly Exalted

PRIDE IN HUMILITY. HILARY OF ARLES: This verse applies to Hebrew slaves who were great and proud and high in their own eyes but in their slavery had become the lowest of the low. It is as if he were saying that life was harder for the rich people with whom they were living than it was for them as their servants. The boasting referred to here is not vain glory but joy in times of temptation. INTRODUCTORY TRACTATE ON THE LETTER OF JAMES.[44]

ENDURING ADVERSITY. BEDE: Everyone who humbly endures adversity for the Lord's sake will receive from him the highest rewards of his kingdom. CONCERNING THE EPISTLE OF ST. JAMES.[45]

HUMBLING OURSELVES. OECUMENIUS: Every good thing comes to us if we humble ourselves before God. COMMENTARY ON JAMES.[46]

HUMILITY THE KEY. THEOPHYLACT: Humility is the distributor of all good things, and apart from it there is nothing which is good. COMMENTARY ON JAMES.[47]

1:10 The Humbling of the Proud

RICHES SNATCHED AWAY. HILARY OF ARLES: Scripture says that "whoever exalts himself will be humbled."[48] Wealth is a rich man's flower, but the elements of the universe are out to snatch it away from him. James says very little about the humble man, but it is enough, for he will receive his glory from

---

[40]ANF 2:26. [41]FC 71:323. [42]PL 93:12. [43]PG 119:460. [44]PL Supp. 3:65. [45]PL 93:12. [46]PG 119:460. [47]PG 125:1140. [48]Lk 14:11.

God. But the rich are condemned at great length, so that no one will be tempted to follow their example. INTRODUCTORY TRACTATE ON THE LETTER OF JAMES.[49]

WEALTH COMES TO AN END. BEDE: James says this ironically, because the rich man will see the wealth in which he gloried, and with which he used to despise the poor in this world, come to an end. He will be humiliated by his eternal condemnation, like the rich man who despised Lazarus. CONCERNING THE EPISTLE OF ST. JAMES.[50]

WHAT PUFFS UP BRINGS DOWN. OECUMENIUS: James calls the rich man both proud and humble at the same time, because what puffs him up also brings him down. COMMENTARY ON JAMES.[51]

1:11 Fading Glory

THE HAPPINESS OF THE UNGODLY VANISHES. BEDE: The flower of the field is pretty and its smell is pleasant for a while, but it soon loses the attraction of its beauty and charm. The present happiness of the ungodly is exactly the same—it lasts for a day or two and then vanishes into nothing. The rising sun stands for the sentence of the strict Judge, which puts a quick end to the transient glory of the reprobate. Of course it is also true that the righteous person flourishes, though not in the same way. The unrighteous flourish for a time, like grass, but the righteous flourish forever, like great trees, as Scripture says: "The righteous flourish like the palm tree."[52] CONCERNING THE EPISTLE OF ST. JAMES.[53]

FADING AWAY. OECUMENIUS: The rich man is said to fade away even while he goes about his business, because anyone engaged in business knows that it can always take an unexpected turn for the worse. COMMENTARY ON JAMES.[54]

1:12 The Crown of Life

DEFYING TRIALS. SULPICIUS SEVERUS: Disasters are the common lot of the saints, who must suffer them. It is by enduring them and overcoming them that the virtue of the righteous has always been noticeable. With invincible strength they have defied all trials—the heavier the sufferings they endured, the more courageous were their victories. LETTER TO EUSEBIUS.[55]

ABLE TO HANDLE ANYTHING. DIDYMUS THE BLIND: James does all he can to encourage people to bear their trials with joy, as a burden which is bearable, and says that perfect patience consists in bearing things for their own sake, not for the hope of some better reward elsewhere. He nevertheless tries to persuade his hearers to rely on the promise that their present state will be put right. The person who has fought the hard battles will be perfectly able to handle anything. Someone who comes through his troubles in this way will be duly prepared to recieve his reward, which is the crown of life prepared by God for those who love him. COMMENTARY ON JAMES.[56]

THE CROWN AWAITS. CHRYSOSTOM: We see no garments or cloaks, but we see crowns

---

[49]PL Supp. 3:65. [50]PL 93:12. [51]PG 119:461. [52]Ps 92:12. [53]PL 93:12-13. [54]PG 119:461. [55]FC 7:143. [56]PG 39:1750-51.

more valuable than any gold, than any contest prizes or rewards, and ten thousand blessings stored up for those who live upright and virtuous lives on earth. ON THE INCOMPREHENSIBLE NATURE OF GOD. 6.7.[57]

THE REWARD OF VIRTUE. BEDE: If anyone is so zealous for continence or good works that he neglects to seek the rewards of eternal recompense in return for them, that person may indeed appear to have a fine linen miter on his head, but he does not have little crowns, for although he certainly displays the image of virtue before other human beings, he does not acquire the reward of virtue with the Lord. ON THE TABERNACLE AND ITS VESSELS 3.8.118.[58]

FAITHFUL UNTIL DEATH. BEDE: This verse is reminiscent of Revelation [2:10]: "Be faithful unto death, and I will give you the crown of life." CONCERNING THE EPISTLE OF ST. JAMES.[59]

1:13 God Does Not Tempt Anybody

GOD DOES NOT DIRECTLY TEMPT. CYRIL OF JERUSALEM: If ever we find ourselves afflicted by illness, grief or trouble, let us not blame God, for God cannot be tempted by evil and does not tempt anyone. Each of us is scourged with the ropes of our own sins.[60] SERMON ON THE PARALYTIC 17.[61]

DECEPTIONS FROM THE DEVIL. AUGUSTINE: By temptation in this context, James meant the bad sort by which we are deceived and subjected to the devil. There is another kind of temptation [mentioned in Deuteronomy 13:3] which is really a kind of testing that comes from God. SERMONS 57.9.[62]

EVIL NOT FROM GOD. BEDE: At this point James moves on from those external temptations which God sends to us for the testing of our faith to those internal ones which assault our souls and which are inspired by the devil. He wants to dispel the notion that the God who puts good thoughts into our minds also fills them with evil intentions. No one who has such wicked thoughts in his mind should ever try to claim that they come from God. CONCERNING THE EPISTLE OF ST. JAMES.[63]

GOD TESTS FOR THE GOOD. ANDREAS: Any testing which comes from God is for good, not for evil. . . . It is quite otherwise with the devil. He tempts in order to kill those whom he has tempted. Furthermore, the devil does not know what is inside us, but God knows and has given everyone his task to accomplish, according to his sovereign will. CATENA.[64]

ABANDONMENT TO OUR OWN STUBBORNNESS. PETER CHRYSOLOGUS: God is said to tempt when he abandons those who stubbornly fall into the snares of temptation. That is how Adam succumbed to the wiles of the tempter when he abandoned the commands of the Creator. SERMONS 70.[65]

1:14 Tempted by One's Own Desires

HEALING OUR NATURE. AUGUSTINE: Against this fault medicinal aid is sought from him who can heal all illnesses of this sort, not by separating an alien nature from us but by healing our own nature. ON CONTINENCE 7.[66]

---

[57]FC 72:167. [58]TTH 18:137. [59]PL 93:13. [60]Cf. Prov 5:22. [61]FC 64:220. [62]WSA 3/3:113. [63]PL 93:13-14. [64]CEC 5. [65]FC 17:122. [66]FC 16:210*.

WILLING CONSENT TO EVIL. AUGUSTINE: The one giving birth is lust, the thing born is sin. Lust does not give birth unless it conceives, and it does not conceive unless it entices and receives willing consent to commit evil. Therefore our battle against lust consists in keeping it from conceiving and giving birth to sin. AGAINST JULIAN 6.15.47.[67]

1:15 Desire Gives Birth to Sin

SIN IS BORN IN PAIN. CHRYSOSTOM: If we sin when we are drunk with pleasure, we do not notice it. But when it gives birth and reaches its goal, then all the pleasure is extinguished and the bitter core of our mind comes to the surface. This stands in contrast to women in labor. For before they give birth, such women have great pain and suffering, but afterwards the pain goes away, leaving their bodies along with the child. But here it is quite different. For until we labor and give birth to our corrupt thoughts, we are happy and joyful. But once the wicked child called sin is born we are in pain as we realize the shame to which we have given birth, and then we are pierced through more deeply than any woman in labor. Therefore I beg you right from the start not to welcome any corrupt thought, for if we do so the seeds will grow inside us, and if we get to that stage, the sin inside us will come out in deeds and strike us dead by condemning us, in spite of all our confessions and tears. For there is nothing more destructive than sin. CATENA.[68]

LUST REQUIRES CONSENT. AUGUSTINE: Each one of us is tempted by our own lust, so let us fight and resist and not give in nor allow ourselves to be lured by it, nor allow it to conceive anything to which it might then give birth. It is like this—lust coaxes and coddles you, it excites and urges you on, positively encouraging you to do something wrong. Do not give in and it will not conceive. If you ponder it willingly and with pleasure, then it will conceive and give birth, and you will die. SERMONS 77A.3.[69]

THREE STAGES OF TEMPTATION. BEDE: There are three stages in temptation. The first is suggestion, the second is experiment, and the third is consent. If we resist the devil's suggestions, then we have victory over temptation and deserve to inherit the crown of life. But if we let the enemy's suggestions gradually take control of us, then we find that we are taken away from the right path and start to indulge in sin. However, if we go no further than initial experiments, we may have offended God, but we have not yet fallen into mortal sin. However, if we continue down the path of depravity and start to embrace evildoing by giving our full consent to it, then we are deserving of death, and the enemy has triumphed over us. CONCERNING THE EPISTLE OF ST. JAMES.[70]

THE BIRTH PANGS OF DEATH. HESYCHIUS: The desires of sinners are the birth pangs of death. CATENA.[71]

---

[67]FC 35:356. [68]CEC 5-6. [69]WSA 3/3:329. [70]PL 93:14. [71]CEC 6.

1:16-27 THE WAY OF RIGHTEOUSNESS

¹⁶*Do not be deceived, my beloved brethren.* ¹⁷*Every good endowment and every perfect gift is from above, coming down from the Father of lights with whom there is no variation or shadow due to change.*^a ¹⁸*Of his own will he brought us forth by the word of truth that we should be a kind of first fruits of his creatures.*

¹⁹*Know this, my beloved brethren. Let every man be quick to hear, slow to speak, slow to anger,* ²⁰*for the anger of man does not work the righteousness of God.* ²¹*Therefore put away all filthiness and rank growth of wickedness and receive with meekness the implanted word, which is able to save your souls.*

²²*But be doers of the word, and not hearers only, deceiving yourselves.* ²³*For if any one is a hearer of the word and not a doer, he is like a man who observes his natural face in a mirror;* ²⁴*for he observes himself and goes away and at once forgets what he was like.* ²⁵*But he who looks into the perfect law, the law of liberty, and perseveres, being no hearer that forgets but a doer that acts, he shall be blessed in his doing.*

²⁶*If any one thinks he is religious, and does not bridle his tongue but deceives his heart, this man's religion is vain.* ²⁷*Religion that is pure and undefiled before God and the Father is this: to visit orphans and widows in their affliction, and to keep oneself unstained from the world.*

a Other ancient authorities read *variation due to a shadow of turning*

OVERVIEW: Above all else, believers in Christ must be careful not to fall into the trap of deception in spiritual matters. Every spiritual gift comes from God and reflects his character as the Father of lights. Every good endowment is an undeserved, a free gift of God for which we pray every day (AUGUSTINE). What God gives is without defect (DIDYMUS). The soul is progressively enlightened in its ascent after the resurrection (ORIGEN), cleansed from wickedness (OECUMENIUS). The procession of Light spreads itself generously toward us in a unitive way (PSEUDO-DIONYSIUS). Nothing can add or subtract from God's glory (NOVATIAN), who is unchanging in his divine essence (SEVERUS). No shadow can cut off God's light (GREGORY THE GREAT). Anyone who stands in this light wishes to share it with others (SYMEON). We must, however, distinguish our begottenness as children of light from the eternal begottenness of the Son (ANDREAS, BEDE, OECUMENIUS).

Therefore, those who possess God's Spirit will be self-controlled in their behavior and will avoid every form of wickedness. Above all, truly spiritual persons will do their utmost to put their faith into practice, since that is the ultimate test of what it means to be born again in Christ. The truth heard is less prone to corruption than the truth spoken (AUGUSTINE). The tongue must be disciplined (BEDE). To be quick to hear implies eagerness to put into practice what has been heard (OECUMENIUS). Two things in particular are indicative of spiritual maturity: the ability to hold one's tongue and a willingness to be generous toward those who are in need. A charitable disposition and charitable behavior must go hand in hand in the life of someone who wants to imitate God's perfect charity. Widows and orphans are especially to be looked after (HERMAS, HILARY OF ARLES). We become more like God in showing acts of mercy (CHRYSOSTOM). Illusions about one's own correctness arise out of the lack of self-control (GREGORY THE GREAT, OECUMENIUS). Imitate God's justice, which is without anger (BEDE). Avoid uncontrollable fury, which leads to a habituation to wickedness (ANDREAS, BEDE, OECUMENIUS). One single uniting Word is addressed to us through many scriptures (AUGUSTINE). We are called to enact in behavior what we hear (AUGUSTINE, OECUMENIUS). We best view our deeper selves in the mirror of the gospel (HILARY OF ARLES). Yet if we behold ourselves in this mirror and then forget it or fail to confirm it in deeds, what we have learned will slip out of our hands (ANDREAS, OECUMENIUS). The doer of the Word delights in the perfect law that liberates from sin and death (AUGUSTINE, OECUMENIUS).

1:16 Do Not Be Deceived

THE DECEPTION. HILARY OF ARLES: This refers to the deception of the heretics who think that because God rules the physical world in darkness and in light, in drought and in rain, in cold and in heat, so he also rules

over human wills with the same determinateness—in good and in bad, in sadness and in joy, in death and in life. Because of this error, James goes on to add that it is "every good endowment and every perfect gift" which comes from the Father of lights. INTRODUCTORY TRACTATE ON THE LETTER OF JAMES.[1]

GOD TEMPTS NO ONE. ANDREAS: "Do not be deceived" into thinking that temptations come from God. CATENA.[2]

1:17a Every Perfect Gift Is from Above

GIFTS WITHOUT DEFECT. DIDYMUS: James calls God the Father of intelligent lights, that is to say, the illuminator of all rational beings, from whom, as the giver of these things, the divine gifts come to human beings. These gifts, James says, are the very best, complete and without defect, undoubtedly perfect. But as there are some people who argue from this that only the good things in life come from God, and not things which are regarded as bad or harmful, we have to recall such passages as "he brought evil on them,"[3] "Evil came down from God onto the gates of Jerusalem"[4] and so on. From these and other similar examples it is clear that bad things as well as good may come about through God's judgment. COMMENTARY ON JAMES.[5]

A WORK OF GOD. AUGUSTINE: If doing something ourselves means that it is not also a work of God, then casting mountains into the

---

[1]PL Supp. 3:66. [2]CEC 6. [3]Baruch 4:18. The implication is not that God directly wills evil upon them but that through their distorted willing they bring, by God's righteous judgment, evil upon themselves. [4]Mic 1:12. [5]PG 39:1751-52.

sea would not be a work of God, since Matthew [17:20] and Luke [17:6] both say that this can be done by the power of faith. ON THE SPIRIT AND THE LETTER 63.[6]

ASKING FOR PERSEVERANCE. AUGUSTINE: You should hope for this perseverance in obedience to the Father of lights, from whom descends every good and perfect gift, and ask for it every day in your prayers, and in so doing have confidence that you are not strangers to the predestination of God's people, for he allows you to do even this. ON THE GIFT OF PERSEVERANCE 22.62.[7]

UNDESERVED GIFT. AUGUSTINE: Man's merit is a free gift, and no one deserves to receive anything from the Father of lights, from whom every good gift comes down, except by receiving what he does not deserve. LETTERS 186.[8]

1:17b Coming Down from the Father of Lights

THE SOUL PROGRESSIVELY ENLIGHTENED. ORIGEN: The soul gradually ascends to the heavens after the resurrection. It does not reach the highest point immediately but goes through many stages during which it is progressively enlightened by the light of Wisdom, until it arrives at the Father of lights himself. HOMILY 27 ON NUMBERS 6.[9]

THE PROCESSION OF LIGHT. PSEUDO-DIONYSIUS: Inspired by the Father, each procession of the Light spreads itself generously towards us, and in its power to unify, it stirs us by lifting us up. It returns us back to the oneness and deifying simplicity of the Father who gathers us in. For as the sacred Word says,

"from him and to him are all things."[10] ON THE CELESTIAL HIERARCHY 1.1.[11]

THE LIGHTS. ANDREAS: The lights are either the rational powers or else those who have been enlightened by the Holy Spirit. CATENA.[12]

1:17c No Variation or Shadow of Change

NO ADDITION OR DIMINUTION TO GOD'S GLORY. NOVATIAN: God never changes or transforms himself into other forms, lest by changing he should somehow appear to be mortal. For the modification implied in change from one thing to another involves a share in death of some sort. Therefore there is never any addition of parts or of glory in him, lest anything should seem to have been wanting to the perfect one in the first place. Nor can there be any diminution in him, for that would imply some degree of mortality in him. ON THE TRINITY 4.4.[13]

GOD UNCHANGING IN HIS BEING. SEVERUS OF ANTIOCH: Hear what God says: "I am, I am and I do not change."[14] He remains always firm and unchanging in his being, and those who have been formed by the gospel and who have been transformed by his commands through the gift and transformation which comes from above, are called to persevere in these precepts as much as their strength permits and not to be swept away by the times in which we live. Therefore Paul also warned people, saying: "Do not be conformed to this world, but be transformed by the renewing of

---

[6]LCC 8:256-57. [7]FC 86:330. [8]FC 30:199. [9]CWS 253. [10]Rom 11:36. [11]CWS 145. [12]CEC 6. [13]FC 67:31. [14]Mal 3:6.

your minds, so that you may prove what the good and acceptable and perfect will of God is."[15] CATENA.[16]

GOD'S LIGHT. GREGORY THE GREAT: This changing is a shadow which conceals the divine light if it goes through certain ups and downs in this life, but because God is un-changing, no shadow can cut off his light. LESSONS IN JOB 2.38.[17]

CLEANSED FROM WICKEDNESS. OECU-MENIUS: Since what comes from us lacks perfection and indeed is very imperfect, nor does it enlighten the soul, think what perfection they will have who acquire it after a happy pilgrimage through life, who with great effort have cleansed their souls from the wickedness they inherited at birth, and who have finally reached the divine splendor. COMMENTARY ON JAMES.[18]

THE ROYAL WAY EXPERIENCED AND SHARED. SYMEON THE NEW THEOLOGIAN: Suppose we had told you that we had freely received grace from the Father of lights, from whom comes every good and perfect gift, but that we do not care for you to receive it also. If so, we would then have deserved to become an object of abhorrence on the part of God and of yourselves. But instead we present to you the truth from Holy Scripture and from experience and show you the royal way. DIS-COURSES 34.6.[19]

1:18 The First Fruits of God's Creatures

THE HIERARCHY OF CREATURES. HILARY OF ARLES: Just as the heavenly powers rule over the angelic creatures, so we human beings rule over the lower creation. INTRODUCTORY TRACTATE ON THE LETTER OF JAMES.[20]

FIRST FRUITS. ANDREAS: The birth here applies in the first instance to the Son and then by extension to the creatures. For to him belong truth and consubstantiality with God, whereas to the creatures belong honor and inheritance. The fact that the same name is used does not mean that the same honor is given, nor should things which are said by extension be taken to mean that they apply in the first instance as well. By "first fruits" James means that we are the first and most highly honored. For by "creatures" he means the visible creation, of which humanity is the most highly honored part. CATENA.[21]

CHANGED TO CHILDREN OF LIGHT. BEDE: God has changed us from being children of darkness into being children of light, not because of any merits of ours but by his own will, through the water of regeneration. But lest we should think that by "begetting" us in this way God has made us somehow a part of his own nature, James goes on to add that the result of the divine activity is that we have become "the first fruits of his creatures," which means that we have been exalted over the rest of creation. CONCERNING THE EPISTLE OF ST. JAMES.[22]

OUR BEGOTTENNESS DISTINGUISHED FROM THAT OF THE SON. OECUMENIUS: Here James reminds us that God is immutable, which is not true of us. For if we have been born it is clear that we have also been changed. How can something be immutable

---

[15]Rom 12:2. [16]CEC 6-7. [17]PL 79:1095. [18]PG 119:464. [19]CWS 352. [20]PL Supp. 3:67. [21]CEC 7. [22]PL 93:15.

if it has gone from nonbeing to being? Furthermore he adds that God has given us birth by the Word of Life, lest we might be tempted to think that his Son was also born in the same way as we are. But according to John, all things were made by the Son, which means that he was not born along with us who have been made by him. COMMENTARY ON JAMES.[23]

1:19 Be Quick to Hear but Slow to Speak

THE TRUTH SPOKEN AND HEARD. AUGUSTINE: Truth is more safely heard than preached. For when it is heard, lowliness is preserved, but when it is preached some bit of boastfulness may steal in almost unawares, and this brings corruption. TRACTATES 57.2.3.[24]

THE DISCIPLINE OF THE TONGUE. BEDE: James is right to say this, for it is stupid to think that someone who is not prepared to learn from others will somehow be well-equipped to preach to them. Someone who wants to become wise must first of all ask for this gift from God, as James has already said. Then he must find himself a good teacher and in the meantime discipline his tongue so that he says nothing useless but restricts himself to preaching the truth which he has recently learned from others. CONCERNING THE EPISTLE OF ST. JAMES.[25]

EAGERNESS TO PRACTICE THE TRUTH. OECUMENIUS: When James says "quick to hear" he is not talking about simple listening but about eagerness to put into practice what has been heard. For he distinguishes quite clearly between the person who is ready to act on what he has heard and the one who is weighed down by laziness and procrastination,

sometimes even to the point of never attempting to do anything at all. COMMENTARY ON JAMES.[26]

1:20 Human Anger, God's Righteousness

LACKING SELF-CONTROL. GREGORY THE GREAT: Because a diseased mind has no control over its own judgment, it thinks that whatever anger suggests must be right. LESSONS IN JOB 5.78.[27]

GOD JUDGES WITH TRANQUILITY. BEDE: Even if anger seems justified in human terms, it can never be right in God's eyes. A human judge who loses his temper, even if his decision is the right one, cannot imitate the justice of God, who always judges in perfect tranquility of mind. CONCERNING THE EPISTLE OF ST. JAMES.[28]

AVOID UNCONTROLLABLE FURY. OECUMENIUS: Unconsidered speech and unguarded wrath do no good at all. David said: "Be angry but do not sin."[29] This means that we must be careful when we get angry not to let it develop into an uncontrollable fury. This is where those who are slow come into their own. It may be wrong to be slow in other things, but when it comes to anger, tardiness is the right policy, because by the time we get round to it the reasons for it may have dissipated. COMMENTARY ON JAMES.[30]

1:21 Turn from Evil and Accept God's Word

---

[23]PG 119:464-65. [24]FC 90:15. [25]PL 93:16. [26]PG 119:465. [27]PL 79:1096. [28]PL 93:16-17. [29]Ps 4:5. [30]PG 119:465.

CONSEQUENCES OF ANGER. HILARY OF ARLES: Filthiness and wickedness arise out of anger. INTRODUCTORY TRACTATE ON THE LETTER OF JAMES.[31]

FILTHINESS AND WICKEDNESS. BEDE: You cannot do good unless you have cleansed yourself from evil first. Filthiness refers primarily to external things which corrupt our hands, whereas wickedness refers primarily to internal things which corrupt our souls. Both must be overcome if we are to do good. CONCERNING THE EPISTLE OF ST. JAMES.[32]

CORRUPTION FROM WITHIN AND WITHOUT. ANDREAS: This refers to the sin which corrupts a man, which dwells in us as the cause of evil. But outside us there is another kind of evil which creeps up on us unawares and is the work of demons who are opposed to us. CATENA.[33]

AVOID HABITUATION TO WICKEDNESS. OECUMENIUS: What James wants to say is this. Although a person may often fall into uncleanness, the faster he gets out of it the better. Otherwise, if he remains in it and carries on, he will make the evil stronger by force of habit and have a harder time washing it away. COMMENTARY ON JAMES.[34]

1:22 Doers of the Word

ONE WORD. AUGUSTINE: James did not say "of the words" but "of the Word," in spite of the fact that there are so many words from the Holy Scriptures which are venerated in the church. SERMONS 71.22.[35]

DOING THE WORD. AUGUSTINE: Neither I nor any other preacher can see into your

hearts . . . but God is looking, for nothing can be hidden from him. . . . Do not deceive yourselves by coming eagerly to hear the Word and then failing to do it. If it is a good thing to hear, it is a much better thing to do. If you do not hear, you cannot do, and therefore you will build nothing. But if you hear and do not do, then what you are building will be a ruin. SERMONS 179.7-8.[36]

BE MINDFUL. ANDREAS: In other words, be mindful of your own salvation! CATENA.[37]

GIVING EFFECT TO WHAT IS HEARD. OECUMENIUS: James knows that some people can get all exited by what they hear, but even in the course of listening their enthusiasm may start to cool off. Therefore he adds these words, so that they may give effect to what they hear. COMMENTARY ON JAMES.[38]

1:23 Hearers of the Word

THE NEW TESTAMENT MIRRORS PERFECTION. HILARY OF ARLES: There are two kinds of mirrors—large and small. In a small mirror you see small things—this is the Old Testament, which leads no one to perfection. But in a big mirror you see great things—this is the New Testament, because in it the fullness of perfection is seen. INTRODUCTORY TRACTATE ON THE LETTER OF JAMES.[39]

CONFIRM THE WORD. ANDREAS: If someone is a hearer of the word only and does not confirm it by his deeds, he will lose the word as

---

[31]PL Supp. 3:67. [32]PL 93:17. [33]CEC 7. [34]PG 119:468. [35]WSA 3/3:259. [36]WSA 3/5:303. [37]CEC 8. [38]PG 119:468. [39]PL Supp. 3:68.

well, for it will slip through his fingers and disappear. CATENA.[40]

FORGETTING THE WORD. OECUMENIUS: James here uses the common mirror as a metaphor for the intellectual mirror, but without going into details. Think of him as saying that someone who hears a sermon but does not put any of it into practice is like a man who having seen himself in the mirror immediately forgets what he looked like. COMMENTARY ON JAMES.[41]

1:24 The Person in the Mirror

REMEMBERING OUR REGENERATION. ANDREAS: We learn what God has made us like, having given us new birth by the washing of regeneration. But if we do not remember what we have seen and apply it in our deeds, then we shall lose the grace which has been given to us. But the one who remembers that he has been born again from on high, that he has been justified, and sanctified and counted among the children of God, will not give himself over to works which reject that grace. CATENA.[42]

FORGETTING THE DIVINE IMAGE IN US. OECUMENIUS: This is like the person who has used the law of Moses to contemplate what he was made like, that is, the image and likeness of God the Creator, but afterwards draws no conclusions about his own behavior from what he has looked at and instead goes back to being just what he was before. COMMENTARY ON JAMES.[43]

1:25 The Perfect Law of Liberty

DELIGHT IN THE LAW OF LIBERTY. AUGUSTINE: The law of liberty is one of love, not fear. Paul too was no longer terrified by the law of

God as a slave would be but was delighted with it, even though he saw another law in his members which was at war against the law of his mind.[44] ON NATURE AND GRACE 57 (67).[45]

GOOD INTENTIONS. BEDE: Spiritual happiness is gained not by empty words but by putting our good intentions into practice. CONCERNING THE EPISTLE OF ST. JAMES.[46]

THE PERFECT LAW LIBERATES. OECUMENIUS: The spiritual law contains something magnificent and altogether desirable, which is able to draw people away even from following it corruptly, and able to make them perfect. The perfect law is liberating because it is the law of Christ, which sets us free from all slavery to the flesh, whether that means observance of the sabbath, circumcision, ritual purifications or whatever. COMMENTARY ON JAMES.[47]

1:26 Bridling the Tongue

THE UNBRIDLED TONGUE. BASIL THE GREAT: Anger causes tongues to become unbridled and speech unguarded. Physical violence, acts of contempt, reviling, accusations, blows and other bad effects too numerous to recount are born of anger and indignation. SERMONS 10.[48]

THE TONGUE CAN UNDO GOOD ACTIONS. BEDE: James says here that even if someone appears to be doing the good works of faith which he has learned he ought to do, none of this matters unless he restrains his tongue from slanders, lies, blasphemies, nonsense,

---

[40]CEC 8. [41]PG 119:468. [42]CEC 8. [43]PG 119:468. [44]Rom 7:22-23. [45]FC 86:74. [46]PL 93:17. [47]PG 119:469. [48]FC 9:448.

verbosity and other things which lead to sin. CONCERNING THE EPISTLE OF ST. JAMES.[49]

TRUE RELIGION. ANDREAS: This rule is the bottom line of true religion. CATENA.[50]

THE PRACTICE OF RELIGION. OECUMENIUS: If you want to be truly religious, do not demonstrate this by your knowledge of the law but by the way you put it into practice. *Religion* appears to mean something more than "faith," in that it offers the knowledge of hidden things and confirmation of what is grasped by faith. COMMENTARY ON JAMES.[51]

1:27 Pure and Undefiled Religion

WHICH FIELDS ARE TO BE BOUGHT. HERMAS: Instead of fields, buy souls that are in trouble, according to your ability. Look after widows and orphans. Do not neglect them. Spend your riches on these kinds of fields and houses. PARABLES 1.8.[52]

BECOME MORE LIKE GOD. CHRYSOSTOM: We can become more like God if we are merciful and compassionate. If we do not do these things, we have nothing at all to our credit. God does not say that if we fast we shall be like him. Rather he wants us to be merciful, as he himself is. "I desire mercy," he says, "and not sacrifice."[53] CATENA.[54]

THE VULNERABILITY OF WIDOWS. HILARY OF ARLES: James calls God the Father because as far as he is concerned there is no other god who made the world (as the Marcionites and other heretics claim). What he says about widows has to be understood in the light of the fact that there were many who tried to rob

them of their possessions, as it says in the Gospel.[55] INTRODUCTORY TRACTATE ON THE LETTER OF JAMES.[56]

THE PRETENSE OF RELIGIOSITY. BEDE: It is good to see that James has added the words "before God, the Father," because there are plenty of people who appear to be religious in the sight of men but who are wicked as far as God is concerned. CONCERNING THE EPISTLE OF ST. JAMES.[57]

A GRADUAL WEANING FROM THE LAW. OECUMENIUS: Here someone might say: If James is a teacher of the covenant established by Christ, why does he not just abolish everything connected with the law, instead of exalting it by supporting those who are experienced in keeping it? Why does he not rebuke them and turn them away from it? To this we answer that James accommodates himself to them and starts where they are. Rather than attack the law head on, he draws them away from it gradually, aware that they are suspicious of new ideas and inclined toward skepticism about them. By doing this he increasingly prepares them to hear what he has to say and then weans them away from observance of the law little by little. COMMENTARY ON JAMES.[58]

THE UNGODLY LED ASTRAY. THEOPHYLACT: In this verse the "world" refers to the common and ungodly people who are led astray by their lusts and errors. COMMENTARY ON JAMES.[59]

---

[49]PL 93:17. [50]CEC 9. [51]PG 119:469-72. [52]FC 1:289. [53]Hos 6:6. [54]CEC 9. [55]Mk 12:40. [56]PL Supp. 3:68-69. [57]PL 93:17. [58]PG 119:472. [59]PG 125:1149-52.

2:1-13 THE EVIL OF DISCRIMINATION

¹*My brethren, show no partiality as you hold the faith of our Lord Jesus Christ, the Lord of glory. ²For if a man with gold rings and in fine clothing comes into your assembly, and a poor man in shabby clothing also comes in, ³and you pay attention to the one who wears the fine clothing and say, "Have a seat here, please," while you say to the poor man, "Stand there," or, "Sit at my feet," ⁴have you not made distinctions among yourselves, and become judges with evil thoughts? ⁵Listen, my beloved brethren. Has not God chosen those who are poor in the world to be rich in faith and heirs of the kingdom which he has promised to those who love him? ⁶But you have dishonored the poor man. Is it not the rich who oppress you, is it not they who drag you into court? ⁷Is it not they who blaspheme the honorable name which was invoked over you?*

⁸*If you really fulfil the royal law, according to the scripture, "You shall love your neighbor as yourself," you do well. ⁹But if you show partiality, you commit sin, and are convicted by the law as transgressors. ¹⁰For whoever keeps the whole law but fails in one point has become guilty of all of it. ¹¹For he who said, "Do not commit adultery," said also, "Do not kill." If you do not commit adultery but do kill, you have become a transgressor of the law. ¹²So speak and so act as those who are to be judged under the law of liberty. ¹³For judgment is without mercy to one who has shown no mercy; yet mercy triumphs over judgment.*

OVERVIEW: Salvation in Christ breaks down all barriers between human beings. It is clear that for James some of the most intractable problems on this score were influenced by economic factors. Rich people in the church were expecting and receiving special considerations from their wealth. This was an insidious attack on the gospel, which especially honored one who was poor in worldly goods but rich in spiritual things. To show contempt for the poor is as much an infraction of the law as murder or adultery, and it is even more serious because it is so common. Christians must learn to fight against the temptations of worldly wealth and concentrate instead on the heavenly blessings, which are the only true riches. Both rich and poor are all of one body in Christ (CHRYSOSTOM). Ostentation and favoritism are reproached (AUGUSTINE, HILARY OF ARLES, OECUMENIUS). God chooses the weak to shame the strong (AUGUSTINE). The nobility are not immune from criticism (SALVIAN). The displaced poor are comforted by God (HILARY OF ARLES), and their energies are especially used of God (OECUMENIUS). Those who base their lives on greed are the poorest of all (CHRYSOSTOM). Loving the neighbor has a literal reference to those immediately present, a spiritual reference to those absent, and a contemplative reference to love itself (HILARY OF ARLES). Treat the neighbor as you would one most dear (ANDREAS). To have fallen from the precept of love is thereby to have offended in all the other commandments (CAESARIUS OF ARLES, AUGUSTINE, ANDREAS). God's righteousness is like a covering over the whole body, hiding all offenses (GREGORY THE GREAT). Adultery and murder are mentioned as extreme examples of offenses against love (HILARY OF ARLES, OECUMENIUS). There can be no favoritism in the law of liberty under which we are to be prepared to be judged (OECUMENIUS). Mercy breaks chains, dispels darkness, extinguishes fire, kills the worm and takes away the gnashing of teeth (CHRYSOSTOM). It is an oil of escape from the demonic (HESYCHIUS). The mercy that one does not show to others will not be shown to him (AUGUSTINE, BRAULIO OF SARAGOSSA). We ask God to forgive us as we forgive others, but if we do not forgive, we shall not be forgiven (OECUMENIUS).

2:1 Impartiality

ALL OF ONE BODY. CHRYSOSTOM: What does it matter if you think highly of yourself, when someone else despises you? Are we not all one body, both great and small? Therefore if in principle we are all one and members of each other, why do you mindlessly exalt yourself? Why do you bring shame on your brother? For just as he is a part of you, so you too are a part of him. CATENA.[1]

HOLDING THE FAITH. BEDE: James here demonstrates that those to whom he is writing were full of faith but empty when it came to works. CONCERNING THE EPISTLE OF ST. JAMES.[2]

FAVORITISM. OECUMENIUS: Anyone who does things by showing favoritism covers himself

with great shame and reproach, for that way he brings disdain not only on his neighbor but much more on himself as well. COMMENTARY ON JAMES.[3]

2:2 Rich and Poor

GOD CHOOSES THE WEAK. AUGUSTINE: Far from me is the notion that in your tabernacle, Lord, the rich should be more highly regarded than the poor, or the noble than the less well-born. You have chosen the weak things of this world to put the strong to shame, and you have chosen things which are dishonorable, despised and of no account, in order to bring to nothing the things which are. CONFESSIONS 8.4.9.[4]

GOLD RINGS. HILARY OF ARLES: What James says here applies not just to rings but to any sign of wealth, for the ring is meant to stand for a treasure house of riches. INTRODUCTORY TRACTATE ON THE LETTER OF JAMES.[5]

2:3 Discrimination

ATTEND TO INWARD FAITH. CHRYSOSTOM: There is no difference between rich and poor in Christ. Pay no attention to the outward appearance, but look for the inner faith instead. CATENA.[6]

2:4 Judging Others by Appearances

THE RICH NOT MORE HOLY. AUGUSTINE: Who could bear to see a rich man chosen to occupy a seat of honor in the church when a

---

[1]CEC 9. [2]PL 93:18. [3]PG 119:473. [4]FC 21:205. [5]PL Supp. 3:69. [6]CEC 10.

more learned and holier man is passed over because he is poor? Is it not a sin to judge by appearances that a rich man is a better man? LETTERS 167.18.[7]

AN ANCIENT STYLISTIC INDICATOR. THEOPHYLACT: The word *and* often occurs here, where we would expect subordinate clauses instead. This was the older way of speaking, which James records for us. COMMENTARY ON JAMES.[8]

2:5 Rich in Faith

CHOOSING THE POOR. AUGUSTINE: It is by choosing the poor that God makes them rich in faith, just as he makes them heirs of the kingdom. It is rightly said that he chose this faith in them, since it was in order to bring it about that he chose them. ON THE PREDES-TINATION OF THE SAINTS 17 (34).[9]

THE NOBILITY NOT IMMUNE TO CRITICISM. SALVIAN THE PRESBYTER: The apostle's testimony is a very serious matter. Do the nobility think that they are immune from his strictures, because he referred only to the rich and not to the noble as well? But there is so great an overlap between these two groups in practice that it makes little difference which one of them the apostle was speaking about. His words certainly ap-ply to both. ON THE GOVERNANCE OF GOD 3.10.[10]

COMFORTING THE DISPLACED POOR. HILARY OF ARLES: Some people say that this is meant to be a comfort to the poor who have been thrown out of the houses of the rich or who dwell in inferior accommodations. Even if they are poor in material things, they may be rich in faith. INTRODUCTORY TRACTATE ON THE LETTER OF JAMES.[11]

THE ENERGIES OF THE POOR. OECUMENIUS: When poor people are not preoccupied with the things of the world, when they come to faith, they often become more energetic and more determined to work at it than rich people do. COMMENTARY ON JAMES.[12]

2:6 The Rich Are Oppressors

THE GREEDY ARE POOREST OF ALL. CHRYSOSTOM: Bear their greed as patiently as you can! Those people destroy themselves, not you. For while they rob you of your money, they strip themselves of God's favor and help. For the one who bases his life on greed and gathers all the wealth of the world around him is in fact the poorest of all. CATENA.[13]

USING POWER TO OPPRESS. BEDE: Here James shows us more clearly who these rich people are, whose humiliation and destruction he talked about earlier. They are people who put their riches before Christ, who are themselves strangers to his teaching and who use their power to oppress those who believe. They take poor people to court and blaspheme the name of Christ. That there were many upper-class people in the time of the apostles who did this kind of thing is clear both from the Acts of the Apostles and from Paul's letters. CONCERNING THE EPISTLE OF ST. JAMES.[14]

2:7 The Rich Blaspheme Christ

---

[7]FC 30:47. [8]PG 125:1152. [9]FC 86:260-61 [10]FC 3:86. [11]PL Supp. 3:70. [12]PG 119:473. [13]CEC 11. [14]PL 93:19.

OPPRESSORS AND IDOLATERS. APOLLINARIUS: This refers to the rulers of the Jews, who enriched themselves on tithes, and also to the leaders of the Romans, who were idolaters at that time. CATENA.[15]

THEY BLASPHEME. HILARY OF ARLES: This is the name of the God of Israel, which was invoked on your behalf in Egypt, as well as in your baptism. INTRODUCTORY TRACTATE ON THE LETTER OF JAMES.[16]

2:8 Love Your Neighbor as Yourself

LITERAL, SPIRITUAL AND CONTEMPLATIVE DIMENSIONS INTERTWINED. HILARY OF ARLES: "Love your neighbor" means three different things. The first is corporal, that is, the literal sense of the words. The second is spiritual, according to which we love those close to us even though we may be absent from them. The third is contemplative, by which love itself is beheld. But we have to understand that one leads to another. The corporal inspires us to go on to the spiritual, and that in turn lifts us up to the contemplative. The spiritual may sometimes regress to the merely corporal, but the contemplative never fails us. The corporal and spiritual forms of love are common to human beings and have analogies in animals, but the contemplative is reserved for humans alone. INTRODUCTORY TRACTATE ON THE LETTER OF JAMES.[17]

AS TOWARD A CHILD OF GOD. ANDREAS: Just as you want to be treated justly and properly by your neighbor, so you must behave toward him as you would towards your kinsman and child of God. What our Savior said about this is absolutely right: "Do unto others as you would have them do unto you. For this

is the law and the prophets."[18] CATENA.[19]

2:9 Discrimination Is Sin

SHOW NO PARTIALITY. HILARY OF ARLES: It is a sin to show any class distinction among persons, for the law says: "You shall not be partial in judgment, you shall hear the small and the great alike."[20] Jesus confirmed this when he said: "Do not judge by appearances, but judge with right judgment."[21] INTRODUCTORY TRACTATE ON THE LETTER OF JAMES.[22]

2:10 Breaking the Law

GUILTY BEFORE THE LAWGIVER. AUGUSTINE: Is it possible that the person who has discriminated between rich and poor is guilty of murder, adultery and sacrilege? That does indeed seem to be the conclusion which James is drawing. Such a man is guilty of every crime, because by offending in one point he has become guilty of them all. LETTERS 167.3.[23]

NEGLECTING LOVE. CAESARIUS OF ARLES: What does it mean to offend in one point and lose all, except to have fallen from the precept of love and thereby to have offended in all the other commandments? Without love none of our virtues amounts to anything at all. SERMONS 100A.12.[24]

GOD'S RIGHTEOUSNESS COVERS THE WHOLE BODY. GREGORY THE GREAT: When we wear a piece of clothing, it covers us all

---

[15]CEC 11. [16]PL Supp. 3:70. [17]PL Supp. 3:70. [18]Mt 7:12. [19]CEC 11. [20]Deut 1:17. [21]Jn 7:24. [22]PL Supp. 3:70. [23]FC 30:34-35. [24]FC 47:96.

over. Righteousness is like this, for it protects itself by good works at every turn and leaves nothing exposed to the ravages of sin. For if someone is righteous in some of the things he does and unrighteous in others, it is rather as if he is covering one side of his body but leaving the other side naked. Such a person is not doing good works, because these works are made evil by the unrighteousness which is present in him. LESSONS IN JOB 19.32.[25]

LOVE IS THE SUM OF THE LAW. ANDREAS: To fail in one point is to lack perfect love, for this is the source of all good deeds. If something in the head is not right, the rest of the body suffers as a result. The entire purpose and plan of God is designed to lead to perfect love. That is the meaning of the commandments such as "Do not commit adultery," "Do not kill" and so on. CATENA.[26]

2:11 Adultery and Murder

EXTREME EXAMPLES. HILARY OF ARLES: Why does James choose these two commandments as his examples? Because they are the ones which deal most closely with loving and with hating one's neighbors. INTRODUCTORY TRACTATE ON THE LETTER OF JAMES.[27]

MURDER AND ADULTERY SHOW HATE. OECUMENIUS: James added these commandments in order to give examples of what he was talking about, which was love. For someone who loves his neighbors as he ought to will neither commit adultery with them nor kill them. When these things are done, they indicate contempt for the neighbor. COMMENTARY ON JAMES.[28]

2:12 Judged by the Law of Liberty

EVERYONE FREE AND EQUAL. HILARY OF ARLES: By the New Testament law everyone is born again, free and equal with one another. INTRODUCTORY TRACTATE ON THE LETTER OF JAMES.[29]

NO FAVORITISM. OECUMENIUS: The law of liberty is the one which does not recognize classes of persons. This is the law of Christ. Whoever shows favoritism is not free but a slave, for "A man is a slave to the one by whom he has been overcome."[30] COMMENTARY ON JAMES.[31]

2:13 Mercy Triumphs Over Judgment

THE ART OF SHOWING MERCY. CHRYSOSTOM: Mercy is the highest art and the shield of those who practice it. It is the friend of God, standing always next to him and freely blessing whatever he wishes. It must not be despised by us. For in its purity it grants great liberty to those who respond to it in kind. It must be shown to those who have quarreled with us, as well as to those who have sinned against us, so great is its power. It breaks chains, dispels darkness, extinguishes fire, kills the worm and takes away the gnashing of teeth.[32] By it the gates of heaven open with the greatest of ease. In short, mercy is a queen which makes men like God. CATENA.[33]

ONE WHO HAS SHOWN NO MERCY. AUGUSTINE: He who judges without mercy will be judged without mercy. And in this sense only is the "same measure" to be understood, that

---

[25]PL 79:1096. [26]CEC 11. [27]PL Supp. 3:71. [28]PG 119:476. [29]PL Supp. 3:71. [30]2 Pet 2:19. [31]PG 119:476. [32]Cf. Mk 9:44-48. [33]CEC 13.

the mercy which he did not show will not be shown to him, and that the judgment which he makes will be eternal, even though the thing judged cannot be eternal. LETTER 102.4.[34]

AN OIL OF ESCAPE. HESYCHIUS: Just as oil enables athletes to escape the hands of their opponents, so mercy prepares those who practice it to avoid and escape the demons. CATENA.[35]

MERCY TRIUMPHS. BRAULIO OF SARAGOSSA: God will never cut us off by his severe judgment. Rather, "mercy triumphs over judgment" and with his accustomed faithfulness, he will unite us in the eternal blessedness of his storehouse, if that is agreeable to him. LETTERS 15.[36]

YOUR JUDGMENT AND GOD'S. HILARY OF ARLES: If you are merciful and lenient to the poor in your judgment, you will have nothing to fear from the judgment of God. INTRODUCTORY TRACTATE ON THE LETTER OF JAMES.[37]

FORGIVING AS WE ARE FORGIVEN. OECUMENIUS: If we forgive others the sins which they have committed against us and give alms to the poor and needy among us, then God's mercy will deliver us from judgment. But if, on the other hand, we are not well-disposed toward those around us, we shall receive the condemnation handed out to the wicked servant, along with the retribution which is mentioned in the Lord's Prayer. For there we ask God to forgive us as we forgive those who have sinned against us,[38] but if we do not forgive them, we shall not be forgiven either. COMMENTARY ON JAMES.[39]

---

[34]FC 18:168. [35]CEC 13. [36]FC 63:42. [37]PL Supp. 3:71. [38]Mt 6:12. [39]PG 119:476-47.

2:14-26 FAITH WITHOUT WORKS IS DEAD

[14]*What does it profit, my brethren, if a man says he has faith but has not works? Can his faith save him?* [15]*If a brother or sister is ill-clad and in lack of daily food,* [16]*and one of you says to them, "Go in peace, be warmed and filled," without giving them the things needed for the body, what does it profit?* [17]*So faith by itself, if it has no works, is dead.*

[18]*But some one will say, "You have faith and I have works." Show me your faith apart from your works, and I by my works will show you my faith.* [19]*You believe that God is one; you do well. Even the demons believe—and shudder.* [20]*Do you want to be shown, you shallow man, that faith apart from works is barren?* [21]*Was not Abraham our father justified by works, when he offered his son Isaac upon the altar?* [22]*You see that faith was active along with his works, and faith was completed by works,* [23]*and the scripture was fulfilled which says, "Abraham*

believed God, and it was reckoned to him as righteousness"; and he was called the friend of God. ²⁴You see that a man is justified by works and not by faith alone. ²⁵And in the same way was not also Rahab the harlot justified by works when she received the messengers and sent them out another way? ²⁶For as the body apart from the spirit is dead, so faith apart from works is dead.

OVERVIEW: The duty to help one's brothers and sisters in need is a paramount obligation of everyone who claims to have faith. Pious talk without equally serious deeds is not only useless but also wicked. Faith is shown through one's deeds (ANDREAS). Those who practice evil but think they have faith are confused (AUGUSTINE). Words alone do not help the hungry (BEDE). Love cares about the body as well as the soul (HILARY OF ARLES, VALERIAN OF CIMIEZ). Opportunities to care for the poor may pass quickly (CAESARIUS OF ARLES). Clemency will be exalted above condemnation for those who are merciful (LEO). Lacking works, faith is dead (ORIGEN, AUGUSTINE, LEO). Works give life to faith (HILARY OF ARLES). They have faith who are willing to follow Christ in his suffering (SYMEON). Words alone do not save (CHRYSOSTOM). Faith shows through deeds (SYMEON). The devils in a sense believe that God exists (BEDE) with trembling and wordy confessions that Christ is Son of God (ANDREAS, CAESARIUS) but not with active love (AUGUSTINE). Worse than the devils are those who presume to have faith but do not even tremble (HILARY OF ARLES). No one receives the gift of justification on the basis of merit derived from works performed beforehand (BEDE). Active faith shines forth through works (CYRIL OF ALEXANDRIA, SALVIAN). It is foolish to presume to believe without acting (OECUMENIUS).

The Fathers were well aware that Paul had spoken of salvation by faith without the works of the law, but they saw no contradiction between that and what James is saying here. The reason for this is that James and Paul are speaking in complementary ways. It is impossible to earn salvation by doing things to please God, and everyone must be clear that we can be saved only by faith. Both belief and action are intrinsic to faith (AUGUSTINE, BEDE, OECUMENIUS). Both Paul and James knew that Abraham was perfect in his faith as well as in his works (BEDE). James is talking here about faith after baptism, for a faith without works can only make us more guilty of sin, seeing that we have received a talent but are not using it profitably (OECUMENIUS). Prebaptismal faith does not of itself require works but only confession and the word of salvation, by which those who believe in Christ are justified. Postbaptismal faith is conjoined with works (ANDREAS). Isaac was an earthly type of Christ being offered up for us all (HILARY OF ARLES). When Abraham bound Isaac to the altar, he did not merely do it as a work that was required of him, but with the faith that in Isaac his seed would be as numberless as the stars of heaven, believing that God could raise him from the dead (CYRIL OF ALEXANDRIA, OECUMENIUS). It was by Abraham's perfect accomplishment of God's command that the active faith that he had in his heart was shown to be perfect (BEDE). His deeds were perfected by his faith (CYRIL OF JERUSALEM). Although orthodox belief is the foundation of our common confession as Christians, it is not good enough merely to mouth the words of a creed or pronounce blessings. Christians must back up what they say with what they do. Otherwise their words will be disregarded and condemned for the hypocrites that they so obviously are.

Abraham gives us a good example, since his faith led him to be willing to sacrifice his son Isaac. Rahab is even more remarkable. As a Gentile and a harlot, she did not have either the right theology or a respectable lifestyle, but God spared her because when the test came, she did the right thing. Rahab was justified by her faith because she performed works of mercy and showed hospitality to God's people (BEDE). Faith saves and then lives by doing its own works (DIDYMUS). Christians must therefore be both inspired and warned by these examples; inspired, because we possess so much more knowledge of the truth than either Abraham or Rahab possessed and can therefore do so much more than they did, but also warned, because if we fail to do even as much as they did, we shall be punished all the more severely for having rejected the knowledge that we have been given (BEDE).

2:14 Faith Without Works

PERSISTENT EVIL. AUGUSTINE: In order to help them, God has put fear in the hearts of believers, lest they think that they might be saved by faith alone, even if they continue to practice these evils. ON CONTINENCE 14.13.[1]

SHOW FAITH BY DEEDS. ANDREAS: If someone does not show by his deeds that he believes in God, his profession of faith is worthless. For it is not the one who just says that he is the Lord's who is a believer, but the one who loves the Lord so much that he is pre-

pared to risk even death because of his faith in him. CATENA.[2]

FAITH ELICITS ACTION. OECUMENIUS: Take note of what spiritual understanding really is. It is not enough to believe in a purely intellectual sense. There has to be some practical application for this belief. What James is saying here does not contradict the apostle Paul, who understood that both belief and action were a part of what he called "faith." COMMENTARY ON JAMES.[3]

2:15 The Hungry and Needy

LOVE HELPS THE BODY. HILARY OF ARLES: These are the words of faith, spoken to those who know that there is only one God, who is the Father of all his children. True love has two sides to it—help for the body and help for the soul. Here James concentrates on the first of these because he is speaking especially to those who are rich. INTRODUCTORY TRACTATE ON THE LETTER OF JAMES.[4]

WORDS ALONE DO NOT HELP. BEDE: It is obvious that words alone are not going to help someone who is naked and hungry. Someone whose faith does not go beyond words is useless. Such faith is dead without works of Christian love which alone can bring it back to life. CONCERNING THE EPISTLE OF ST. JAMES.[5]

2:16 Actions Speak Louder Than Words

CARE FOR THE BODY. VALERIAN OF CIMIEZ: Who does not hate this kind of [merely ver-

---

[1]FC 16:228-29. [2]CEC 14. [3]PG 119:477. [4]PL Supp. 3:71. [5]PL 93:21.

bal] "mercy"? In it an idle piety flatters the sick with elegant language. Fruitless tears are offered to heaven. What does it profit to bewail another man's shipwreck if you take no care of his body, which is suffering from exposure? What good does it do to torture your soul with grief over another's wound if you refuse him a health-giving cup? SERMONS 7.5.[6]

WORKS OF COMPASSION. LEO THE GREAT: Since mercy will be exalted over condemnation and the gifts of clemency will surpass any just compensation, all the lives led by mortals and all different kinds of actions will be appraised under the aspect of a single rule. No charges will be brought up where works of compassion have been found in acknowledgment of the Creator. SERMONS 11.1.[7]

OPPORTUNITY FOR COMPASSION PASSES. CAESARIUS OF ARLES: Christ says: "My justice can give you nothing except what your works deserve. To no purpose do you cry out, now that you are dead and in the power of another, for when you had opportunities and saw me in the person of the poor, you were blind." SERMONS 31.4.[8]

2:17 Faith Without Works Is Dead

LACKING WORKS, FAITH IS DEAD. ORIGEN: If someone dies in his sins he has not truly believed in Christ, even if he has made a profession of faith in him, and if faith is mentioned but it lacks works, such faith is dead, as we have read in the epistle which circulates as the work of James. COMMENTARY ON JOHN 19.152.[9]

KEEP THE COMMANDMENTS. AUGUSTINE: I do not understand why the Lord said, "If you

want to enter into eternal life, keep the commandments,"[10] and then mentioned the commandments relating to good behavior, if one is able to enter into eternal life without observing them. ON FAITH AND WORKS 15.25.[11]

THE STRENGTH OF FAITH. LEO THE GREAT: While faith provides the basis for works, the strength of faith comes out only in works. SERMONS 10.3.[12]

WORKS GIVE LIFE TO FAITH. HILARY OF ARLES: Works give life to faith, faith gives life to the soul, and the soul gives life to the body. INTRODUCTORY TRACTATE ON THE LETTER OF JAMES.[13]

ASHAMED TO FOLLOW CHRIST IN SUFFERING. SYMEON THE NEW THEOLOGIAN: If we are ashamed to imitate Christ's sufferings, which he endured for us, and to suffer as he suffered, it is obvious that we shall not become partakers with him in his glory. If that is true of us, we are believers in words only and not in deeds. DISCOURSES 6.10.[14]

2:18 Show Your Faith by Your Works

WORDS ALONE DO NOT SAVE. CHRYSOSTOM: Even if somebody believes rightly in the Father and the Son, as well as in the Holy Spirit, if he does not lead the right kind of life, his faith will not benefit him at all as far as his salvation is concerned. For although Jesus says: "This is eternal life, to know you, the only true God,"[15] we must not think that

---

[6]FC 17:349. [7]FC 93:47. [8]FC 31:157. [9]FC 89:202. [10]Mt 19:17 [11]FC 27:252. [12]FC 93:45. [13]PL Supp. 3:72. [14]CWS 128. [15]Jn 17:3.

merely uttering the words is enough to save us. For our life and behavior must be pure as well. CATENA.[16]

FAITH REFLECTED BY DEEDS. SYMEON THE NEW THEOLOGIAN: Faith is shown by deeds like the features of the face in a mirror. DISCOURSES 29.4.[17]

2:19 Even the Devils Believe—and Shudder

HOW DEMONS BELIEVE. AUGUSTINE: Those who believe and act according to true faith do live and are not dead, but those who do not believe, or else who believe like the demons, trembling but living evilly, proclaiming the Son of God but not having love, must rather be accounted dead. TRACTATES 22.7.2.[18]

THEY BELIEVE AND TREMBLE. AUGUSTINE: Will the devils see God? Those who are pure of heart will see him, and who would say that the devils are pure of heart? Nevertheless, they believe and tremble. COMMENTARY ON THE SERMON ON THE MOUNT 53.10.[19]

WORKS ATTEST FAITH. SALVIAN THE PRESBYTER: Good works are witnesses to the Christian faith, because otherwise a Christian cannot prove that he has that faith. If he cannot prove it, it must be considered completely nonexistent. ON THE GOVERNANCE OF GOD 4.2.[20]

BELIEF THAT LACKS REVERENCE. HILARY OF ARLES: Those who believe but who do not fear God are even worse than the devils. And those who believe and tremble but who do not practice what they preach are just like the devils. INTRODUCTORY TRACTATE ON THE LETTER OF JAMES.[21]

FAITH WITHOUT LOVE IS DEMONIC. BEDE: You can believe what God says, you can believe that God exists, and you can believe in him, which means that you love him so much that you want to do what he tells you. There are many evil people around who can manage the first two of these. They believe that God means what he says, and they are quite prepared to accept that he exists. But it takes someone who is not just a nominal Christian but who is one in deed and in living to love God and to do what he commands. Faith with love is Christian, but faith without love is demonic. CONCERNING THE EPISTLE OF ST. JAMES.[22]

LIP SERVICE TO FAITH. ANDREAS: James gives us the example of the devils, saying that those who profess faith with their lips only are really no better than they are. For even they believe that Christ is the Son of God, that he is the Holy One of God and that he has authority over them. CATENA.[23]

THE FAITH OF DEMONS. CAESARIUS OF ARLES: The apostle says that a man who believes and does not act has the faith of demons. If that is true, imagine the fate of a man who does not believe at all. SERMONS 12.5.[24]

2:20 Faith Apart from Works Is Barren

PAUL AND JAMES COMPLEMENTARY. AUGUSTINE: Holy Scripture should be interpreted in

---

[16]CEC 15. [17]CWS 312. [18]FC 79:203. [19]FC 11:219. [20]FC 3:92. [21]PL Supp. 3:72. [22]PL 93:22. [23]CEC 14-15. [24]FC 31:72.

a way which is in complete agreement with those who understood it and not in a way which seems to be inconsistent to those who are least familiar with it. Paul said that a man is justified through faith without the works of the law, but not without those works of which James speaks. ON THE CHRISTIAN LIFE 13.[25]

UPRIGHT LIVING. CYRIL OF ALEXANDRIA: Just as faith without works is dead, so the reverse is also true. Therefore let integrity in faith shine forth along with the glories of upright living. LETTERS 55.2.[26]

INTERPRETING PAUL AND JAMES TOGETHER. BEDE: Although the apostle Paul preached that we are justified by faith without works, those who understand by this that it does not matter whether they live evil lives or do wicked and terrible things, as long as they believe in Christ, because salvation is through faith, have made a great mistake. James here expounds how Paul's words ought to be understood. This is why he uses the example of Abraham, whom Paul also used as an example of faith, to show that the patriarch also performed good works in the light of his faith. It is therefore wrong to interpret Paul in such a way as to suggest that it did not matter whether Abraham put his faith into practice or not. What Paul meant was that no one obtains the gift of justification on the basis of merit derived from works performed beforehand, because the gift of justification comes only from faith. CONCERNING THE EPISTLE OF ST. JAMES.[27]

YOU FOOLISH PERSON! OECUMENIUS: According to James, someone who thinks that it is possible to believe without acting accordingly is out of his mind. COMMENTARY ON JAMES.[28]

2:21 Abraham and Isaac

WHAT ABRAHAM TOOK ON THE MOUNT OF SACRIFICE. HILARY OF ARLES: When Abraham went up the mountain to sacrifice Isaac, he took four things with him—a sword, fire, a heavy heart and a pile of wood. What does the fire stand for if not the suffering of Christ? What does the sword signify, if not death? What does the wood indicate, if not the cross? And what is the importance of Abraham's heavy heart, if it does not stand for the compassion of the Father and the angels as they beheld the death of Christ? Isaac was an earthly type of Christ and was offered up for us all. According to tradition this occurred on 25 March, the day on which the world was created, the day on which the last judgment will occur. The place where it happened was none other than the one which God would later choose for the site of his temple on Mount Zion, which is so called because Zion means "mirror of life," for it was there that Abraham saw as in a mirror the life which was to be revealed in the New Testament. INTRODUCTORY TRACTATE ON THE LETTER OF JAMES.[29]

ABRAHAM'S BELIEVING AND DOING. BEDE: James makes deft use of the example of Abraham in order to provoke those Jews who imagined that they were worthy followers of their great ancestor. In order to show them that they did not come up to the mark in times of trial and to test their faith by specific examples, James takes Abraham as his model. For what greater trial could there be than to demand that a man sacrifice his

---

[25]FC 16:36. [26]FC 77:15. [27]PL 93:22. [28]PG 119:480. [29]PL Supp. 3:73.

beloved son and heir? How much more would Abraham have preferred to give all the food and clothing he possessed to the poor than to be forced to make this supreme sacrifice at God's command? James is merely echoing what it says in Hebrews: "By faith Abraham, when he was tested, offered up Isaac, and he who had received the promises was ready to offer up his only son, of whom it was said, 'Through Isaac shall your descendants be named.'"[30] Looking at one and the same sacrifice, James praised the magnificence of Abraham's work, while Paul praised the constancy of his faith. But in reality the two men are saying exactly the same thing, because they both knew that Abraham was perfect in his faith as well as in his works, and each one merely emphasized that aspect of the incident which his own audience was most in need of hearing. CONCERNING THE EPISTLE OF ST. JAMES.[31]

DISTINGUISHING PRE- AND POSTBAPTIS-MAL FAITH. ANDREAS: Now someone might object to this and say: "Did Paul not use Abraham as an example of someone who was justified by faith, without works? And here James is using the very same Abraham as an example of someone who was justified, not by faith alone, but also by works which confirm that faith." How can we answer this? And how can Abraham be an example of faith without works, as well as of faith with works, at the same time? But the solution is ready to hand from the Scriptures. For the same Abraham is at different times an example of both kinds of faith. The first is prebaptismal faith, which does not require works but only confession and the word of salvation, by which those who believe in Christ are justified. The second is postbaptismal faith, which is combined with

works. Understood in this way, the two apostles do not contradict one another, but one and the same Spirit is speaking through both of them. CATENA.[32]

ABRAHAM'S ACTIVE FAITH. CYRIL OF ALEXANDRIA: On the one hand, the blessed James says that Abraham was justified by works when he bound Isaac his son on the altar, but on the other hand Paul says that he was justified by faith, which appears to be contradictory. However, this is to be understood as meaning that Abraham believed before he had Isaac and that Isaac was given to him as a reward for his faith. Likewise, when he bound Isaac to the altar, he did not merely do the work which was required of him, but he did it with the faith that in Isaac his seed would be as numberless as the stars of heaven, believing that God could raise him from the dead.[33] CATENA.[34]

2:22 Faith Is Completed by Works

NOTHING COMPARABLE TO GOD'S LOVE. CYRIL OF ALEXANDRIA: He has sacrificed the spiritual victim and announced that the laws of nature have been overcome. He has opened up the heart of his unquenchable love for humanity and shown that nothing on earth can compare with the love of God. CATENA.[35]

HIS VIBRANT FAITH ENACTED. BEDE: Abraham had such a vibrant faith in God that he was ready to do whatever God wanted him to. This is why his faith was reckoned to him as righteousness, and it was in order that we

---

[30]Heb 11:17-18. [31]PL 93:23. [32]CEC 16. [33]Rom 4:18-25. [34]CEC 17. [35]CEC 17.

might know the full meaning of this that God ordered Abraham to sacrifice his son. It was by his perfect accomplishment of God's command that the faith which he had in his heart was shown to be perfect. CONCERNING THE EPISTLE OF ST. JAMES.[36]

2:23 Abraham, the Friend of God

PROVED FAITHFUL. CLEMENT OF ROME: Abraham, who was called the friend of God, proved himself faithful by becoming obedient to the words of God. LETTER TO THE CORINTHIANS 10.1.[37]

HIS DEEDS PERFECTED BY FAITH. CYRIL OF JERUSALEM: Abraham was justified not by works but by faith. For although he had done many good things, he was not called a friend of God until he believed, and every one of his deeds was perfected by faith. CATECHETICAL LECTURES 5.5.[38]

GREAT FAITH AND WORKS. AUGUSTINE: That Abraham believed God deep in his heart is a matter of faith alone, but that he took his son to sacrifice him . . . is not just a great act of faith but a great work as well. SERMONS 2.9.[39]

APPROVED FOR HIS FAITH AND WORKS. OECUMENIUS: Abraham is the image of someone who is justified by faith alone, since what he believed was credited to him as righteousness. But he is also approved because of his works, since he offered up his son Isaac on the altar.[40] Of course he did not do this work by itself; in doing it, he remained firmly anchored in his faith, believing that through Isaac his seed would be multiplied until it was as numerous as the stars. COMMENTARY ON JAMES.[41]

2:24 Justified by Works As Well As Faith

RIGHTEOUSNESS AS A REWARD. CYRIL OF ALEXANDRIA: The person who in faith honors the God and ruler of all has righteousness as his reward. CATENA.[42]

WORKS OF FAITH. BEDE: The works mentioned here are works of faith. No one can have perfect works unless he has faith, but many have perfect faith without works, since they do not always have time to do them.[43] CONCERNING THE EPISTLE OF ST. JAMES.[44]

NOT WORKS OF LAW. THEOPHYLACT: The works of which James speaks are not those of the law but those of righteousness and the other virtues. COMMENTARY ON JAMES.[45]

2:25 Rahab's Story

NUMBERED AMONG THE SAINTS. PACHOMIUS: Rahab was a prostitute, but even so she was numbered among the saints. COMMUNION 3.25.[46]

A FLOWER IN THE MUD. SEVERIAN OF GABALA: Listen to the testimony of Scripture. In the midst of prostitution there was a pearl, in the mire there was burnished gold, in the mud there was a flower blooming with godliness. A godly soul was concealed in a land of impiety. CATENA.[47]

RAHAB JUSTIFIED BY HER FAITH. BEDE: There must have been some people who

---

[36]PL 93:23-24. [37]FC 1:17. [38]FC 61:141. [39]WSA 3/1:181. [40]Gen 22:10-18. [41]PG 119:481. [42]CEC 18. [43]If they die before having time to do good works, as in the case of martyrs. [44]PL 93:24. [45]PG 125:1161. [46]CS 47:23. [47]CEC 18.

would have argued that Abraham was a special case, since nobody would now be asked to make such a sacrifice, and that therefore his example does not really count. To answer this objection, James looks through the Scriptures and refers to the case of Rahab, a wicked woman and a foreigner to boot, who nevertheless was justified by her faith because she performed works of mercy and showed hospitality to members of God's people, even though her own life was thereby put in danger. CONCERNING THE EPISTLE OF ST. JAMES.[48]

2:26a As the Body Apart from the Spirit Is Dead

SPIRIT BRINGS LIFE TO THE BODY. DIDYMUS THE BLIND: Just as the spirit joins itself to the body and by doing so brings the latter to life, so works, joined to faith, give life to it as well. Furthermore, it is to be understood that faith without works is not faith at all, just as a dead man is not really a human being. But how can some say that because the spirit which gives life to the body is more honorable than the body, therefore works are more honorable than faith? I have looked into this matter in some detail and shall try to explain my position on this. It is undoubtedly true that the spirit is nobler than the body, but this does not mean that works can be put before faith, because a person is saved by grace, not by works but by faith. There should be no doubt but that faith saves and then lives by doing its own works, so that the works which are added to salvation by faith are not those of the law but a different kind of thing alto-

gether. COMMENTARY ON JAMES.[49]

2:26b So Faith Apart from Works Is Dead

DOCTRINE AND LIFE. CHRYSOSTOM: Faith without works is dead, and works without faith are dead also. For if we have sound doctrine but fail in living, the doctrine is of no use to us. Likewise if we take pains with life but are careless about doctrine, that will not be any good to us either. It is therefore necessary to shore up the spiritual edifice in both directions. SERMONS ON GENESIS 2.14.[50]

WHILE REMEDIES REMAIN. CAESARIUS OF ARLES: In order that we may bear the name Christian as a remedy, not leading to judgment, let us take up good works while the remedies are still within our power. SERMONS 13.1.[51]

FAITH AFTER BAPTISM. OECUMENIUS: James is talking here about faith after baptism, for a faith without works can only make us more guilty of sin, seeing that we have received a talent but are not using it profitably. The Lord himself demonstrated the need for works after baptism by going into the desert to do battle with the devil.[52] Paul also exhorts those who have entered into the mystery of faith to "strive to enter his peace,"[53] as if faith by itself were not enough. Holiness of life is also necessary, and for that great efforts are required. COMMENTARY ON JAMES.[54]

---

[48]PL 93:24. [49]PG 39:1752. [50]FC 74:37. [51]FC 31:75. [52]Mt 4:1-11. [53]Heb 4:4. [54]PG 119:481.

3:1-12 CONTROLLING THE TONGUE

[1]*Let not many of you become teachers, my brethren, for you know that we who teach shall be judged with greater strictness.* [2]*For we all make many mistakes, and if any one makes no mistakes in what he says he is a perfect man, able to bridle the whole body also.* [3]*If we put bits into the mouths of horses that they may obey us, we guide their whole bodies.* [4]*Look at the ships also; though they are so great and are driven by strong winds, they are guided by a very small rudder wherever the will of the pilot directs.* [5]*So the tongue is a little member and boasts of great things. How great a forest is set ablaze by a small fire!*

[6]*And the tongue is a fire. The tongue is an unrighteous world among our members, staining the whole body, setting on fire the cycle of nature,[b] and set on fire by hell.[c]* [7]*For every kind of beast and bird, of reptile and sea creature, can be tamed and has been tamed by humankind,* [8]*but no human being can tame the tongue—a restless evil, full of deadly poison.* [9]*With it we bless the Lord and Father, and with it we curse men, who are made in the likeness of God.* [10]*From the same mouth come blessing and cursing. My brethren, this ought not to be so.* [11]*Does a spring pour forth from the same opening fresh water and brackish?* [12]*Can a fig tree, my brethren, yield olives, or a grapevine figs? No more can salt water yield fresh.*

b Or *wheel of birth*   **c** Greek *Gehenna*

OVERVIEW: Nothing can destroy a fellowship more quickly than verbal abuse and gossip. The tongue is the most powerful weapon that we have, both for good and for evil. It is a matter for wonder that such a small part of the body can do such great things. It can preach the Word of God, win nations for Christ and glorify the name of our Creator. But it can also destroy character, divide churches and kill the soul. Human beings have learned to tame horses and ships, but their own tongues are another matter. Yet the tongue only reflects what is going on in the heart and soul of the person who is speaking, and it is this fact that is the real danger. For if a person claims to be a believer but then says things that contradict that claim, the truth is that he or she is not a Christian. No one is perfect, and we must be ready to make allowances for the failings of others rather than criticize them. Moreover, teachers will be judged by a higher standard, and therefore they must take special care not to fall into the trap of verbal abuse.

Christ chose only twelve teachers, and some of them did not come through (HILARY OF ARLES). The deeds of teachers must correspond with their words (CHRYSOSTOM, OECUMENIUS). Some are too eager to teach, so as to lead to false teaching (ISHO'DAD, BEDE). James singles out the tongue as a special instrument for either great good or great evil (DIDYMUS,

JEROME, BEDE). No one is free from sins of the tongue (AUGUSTINE, OECUMENIUS). Yet the saints seek to allay God's judgment on their speech (SEVERUS, CYRIL OF ALEXANDRIA) and pray for the healing of their speech (PACHOMIUS). We may be imperfect, but we can still seek to avoid deception, cursing, pride, boasting, quarreling, lying and perjury (BEDE). Sins of the tongue are many (BASIL). So put brakes on the mouth (AUGUSTINE, BEDE). The tongue is like a fire (HILARY OF ARLES) that can destroy a whole forest of good works just by saying evil things (BEDE). The tongue can infect like gangrene (PACHOMIUS, OECUMENIUS). The metaphor of the horse with bit in mouth (CHRYSOSTOM) is complemented by that of the ruddered ship (ANDREAS, OECUMENIUS): the great ship of life is blown by strong winds of passion yet directed by a small rudder—the intention of the heart (BEDE). Taming the tongue is harder than taming a wild beast (AUGUSTINE, ANDREAS). Like a sword, the tongue is capable of wounding (CHRYSOSTOM, HESYCHIUS). It is not made for cursing (ANDREAS). If mixed, the bitter water overcomes the sweet water (BEDE). Yet the bad tongue can be converted, as in the case of Paul (ANDREAS).

3:1a Let Not Many of You Become Teachers

CHRIST CHOSE ONLY TWELVE. HILARY OF ARLES: The apostle here prohibits a large number of teachers, for even our Lord Jesus Christ chose only a few for this role. He had only twelve disciples, and not all of them went on to become teachers of the gospel. INTRODUCTORY TRACTATE ON THE LETTER OF JAMES.[1]

A WARNING AGAINST FALSE TEACHING.

ISHO'DAD OF MERV: James is not trying to limit the number of teachers but rather to warn them against the dangers of false doctrines. COMMENTARIES.[2]

3:1b Teachers Judged with Greater Strictness

LET WORDS AND DEEDS CORRESPOND. CHRYSOSTOM: Teaching without setting an example is not only worthless but also brings great punishment and judgment on the one who leads his life with such heedlessness, throwing out the pride of those who do not want to practice what they preach. So reject the teaching of those who teach without setting an example and pass judgment on them. Yet if there is no contradiction between what he says and what he does, and he is able to control his entire body, then do not condemn him. For if he teaches such things and surrounds the right words of his faith with outstanding deeds corresponding to it, it is clear that he is fully in charge of his body and has no love for the things of the world. CATENA.[3]

MORE SEVERE JUDGMENT. OECUMENIUS: If a person does not practice what he preaches, he will be judged more severely, since his teaching has borne no fruit. For such a person is condemned along with the one who has sinned with his tongue. COMMENTARY ON JAMES.[4]

THE UNDERLYING TEXT. BEDE: James indicates that judgment which was pronounced long ago [in Psalm 50:16-17]. ON THE

---

[1]PL Supp. 3:75. [2]CIM 36-37. [3]CEC 18. [4]PG 119:481.

TABERNACLE AND ITS VESSELS 3.1.95.[5]

OVEREAGERNESS TO TEACH. BEDE: In the days of the apostles there were many who were eager to go out preaching the Word of God but who lacked proper instruction. One of them was Apollos, who preached Christ perfectly well but who for some reason knew only the baptism of John. But because he was a wise person, it was not long before a teacher appeared and led him into greater truth, which he readily accepted and thus became even better at his preaching task. There were others who were much less skilled who went to Antioch from Judea and told people there that they had to be circumcised according to the law of Moses if they wanted to be saved, a message which gave orthodox preachers no little trouble. It is this second kind of teacher that James wants to remove from office, so that they will not be a hindrance to those who are trying to preach the gospel in the right way. For just as someone who serves well obtains a good report, so someone who tries to usurp the right to teach when he is not prepared to do so deserves greater punishment than the one he would have received if he had kept his wickedness to himself. CONCERNING THE EPISTLE OF ST. JAMES.[6]

3:2 We All Make Mistakes

OUR IMPERFECTION. AUGUSTINE: Who then would ever dare to call himself perfect? SERMONS 23.[7]

ALLAYING GOD'S JUDGMENT. SEVERUS OF ANTIOCH: If one of Christ's own disciples can talk like this,[8] we must make it our business to press toward the opposite direction, so as to allay the God and judge of all things for those times when in the weakness of our humanity we have fallen into wrongdoing, failing to pay heed to our salvation. CATENA.[9]

AVOID FOOLISH TALK. CYRIL OF ALEXANDRIA: The effective proof of a sound mind and perfect thought is to have nothing faulty on our tongue and to keep our mouths closed when necessary. For it is better to be guided by worthy speech, which is able to know and to express the fullness of all praise. For the most useful talent is to be able to speak wisdom when talking about how to live well. Foolish talk should be foreign to the saints. CATENA.[10]

PRAY FOR HEALING. PACHOMIUS: We all fall very often, but let us pray to the merciful God, and if we watch over ourselves in the future, he will heal us. COMMUNION 1.68.[11]

PERFECT SILENCE. HILARY OF ARLES: Perfection consists of righteousness, and silence is the way to achieve it. This is why James connects perfection with keeping one's mouth shut. INTRODUCTORY TRACTATE ON THE LETTER OF JAMES.[12]

CONTROL THE TONGUE. BEDE: James reminds us here that even good people are not perfect and that we all need to be led by the grace of the Holy Spirit, for there is no one[13] who can go through life without ever sinning at all. Nevertheless, there are different kinds of sins, and James singles out one area of our

---

[5]TTH 18:108. [6]PL 93:25. [7]WSA 3/2:57. [8]Saying that we all make mistakes. [9]CEC 18. [10]CEC 19. [11]CS 45:90. [12]PL Supp. 3:75. [13]Among fallen humanity.

lives where perfection is attainable, namely, control of the tongue. We may be imperfect, but we can still learn to avoid deception, abuse, cursing, pride, boasting, envy, quarreling, lying, perjury and so on. CONCERNING THE EPISTLE OF ST. JAMES.[14]

SINS OF THE TONGUE. OECUMENIUS: James shows from the faults of the tongue that there is nobody who goes through life without sinning. From this he proves that nobody is perfect. COMMENTARY ON JAMES.[15]

3:3 Bits into the Mouths of Horses

SO GOD TAMES HUMANITY. AUGUSTINE: Note that the comparison is taken from the beasts which we are able to tame. The horse does not tame itself, nor does a man do so. A man is needed in order to tame a horse, and in the same way, God is needed in order to tame a man. COMMENTARY ON THE SERMON ON THE MOUNT 55.2.[16]

PUTTING BRAKES ON THE MOUTH. BEDE: In other words, says James, how much more appropriate is it to put a brake in our own mouths so that we say only what agrees with the teachings of our Creator, and by controlling our tongues guide our doings in the right way also? CONCERNING THE EPISTLE OF ST. JAMES.[17]

3:4 The Great Ship's Small Rudder

GREAT SHIPS, STRONG WINDS, SMALL RUDDER. BEDE: These great ships stand for the minds of people in this life, whether they are good or bad. The strong winds which threaten them are the desires of these minds, by which they are naturally forced to act and

which bring them either to a good or to a bad end. The rudder which directs them is the intention of the heart by which the elect cross the waves of this life and finally reach the harbor of their heavenly home. CONCERNING THE EPISTLE OF ST. JAMES.[18]

GUIDING THE TONGUE. ANDREAS: James says that if we can contain the spirits of a horse by putting a bit into his mouth and control the direction of a ship with a small rudder, how much more ought we to be able to guide the tongue by right words toward doing good. CATENA.[19]

THE ANALOGIES WORK TOGETHER. OECUMENIUS: This confirms what has been said about the tongue and adds something more to it, for the person who can domesticate an animal in so simple a manner will also master that which is more difficult to control. It is probable that James chose this example because somebody asked him why it was so difficult to contain something as small as the tongue. The text also implies that we should go on from merely controlling our tongues and find a higher use for them. For just as a domesticated horse is then used for better purposes, as is a ship under control, so our tongues ought to be used for saying the right thing at the right time. COMMENTARY ON JAMES.[20]

3:5 The Power of the Tongue

THE TONGUE AND THE BODY. DIDYMUS THE BLIND: In attacking what they say, James singles out the tongue, which is the instrument

---

[14]PL 93:25-26. [15]PG 119:484. [16]FC 11:234. [17]PL 93:26. [18]PL 93:26. [19]CEC 19-20. [20]PG 119:484.

of speech. But since their thoughts are present in the body as a whole, it ought to be understood that his remarks apply to the entire body. COMMENTARY ON JAMES.[21]

THE TONGUE KNOWS GREAT GOOD AND GREAT EVIL.

JEROME: The sword kills the body, but the tongue kills the soul. The tongue knows no moderation—either it is a great good or it is a great evil. It is a great good when it acknowledges that Christ is God, and a great evil when it denies that. Let no one deceive himself into thinking that he has never sinned, for if I have sinned, it is with my tongue. What more monstrous sin is there than blasphemy against God? The devil did not fall because he committed theft, murder or adultery; he fell because of his tongue. He said: "I will scale the heavens; above the stars I will set up my throne, I will be like the most high."[22] SERMONS 41.[23]

THE MISERY OF THE TONGUE.

JEROME: The more the tongue has sinned, the more it is miserable. SERMONS 86.[24]

THE VARIABLE CAPACITY OF THE TONGUE.

BEDE: The tongue can indeed boast of great things if it is properly controlled. But if the tongue is evil it will only be able to boast of evil things, which are not great at all. CONCERNING THE EPISTLE OF ST. JAMES.[25]

3:6 The Tongue Is a Fire

SINS OF THE TONGUE ARE MANY.

BASIL THE GREAT: If you love life, fulfill the commandment of life. "The one who loves me," said Jesus, "keeps my commandments,"[26] and the first commandment is this: "Keep your tongue from evil, and your lips from speaking guile."[27]

For the sin which is caused by the tongue is very active and many-sided, being active in wrath, lust, hypocrisy, judgment and deception. Do we need to recall the many names which are given to sins of the tongue? For from it come slanders, coarse jokes, idiocies, irrelevant accusations, bitterness, swearing, false witness—the tongue is the creator of all these evil things and more. CATENA.[28]

GUARDING THE TONGUE.

CHRYSOSTOM: Therefore, guard the tip of the tongue, for it is like a majestic stallion. For if you put a bit in its mouth and teach it to walk in order, it adapts to this and is satisfied. But if you let it run wild, it becomes the vehicle of the devil and his angels. CATENA.[29]

THE TONGUE ABLAZE.

BEDE: The tongue is a fire which can destroy a whole forest of good works just by saying things which are evil. This fire is the exact opposite of that saving fire which is also like a tongue and which consumes all the dross and chaff of our vices, revealing the secrets of the heart. The saints are inflamed by it, they burn with love because of it, and by their preaching they set others ablaze like tongues of fire. CONCERNING THE EPISTLE OF ST. JAMES.[30]

LEADING INTO RASHNESS.

ANDREAS: James did not say that the course of our life ignites the tongue but that the tongue ignites the course of our life. For it causes us to make wrong decisions and leads us into rashness. By it, our life is thrown off course and subjected to many kinds of wickedness. CATENA.[31]

---

[21]PG 39:1753. [22]Is 14:13-14. [23]FC 48:306, in reference to Is 14:13-14. [24]FC 57:204. [25]PL 93:26. [26]See Jn 14:21. [27]Ps 34:13; 1 Pet 3:10. [28]CEC 21. [29]CEC 20. [30]PL 93:27. [31]CEC 20.

GANGRENE TO THE SOUL. PACHOMIUS: The bragging tongue fouls the whole body and is gangrene to the soul. COMMUNION 3.38.[32]

INIQUITY BURNS. HILARY OF ARLES: Iniquity stains us in the same way as wood is scorched by fire, and hell burns as if it were a fire. INTRODUCTORY TRACTATE ON THE LETTER OF JAMES.[33]

A WORLD OF EVIL. OECUMENIUS: The tongue is described as a "world" of evil, because the word *world* implies a large quantity. The phrase should thus be interpreted as "a great evil." COMMENTARY ON JAMES.[34]

3:7 Taming the Animals

TAMING THE WILD TONGUE. BEDE: We read in Pliny of how a householder managed to tame an immense asp, so that the snake emerged each day from its hole and brought the day's food to the man's table. We also read in Ammianus Marcellinus of a domesticated tigress which was sent to the emperor Anastasius from India. James emphasizes that that kind of thing is child's play compared with the art of taming the tongue, because the tongue is much wilder and more ferocious than any animal. CONCERNING THE EPISTLE OF ST. JAMES.[35]

CONTROLLING THE TONGUE. ANDREAS: James says that it is unnatural that we should be able to domesticate all the creatures but not be able to control our own tongues. CATENA.[36]

3:8 Taming the Tongue

CAPABLE OF WOUNDING. CHRYSOSTOM: The tongue is a piercing sword. But let us not wound others with it; rather let us cut off our own gangrene. CATENA.[37]

TAMING THE TONGUE HARDER THAN TAMING THE BEAST. AUGUSTINE: I do not believe that this passage can bear the interpretation which Pelagius wants to put on it. He says that this is stated as a reproach, as if one were to say: "Is no one therefore able to control his tongue?" As if it were easier to tame the tongue than to tame wild beasts. But I do not believe that this is the meaning. If James had wanted to say that, he would have done so, but instead he was determined to show what a great evil a man's tongue can be, so great that it cannot be tamed by anyone, even though that is not true of wild beasts. He said this not in order that we should tolerate this evil but in order that we should ask for divine grace to tame our tongue. ON NATURE AND GRACE 15 (16).[38]

THE SHARPNESS OF THE SWORD. HESYCHIUS: Just as a sword, if it is sharpened, is more easily able to kill, so the tongue, which has great difficulty in keeping itself quiet and cannot easily be controlled, becomes more insolent if it learns from bad people how to deceive, how to slander and how to incriminate. CATENA.[39]

3:10 Blessing and Cursing

THE TONGUE NOT FOR CURSING. ANDREAS: Nothing bitter should come out of a mouth which has uttered the praise of so great a mystery, nor should the tongue say anything which

---

[32]CS 47:31. [33]PL Supp. 3:76. [34]PG 119:488. [35]PL 93:28. [36]CEC 22. [37]CEC 23. [38]FC 86:32-33. [39]CEC 23.

is unworthy of a holy mouth. Let us keep it pure and not use it to curse. For if those who rail against God will not inherit the kingdom, how much more will this be true of those who curse? CATENA.[40]

3:11 Good and Bad Water from the Same Spring

SWEET SPRING WATER. HILARY OF ARLES: The spring is the heart of man, the flowing stream of water is his speech, and the opening through which it pours is his mouth. The sweet water is sound doctrine, while the bitter water is just the opposite. INTRODUCTORY TRACTATE ON THE LETTER OF JAMES.[41]

IF MIXED, THE BITTER OVERCOMES THE SWEET WATER. BEDE: Not only is it impossible for sweet and bitter water to come out of one and the same fountain, but it is also true that if the two get mixed, it is the bitter which will affect the sweet, not the other way round. Put blessing and cursing together, and cursing will win out every time. Bad habits corrupt good manners, and wicked talk has the same effect. CONCERNING THE EPISTLE OF ST. JAMES.[42]

3:12 Can a Fig Tree Produce Olives?

MIXING HUMAN AND DIVINE THINGS. ANDREAS: For being power-hungry and filled with the wisdom of the world, they preached with the force and zeal of orthodox teachers, gathering a crowd with no trouble at all and deceiving them, mixing human things with the divine, so that the hearers might be dazzled by the newness of what was being said. That is how heresy arose. But James forbids that kind of teaching and whatever comes from a wisdom which is not divine but diabolical. He said all this in order to praise good teaching, the wisdom which comes from humility in words and in useful deeds. CA-TENA.[43]

THE HEART AND THE TONGUE. BEDE: It is clear from this that a heart which is not right with God cannot bring forth the words or the works of righteousness. On the contrary, if the heart is wicked, everything it says and does will be wicked also. CONCERNING THE EPISTLE OF ST. JAMES.[44]

---

[40]CEC 23. [41]PL Supp. 3:76. [42]PL 93:28-29. [43]CEC 23-24. [44]PL 93:29.

3:13-18 TRUE WISDOM

[13]*Who is wise and understanding among you? By his good life let him show his works in the meekness of wisdom.* [14]*But if you have bitter jealousy and selfish ambition in your hearts, do not boast and be false to the truth.* [15]*This wisdom is not such as comes down from above, but is*

earthly, unspiritual, devilish. [16]*For where jealousy and selfish ambition exist, there will be disorder and every vile practice.* [17]*But the wisdom from above is first pure, then peaceable, gentle, open to reason, full of mercy and good fruits, without uncertainty or insincerity.* [18]*And the harvest of righteousness is sown in peace by those who make peace.*

OVERVIEW: James picks up the theme of wisdom from the first chapter and discusses it in greater detail here. True wisdom is a gift of God, and therefore it reflects his character. By your humble and wise actions show who you are (BEDE). People who boast or who display signs of jealousy and selfishness do not have God's wisdom but a false imitation that comes from the world, the flesh and the devil. This false wisdom is a lie that leads to every kind of evil practice, and Christians must do their utmost to avoid it. God's wisdom has many important features, but it is most noticeable when it brings peace within and among believers. Bitterness and jealousy are demonically conceived (CASSIODORUS) and taint everything they touch (BEDE). As long as the soul seeks earthly glory, it is deprived of spiritual grace (BEDE). As filth blinds, so does ambition (CHRYSOSTOM). Gracious wisdom, born of pure thoughts (BEDE), comes from above, not from our power (AUGUSTINE). Having labored in this world, rejoice in the harvest of right-eousness in the world to come (ORIGEN). Those who desire peace sow the earth with the best seed and by their daily actions gain an increase that entitles them to inherit the fruits of right-eousness in eternal life (BEDE).

3:13 The Meekness of Wisdom

BY YOUR GOOD LIFE SHOW YOUR WORKS. BEDE: Just as James has imposed silence on unworthy teachers and on those who want to obtain a teaching post without having the right qualifications of right living and circumspect behavior, so he also exhorts those who are wise and self-disciplined, or who at least think they are such, to demonstrate that fact by living out what they profess more than by trying to teach others. For someone who lives in a humble and wise way will give more evidence of his standing before God than any number of words could ever do. CONCERNING THE EPISTLE OF ST. JAMES.[1]

3:14 Jealousy and Ambition

JEALOUSY ELICITS STRIFE. CASSIODORUS: The mature faithful should not have any bitterness or jealousy in them, since such things are not given by God but are conceived by diabolical fraud. For where there is jealousy there is strife, disloyalty and every kind of evil which divine authority condemns. SUMMARY OF JAMES.[2]

3:15 Worldly Wisdom

SEEKING EARTHLY GLORY. BEDE: Paul also says: "The unspiritual man does not know the things which come from the Spirit of God."[3] Contentious and proud wisdom is rightly described as earthly, unspiritual and devilish because as long as the soul seeks earthly glory it is deprived of spiritual grace and remains cut off from God. For now it thinks only what

---

[1]PL 93:30. [2]PL 70:1379. [3]1 Cor 2:14.

comes naturally to it since it originally fell.[4] It is persuaded by the delusion of an evil spirit to do things which are wicked and harmful. CONCERNING THE EPISTLE OF ST. JAMES.[5]

3:16 Disorder and Every Vile Practice

FILTH AND AMBITION BLIND. CHRYSOSTOM: Let us cleanse the eyes of our souls of all filth. For just as filth and mud blind the eyes of the flesh, so too worldly concerns and discussions about moneymaking can dull the hearing of our minds more effectively than any filth, and not only corrupt them but do wicked things as well. CATENA.[6]

JEALOUSY TAINTS EVERYTHING IT TOUCHES. BEDE: The heart is like a root and contains within itself all the fruit of the action which proceeds from it. Someone who operates from a spirit of jealousy and strife will do nothing which is not tainted with evil, however good it may appear to others. CONCERNING THE EPISTLE OF ST. JAMES.[7]

3:17 The Wisdom from Above

NOT FROM OUR POWER. AUGUSTINE: This is the wisdom which tames the tongue, descending from above, not springing from the human heart. Would anyone dare to snatch it away from the grace of God and, with overweening pride, place it in the power of man? ON NATURE AND GRACE 16 (17).[8]

BORN IN PURE THOUGHTS. BEDE: The wisdom from above is pure because it thinks only pure thoughts, and it is peaceable because it does not dissociate itself from others on account of its pride. The other virtues mentioned here are the common possession of any wise person, and they will manifest themselves in a life full of mercy and other good works. CONCERNING THE EPISTLE OF ST. JAMES.[9]

3:18 The Harvest of Righteousness Sown in Peace

REJOICE IN THE HARVEST TO COME. ORIGEN: You shall rejoice in the morning, that is, in the world to come, if you have gathered the fruits of righteousness by weeping and labor in this world. SERMONS ON GENESIS 10.3.[10]

SOW THE EARTH WITH THE BEST SEED. BEDE: Everything we do in this life contains within it the seed of future reward. Paul says the same thing when he writes: "Whatever a man sows, that will he also reap."[11] Therefore it is rightly said that the fruit of righteousness is sown in peace by those who make peace. For the fruit of righteousness is eternal life, which is the reward for good works, so that those who desire peace and implement it sow the earth with the best seed there is, and by their daily actions gain an increase which entitles them to inherit the fruits of life in heaven. The reprobate also reap what they sow, because they will also receive their just reward at the judgment. But that reward will not be the fruits of eternal life, but corruption, because they will reap the eternal punishment due to the corruption in which they passed their lives on earth. CONCERNING THE EPISTLE OF ST. JAMES.[12]

---

[4]In the garden of Eden. [5]PL 93:30. [6]CEC 24. [7]PL 93:30. [8]FC 86:33. [9]PL 93:31. [10]FC 71:163. [11]Gal 6:7. [12]PL 93:31.

4:1-10 EFFECTIVE PRAYER

[1]*What causes wars, and what causes fightings among you? Is it not your passions that are at war in your members?* [2]*You desire and do not have; so you kill. And you covet*[d] *and cannot obtain; so you fight and wage war. You do not have, because you do not ask.* [3]*You ask and do not receive, because you ask wrongly, to spend it on your passions.* [4]*Unfaithful creatures! Do you not know that friendship with the world is enmity with God? Therefore whoever wishes to be a friend of the world makes himself an enemy of God.* [5]*Or do you suppose it is in vain that the scripture says, "He yearns jealously over the spirit which he has made to dwell in us"?* [6]*But he gives more grace; therefore it says, "God opposes the proud, but gives grace to the humble."* [7]*Submit yourselves therefore to God. Resist the devil and he will flee from you.* [8]*Draw near to God and he will draw near to you. Cleanse your hands, you sinners, and purify your hearts, you men of double mind.* [9]*Be wretched and mourn and weep. Let your laughter be turned to mourning and your joy to dejection.* [10]*Humble yourselves before the Lord and he will exalt you.*

d Or you kill and you covet

OVERVIEW: There is nothing wrong with wanting to enjoy God's creation, but everything depends on recognizing what those good things are and seeking them in the right way. Do not become fixated on making comparisons between what you own and what your neighbor owns (DIONYSIUS OF ALEXANDRIA). This intensifies the struggle within (BEDE). When someone desires something inordinately, it tends to ensure the receiving of the opposite (OECUMENIUS). God will see to it that petitions arising from bad motives will not be fulfilled (AUGUSTINE, ANDREAS). So pray for right motives (BEDE). The godly petitioner asks only for what is compatible with the divine promises (DIDYMUS), for what pleases God and for what God will freely give (PSEUDO-DIONYSIUS). There can be no enduring coexistence of virtue with evil (ORIGEN,

DIDYMUS), and so it has been since the fallen angels and Adam (HILARY OF ARLES). Our enmities tend to make us morally blind (OECUMENIUS, SYMEON). So make the proper use of wisdom (OECUMENIUS).

God yearns jealously over the spirit that he has made to dwell in us. This is so whether it refers to God's Spirit or the spirit in us that draws us toward God (SEVERIAN, BEDE). Beware of self-conceit (JEROME, AUGUSTINE). Draw near to gracious people (CLEMENT OF ROME). God wants to dwell in you (CAESARIUS OF ARLES), but this indwelling can occur only in a humble, merciful heart (MACARIUS OF EGYPT, VALERIAN). God resists the proud who trust in their own strength but gives grace to the humble because they recognize their need and ask him for help (DIDYMUS, HESYCHIUS, BEDE, OECUMENIUS). God dwells in us (AMbrose) that he might destroy the death that has come upon us and give us more grace (ANDREAS).

Meanwhile we must fight against demonic captivity (CAESARIUS OF ARLES), a struggle in which one cannot be double-minded (OECUMENIUS). Those who remain unashamed of their sin are miserable, not so much because they have fallen from grace but because they have remained in their fallen state (CHRYSOSTOM). Mourn your sins (LEANDER). Be ready to repent while there is time (BEDE). The most important blessings that we can ever receive are spiritual ones, and Christians must be sufficiently detached from the cares of this world that they can recognize this and pray for that kind of blessing. There is no room here for compromise. To embrace the world is to reject God. By *world* James means the desires of ungodly people, who are at war with the Spirit of God. The only way to deal with this effectively is to humble ourselves and turn back to God in prayer and supplication. If we do this, we shall be full of contrition, and our prayers will be punctured by weeping rather than by laughter. Only if we come to God as abject penitents will he be willing to help us, but when we have that attitude, then we shall discover that far from rejecting us, he lifts us up and receives us with great joy and gladness into his heavenly kingdom.

4:1a The Cause of Infighting

EXCESSIVE COMPARISON. DIONYSIUS: When a man has bought a large enough field and sees that his neighbor's is larger still, he wants to increase his own so as to make his house greater. CATENA.[1]

THE TEST OF TEACHING. ANDREAS: James shows that the teaching[2] is not working, for they are all carnal and doing the most wicked things. CATENA.[3]

4:1b Your Passions at War

THE STRUGGLE WITHIN. BEDE: Your passions are at war in your members whenever your hands or your tongue or some combination of your bodily parts obeys the promptings of your depraved mind. It is also possible that the passions mentioned here are in fact good desires, pointing towards the riches and benefits of God's kingdom. On account of these and many other such things there is often a struggle between good and evil going on in our minds. CONCERNING THE EPISTLE OF ST. JAMES.[4]

4:2 You Do Not Have Because You Do Not Ask

ASK FOR RIGHT MOTIVES. BEDE: The reason that you struggle but fail to obtain what you want is that you do not ask God to give these things to you. For if you ask him with the right motives, he will give you not only everything you need here on earth but also what you need to get to heaven. CONCERNING THE EPISTLE OF ST. JAMES.[5]

THE OPPOSITE OBTAINED FROM WRONG DESIRES. OECUMENIUS: James proceeds here by way of thesis and antithesis. The thesis, that is, what they desire, is absurd to begin with, but the way they go about getting what they want ensures the exact opposite. Murder

---

[1]CEC 25. [2]The skewed teaching that the people have received. [3]CEC 25. [4]PL 93:31-32. [5]PL 93:32.

and fighting are not good things, but neither do the good things which they desire follow from them. Note also that here James speaks of murder and of fighting as spiritual things, not physical ones. It would be bad enough to think this kind of thing about robbers, but how much worse it is when we are dealing with people who have a certain amount of faith and who have turned to God. These are people who are trying to kill the soul and to fight against godliness. COMMENTARY ON JAMES.[6]

4:3 You Ask but Do Not Receive

ASK IN THE RIGHT SPIRIT. DIDYMUS THE BLIND: The Savior said: "Ask and you will receive. Everyone who asks will receive."[7] How can it be then that some people pray but do not get what they ask for? To this it must be answered that if someone comes to prayer in the right way, omitting none of the prerequisites for intercession, he will receive everything he asks for. But if someone appears to be going beyond the permissible bounds laid down for intercession, he will appear to be asking for something in the wrong way and therefore will not obtain it. COMMENTARY ON JAMES.[8]

ABUSIVE INTENTIONS. AUGUSTINE: If someone intends to misuse what he receives, he will not receive it. Instead, God will pity him. TRACTATES 73.1.[9]

GOD GRASPS OUR WORTHINESS TO RECEIVE. ANDREAS: It appears that some ask but do not receive. God ignores those who attack him and those who ask wrongly, according to their own desires. But someone will say that even those who ask for divine

wisdom and virtue do not receive them. In reply it must be said that such people may be worthy to receive these good things, but they must do so in the right way. Perhaps they want such things merely for the pleasure of having them, and if so, they will not get them. CATENA.[10]

ASKING FOR WHAT PLEASES GOD. PSEUDO-DIONYSIUS: The hierarch,[11] being a man of God, asks only for what is compatible with the divine promises, for what pleases God and for what God will freely give. He thereby demonstrates to God the lover of good that his own conduct is always modeled on the Good and shows those who are present what kinds of gifts the saints will receive. ON THE ECCLESIASTICAL HIERARCHY 7.3.7.[12]

FALSE PETITIONS. BEDE: Those who continue in their sins ask wrongly. They entreat the Lord ill-advisedly to forgive them sins which they are not prepared to forgive in others. HOMILIES ON THE GOSPELS 2.14.[13]

4:4 Friendship with the World Is Enmity with God

VIRTUE AND EVIL. ORIGEN: Since evil forms a friendship with the world and virtue a friendship with God, virtue and evil cannot coexist. CATENA.[14]

GOD AND MAMMON OPPOSITES. DIDYMUS THE BLIND: Whoever loves the world by committing sin is revealed as an enemy of God,

---

[6]PG 119:492. [7]Mt 7:7-8. [8]PG 39:1753. [9]FC 90:84. [10]CEC 26. [11]One who stands within the right ordering of God's providential design. [12]CWS 256. [13]HOG 2:127. [14]CEC 26.

just as, on the other hand, one who affirms friendship with God by not sinning is a constant enemy of the world. Therefore, just as it is impossible to serve both God and mammon,[15] so it is also impossible to be a friend of the world and of God at the same time. COMMENTARY ON JAMES.[16]

EVEN THE SON FACED THESE ENMITIES.

AUGUSTINE: It was because of these enmities toward God that not even his only-begotten Son was spared. TRACTATES 101.2.[17]

THE UNDOING OF THE FALLEN ANGELS.

HILARY OF ARLES: Love of honor and pride and boastfulness is hostile to God, for these things were the undoing of the fallen angels as well as of the first human couple, which is why to this day they are described as "enemies of God." INTRODUCTORY TRACTATE ON THE LETTER OF JAMES.[18]

TOLERATING ADULTEROUS TEACHERS.

OECUMENIUS: James calls these people adulterers, not because they practiced physical adultery but because they corrupted the commands which were instituted by God and turned away to other loves. They were even prepared to tolerate an adulterous teacher, even if it was clear that he was as deep in the mud as any pig. COMMENTARY ON JAMES.[19]

ENMITY TENDS TOWARD BLINDNESS.

SYMEON THE NEW THEOLOGIAN: When one is at enmity toward someone else, he has no idea how to explain to others what that person approves of or likes, nor is he able to instruct them concerning his desires. DISCOURSES 2.11.[20]

4:5 The Spirit He Has Made to Dwell in Us

THE SPIRIT DRAWS US TOWARD GOD.

SEVERIAN OF GABALA: What this means is that the Spirit in us tends toward fellowship with God. He turns us away from the love of the world and gives us ever more grace. CATENA.[21]

WHETHER THIS IS THE HUMAN SPIRIT.

BEDE: Some think that this refers to God's Spirit, which does battle inside us against envy and tries to rid us of it. Others, however, think that it refers to the human spirit and is a warning to us not to desire or to attach ourselves to the lusts of this world, because as long as the spirit of our mind desires earthly things it does so with envy, because it envies the fact that others have what it wants to obtain. CONCERNING THE EPISTLE OF ST. JAMES.[22]

USE WISDOM RIGHTLY.

OECUMENIUS: James is here using an abbreviated form of speech in order to convey his meaning. What he is saying is this: "I have thus far been warning you in my own words to make the right and proper use of your wisdom that you might not abuse it in your pride by corrupting it or misinterpreting it by your overly clever preaching." COMMENTARY ON JAMES.[23]

4:6 God Opposes the Proud but Gives Grace to the Humble

DRAW NEAR TO GRACIOUS PEOPLE.

CLEMENT OF ROME: Scripture says that God resists the arrogant but gives grace to the humble. We should associate with those to whom

---

[15]Mt 6:24. [16]PG 39:1754. [17]FC 90:235. [18]PL Supp. 3:78. [19]PG 119:492. [20]CWS 56. [21]CEC 29. [22]PL 93:33. [23]PG 119:496.

God's grace has been given. LETTER TO THE
CORINTHIANS 1.30.2-3.[24]

AGAINST THOSE WHO DEMEAN MARRIAGE.
CLEMENT OF ALEXANDRIA: There are those
who say openly that marriage is fornication.
They lay it down as a dogma that it was instituted by the devil. They are arrogant and claim
that they are emulating the Lord, who did not
marry and had no worldly possessions. It is
their boast that they have a deeper understanding of the gospel than anyone else. To them
Scripture says that God is against the proud
and gives grace to the humble. STROMATEIS
3.49.1-2.[25]

WARNING AGAINST SELF-CONCEIT. AUGUS-
TINE: Give me someone professing perpetual
continence, who is free from all vices and
blemishes of conduct. For her I fear pride
—I dread the swelling of self-conceit from
so great a blessing. The more there is in her
which she is satisfied with, the more I fear
that in pleasing herself she will displease the
one who resists the proud but gives grace to
the humble. HOLY VIRGINITY 34.[26]

ARROGANCE. JEROME: One who holds his
head high in arrogance hates God. SERMONS
15.[27]

THE TRUE SIGN OF A CHRISTIAN. MACAR-
IUS OF EGYPT: The true sign of a Christian is
the following: to feed the hungry and give
drink to the thirsty, to endure hunger and
thirst, to be poor in spirit, humble and con-
temptible in one's own eyes. FIRST SYRIAC
EPISTLE 2.[28]

GOD WANTS TO DWELL IN YOU. CAESARIUS
OF ARLES: Be humble, in order that God may

rest in you, which he wants to do. SERMONS
210.5.[29]

PRIDE AND HUMILITY. VALERIAN OF CIM-
IEZ: One man is invited to grace in proportion
to his love of humility. Another is consigned to
punishment in proportion to his sin of pride.
So if the swelling of pride is taking place in anyone, let him combat it, lest he draw the arms of
heavenly justice against himself. SERMONS
14.2.[30]

THE PROUD TRUST THEIR OWN STRENGTH.
BEDE: God punishes robbers, perjurers, glut-
tons and other sinners because they are in contempt of his commandments, but it is said that
he resists the proud in a special way. This is
because those who trust in their own strength,
who neglect to submit themselves to God's
power, who really think that they can almost
save themselves and therefore have no time to
seek help from above—these are all deserving
of greater punishment. On the other hand,
God gives grace to the hum-ble because they
recognize their need and ask him for help to
overcome the plague of their sins, and for this
reason they deserve to be healed. It ought to be
noted that James quotes this verse from Proverbs according to the Septuagint, as does Peter
in his letter. The Latin text, which is based on
the He-brew original, reads: "Toward the scor-
ners he is scornful, but to the humble he shows
favor."[31] CONCERNING THE EPISTLE OF ST.
JAMES.[32]

ENMITY WITH GOD. OECUMENIUS: It is not

---

[24]LCC 1:57. [25]FC 85:286. [26]FC 27:184-85. [27]FC 48:111. [28]*AHSIS* 455. [29]FC 66:96-97. [30]FC 17:391. [31]Prov 3:34. [32]PL 93:33.

absurd to say that contempt for divine doctrine and an inordinate love for the world derive from pride and are the substance of enmity against God. God resists the proud, because it is normal to resist one's enemies, and the proud must be counted among them. COMMENTARY ON JAMES.[33]

4:7 Submit to God and Resist the Devil

GIVING MORE GRACE. ANDREAS: If death came into the world by the malice of the devil, and Christ dwells in the inner man according to the Scriptures, this is the reason why he dwells in us, that he might destroy the death which has come upon us through the devil's cunning. And not only this, but that he might give us more grace as well. For he said: "I have come that they might have life, and have it more abundantly."[34] CATENA.[35]

FIGHT AGAINST CAPTIVITY. CAESARIUS OF ARLES: Let us fight as hard as we can, with the Lord's help, against that most harsh captivity of the soul [which is the devil's ability to divert our thoughts away from spiritual concerns]. SERMONS 77.7.[36]

4:8a Draw Near to God

GOD IS NEAR. AMBROSE OF MILAN: God is near, and he does not drive away those who draw near to him. THE PRAYER OF JOB AND DAVID 3.11.29.[37]

NEARNESS TO GOD. BEDE: Draw near to God in humility, by walking in his footsteps, and he will draw near to you in his mercy, setting you free from all anxiety. For nobody is far away from God in terms of physical distance; the problem is one of attitudes and emotions.

For the person who is anxious to do what is right is always near to God, whereas the one who is lost in his wickedness is far away from him, regardless of where either one happens to live. CONCERNING THE EPISTLE OF ST. JAMES.[38]

4:8b Purify Your Hearts

DOUBLE-MINDED. OECUMENIUS: James describes as double-minded those who do not want to live in a committed way but who are tossed about by the iniquities of men. It is clear from what Job says that the mind here stands for our very life: "skin for skin," [Satan says], "all that a man has he will give for his own soul."[39] COMMENTARY ON JAMES.[40]

4:9 Mourn and Weep

FIRST, CONFESS. CHRYSOSTOM: The person who repents after sinning is worthy of blessings, not of mourning, as he returns to the company of the righteous. First, confess your sins that you may be justified, for if someone is not ashamed of his sin he is miserable, not so much because he fell from grace but because he has remained in his fallen state. And if it is a wicked thing not to repent after sinning, what punishment will someone deserve who sins as a matter of course? If a person overcome with the need to repent is unclean, what forgiveness will there be for someone who suffers because he remains in his sins? CATENA.[41]

---

[33]PG 119:496. [34]Jn 10:10. [35]CEC 30. [36]FC 31:359. [37]FC 65:387. [38]PL 93:34. [39]Job 2:4. [40]PG 119:497. [41]CEC 30-31.

MOURN YOUR SINS. LEANDER: Flee laughter as a sin[42] and change temporal joy into mourning so that you may be blessed, for those who mourn are blessed and shall be comforted.[43] THE TRAINING OF NUNS 21.[44]

READINESS TO REPENT. BEDE: Do not rejoice in the things of this world, but remember the sins which you have committed and spend the short time which is allotted to you on this earth looking for the joys of the heavenly kingdom. You do not want to find that your pursuit of earthly enjoyment produces a situation in which you will be a beggar in eternity, weeping and wailing forever in your torment. CONCERNING THE EPISTLE OF ST. JAMES.[45]

4:10 Humble Yourselves

COMBATING PRIDE. DIDYMUS THE BLIND: Pride is the greatest of all evils. To the extent that humility can oppose it, it is a great good. And when both of these are consciously and deliberately at work, good I mean and evil, everyone who humbles himself before God and rejects the proud will be raised up, and his humility will take him to the heights.[46] CATENA.[47]

THE HUMBLE ARE BLESSED. HESYCHIUS: It is a blessed thing to humble oneself before the Lord. For James says: "Humble yourselves before the Lord, and he will exalt you." Whenever we are thus humbled, even if we are tempted by demons and even if we are attacked by those who hate virtue, we have God to deliver us, as long as we do not forget his law or curse him in our sufferings. CATENA.[48]

---

[42]When repenting, your mind should be at the greatest distance from an attitude that laughs about the sin. [43]Mt 5:5. [44]FC 62:215. [45]PL 93:34. [46]Of glory. [47]CEC 30. [48]CEC 31.

4:11-17 PRACTICAL CHRISTIAN LIVING

[11]*Do not speak evil against one another, brethren. He that speaks evil against a brother or judges his brother, speaks evil against the law and judges the law. But if you judge the law, you are not a doer of the law but a judge.* [12]*There is one lawgiver and judge, he who is able to save and to destroy. But who are you that you judge your neighbor?*

[13]*Come now, you who say, "Today or tomorrow we will go into such and such a town and spend a year there and trade and get gain";* [14]*whereas you do not know about tomorrow. What is your life? For you are a mist that appears for a little time and then vanishes.* [15]*Instead you ought to say, "If the Lord wills, we shall live and we shall do this or that."* [16]*As it is, you boast in your arrogance. All such boasting is evil.* [17]*Whoever knows what is right to do and fails to do it, for him it is sin.*

OVERVIEW: Humble persons understand that they are in no position to pass judgment on others, and they will not do so. On the contrary, they recognize that they are also under judgment and will be more concerned to put their own lives right than to go about criticizing others. Christians must also watch how they plan their lives. It is all too easy to map out a future in which God has no place, but we must remember that everything we do is bound by the limits of time and of his will. To forget this is to fall back into the sin of pride, which can only lead to our destruction. Many would prefer to mind the business of others more than their own (CYRIL OF ALEXANDRIA). Such pride ultimately arises from contempt of others (OECUMENIUS). Our knowing complicates our sinning (AUGUSTINE). The faith rightly proclaimed must first be lived (OECUMENIUS). There is only one law and one lawgiver (HILARY OF ARLES, BEDE, THEOPHYLACT). View your life in terms of the wider perspective of God's grace (CYRIL OF ALEXANDRIA, OECUMENIUS). James is aware of how fleeting and empty our present life is (AUGUSTINE, OECUMENIUS). Grace enables good effort (CHRYSOSTOM).

4:11 Do Not Speak Evil

WICKED ACTS GIVE BIRTH TO ARROGANCE. CYRIL OF ALEXANDRIA: Every wicked act dulls the sense of our thoughts and gives birth to arrogance. For although it is necessary for each one to examine himself and behave according to God's will, many people do not do this but prefer to mind the business of others. If they happen to see others suffering, it seems that they forget their own weaknesses and set about criticizing them and slandering them. They condemn them, not knowing that they suffer from the same things as the people they have criticized, and in so doing they condemn themselves. The wise Paul writes exactly the same thing: "If you judge another in something, you condemn yourself, for the one who judges does the same things."[1] CATENA.[2]

PRIDE ARISES FROM CONTEMPT. OECUMENIUS: James knows that haughtiness and pride arise from contempt and disdain toward the meek, which pushes those who behave that way to despise them completely. He wants to turn his hearers aside from this. COMMENTARY ON JAMES.[3]

4:12 The One Lawgiver and Judge

ONLY ONE LAWGIVER. HILARY OF ARLES: The law of the Bible was given through many agents, like Moses and Elijah and John the Baptist, but ultimately it is still only one law, and there is only one lawgiver. INTRODUCTORY TRACTATE ON THE LETTER OF JAMES.[4]

THE ARROGANCE OF JUDGING. BEDE: James says it is arrogant to judge another person and not to consider the uncertain state of our own weakness and time-bound life. CONCERNING THE EPISTLE OF ST. JAMES.[5]

DO NOT DESPISE THE LAW. THEOPHYLACT: Who would endure having to live under a law which he despises? Therefore do not be a despiser of the law, says James, and do not look for some other legislator, who will prescribe the opposite. For there is only one law-

---

[1]Rom 2:1. [2]CEC 31. [3]PG 119:497. [4]PL Supp. 3:79. [5]PL 93:34-35.

giver, God, who can both condemn and deliver sinners. COMMENTARY ON JAMES.[6]

4:13 *You Do Not Know about Tomorrow*

PUT YOUR LIFE IN PERSPECTIVE. CYRIL OF ALEXANDRIA: Some people go on endless journeys for the sake of business and the profits which they can make thereby, enduring even sea travel for their sake. Some fight in order to get some advantage over others by increasing their power. Still others fatten their purses by cheating and by extortion, bringing down fire and brimstone on their heads. CATENA.[7]

THE WIDER PLAN. OECUMENIUS: James does not take away our free will but points out that everything we do is part of a wider plan which is governed by God's grace. Even if we are able to run around and get on with the business of this life, we must not attribute this ability to our own efforts but accept that we can do these things only by the blessing of God. COMMENTARY ON JAMES.[8]

4:14 *You Are a Mist That Vanishes*

THE VAPOR OF TEMPORAL GOODS. AUGUSTINE: Restoring health for a time to a man's body amounts to no more than extending his breath for a little while longer. Therefore it should not be considered of great importance, because it is temporal, not eternal. SERMONS 124.1.[9]

OUR TEMPORAL LABOR VANISHES. OECUMENIUS: James says this in order to indicate just how fleeting and empty our present life is. He wants to make us ashamed of the fact that we spend all our time engaged in its vanity, and

in the evils of this age and in things which, as soon as they are accomplished, disappear, and all our labor vanishes with them. COMMENTARY ON JAMES.[10]

4:15 *Say "If the Lord Wills"*

GRACE COMPLEMENTS HUMAN EFFORT. CHRYSOSTOM: James is not trying to take away our freedom to decide, but he is showing us that it is not just what we want that matters. We need God's grace to complement our efforts and ought to rely not on them but on God's love for us. As it says in Proverbs: "Do not boast about tomorrow, for you do not know what a day may bring forth."[11] CATENA.[12]

4:16 *Boasting in Arrogance*

IN BAPTISM WE RENOUNCE THE DEVIL. OECUMENIUS: Vain boasting comes from pride, and its ultimate source is the devil. Those who have been baptized into Christ ought not to take any kind of inspiration from Satan. COMMENTARY ON JAMES.[13]

4:17 *Knowing Right but Doing Wrong*

GRACE ENABLES DOING GOOD. CHRYSOSTOM: James does not remove the power to do good, but he shows that it is not just a matter of one's own will. To do good as we ought, we need the grace of God. CATENA.[14]

KNOWING COMPLICATES SINNING. AUGUSTINE: Does the one who does not know how

---

[6]PG 125:1177. [7]CEC 32. [8]PG 119:500. [9]*WSA* 3/4:248. [10]PG 119:500. [11]Prov 27:1. [12]CEC 32. [13]PG 119:501. [14]CEC 32.

to do good and does not do it commit a sin? He certainly does, but the one who knows what is good and does not do it sins more grievously. ADULTEROUS MARRIAGES 9.[15]

THE FAITH PROCLAIMED MUST BE LIVED.
OECUMENIUS: Good deeds ought to come

before preaching, so that it will be clear that it is a righteous man who is proclaiming the faith which is being expounded. COMMENTARY ON JAMES.[16]

---

[15]FC 27:71. [16]PG 119:501.

5:1-6 THE CORRUPTING POWER OF WEALTH

[1]*Come now, you rich, weep and howl for the miseries that are coming upon you.* [2]*Your riches have rotted and your garments are moth-eaten.* [3]*Your gold and silver have rusted, and their rust will be evidence against you and will eat your flesh like fire. You have laid up trea-sure[e] for the last days.* [4]*Behold, the wages of the laborers who mowed your fields, which you kept back by fraud, cry out; and the cries of the harvesters have reached the ears of the Lord of hosts.* [5]*You have lived on the earth in luxury and in pleasure; you have fattened your hearts in a day of slaughter.* [6]*You have condemned, you have killed the righteous man; he does not resist you.*

e Or *will eat your flesh, since you have stored up fire*

OVERVIEW: Once again James picks up a theme that he has already dealt with: the question of human riches. People with a lot of money should consider what it is that they have—a wasting resource that they cannot take with them when they die and that even now is in a state of constant decay. The love of money is the root of all evil and will lead people to defraud and even kill those who are less fortunate than they are. The rich must repent while there is still time (HILARY OF ARLES), casting their bread upon waters (OECUMENIUS). God's love is delay-ing judgment to give them time for repentance

(HESYCHIUS). Perishable riches (BEDE) can nei-ther hurt a good person or help a bad person (CAESARIUS OF ARLES). Luxury comes to noth-ing (CHRYSOSTOM). God's power ultimately puts to right all human injustices (HILARY OF ARLES, BEDE, THEOPHYLACT). Pray for a soul set free from excess (CHRYSOSTOM). It is time to give generously where we have given only spar-ingly (CAESARIUS OF ARLES). Human injustices are viewed in the light of the injustice done to the righteous Man, Christ (THEOPHYLACT).

5:1 You Rich, Weep and Howl

JUDGMENT DELAYED. HESYCHIUS: God delays the judgment because of his love for humanity, so that those who repent may not suffer along with those who are condemned. CATENA.[1]

REPENT WHILE STILL TIME. HILARY OF ARLES: The rich must repent while there is still time for them to do so. James is speaking here of those rich people who have shown themselves to be too stingy to offer any help to the poor. INTRODUCTORY TRACTATE ON THE LETTER OF JAMES.[2]

CAST BREAD UPON WATERS. OECUMENIUS: James makes their possession of wealth and their stinginess a source of lamentation for those who store up their riches for burial and loss rather than give them to the needy. For the person who gives his wealth to the poor does not lose it but keeps every penny. This is why the Preacher said: "Cast your bread upon the waters,"[3] that is, upon the apparent corruption and decadence of this world, and it will not be lost, but rather it will preserve us from destruction. COMMENTARY ON JAMES.[4]

5:2 Wealth Rots Away

RICHES CANNOT HELP A BAD PERSON. CAESARIUS OF ARLES: Riches cannot harm a good person, because he spends them kindly. Likewise they cannot help an evil person as long as he keeps them avariciously or wastes them in dissipation. SERMONS 35.4.[5]

WEALTH PERISHES. BEDE: It is not just that the fires of hell will torture rich people who have been ungodly and unmerciful, but their wealth too, with which they could have done all the good needed to redeem them,[6] will also

perish and disappear even before they themselves are judged. CONCERNING THE EPISTLE OF ST. JAMES.[7]

5:3 Wealth Condemns the Wealthy

LUXURY COMES TO NOTHING. CHRYSOSTOM: Let us go in by the narrow way. How long will luxury last? How long will there be licentiousness? Have not the heedless among us been warned? What about the mockers and the procrastinators? Will not their banquets and gluttony and self-satisfaction, not to mention their wealth, their possessions and their property all disappear? What reward have they got? Death. And what will their end be? Dust and ashes, urns and worms. CATENA.[8]

YOUR RICHES HAVE ROTTED. HILARY OF ARLES: It is true of course that gold does not rust, but James is comparing it to material things which do rust in the course of time. INTRODUCTORY TRACTATE ON THE LETTER OF JAMES.[9]

THEIR TREASURE THEIR CONDEMNATION. BEDE: By refusing to give alms the rich think that they have done well in saving their treasure, and indeed they have, though they have not seen what it will be used for, namely, their own condemnation. CONCERNING THE EPISTLE OF ST. JAMES.[10]

5:4 Wages Kept Back by Fraud

---

[1]CEC 33. [2]PL Supp. 3:80. [3]Eccles 11:1. [4]PG 119:501-4. [5]FC 31:175. [6]They could have used their wealth for good works, confirming their justification by faith in God's redemption, as is clear from many other passages in Bede. [7]PL 93:36. [8]CEC 33. [9]PL Supp. 3:80. [10]PL 93:36.

DUE WAGES UNPAID. BEDE: Think how great is the wickedness of those who not only refuse to share their wealth with the poor and needy but who go one step further and refuse to pay their workers the wages which are due to them! CONCERNING THE EPISTLE OF ST. JAMES.[11]

PREPARED FOR DESTRUCTION. THEOPHYLACT: This accusation is a digression directed against the Jewish leaders who robbed the poor and covered themselves with all manner of riches. But they were being prepared for destruction at the hands of the Romans, not least because they condemned our Lord to death. COMMENTARY ON JAMES.[12]

The Cries of the Harvesters

THE EARS OF THE LORD. HILARY OF ARLES: What James means here is not that God has ears but that he can use his power to put right the wrongs which exist on earth. INTRODUCTORY TRACTATE ON THE LETTER OF JAMES.[13]

5:5 Luxury and Pleasure

THE SOUL SET FREE FROM GLUTTONY. CHRYSOSTOM: What then? Has luxury been condemned? It certainly has—so why do you continue to strive for it? A man has made bread, but the excess has been trimmed away. A man has made wine, but the excess has been cut off there also. God desires that we should pray not for impure food but for souls set free from excess. For everything that God has created is good, and nothing which has been received with thanks is to be despised. CATENA.[14]

TIME TO GIVE ALMS. CAESARIUS OF ARLES: These things which Christ threatened through the apostle should terrify us very much, but we should not despair of the mercy of God. Those of us who have been careless up to now can, with God's help, correct ourselves, provide that we are willing to dispense more generously those alms which we have given sparingly up to now. SERMONS 199.5.[15]

5:6 You Have Killed the Righteous Man

WHO IS THE RIGHTEOUS MAN? THEOPHYLACT: It cannot be denied that this verse refers to Christ, especially since James adds that there was no resistance. Nevertheless it also includes others who suffered at the hands of the Jews, and he may even have been speaking prophetically about his own approaching death. COMMENTARY ON JAMES.[16]

---

[11]PL 93:36. [12]PG 125:1184. [13]PL Supp. 3:80. [14]CEC 34. [15]FC 66:56. [16]PG 125:1184.

5:7-11 THE LORD'S IMMINENT RETURN

⁷Be patient, therefore, brethren, until the coming of the Lord. Behold, the farmer waits for the precious fruit of the earth, being patient over it until it receives the early and the late rain. ⁸You also be patient. Establish your hearts, for the coming of the Lord is at hand. ⁹Do not grumble, brethren, against one another, that you may not be judged; behold, the Judge is standing at the doors. ¹⁰As an example of suffering and patience, brethren, take the prophets who spoke in the name of the Lord. ¹¹Behold, we call those happy who were steadfast. You have heard of the steadfastness of Job, and you have seen the purpose of the Lord, how the Lord is compassionate and merciful.

OVERVIEW: The return of Christ was a constant hope in the early church, where there was a strong conviction that they were living in the last days before the end. To those who were suffering, the wait seemed interminable, but it was important to develop a proper sense of perspective. The example of the patience of Job and the Old Testament prophets was held out to Christians as proof that what they were hoping for would eventually come and that when it finally arrived the wait would seem like no time at all. Although God now waits for our repentance (CYRIL OF ALEXANDRIA), he may come quickly at any time to dispense justice (BEDE). As in the case of Job, the devil is allowed to put us on trial, not merely in order to take our possessions away but that when that happens he can force us to curse God because of it (CHRYSOSTOM). Our hope is for eternal, not temporal, rewards (AUGUSTINE, BEDE).

5:7 Wait Patiently for the Lord to Come

GOD WAITS FOR REPENTANCE. CYRIL OF ALEXANDRIA: If God delays the punishment of sinners, waiting for them to repent, it is not because his character has changed, so that now he loves sin. Rather he is giving them time to repent. CATENA.[1]

5:8 The Lord Is Coming Soon

LONGSUFFERING AND PATIENCE. CHRYSOSTOM: Longsuffering toward one another and patience to those outside. Longsuffering is what we show toward those who can return it, and patience is how we act toward those who cannot do the same to us. CATENA.[2]

5:9 Your Judge Is Almost Here

HE WILL COME QUICKLY. BEDE: The just Judge will give you the rewards of your patience and will punish your adversaries with what they deserve. He sits at the door where he can watch everything you do, and he will come quickly to give each one whatever he or she deserves. CONCERNING THE EPISTLE OF ST. JAMES.[3]

---

[1]CEC 34. [2]CEC 34-35. [3]PL 93:38.

STOP HARMING THE POOR. ISHO'DAD OF MERV: James means that we should stop mocking the poor and doing them harm, complaining about them at the same time, because we shall be judged according to our cruelty and condemned by the righteous judge. COMMENTARIES.[4]

5:10 An Example of Suffering and Patience

WITHOUT COMPLAINT. BEDE: James tells us to look to the prophets, who never did anything wrong and who spoke the words of God's Spirit to the people but who nevertheless suffered a terrible end at the hands of unbelievers—Zechariah, Uriah and the Maccabees, for example, not to mention John the Baptist, Stephen, James the son of Zebedee and many others in the New Testament. They did not complain at such an end but were willing to endure it. Others put up with long labors without complaining, for example, Noah, who spent a hundred years building his ark, and Moses, who took forty years to lead his people out of slavery and into the promised land. CONCERNING THE EPISTLE OF ST. JAMES.[5]

5:11 The Joy of Endurance

THE EXAMPLE OF JOB. CHRYSOSTOM: It is a great thing if we can give thanks with great joy. But there is such a thing as giving thanks out of fear, and also such a thing as giving thanks in grief. This is what Job did when, in great suffering, he thanked God, saying: "The Lord has given, the Lord has taken away."[6] Let no one say that he was not grieving over what had happened to him or that he did not feel it deeply. Do not take away the great praise due to the righteous. . . . How great is this praise? Tell me, in what circumstances do you bless Job? Is it when he had all those camels and flocks and herds? Or is it when he says: "The Lord has given and the Lord has taken away"? For the devil also harms us not in order to take our possessions away so that we have nothing left but so that when that happens he can force us to curse God because of it. CATENA.[7]

HOPE FOR ETERNAL REWARDS. AUGUSTINE: James means: "Bear your temporal misfortunes as Job did, but do not hope for temporal goods as a reward for your patience, such as were returned to him double. Rather hope for the eternal goods which the Lord went before us to secure." LETTERS 140.10.[8]

THE CROWN AFTER DEATH. BEDE: God shows his compassion toward us by setting us free from our temptations in this life and by glorifying the living before others because of the constancy of their faith. After their deaths he crowns them in secret, so that the memory which they deserve will not be taken away from them by other people. CONCERNING THE EPISTLE OF ST. JAMES.[9]

---

[4]CIM 37. [5]PL 93:38. [6]Job 1:21. [7]CEC 35. [8]FC 20:79. [9]PL 93:38.

5:12-20 SPIRITUAL GUIDANCE

¹²*But above all, my brethren, do not swear, either by heaven or by earth or with any other oath, but let your yes be yes and your no be no, that you may not fall under condemnation.*

¹³*Is any one among you suffering? Let him pray. Is any cheerful? Let him sing praise.* ¹⁴*Is any among you sick? Let him call for the elders of the church, and let them pray over him, anointing him with oil in the name of the Lord;* ¹⁵*and the prayer of faith will save the sick man, and the Lord will raise him up; and if he has committed sins, he will be forgiven.* ¹⁶*Therefore confess your sins to one another, and pray for one another, that you may be healed. The prayer of a righteous man has great power in its effects.* ¹⁷*Elijah was a man of like nature with ourselves and he prayed fervently that it might not rain, and for three years and six months it did not rain on the earth.* ¹⁸*Then he prayed again and the heaven gave rain, and the earth brought forth its fruit.*

¹⁹*My brethren, if any one among you wanders from the truth and some one brings him back,* ²⁰*let him know that whoever brings back a sinner from the error of his way will save his soul from death and will cover a multitude of sins.*

OVERVIEW: James closes his letter with a brief sketch of how we should conduct our relationship with God. First of all, it is important to avoid demeaning God's name, which points to his power and presence in the world. Let the witness of your life be stronger than any oath (CYRIL OF ALEXANDRIA). An oath adds nothing to a simple yes or no (CHRYSOSTOM) and tends toward disaster as seen in the case of Herod (BEDE). We must not give the creation more value than it has by deifying it (CYRIL OF ALEXANDRIA). The need of an oath comes from an unsure conscience (LEANDER). Pray and praise God whether in good times or bad (ANDREAS, BEDE).

In time of suffering and illness we must turn to God, and if our sins are too great for us to deal with on our own, we must call the elders of the church to come and assist us. The apostolic tradition calls for the elders to anoint the sick with the oil of mercy and pray for their healing (HILARY OF ARLES, BEDE, OECUMENIUS). The prayer of faith is efficacious (CAESARIUS OF ARLES) when it gives expression to the petition of the whole consenting church (HILARY OF ARLES). Do not leave sin unconfessed and ignored either in your own house or another's (AUGUSTINE). And do not bore others with every detail (BRAULIO OF SARAGOSSA). The Lord himself who had no sin sets the example for sinners to pray for our sins (AUGUSTINE). Prayers of the righteous are beneficial (PSEUDO-DIONYSIUS), especially when one does works fitting to the prayer (MAXIMUS THE CONFESSOR). God loves to be asked (BEDE). The effectiveness of prayer offered by the right people in the right way can never be underestimated, as the case of Elijah reminds us. We are called to persevere in prayer like Elijah (HILARY OF ARLES), who was on fire with zeal for God (CHRYSOSTOM, THEODORET).

The most important thing of all is to recover the lost sheep who have gone astray, and those who do this will give incontrovertible proof of the fact that they are ready to reign with Christ in his eternal kingdom. One who converts others will save his own soul (ORIGEN, HILARY OF ARLES). Out of love (BEDE) the shepherd of souls rescues and delivers souls from death (GREGORY THE GREAT, SYMEON). Unless we protect what has been sown in us by constant care, the devil will snatch it away (CHRYSOSTOM).

5:12a Do Not Swear

AN OATH ADDS NOTHING. CHRYSOSTOM: What if someone swears an oath and claims that he was forced to do so? The fear of God is more powerful than any force. For though you may start out by swearing all kinds of promises, you will not keep any of them. Moreover, you would not dare to swear or give an oath in matters of human law, which you accept whether you want to or not. You would certainly never claim that you were forced into doing so. Now the person who has heard the blessings of God and who has prepared himself as Christ has commanded will never claim any need to do anything of the kind, for he is respected and honored by all. What is needed beyond a simple yes and no? An oath adds nothing to these, for no one has to be told that evil is the source of both excess and its deficient opposite. An oath is a form of excess. CATENA.[1]

DO NOT DEIFY CREATION. CYRIL OF ALEX-

ANDRIA: Let the witness of our life be stronger than an oath, and if some shameless person dares to ask an oath from you, let your yes be yes and your no be no, instead of swearing an oath. James forbids us to swear by heaven or by earth for this reason, that we should not give the creation more value than it has by deifying it. For those who swear, swear by something greater than themselves, as the apostle says.[2] CATENA.[3]

HEROD'S OATH RECALLED. BEDE: This is the judgment to which Herod fell victim, so that he found that he had either to break his oath or commit another shameful act in order to avoid breaking it. HOMILIES ON THE GOSPELS 2.23.[4]

5:12b Let Your Yes Be Yes

THE UNSURE CONSCIENCE. LEANDER: Jesus said: "Let your yes be yes and your no, no." Any more than this is evil. So do not swear for good reason, because that is evil. It is said to be evil because the need of an oath comes from an unsure conscience. It is necessary to extract an oath from one whose sincerity is in doubt, but why should you bind yourself by an involuntary oath when you are bound to show with your lips the sincerity of your heart? Speak the truth from your heart and you will not need an oath. THE TRAINING OF NUNS 29 (19).[5]

5:13 Prayer and Praise

IN GOOD TIMES OR BAD. ANDREAS: What should you do when you are in trouble? Call on

---

[1]CEC 36. [2]Heb 6:13. [3]CEC 36. [4]HOG 2:233. [5]FC 62:224.

God. And what should you do when you are happy? Praise him. CATENA.[6]

PRAY FOR GRACE. BEDE: Just as James forbade people to complain to each other about their sufferings, so now he goes on to say how they should behave. If someone has suffered an injury, he ought to go to the church and pray that God will send him the grace of his comfort, so that the sadness of this world, which leads to death, will not overtake him. CONCERNING THE EPISTLE OF ST. JAMES.[7]

5:14 The Anointing of the Sick by Elders

THE OIL OF MERCY. HILARY OF ARLES: This sickness is the sickness of sin. If someone is struck down by his own thoughts, then he should pray on his own, but if he has committed some sin he should ask for the church's prayers. The custom mentioned here is followed even today, for the grace of mercy is symbolized by oil. INTRODUCTORY TRACTATE ON THE LETTER OF JAMES.[8]

PRAY FOR THE SICK. BEDE: Just as he has already advised the person who has been injured, so now James gives his advice to the one who is ill. In order to prevent the foolishness of complaining, he told the injured person to pray and sing, and now he tells the person who is sick, either in body or in faith, to call the elders in proportion to the gravity of the illness which he is enduring. James does not advise this person to call the younger members of the church because they are less experienced in such matters and run the risk of saying or doing something which will make matters worse. We read in the New Testament that the apostles did this sort of thing, and the custom is retained in the church, that the priests will anoint a person who is ill and pray for his healing. And this is not the prerogative of the priests only, for in cases of necessity any Christian may do this, provided that he uses only oil which has been consecrated by the bishop. And of course anyone who anoints a sick person in this way must invoke the name of God over him while doing so. CONCERNING THE EPISTLE OF ST. JAMES.[9]

AN APOSTOLIC PRACTICE. OECUMENIUS: The apostles did this even during the time when our Lord was still on earth. They anointed the sick with oil and healed them.[10] COMMENTARY ON JAMES.[11]

5:15 The Prayer of Faith Will Save the Sick

HEALTH AND FORGIVENESS. CAESARIUS OF ARLES: Whenever some illness comes upon a man, he should hurry back to the church. Let him receive the body and blood of Christ, be anointed by the presbyters with consecrated oil and ask them and the deacons to pray over him in Christ's name. If he does this, he will receive not only bodily health but also the forgiveness of his sins. SERMONS 19.5.[12]

ASK IN MY NAME. HILARY OF ARLES: The prayer of faith is the consensus of the whole church, as it is said in the Gospel: "Whatever you ask in my name shall be done for you."[13] INTRODUCTORY TRACTATE ON THE LETTER OF JAMES.[14]

5:16a Confess Your Sins to One Another

---

[6]CEC 36-37. [7]PL 93:39. [8]PL Supp. 3:81. [9]PL 93:39. [10]Mk 6:13. [11]PG 119:508. [12]FC 31:101. [13]Jn 16:23. [14]PL Supp. 3:81.

LEAVING SIN UNCONFESSED. AUGUSTINE: Everyone claims this consideration from others whenever possible, for what each of us would punish if it occurred in our house, we want to leave unpunished in someone else's house. For if we are called to a friend's house and find him about to punish someone over whom he has power, it is considered most inhumane for us not to intervene. LETTERS 153.[15]

CONFESS AND BELIEVE. BEDE: We must use our common sense in applying this commandment. As far as small, everyday sins are concerned, we ought to admit them to one another and believe that we are saved from them by praying for each other. But if we have sinned in a more serious way, then we ought to follow the principle of showing our leprosy to the priest and do penance for it as much and for as long as he thinks is right. CONCERNING THE EPISTLE OF ST. JAMES.[16]

BORING AND DETAILED CONFESSION NOT NEEDED. BRAULIO OF SARAGOSSA: Since it would be a long and unpleasant task to reveal my sinful ways to you and to tell you everything in detail, it must suffice for me to reveal to your most holy mind that I am not what you believe, though I beg you to pray to God that he might make me what you believe. LETTERS 44.[17]

5:16b Pray That You May Be Healed

THE LORD'S EXAMPLE. AUGUSTINE: The Lord himself sets an example for us in this also. For if he who neither has, nor had, nor will have any sin prays for our sins, how much more ought we to pray for each other's sins! And if he for whom we have nothing to for-give forgives us, how much more should we forgive one another, knowing that we cannot live on earth without sinning! TRACTATES 58.2.[18]

PRAYERS OF THE RIGHTEOUS. PSEUDO-DIONYSIUS: Scriptural truth has passed on to us the fact that the prayers of the righteous are of use only to those who are worthy of them, and only in this life, not after death. ON THE ECCLESIASTICAL HIERARCHY 7.3.6.[19]

DOING WORKS FITTING TO THE PRAYER. MAXIMUS THE CONFESSOR: There are two ways in which the prayer of a righteous man is effective. The first is when the person praying does so by offering to God his works done according to his commands. Then the prayer is not just a matter of words, blurted out meaninglessly with the empty echo of the tongue, but powerful and living and inspired with the spirit of the commandments. For the true basis of prayer and supplication is the fulfillment of the commandments by virtue. This makes the prayer of a righteous person strong and full of power. The second way is when the person who asks for the prayers of a righteous man fulfills the works of prayer, above all by putting his life right. Then he makes the prayer of the righteous man strong, because it is reinforced by his own wonderful conversion. For there is nothing to be profited by a person who makes use of the prayer of a righteous man if he is himself already more inclined to virtue than to vice. CATENA.[20]

ASK GOD. BEDE: God loves to be asked, so

---

[15]FC 20:288. [16]PL 93:39-40. [17]FC 63:100. [18]FC 90:23. [19]CWS 254. [20]CEC 37.

that he can give. HOMILIES ON THE GOSPELS 2.14.[21]

COOPERATING WITH THE INTENT OF THE PETITIONER. THEOPHYLACT: The prayer of a righteous man is effective as long as the person who is being prayed for cooperates with his intentions. For if other people are praying for us while we are wasting our time in idleness and debauchery, their prayers will be useless. COMMENTARY ON JAMES.[22]

5:17a *The First Prayer of Elijah*

A MAN LIKE OURSELVES. BEDE: If Elijah got what he prayed for, just think how much the persistent prayer of a righteous person is worth in the sight of God! But just in case you think that you could never measure up to someone as holy as Elijah, James adds that he was a man, just as we are, even if he was second to none in his virtue. CONCERNING THE EPISTLE OF ST. JAMES.[23]

5:17b *It Did Not Rain*

PERSEVERE IN PRAYER. HILARY OF ARLES: The apostle regards himself as inferior to the prophets, who performed such miracles. The three years and six months represent the time of the antichrist, but the three years may also stand for the three ages of human history from the creation to the time of David, or they may symbolize the patriarchs, the prophets and the apostles. The miracle mentioned here is meant to encourage believers to persevere in their struggle against the unrighteous, for as in the case of Elijah, even if only one person prays, his prayer represents the common mind of all the righteous. INTRODUCTORY TRACTATE ON THE LETTER OF JAMES.[24]

5:18 *Elijah's Second Prayer*

THE HEAVENS GAVE RAIN. CHRYSOSTOM: The word of the prophet went forth and suddenly the air was changed, the sky became bronze, not because its nature was altered but because of the electric effect which was produced. Suddenly the elements were transformed, as the prophet's word fell like a fiery bolt on the hollow parts of the earth, and immediately everything dried up, became a desert and disappeared. CATENA.[25]

ON FIRE WITH ZEAL FOR GOD. THEODORET OF CYR: It is rash to think that anything which spiritual men say is excessive or badly stated, for what is said is not mindless or superficial. For this man was a prophet, and the greatest of the prophets, on fire with zeal for God. What he said, he said by the inspiration of God's Spirit, which explains its extraordinary character. CATENA.[26]

5:19 *If Anyone Wanders from the Truth*

WHAT WE SHOULD DO. BEDE: Earlier on in his letter James warned us to restrain our tongues from wicked or pointless statements, but now at the end he takes the opportunity to show us what we should be doing with them instead. CONCERNING THE EPISTLE OF ST. JAMES.[27]

YOUR MOUTH LIKE GOD'S. OECUMENIUS: Jeremiah said: "If you separate what is precious from what is vile, you will be like my own mouth,"[28] for whoever proclaims God's

---

[21]HOG 2:126. [22]PG 125:1188. [23]PL 93:40. [24]PL Supp. 3:82. [25]CEC 38. [26]CEC 39. [27]PL 93:40. [28]Jer 15:12.

words becomes in effect his mouth. COMMEN-TARY ON JAMES.[29]

5:20 Whoever Brings Back a Sinner

CONVERTING OTHERS. ORIGEN: A man who converts others will have his own sins forgiven. SERMONS ON LEVITICUS 2.4.[30]

HOW TO CONVERT OTHERS. CHRYSOSTOM: And how do you go about converting someone? It is like the seeds sown by farmers. They are sown once, but they do not survive forever unless they are carefully nurtured. And unless the tillers of the soil protect the seeds, they will be exposed to the birds and to every seed-eating creature. We are just like this, unless we protect what has been sown in us by constant care, for the devil will snatch it away and our own lethargy will destroy it. The sun dries it up, the rain drowns it, and weeds choke it, so that it is not enough for the sower to pass by once only. Rather he must tend it often, driving away the birds of the air, pulling up the weeds and filling up the rocky places with much soil. He must prevent, block off and eject any form of destruction. Where soil is concerned, everything depends on the farmer, for without him it remains lifeless, ready only to suffer harm. It is not like that with spiritual soil however. For in spiritual matters it is not all up to the teachers; at least half the effort must come from the pupils. It is up to us the teachers to sow the seed but up to you the pupils to do the rest. CATENA.[31]

RESCUING A SOUL FROM DEATH. GREGORY THE GREAT: If it is a great thing to rescue someone's body when it is on the point of death, how much greater is it to deliver someone's soul from death, so that it might live forever in the heavenly country? LESSONS IN JOB 19.31.[32]

PREACH IN ORDER TO CONVERT. HILARY OF ARLES: Someone who preaches to sinners in order to convert them will save his soul, even if the people he preaches to are not actually converted. INTRODUCTORY TRACTATE ON THE LETTER OF JAMES.[33]

THE MOTIVE OF LOVE. BEDE: James does all he can here to ensure that imperfect people like ourselves do not gloat over winning others away from their wicked ways and converting them to the truth by reminding us that we should be engaged in such work out of love for our brothers and sisters. CONCERNING THE EPISTLE OF ST. JAMES.[34]

PHYSICIAN AND SHEPHERD. SYMEON THE NEW THEOLOGIAN: As a physician you must cure the passions and diseases of those who are sick in soul; as a shepherd you must bring back those who have strayed. DISCOURSES 18.16.[35]

---

[29]PG 119:509. [30]FC 83:47. [31]CEC 39. [32]PL 79:1386. [33]PL Supp. 3:83. [34]PL 93:41. [35]CWS 222.

THE FIRST EPISTLE OF PETER

1:1-2 PETER INTRODUCES HIMSELF

> ¹*Peter, an apostle of Jesus Christ,*
> *To the exiles of the Dispersion in Pontus, Galatia, Cappadocia, Asia, and Bithynia,* ²*chosen and destined by God the Father and sanctified by the Spirit for obedience to Jesus Christ and for sprinkling with his blood:*
> *May grace and peace be multiplied to you.*

OVERVIEW: With few exceptions, the Fathers believed that this letter was written by the apostle Peter and sent to Jewish Christians in the Diaspora (EUSEBIUS OF CAESAREA, DIDYMUS, ANDREAS, OECUMENIUS). They recognized that the letter has close resemblances to James, and they accounted for this by saying that both men were apostles to the Jews, though Peter seems to have concentrated more on those who lived outside Palestine (ANDREAS). Peter explains his calling from God with a trinitarian promise, and the Fathers were quick to pick this up (ANDREAS, BEDE). They recognized him as the chief of the apostles and believed that this letter had been sent from Rome. Foreknowledge is God's knowledge of things God foresees as coming to pass (DIDYMUS). The Peter of this letter was compared with the Peter of Acts (ISHO'DAD).

1:1 An Apostle Speaks to the Exiles of the Dispersion

THE TRAJECTORY OF PETER'S GENTILE MISSION. EUSEBIUS OF CAESAREA: Peter seems to have preached in Pontus, Galatia, Bithynia, Cappadocia and Asia to the Jews of the dispersion, and afterwards, having come to Rome, he was crucified head downwards, for he himself had asked to suffer so. HISTORY OF THE CHURCH 3.1.[1]

A PILGRIM AND STRANGER. DIDYMUS THE BLIND: Why does Peter, an apostle to the Jews, write to those who are scattered in the dispersion, when most of them were still living in Judea at that time? To understand his meaning, we have to compare what he says with texts like "I am a pilgrim and stranger on earth, as were all my forefathers."[2] The souls of all are like strangers who are joined to bodies for as long as they dwell in time. If these souls were thought

---

[1]FC 19:138. [2]Ps 39:12.

to be the substance of the body, they would be natives on earth. But these souls are concealed in a covering of flesh and are in fact like strangers on earth. They feel the pains of the flesh because they are quite assimilated into natural bodies. This is why terrors are brought on the inhabitants of the earth, which affect both the things which are earthly in themselves and the souls which are covered in an earthly image. COMMENTARY ON 1 PETER.[3]

TO JEWS IN DIASPORA. ANDREAS: This apostle was appointed to preach to those of the circumcision, but he deliberately did not limit his preaching to those who lived in Judea. Instead, by sending this circular letter, he sought to preach to Jews scattered all over the world, to the effect that they must hold onto the faith which they have received, for by keeping it they would inherit many great, good, eternal and heavenly things. CATENA.[4]

TO ALL JEWS EVERYWHERE. OECUMENIUS: Like James, Peter was an apostle to the Jews, but he was sent to all Jews everywhere, and not just to those who lived in Palestine. COMMENTARY ON 1 PETER.[5]

COMPARED WITH THE PETER OF ACTS. ISHO'DAD OF MERV: This epistle is by somebody called Peter, but although its teaching is more sublime and perfect in both style and arrangement than James, it is very inferior to the exactness of the teachings of Peter as they are found in the Acts of the Apostles. COMMENTARIES.[6]

1:2a Destined by God the Father

FOREKNOWLEDGE HAS BECOME KNOWLEDGE. DIDYMUS THE BLIND: What Peter says

agrees with the statements of Paul, such as: "He has chosen us in himself before the foundation of the world, to be holy and spotless before him in love, predestinating us to be adopted as sons."[7] . . . Foreknowledge is not to be regarded as anything other than the contemplation of the future. It becomes knowledge as the things which are foreseen come to pass. Therefore, although the people to whom Peter was writing had once been chosen according to God's foreknowledge, by the time he was writing to them their election had already taken place. COMMENTARY ON 1 PETER.[8]

BEFORE BIRTH I KNEW YOU. OECUMENIUS: Peter is showing here that although he is later in time, he is in no way inferior to the prophets of old. For he is the equal of Jeremiah, to whom God said: "Before I formed you in the womb, I knew you."[9] He goes on to say that he has been sent by the sanctifying power of the Holy Spirit, whose mission was to separate, by spiritual gifts, those who were obedient to the gospel of Christ's suffering and who were sprinkled by his blood, from all other peoples. COMMENTARY ON 1 PETER.[10]

1:2b Sanctified by the Spirit for Obedience to Jesus Christ

THE SPIRIT KNOWS ETERNALLY. ORIGEN: We must not suppose that the Spirit knows God as we do, only through the historic revelation of the Son. For if the Holy Spirit knows God only in this way, then he has passed from ignorance to knowledge, and it is certainly as

---

[3]PG 39:1755. [4]CEC 41-42. [5]PG 119:513. [6]CIM 38; note the discussion of Isho'dad in the introduction. [7]Eph 1:4-5. [8]PG 39:1755-56. [9]Jer 1:5. [10]PG 119:513.

impious as it is foolish to confess him as the Holy Spirit and then ascribe a prior ignorance to him. On First Principles 1.3.4.[11]

Father, Son and Spirit. Andreas: See how Peter says that he was called to be an apostle of Jesus Christ by the foreknowledge of God the Father. Furthermore, he explains what his apostleship is like by saying that it is in the sanctification of the Spirit, for obedience and sprinkling with the blood of Jesus Christ. Moreover, we who believe in him have also been sanctified by the Spirit, and he sprinkles us too with his blood in order to cleanse us. For how can we not know that God sanctifies us by his own Spirit and cleanses us believers with his own blood? For Christ was God in human flesh. Catena.[12]

For Obedience to Jesus Christ. Bede: They were chosen for the purpose of being sanctified by the Holy Spirit so that once they had been cleansed from all their sins, those who had perished by their disobedience might start to obey the Lord Jesus Christ and, by being sprinkled with his blood, escape the power of Satan. On 1 Peter.[13]

1:2c Grace and Peace

Children of Peace. Basil the Great: May it be granted to us, after we have struggled nobly and subdued the spirit of the flesh, which was at enmity with God, when our soul is in a calm and tranquil state, to be called the children of peace and to share the blessing of God in peace. Sermons 13.8.[14]

---

[11]OFP 33. [12]CEC 42. [13]PL 93:42. [14]FC 46:211.

1:3-9 THE LIVING HOPE OF THOSE WHO HAVE BEEN BORN AGAIN

[3]*Blessed be the God and Father of our Lord Jesus Christ! By his great mercy we have been born anew to a living hope through the resurrection of Jesus Christ from the dead,* [4]*and to an inheritance which is imperishable, undefiled, and unfading, kept in heaven for you,* [5]*who by God's power are guarded through faith for a salvation ready to be revealed in the last time.* [6]*In this you rejoice,[a] though now for a little while you may have to suffer various trials,* [7]*so that the genuineness of your faith, more precious than gold which though perishable is tested by fire, may redound to praise and glory and honor at the revelation of Jesus Christ.* [8]*Without having seen[b] him you[c] love him; though you do not now see him you[c] believe in him and rejoice with unutterable and exalted joy.* [9]*As the outcome of your faith you obtain the salvation of your souls.*

a Or *Rejoice in this* b Other ancient authorities read *known* c Or omit *you*

Overview: The resurrection of Christ has made it possible for human beings to be born again and to become the heirs of God's promises. This inheritance is being kept in heaven for us and will be fully revealed at the end of time. Christ rises again in us according to our faith, just as earlier he died in us because of our unbelief (Clement of Alexandria). This is a living hope in an incorruptible inheritance (Oecumenius). His mercy is great enough to be able to forgive every sin committed in thought, word and deed, from the beginning to the end of the world (Hilary of Arles). When God is the giver, the things given are incomparably good (Andreas). He died that we should no longer be afraid of death (Bede). It is an inheritance foreknown (Origen), a blessing that is infinite (Hilary of Arles), incorruptible and never fading (Didymus). The blessed never grow tired of it (Bede).

Meanwhile we must persevere through the trials of this life, which are designed to purify our faith and to make us concentrate more fully on Christ and the joy he brings. Having begun in faith, the Christian continues in hope, which will one day be fulfilled in the perfect love of God. Yet some grow cold thinking of an earthly Jerusalem (Andreas). Your room in heaven is ready, so make yourself ready (Bede). Once you have entered your eternal reward, the time spent suffering here below will seem like no time at all (Bede, Andreas), as when a mother gives birth (Origen). So persevere through this temporary grief (Didymus). Just as gold is tested by fire and becomes useful, so also you who live in the world are tried in it (Hermas). The righteous suffer that they may be crowned with glory, but sinners suffer in order to bring judgment on their sins (Chrysostom). Even now the patience of the saints (Bede) shines like refined gold (Athanasius, Hilary of Arles). If you love him now when you have not seen him, think how much you will love him when you finally do see him, when he appears in his glory (Oecumenius, Hilary of Arles, Bede). It is now by faith that your soul exults already in salvation (Clement of Alexandria, Origen, Cyril of Alexandria).

1:3a Blessed Be God

When God Is the Giver. Andreas: They have received immortality and the hope of eternal life. These good things in heaven are better than human things. For this reason they praise God the Father, who shows his great mercy in doing these things faithfully. When God is the giver, the things given are both better and certain to materialize. The statement also has relevance to the Old Testament, for in it God gave the land of the Canaanites to those who believed in him. Catena.[1]

1:3b By His Great Mercy

His Mercy Great Enough. Hilary of Arles: Peter means that God has acted to redeem us without any help from us. His mercy is great enough to be able to forgive every sin which has been committed in thought, word and deed, from the beginning to the end of the world. Introductory Commentary on 1 Peter.[2]

1:3c Born to a Living Hope Through the Resurrection

---

[1]CEC 42. [2]PL Supp. 3:84.

The Blessings God Gives. Oecumenius: What exactly are the blessings which God has given us in Christ? First, there is hope, not the kind of hope which he gave to Moses, that the people would inherit a promised land in Canaan, for that hope was temporal and corruptible. Rather God gives us a living hope, which has come from the resurrection of Christ. Because of that, he has given all those who believe in Jesus the same resurrection. This is a living hope and an incorruptible inheritance, not stored up here on earth but in heaven, which is much greater. Commentary on 1 Peter.[3]

Christ Rises in Us. Clement of Alexandria: If God first generated us out of matter, the Father of our Lord later regenerated us into a better life. Christ rises again in us according to our faith, just as earlier he died in us because of our unbelief. It was furthermore said that no soul, whether it is righteous or evil, will ever return to a corruptible body in this life, lest by taking on flesh it should once more acquire the opportunity to sin, but rather that both good and evil souls will return in the resurrection body. For soul and body are joined together each according to its proper nature. They fit together rather like stuffing in food, or a construction of stones. Adumbrations.[4]

Rising with Him. Bede: Peter offers praise to God the Father in such a way as to make it perfectly clear that our Lord and Savior is both God and man. He calls God the Father of our Lord precisely because he does not doubt that our Lord had always existed with him as his Son. It is right for us to bless God because although on the strength of our own merits we deserve nothing but death, he has

regenerated us by his mercy to a new life. He has done this by the resurrection of his Son who loved our life so much that he gave himself up to death for our sake. When that death was overcome by his resurrection, he offered it to us as a model which might give us hope of rising again ourselves. For he died in order that we should no longer be afraid of death, and he rose again so that we might have a hope of rising again through him. On 1 Peter.[5]

1:4a To an Inheritance Imperishable

The Inheritance Foreknown. Origen: For God foresaw that the faith and behavior of people would be put right by the teaching of the gospel, and so he chose them in Christ before the foundation of the world, predestinating them to be his children by partaking of the Spirit of sonship. For foreknowledge means no more than seeing what is inside a person. It is now no longer foreknowledge in effect but knowledge of something real which has been foreseen. Those to whom Peter is writing were chosen according to foreknowledge, but the calling does not come to people who are hidden from view, for their innate awareness removes any doubt about their true nature. Catena.[6]

An Inheritance Unfading. Didymus the Blind: In order to show how the inheritance of the blessed will continue forever, Peter calls it incorruptible and unfading, demonstrating by this that it is a pure and divine inheritance

---

[3]PG 119:516. [4]FGNK 3: 79. This is the Latin translation of select portions of a longer, lost text, *Hypotypoeis*—brief interpretations of Scripture translated by the scholars associated with Cassiodorus about A.D. 540. [5]PL 93:42. [6]CEC 42.

which will remain uncontaminated in the eyes of those who care nothing for their present wealth, knowing that they have something better and eternal waiting for them. Commentary on 1 Peter.[7]

Of the Second Adam. Hilary of Arles: An incorruptible inheritance must be an infinite one, since everything finite is corruptible. The inheritance of the first Adam was corrupted by sin, but the inheritance of the second Adam can never be touched by the stain of sin. Introductory Commentary on 1 Peter.[8]

Of the Blessed. Bede: God has revealed the doctrine of truth, enjoined the path of good work and both promised and delivered the blessing of an inheritance that is always unfading and uncorrupted. On the Tabernacle and Its Vessels 1.8.35.[9]

1:4b Kept in Heaven for You

Imperishable, Undefiled, Unfading. Bede: Our inheritance is imperishable because it is a heavenly life which neither age nor illness nor death nor any plague can touch. It is undefiled because no unclean person can enter into it. It is unfading, because the heavenly blessings are such that even after long enjoyment of them the blessed never grow tired, whereas those who live in earthly luxury eventually have their fill of it and turn away from it. On 1 Peter.[10]

1:5a Guarded by Faith

Kept by Faith. Andreas: Peter says that God has blessed us greatly and that he has done so through his Son. Furthermore, he says that those who receive these things are those who are protected in the power of God, as Christ himself prayed: "Holy Father, protect them."[11] If the inheritance is kept in heaven for believers, some grow cold thinking that it has been left for us in the earthly Jerusalem, assuming that the rewards of the kingdom will be acquired by the appearance of luxury every thousand years. They should be asked why they say that this bodily luxury is immortal and unfading but at the same time they limit it to every thousandth year. They need to be told that these words show that the inheritance is in the kingdom of heaven and that it cannot be known by the senses of mortal beings. We have been assured that we shall receive all these great things by the Father himself, who is the one who gives them. For it is certain by other means also that he will bless us with these things through his own Son, and not simply through the Son but through his resurrection. For if everything has been granted to us, what is there left to give? The inheritance is immortal and unfading, and what is even greater, it is not here on earth but in heaven. Catena.[12]

1:5b A Salvation Ready to Be Revealed

Make Yourself Ready. Bede: Your place in the kingdom of heaven is ready, your room in the Father's house is prepared, your salvation in heaven awaits you. All you have to do, if you want to receive them, is to make yourself ready. But since no one can do this by his own efforts, Peter reminds us that we are kept in the power of God by faith. Nobody can keep

---

[7]PG 39:1756. [8]PL Supp. 3:84-85. [9]TTH 18:37. [10]PL 93:43. [11]Jn 17:11. [12]CEC 43.

doing good works in the strength of his own free will. So we must all ask God to help us, so that we may be brought to perfection by the One who made it possible for us to do good works in the first place. ON 1 PETER.[13]

1:6 For a Little While You Suffer Various Trials

IN SUFFERING YOU GIVE BIRTH. ORIGEN: Read "grieve" in this verse in the sense of "suffer," as in "in grief you shall bring forth children."[14] For a woman experiences grief not in bearing children but rather in suffering before birth. EXHORTATION TO MARTYRDOM 39.[15]

PERSEVERANCE TO THE END. DIDYMUS THE BLIND: Those who are afflicted in various ways because of Christ and who persevere to the end have their faith tested and proved. They ought therefore to rejoice, even if some of their labor appears to be involuntary. Peter calls this kind of labor grief, a word which he uses in one of the two meanings described by the apostle Paul, who said that there is one grief which leads to death and another which leads to repentance.[16] Obviously it is the second of these which is meant here. COMMENTARY ON 1 PETER.[17]

RELIEF IS NEAR. ANDREAS: Right now we have to suffer for the sake of the preaching, but relief for those who toil is near. CATENA.[18]

TRIALS FOR A TIME. BEDE: Peter says that we must still suffer for a little while, because it is only through the sadness of the present age and its afflictions that it is possible to reach the joys of eternity. He stresses the fact that this is only "for a little while," because once we have entered our eternal reward, the years we spent suffering here below will seem like no time at all. ON 1 PETER.[19]

1:7 Genuine Faith Tested by Fire

GOLD TRIED BY FIRE. HERMAS: Just as gold is tried by fire and becomes useful, so also you who live in the world are tried in it. So then, you who remain in it and pass through the flames will be purified. For just as gold casts off its dross, so also you will cast off all sorrow and tribulation, becoming pure and useful for the building of the tower. SHEPHERD, VISIONS 3.1.[20]

THE SAINTS SHINE LIKE REFINED GOLD. ATHANASIUS: Because the saints saw that the divine fire would cleanse them and benefit them, they did not shrink back from or get discouraged by the trials which they faced. Rather than being hurt by what they went through, they grew and were made better, shining like gold that has been refined in a fire. FESTAL LETTERS 10.[21]

NOT ALL SUFFER NOW. CHRYSOSTOM: The righteous suffer so that they may be crowned with glory, but sinners suffer in order to bring judgment on their sins. But not all sinners pay the price of their sins in this life, but await the resurrection. And not all the righteous suffer now, lest you think that evil is to be praised and you come to hate the good. CATENA.[22]

FAITH MORE PRECIOUS THAN GOLD. HILARY OF ARLES: The glory of the redeemed will never fade after they have been raised

---

[13]PL 93:43. [14]Gen 3:16. [15]CWS 70. [16]2 Cor 7:10. [17]PG 39:1756-57. [18]CEC 43. [19]PL 93:43. [20]FC 1:259. [21]ARL 168. [22]CEC 44.

from the dead, for it will have withstood the fire of temptation, whereas the gold of this world is said to rust.[23] INTRODUCTORY COMMENTARY ON 1 PETER.[24]

PATIENCE LIKE GOLD. BEDE: It is appropriate that Peter should compare Christian patience with gold, because just as there is no metal more precious than that, so patience is worthy of all honor in the sight of God. ON 1 PETER.[25]

1:8a Without Having Seen Him You Love Him

WHEN HE APPEARS. OECUMENIUS: If you love him now when you have not seen him but have only heard about him, think how much you will love him when you finally do see him and when he appears in his glory! For if his suffering and death have drawn you to him, how much more will you be attracted by his incredible splendor, when he will grant you the salvation of your souls as your reward. COMMENTARY ON 1 PETER.[26]

1:8b With Unutterable Joy

THE SWEETNESS OF HEAVENLY BLESSING. HILARY OF ARLES: Not even a thousand iron-clad tongues can sound out the sweetness of the heavenly blessings. INTRODUCTORY COMMENTARY ON 1 PETER.[27]

EXALTED JOY. BEDE: To ask joy of this sort is not to plead only with your words for entry into the heavenly fatherland but also to strive with labor to receive it. HOMILIES ON THE GOSPELS 2.12.[28]

1:9 The Outcome of Faith

MADE INCORRUPTIBLE BY GRACE. CLEMENT OF ALEXANDRIA: It appears from this that the soul is not naturally incorruptible but is made so by the grace of God, through faith, righteousness and understanding. ADUMBRATIONS.[29]

THE SOUL PRAYS AND SINGS. ORIGEN: If it is the mind which prays and sings in the spirit and the mind which receives perfection and salvation, how is it that Peter says: "As the outcome of your faith you obtain the salvation of your souls"? If the soul neither prays nor sings with the spirit, how shall it hope for salvation? ON FIRST PRINCIPLES 2.8.3.[30]

THE HARBINGER OF SALVATION. CYRIL OF ALEXANDRIA: Unbelief is a horrible and wicked thing, but faith is the highest good, for it is the harbinger of our entire salvation. CATENA.[31]

---

[23]Jas 5:3. [24]PL Supp. 3:85. [25]PL 93:43. [26]PG 119:520. [27]PL Supp. 3:85. [28]HOG 2:111. [29]FGNK 3:79-80. [30]OFP 122. [31]CEC 44.

1:10-12 THE HERITAGE OF THE PROPHETS

[10]*The prophets who prophesied of the grace that was to be yours searched and inquired about this salvation;* [11]*they inquired what person or time was indicated by the Spirit of Christ within them when predicting the sufferings of Christ and the subsequent glory.* [12]*It was revealed to them that they were serving not themselves but you, in the things which have now been announced to you by those who preached the good news to you through the Holy Spirit sent from heaven, things into which angels long to look.*

OVERVIEW: The Old Testament prophets were not ignorant of the promises of God, but they lived at a time when it had not yet been revealed when and how those promises would be fulfilled. For that reason, their writings display the fruits of an intense search for details about the coming of Christ. They knew that they would not live to see that happen, but they wanted to leave a legacy for us, so that we who have come after the revelation of Christ to the world are able to understand the meaning of that witness more fully and enjoy its fruits more deeply than would otherwise have been possible. The prophets inquired of the grace that would be later revealed (BEDE). Their share in salvation was not inferior to that of persons of faith today (DIDYMUS). The Spirit of Christ was in the prophets (CLEMENT OF ALEXANDRIA) in their prediction of the incarnate Lord (ANDREAS), his suffering (OECUMENIUS) and his glory (BEDE). It is not necessary to have seen Jesus in the flesh, for there were many unbelievers who did so and who later transgressed (THEODORET). The fulfillment that the prophets desired would not occur in their time but in ours (BEDE).

1:10 The Prophets Inquired

PROPHETS AND BELIEVERS RECEIVE THE SAME SALVATION. DIDYMUS THE BLIND: Some say that the promises and the salvation of the saints who lived before the coming of the Savior was inferior to those given to people who came afterwards and who saw Jesus in the flesh, who heard his teaching and beheld the miracles he did in his body. We must however show that this opinion is false. Christ comes in two ways. One is through the intellect, by which God is received as a divine Word. The other is through the senses, by which he appears as a historical person coming out of the womb of Mary. But the first way is more purely divine than the second, which was made necessary by the sinful behavior of mankind. For God comes to all the saints through the intellect and by his word, whether they lived before or after the coming of Christ, sanctifying each one according to his deeds. Those who lived before the coming of Christ were less informed, not because of their wickedness but because of God's dispensation of time. Therefore it is said that the prophets examined how and at what time the salvation of their souls would be fulfilled by the sufferings of Christ and his subsequent glory. They preached these things, knowing that they were not going to be revealed directly to them but would appear at some future time. Therefore it is wrong to say that their sanctification was somehow inferior to ours. COMMENTARY ON 1 PETER.[1]

THEY PROPHESIED OF THE COMING GRACE. BEDE: The prophets inquired and sought out whatever information they could obtain from the Lord or from angels, in the secret recesses of their hearts, about the future grace of the gospel and about how and when eternal salvation would come into the world. They then prophesied by speaking openly to other people and revealing to them what they had learned through their own private contemplation. ON 1 PETER.[2]

1:11 Predicting the Sufferings of Christ

THE SPIRIT OF CHRIST WITHIN THEM. CLEMENT OF ALEXANDRIA: Here is it stated that the prophets spoke with wisdom and that the Spirit of God was in them because they belonged and were subject to Christ. For the Lord works through archangels and their associate angels, who are called the spirit of Christ. ADUMBRATIONS.[3]

PROPHETS PREDICTED THE INCARNATION. ANDREAS: The apostle insists that the one who spoke by the prophets was the Holy Spirit of Christ. Nor was Christ a mere man, as the heretics say, but he was the incarnate Son of God, consubstantial with the Father. "Christ the power of God and the wisdom of God."[4] . . . For this reason the Savior said: "Many prophets and righteous men desired to

see what you are seeing, and they did not see it."[5] CATENA.[6]

THE SUBSEQUENT GLORY. BEDE: Christ has already been glorified twice, once in his resurrection from the dead and again in his ascension into heaven. There will also be a third time, when he comes again in his majesty, as well as in that of the Father and the holy angels, to judge each of us according to our works. ON 1 PETER.[7]

THEY PREDICTED HIS SUFFERINGS. OECUMENIUS: The Spirit of Christ predicted his sufferings to Isaiah: "He was led like a sheep to the slaughter,"[8] and he predicted the resurrection to Hosea: "On the third day we shall be raised up before him, and we shall go on to know the Lord, and we shall find him like the ready morning."[9] COMMENTARY ON 1 PETER.[10]

1:12a The Prophets Served You

THEY FORETOLD THE FUTURE GLORY. AMBROSE OF MILAN: The mysteries of the more perfect sacraments are of two kinds. . . . Of one kind are the things which the prophets foretold about the future glory, for they were revealed to them. And the saints have preached the good tidings "by the spirit of God sent from heaven. Into these things angels desire to look," as the apostle Peter says. LETTERS TO LAYMEN 66.[11]

ABRAHAM AND MOSES SAW THE FUTURE. THEODORET OF CYR: Some thought that the

---

[1]PG 39:1757-58. [2]PL 93:44. [3]FGNK 3:80. [4]1 Cor 1:24. [5]Mt 13:17. [6]CEC 44. [7]PL 93:44. [8]Is 53:7. [9]Hos 6:3; see LXX. [10]PG 119:520. [11]FC 26:402.

promise and the salvation of those who lived before the coming of Christ was inferior, on the grounds that those who saw him in the flesh and observed the miracles which he did had a greater reward. This is why Peter had to show that their impression was wrong. For how could Abraham be inferior to someone who lived after the coming of Christ, when he saw the day of the Lord and that everyone who would be made perfect by the Lord would depart into his bosom? How could Moses and Elijah be inferior, when they appeared with the Lord at his transfiguration, even though they did not see him in the flesh? Peter insists that it is not necessary to have seen Jesus in the flesh, for there were many unbelievers who did so, some of whom were bold enough to transgress the old covenant. And this has been said for the benefit of those who, even if they have not seen or heard what the Lord said in the flesh, nevertheless have a divinely inspired love for those things. If someone receives the salvation sought by the prophets, it is that which they all longed for at the end of time. For everything else was created by him, but this was not made by anyone. It was not possible for the holy angels or for any of the blessed rational creatures to partake of it beforehand, though they all longed to glimpse the things which would be revealed in the last days. Catena.[12]

1:12b Those Who Preached the Good News

The Comforter. Clement of Alexandria: These things were announced by the Holy Spirit, who is the comforter of whom Jesus said that, unless he himself went away, the Comforter would not come.[13] The angels who want to glimpse these things are not the ones who fell, despite what many people think. Rather, these are the angels who desire to obtain the fullness of his perfection. Adumbrations.[14]

1:12c Things into Which Angels Long to Look

The Mysteries Accomplished. Irenaeus: There is one Son who accomplished the Father's will and one human race in which the mysteries of God are accomplished, which an-gels long to behold. Against Heresies 5.36.3.[15]

Angelic Love. Hilary of Arles: The angels long to look into these things because of the greatness of their love. They meditate on the Spirit and go on doing so forever, because love never comes to an end. Introductory Commentary on 1 Peter.[16]

The Longing of Angels and Humans. Niceta of Remesiana: If the angels desire to look upon him, should not human beings be all the more afraid to despise him? The Power of the Holy Spirit 19.[17]

Desiring and Seeing. Gregory the Great: The angels both desire to see God and see him at the same time. For if they desired to see him but in such a way that their desire remained unsatisfied, they would be anxious and in suffering, but they are not. On the contrary, they are blessed and far removed from any kind of suffering or anxiety, since suffering and blessing do not go together. Lessons in Job 18.91.[18]

---

[12]CEC 45-46. [13]Jn 16:7. [14]FGNK 3:80. [15]LCC 1:397. [16]PL Supp. 3:86. [17]FC 7:39. [18]PL 79:1097.

Fulfillment to Come. Bede: Among all the other things which were revealed to the prophets was the message that the fulfillment which they desired would not occur in their time but in yours, for you have been born at the end of the ages. Peter tells his hearers this so that they will value their salvation, knowing that the prophets and righteous people who lived before them were so eager to be on earth when it arrived. On 1 Peter.[19]

---

[19]PL 93:44.

1:13-26 HOLINESS AND HOPE

[13]*Therefore gird up your minds, be sober, set your hope fully upon the grace that is coming to you at the revelation of Jesus Christ.* [14]*As obedient children, do not be conformed to the passions of your former ignorance,* [15]*but as he who called you is holy, be holy yourselves in all your conduct;* [16]*since it is written, "You shall be holy, for I am holy."* [17]*And if you invoke as Father him who judges each one impartially according to his deeds, conduct yourselves with fear throughout the time of your exile.* [18]*You know that you were ransomed from the futile ways inherited from your fathers, not with perishable things such as silver or gold,* [19]*but with the precious blood of Christ, like that of a lamb without blemish or spot.* [20]*He was destined before the foundation of the world but was made manifest at the end of the times for your sake.* [21]*Through him you have confidence in God, who raised him from the dead and gave him glory, so that your faith and hope are in God.*[d]

[22]*Having purified your souls by your obedience to the truth for a sincere love of the brethren, love one another earnestly from the heart.* [23]*You have been born anew, not of perishable seed but of imperishable, through the living and abiding word of God;* [24]*for*

> *"All flesh is like grass*
> *and all its glory like the flower of grass.*
> *The grass withers, and the flower falls,*
> [25]*but the word of the Lord abides for ever."*

That word is the good news which was preached to you.

d Or *so that your faith is hope in God*

Overview: The duty of the Christian is to live in the hope that Christ will soon return to fulfill his promises. In practical terms that means that we must strive to be holy, because

God himself is holy. Having been rescued from the vanity and folly of this world, it is our privilege to be able to purify our souls by obeying the truth. The effort that we devote to this ought to reflect the price that has been paid for our lives. This price cannot be measured in silver and gold, because we have been redeemed by the precious blood of Christ, the incarnate Son of God himself. That knowledge ought to fire our devotion and ensure that we shall do our utmost to reflect in our behavior the kind of new people that God wants us to be. Those called and baptized should live here and now as obedient children of God, ready to receive grace (DIDYMUS, BEDE), holding fast to faith (ANDREAS), being conformed not to the world but to God's will (THEOPHYLACT), imitating God's holiness (ANDREAS). The time we have been given on earth is limited (AMBROSE), given to allow us to act in ways worthy of our sonship to the Father (OECUMENIUS, BEDE). You owe that price with which you have been bought, even though God does not demand it. What Christ claims from you is his own (AMBROSE, CAESARIUS OF ARLES, MAXIMUS OF TURIN).

1:13 The Grace That Is Coming

GIRD YOUR MINDS. ANDREAS: Having spoken of the greatness of the blessings of the Father's gift, the sufferings of Christ, the Holy Spirit's prediction concerning him, the prophets' proclamation, the desire of the angels—having said all this, Peter tells us to hold on to them all by faith. CATENA.[1]

BE READY TO RECEIVE GRACE. BEDE: You must do this, Peter says, because you have been promised that you will see the revelation of Jesus Christ, which the angels now look

upon, after your death. The greater the grace which has been promised to you is, the more you ought to make sure that you are worthy to receive it. You must be pure and chaste in your minds, waiting for the Lord to come, for if someone is unable to please God now, it is certain that he will not receive the reward promised to the righteous when Christ comes again. ON 1 PETER.[2]

1:14 Obedient Children

BE OBEDIENT NOW. BEDE: It follows naturally that Peter expects those who were called and chosen by having been sprinkled with Christ's blood to be obedient. They should live as obedient children of God right here and now. ON 1 PETER.[3]

YOUR FORMER IGNORANCE. THEOPHYLACT: To be conformed to the things of this world means to be surrounded by them. Even today there are some weak-willed people who say that when they are in Rome, they have to do as the Romans do. But whether they do this knowingly or in ignorance, the message here is clear. We are to abandon this world and be conformed to the One who alone is truly holy. COMMENTARY ON 1 PETER.[4]

1:15 Holiness

GRACE EMPOWERS HOLINESS. DIDYMUS THE BLIND: Since God, who called us to salvation by the gospel, is holy, those who obey his calling must also become holy in all their thoughts and behavior, especially since he who calls us to this also provides the neces-

---

[1]CEC 46. [2]PL 93:45-46. [3]PL 93:46. [4]PG 125:1201.

sary sanctification himself. COMMENTARY ON 1 PETER.[5]

IMITATE GOD'S HOLINESS. ANDREAS: Those who seek to imitate the Holy God must be holy themselves. CATENA.[6]

1:16 Be Holy as God is Holy

BECOME LIKE GOD. ANDREAS: God insists that we become like him. In God's holiness lies our salvation. Therefore those who are truly holy now in Christ are prepared for true life in him. CATENA.[7]

BE PERFECT. BEDE: This is exactly what Jesus meant when he said: "Be perfect, as your heavenly Father is perfect."[8] ON 1 PETER.[9]

1:17 Fear God

TIME ON EARTH LIMITED. AMBROSE OF MILAN: You have been given time on this earth, not eternity. Use the time as those who know that they are setting out from here. LETTERS TO PRIESTS 59.[10]

JUDGE AS FATHER. DIDYMUS THE BLIND: If the one whom we call the Father is also our judge, and if he pays no attention to classes of persons, let us hasten to do our best in the time of our sojourn here on earth, with all fear and holy behavior. In this way we shall recognize that the same Father is the one who gives us promises, and we shall persevere without any punishment. COMMENTARY ON 1 PETER.[11]

THE JUDGMENT OF THE FATHER AND THE SON. ANDREAS: If the Father judges no one but has given all judgment to the Son, what are we to think about this passage? For if it is

the Father who is indicated here, how is he a judge, judging everyone according to his work? But if it is the Son who judges, taking all judgment on himself, why does Peter mention the Father? The solution here is that if the Father and the Son are one Godhead, the judgment of the Son is the judgment of the Father also, but the Son can also be called the Father of the creatures, having given them birth by partaking in holiness. For on many occasions he called his disciples his children, and to others he said things like: "Child, your sins are forgiven,"[12] and "Daughter, your faith has saved you."[13] CATENA.[14]

SONS OF THE FATHER. BEDE: God is not like an earthly father, who is more inclined to pardon his erring sons than he is to spare other members of his household. God the Father is so holy and just that he adopts as his sons not only humble and obedient servants but also enemies who have lifted up their hands against him. On the other hand, he has also disinherited those who appeared to enjoy the benefits of sonship because of their disobedience. ON 1 PETER.[15]

WORTHY OF THE FATHER. OECUMENIUS: Those who desire the adoption of sons must do the things which are worthy of the Father. COMMENTARY ON 1 PETER.[16]

1:18a You Were Ransomed

YOU OWE THE PRICE. AMBROSE OF MILAN: You owe that price with which you have been bought. Even though God does not always

---

[5]PG 39:1759. [6]CEC 46. [7]CEC 46. [8]Mt 5:48. [9]PL 93:46. [10]FC 26:353. [11]PG 39:1760. [12]Mt 9:2. [13]Mt 9:22. [14]CEC 46-47. [15]PL 79:46. [16]PG 119:524.

demand it, you still owe it. Buy Christ for yourself, not with what few men possess but with what all men possess by nature but few offer on account of fear. What Christ claims from you is his own. He gave his life for all men. He offered his death for all men. Pay on behalf of your creator what you are going to pay by law. He is not bargained for at a low price, and not all men see him readily. On Joseph 7.42.[17]

Pay Attention to the Price. Caesarius of Arles: If the unfortunate Jews observe the sabbath in such a way that they do not dare to do any secular work on it, how much more should those who have been "redeemed, not with gold or silver, but with the precious blood of Christ," pay attention to their price and devote themselves to God on the day of his resurrection, thinking more diligently of the salvation of their souls? Sermons 73.4.[18]

Bought with a Price. Maximus of Turin: If the price of our life is the blood of the Lord, see to it that it is not an ephemeral earthly field which has been purchased but rather the eternal salvation of the whole world. Sermons 59.2.[19]

The Price of Your Redemption. Bede: The greater the price of your redemption, the more respectful to God you ought to be, and not risk offending your Redeemer by falling back into your previous life of wickedness. On 1 Peter.[20]

1:19 The Precious Blood of Christ

A Soul Made Clean. Clement of Alexandria: This recalls the ancient ceremonies of the Levites and the priests, and relates to a soul made clean by righteousness, which is offered to God. Adumbrations.[21]

Bought at a Price. Chrysostom: We are God's creatures, but because of sin we have passed under the rule of the devil. Because of that, the Savior has bought us back with his own blood—"you are bought with a price."[22] Indeed, we have been bought with Christ's precious blood. Think of a righteous and good householder who does not regard a wicked servant as worthy to serve in his house but hands him over to someone who will correct him. If he then sees his servant being punished by a wicked master and saying: "I will go back to my first master, for he was good to me then and he will be good to me now," he will give him back his honor and redeem him, so that he might become a productive person. This is what God has done for us. How is it that we both belong to him and do not belong to him at the same time?[23] As creatures we belong to him, but as sinners we have become alien to him and do not belong to him any more. Do not think that you belong to God if you are a sinner, for in that case the devil has got hold of you, and you are his creature. The man of sin, the son of destruction, it is he who has bought you, with blood which is not precious but impure. Indeed, you have been bought by sin, you have been bought by harlotry, and you are impure. Catena.[24]

1:20 Predestination and Fulfillment

---

[17]FC 65:217. [18]FC 31:344-45. [19]ACW 50:142. [20]PL 93:46. [21]FGNK 3:80. [22]1 Cor 6:20. [23]Cf. the struggle set forth in Rom 7. [24]CEC 47.

Belonging to Christ. Augustine: Those belonging to the grace of Christ, who are foreknown, predestined and chosen from before the foundation of the world, shall die only insofar as Christ himself died for us, that is, by the death of the flesh only, not of the spirit. On the Trinity 13.15.[25]

Fully and Perfectly Revealed. Oecumenius: Christ existed in earlier times and even before the foundation of the world, when he was hidden by divine providence until the right time should come. He was manifested to the prophets who did their best to examine these matters, as Peter has already mentioned, and now he is even more manifest, since he has been fully and perfectly re-vealed. Furthermore, Peter adds that he has been revealed for our sake. Commentary on 1 Peter.[26]

1:21 Confidence in God

Holding Everything in Common. Andreas: Peter did not stop at Christ's death but went on immediately to remember his resurrection as well. Just because you hear that the Father has raised the Son, do not retort that the Son cannot raise himself. For listen to what Christ says: "Destroy this temple and in three days I shall raise it up again"[27] and again: "I have power to lay down my life, and I have power to take it up again."[28] The apostle says these things in order to teach us that the Father and the Son hold everything in common. Catena.[29]

1:22 Love One Another

Purity from Within. Hilary of Arles: Why does Peter talk about purifying our souls but says nothing about the body? The reason for this is that true purity comes from within. If the soul is clean, the body will be cleansed as well. Introductory Commentary on 1 Peter.[30]

Obeying by the Power of the Spirit. Oecumenius: This means: "When you have pulled yourselves together and determined to obey the truth by the power of the Spirit." For it is also possible to "obey" in evil and vicious matters, but that is not in the Spirit. And since there is a purification or preparation which must come before obedience, Peter wants to bring in as many extra helpers as possible. This is the role of brotherly love, which makes our neighbors also partakers of the good things which we have found. Commentary on 1 Peter.[31]

1:23 Born Again

Birth from the Spirit. Didymus the Blind: Peter uses the words *regeneration* and *restitution* to signify the introduction of birth after the destruction of the first generation of mankind. For how could that not have been destroyed, seeing that it is corrupt, in order to make room for the incorruptible which is coming and which will remain forever? For there is a first birth, in the descent of Adam, which is mortal and therefore corruptible, but there is also a later birth which comes from the Spirit and the ever-living Word of God. Commentary on 1 Peter.[32]

The Unending Word. Andreas: The Gos-

---

[25]FC 45:398. [26]PG 119:525. [27]Jn 2:19. [28]Jn 10:18. [29]CEC 48. [30]PL Supp. 3:87. [31]PG 119:528. [32]PG 39:1761.

pel says: "Heaven and earth will pass away, but my words will not pass away, says the Lord Jesus Christ."[33] CATENA.[34]

REDEMPTION AND BAPTISM. BEDE: Just as the gift of the Lord's passion, by which we have been redeemed, is imperishable, so too is the sacrament of the sacred font[35] by which we have been born again. The two things are so intimately connected that it is impossible to be saved by one without the other. For just as the Lord, during the time of his incarnation, redeemed us all on a single occasion by the shedding of his blood, so we must now in our time become partakers of that regeneration by being born again through baptism. It is well said of this regeneration that it does not come from corruptible seed but operates by the word of the living and eternal God. ON 1 PETER.[36]

THE SPIRIT'S PROMISE. ISHO'DAD OF MERV: Your birth is not human and is far removed from corruption and death, because the Holy Spirit is its mediator, and as John said, you have been born not of the will of man but of God.[37] The living word is the Spirit's promise of everlasting life. COMMENTARIES.[38]

1:24 All Flesh Is Like Grass

THE NATURE OF FLESH. EUSEBIUS OF CAESAREA: This is the nature of all flesh, and the portrait of a man made from clay, I mean someone who loves his own body and lives according to the flesh. Like the grass of the field and like beautiful flowers he will soon wither and die. CATENA.[39]

LONGING FOR DIVINE LIFE. GREGORY OF NYSSA: If someone despises whatever is held in honor among men and longs only for the divine life, is he likely to think of the grass which exists today and is gone tomorrow as something worth striving for? ON VIRGINITY 4.[40]

PRIDE AND GLORY EXTINGUISHED. THEODORET OF CYR: Just like grass, the people have dried up and their flower has fallen. God here foretold the salvation of the Gentiles and the sterility of the Jews. For by nature the human race is like grass, and the flowers of the grass are our pride and glory. But just as when the grass withers the flowers fall off, so when men die, their pride and glory are extinguished. CATENA.[41]

TWO SIDES OF HUMANITY. HILARY OF ARLES: Here we see the two sides of the human being. The outer man is like the flower of the field which is mortal and will pass away, whereas the inner man lives forever by the power of the living God. INTRODUCTORY COMMENTARY ON 1 PETER.[42]

1:25 The Word of the Lord Abides Forever

THE WORD REMAINS. CLEMENT OF ALEXANDRIA: The Word of God remains forever—both prophecy and divine teaching. ADUMBRATIONS.[43]

GUIDED TOWARD SALVATION. ANDREAS: God foresaw and forewarned us about all the above, but although he sees our great disobedience, the Lord of all persists in guiding us toward salvation. CATENA.[44]

---

[33]Mt 24:35. [34]CEC 48. [35]Baptism. [36]PL 93:46. [37]Jn 1:13. [38]CIM 38. [39]CEC 49. [40]FC 58:23. [41]CEC 49-50. [42]PL Supp. 3:87-88. [43]FGNK 3:80. [44]CEC 50.

2:1-10 GOD'S NEW PEOPLE

¹So put away all malice and all guile and insincerity and envy and all slander. ²Like new-born babes, long for the pure spiritual milk, that by it you may grow up to salvation; ³for you have tasted the kindness of the Lord.

⁴Come to him, to that living stone, rejected by men but in God's sight chosen and precious; ⁵and like living stones be yourselves built into a spiritual house, to be a holy priesthood, to offer spiritual sacrifices acceptable to God through Jesus Christ. ⁶For it stands in scripture:

"Behold, I am laying in Zion a stone, a cornerstone chosen and precious,

and he who believes in him will not be put to shame."

⁷To you therefore who believe, he is precious, but for those who do not believe,

"The very stone which the builders rejected

has become the head of the corner,"

⁸and

A stone that will make men stumble,

a rock that will make them fall";

for they stumble because they disobey the word, as they were destined to do.

⁹But you are a chosen race, a royal priesthood, a holy nation, God's own people,ᵉ that you may declare the wonderful deeds of him who called you out of darkness into his marvelous light. ¹⁰Once you were no people but now you are God's people; once you had not received mercy but now you have received mercy.

e Greek *a people for his possession*

OVERVIEW: Having described what it means to be born again in Christ, Peter outlines what those born anew are called to strive for in their lives. We must grow to be more like Christ, and we must also be built into the structure of his temple, which is the church. Since you are children of God, act like it (DIDYMUS, BEDE). Be immune to all deceit, pretense, envy and disparagement, which are the opposite of the truth preached to you (HILARY OF ARLES, OECUMENIUS). The new-born baby must first drink milk before growing stronger (ANDREAS). The pure spiritual milk you long for is found in the Scripture taken in its literal, moral and spiritual sense (HILARY OF ARLES), in the elementary teaching of the gospel (BEDE). Therefore taste the kindness of the Lord in the vital nourishment of the bread of life (BASIL, BEDE).

Believers are being fashioned together into a single living edifice (ORIGEN), a spiritual house (DIDYMUS, ANDREAS), cemented by charity (Augustine), having the same mind together with Christ (Theodoret). Believers all stand as if in one house, built on a good foundation (Hilary of Arles, Bede), in relation to a single, living cornerstone (Andreas). There is no unity of the edifice without its unique cornerstone, Jesus Christ (Hilary of Arles, Bede), who binds together believers of all cultures into one community of faith (Augustine, Cyril of Alexandria). Christ gives honor to those who join themselves to him in faith and reveals himself as a reliable foundation, but to those who do not believe he is a stone of stumbling and a rock of offense, considered worthless by the builders who have rejected him (Didymus). He will reject those who reject his divine sonship (Chrysostom, Hilary of Arles, Bede). They stumble because of their own unwillingness to believe (Didymus). Though their decisions are foreknown by God, God is not to be held responsible for this, for no cause of damnation can come from him who wants everyone to be saved. It is they who have made themselves into vessels of wrath and unbelief has followed naturally from that (Oecumenius, Andreas).

Christians are integrated into a new nation, which is described here as a royal priesthood. This means that we share in the government of his kingdom because we have benefitted from the sacrifice that he made on our behalf. We are a royal people because we have been called to share Christ's kingdom (Bede). We are a priesthood because of the offering that is made in prayers by which the people are offered to God (Clement of Alexandria, Origen). The gospel unites the kingly and priestly offices in Christ (Didymus). All believers are therefore anointed (Augustine), being made kings by the sign of the cross and priests by the anointing of the Holy Spirit (Leo) and a holy people by participating in God's holiness (Severus, Andreas). Believing Gentiles are now rightly called God's people (Origen, Didymus), united by faith (Andreas), brought near to God by the blood of Christ (Bede). The Christian church has been formed on this spiritual foundation by people from every corner of the world, thereby fulfilling the prophecy of Hosea, who foretold that a time would come when God would create a new nation that would glorify him forever (Didymus, Bede).

2:1 Turn Away from Evil

Be Born Again. Didymus the Blind: This verse upsets the heretics, who like to think that natures are good or bad in themselves and therefore cannot be changed. But what Peter says is fully in line with the words of Jesus: "You must be born again."[1] Commentary on 1 Peter.[2]

Lay Aside Malice. Hilary of Arles: As you have been born again by the Word of the living God, lay aside all malice, for an infant has no malice in him. Introductory Commentary on 1 Peter.[3]

Act Like Children of God. Bede: Peter says that now that you have been born again and have become children of God through baptism, you ought to become like newborn children in the innocency of your life and behavior. On 1 Peter.[4]

Born to an Incorruptible Life. Oecumenius: These few words say a great deal, for

---

[1]Jn 3:7. [2]PG 39:1761-62. [3]PL Supp. 3:88. [4]PL 93:47.

it is unworthy of those who have been born again to an incorruptible life to be ensnared by evil and to prefer things which have no existence to that which truly exists. For evil is not a substance but merely clings to substances as if it were part of them. Peter says that believers ought to be immune to all deceit, pretense, envy and disparagement. Deceit and pretence are the exact opposite of the truth which was preached to you. If envy and disparagement find a home inside you, who are bound by the tie of brotherly love, how will you be able to bear the attacks of the heretics? COMMENTARY ON 1 PETER.[5]

2:2 Newborn Babies

LONG FOR SPIRITUAL MILK. HILARY OF ARLES: Milk has three forms which can be compared to doctrine, that is, the liquid, cheese and butter. Liquid milk is the literal sense of Scripture, cheese is the moral sense, and butter is the spiritual sense. Find a good teacher and you will soon learn these things. INTRODUCTORY COMMENTARY ON 1 PETER.[6]

NEWBORN BABIES DRINK MILK. ANDREAS: The divine law wants us to be perfect, but on the way toward perfection it has us first drink milk, as if we were newborn babies, and by that milk we shall grow toward salvation. Paul spoke to the same effect when he said: "Do not be children in understanding, but be innocent in wrongdoing. In understanding be adults."[7] For it is not possible to advance toward purity, or toward maturity in understanding, or toward adulthood as a worker approved by God, unless you renounce evil and become like an innocent child. CATENA.[8]

ELEMENTARY DOCTRINE. BEDE: In accordance with the apostolic principle of discretion, to disciples who are still ignorant the priests supply elementary doctrine, which is the rational milk without guile. But they also provide the solid food of more sublime doctrine to those who are more nearly perfect. ON THE TABERNACLE AND ITS VESSELS 2.10.81.[9]

2:3 You Have Tasted the Kindness of the Lord

TASTE THE BREAD OF LIFE. BASIL THE GREAT: Everywhere we notice that the various facets of the soul are designated by outward things. Thus when our Lord is described as the true bread and his flesh as the true food, we must understand this as meaning that the pleasure of right reason is like the taste of bread. Just as it is impossible for someone to know what honey is like simply by being told about it, because he must taste it in order to find out, so too the goodness of the heavenly bread is not properly communicated by teaching alone. We must taste the goodness of the Lord by our own experience. CATENA.[10]

LONG FOR VITAL NOURISHMENT. BEDE: It is hardly surprising if someone who has never tasted the kindness of the Lord fails to avoid the filth and corruption of this world. But if your hearts and minds have been cleansed from wickedness, then it is natural for you to long for the vital nourishment of Christ. ON 1 PETER.[11]

2:4 That Living Stone

---

[5]PG 119:529. [6]PL Supp. 3:88. [7]1 Cor 1:20. [8]CEC 50-51. [9]TTH 18:90. [10]CEC 51. [11]PL 93:47.

COME TO HIM. DIDYMUS THE BLIND: Those who have accepted the gospel and who have been born again of incorruptible seed are an elect and approved race. At the same time they have been made living stones, built on top of the living Stone, who is chosen and honored, the foundation of the apostles and the prophets, in order to build a spiritual house for God toward whom they are being led and to whom spiritual sacrifices are offered. COMMENTARY ON 1 PETER.[12]

THE CHIEF CORNERSTONE. ANDREAS: This refers to the scribes and the Pharisees and the whole body of the Sanhedrin, about whom it was said: "The stone which the builders rejected has become the chief cornerstone."[13] CATENA.[14]

2:5a Built into a Spiritual House

CEMENTED BY CHARITY. AUGUSTINE: The Lord will repay his faithful followers who are so lovingly, so cheerfully, so devotedly carrying out these works, to the effect that he includes them in the construction of his own building, into which they hasten to fit as living stones, fashioned by faith, made solidly firm by hope, cemented together by charity. SERMONS 337.[15]

HAVING THE SAME MIND. THEODORET OF CYR: This is how Peter describes the way in which those who have been accepted by God are integrated into the church. It is by sharing a common origin, and by being in harmony with one another, by thinking and by saying the same things, by having the same mind and the same thoughts, that we are built into one house for the Lord. CATENA.[16]

2:5b To Be a Holy Priesthood

FASHIONED INTO A LIVING STONE. ORIGEN: Even though a man may have departed out of this life insufficiently instructed but with a record of acceptable works, he can be instructed in that Jerusalem, the city of the saints, that is, he can be taught and informed and fashioned into a "living stone," a stone precious and elect, because he has borne with courage and endurance the trials of life and the struggle for piety. ON FIRST PRINCIPLES 2.11.3.[17]

A HOUSE OF GOD. ORIGEN: We learn from Peter that the church is a body and a house of God built from living stones. COMMENTARY ON JOHN 10.266.[18]

BUILT ON A GOOD FOUNDATION. HILARY OF ARLES: You have been built on a good foundation, that of the apostles, prophets and patriarchs. INTRODUCTORY COMMENTARY ON 1 PETER.[19]

IN ONE EDIFICE. BEDE: The temple which Christ built is the universal church, which he gathers into the one structure of his faith and love from all the believers throughout the world, as it were from living stones. HOMILIES ON THE GOSPELS 2.24.[20]

2:6 The Cornerstone in Zion

NO BUILDING WITHOUT CORNERSTONE. AUGUSTINE: Without the cornerstone which is Christ, I do not see how men can be built

---

[12]PG 39:1762. [13]Ps 118:22. [14]CEC 51. [15]WSA 3/9:271. [16]CEC 51. [17]OFP 149. [18]FC 80:314. [19]PL Supp. 3:89. [20]HOG 2:249.

into a house of God, to contain God dwelling in them, without being born again, which cannot happen before they are born the first time. LETTERS 187.31.[21]

BELIEVERS OF ALL CULTURES. CYRIL OF ALEXANDRIA: Peter calls our Lord Jesus Christ a chosen and precious stone, fashioned by the glory and splendor of divinity. He calls it the cornerstone, because through one faith it binds together in unity the two peoples, Israel and the Gentiles. CATENA.[22]

ONLY ONE CORNERSTONE. HILARY OF ARLES: Everything in this prophecy is written about Christ. There are many living stones in God's temple, but here we are contemplating only the One. INTRODUCTORY COMMENTARY ON 1 PETER.[23]

CHRIST THE ROCK. BEDE: Peter reinforces the reliability of Christ as our Lord and Savior by reminding us that he was called a rock by the prophets. ON 1 PETER.[24]

2:7 The Head of the Corner

BELIEF AND REJECTION. DIDYMUS THE BLIND: Just as the Lord is the true light who has come into the world for judgment, so that at his coming he may give sight to the blind and blind those who see in the wrong way, so he is also a chosen cornerstone, giving honor to those who join themselves to him in faith and revealing himself to them as a reliable foundation, but to those who do not believe he is not precious but a stone of stumbling and a rock of offense, considered worthless by the builders who have rejected him. These builders are the scribes and the Pharisees. CATENA.[25]

THE REVERSAL. CHRYSOSTOM: These words refer to Christ, who himself prophesied in the Gospels, saying: "Have you not read, 'The stone which the builders rejected, the same has become the head of the corner?'"[26] CATENA.[27]

SONS OR STONES? HILARY OF ARLES: Those of you who believe in Christ are more than just stones—you are sons of God! INTRODUCTORY COMMENTARY ON 1 PETER.[28]

THOSE WHO REJECT HIM. BEDE: Just as those who refused to make Christ the foundation of their heart in effect condemned him by their actions, so too will they be condemned by him when he comes again, for then he will be unwilling to receive those who rejected him into his house, which is in the heavens. ON 1 PETER.[29]

2:8a The Stone of Stumbling

WICKEDNESS BRINGS DAMNATION. ANDREAS: They stumble because of their wicked mind and because they were chosen for damnation. For it is that which has brought them to this position. CATENA.[30]

2:8b They Disobey the Word

THEIR OWN UNWILLINGNESS. DIDYMUS THE BLIND: The position in which they find themselves is one which they have chosen, for it starts with their unbelief. For just as the world, which has been placed under evil, is

---

[21]FC 30:246. [22]CEC 51-52. [23]PL Supp. 3:89. [24]PL 93:49. [25]CEC 52-53. [26]Mt 21:42. [27]CEC 52. [28]PL Supp. 3:90. [29]PL 93:50. [30]CEC 53.

not evil by nature but has attained this position by its own desire, so also those who are being talked about here have been so placed because of their own unwillingness to believe, for they are cousins of those who have been handed over to the wickednesses of their desires. For God was very patient with those who despised his goodness and mercy, but in the end he left them to follow their own will. COMMENTARY ON 1 PETER.[31]

GOD WILLS EVERYONE TO BE SAVED. OECUMENIUS: God is not to be held responsible for this, for no cause of damnation can come from him who wants everyone to be saved. It is they who have made themselves into vessels of wrath, and unbelief has followed naturally from that. Therefore they have been established in the order for which they have prepared themselves. For if a human being is made with free will, that free will cannot be forced, nor can anyone accuse him who has decreed their fate of having done anything to them which they did not fully deserve as a result of their own actions. COMMENTARY ON 1 PETER.[32]

2:9 A Chosen Race, a Royal Priesthood

A ROYAL PEOPLE. CLEMENT OF ALEXANDRIA: That we are a chosen people is clear enough, but Peter said that we are a royal people because we have been called to share Christ's kingdom and we belong to him. We are a priesthood because of the offering which is made in prayers and in the teachings by which souls which are offered to God are won. ADUMBRATIONS.[33]

THE APPROACH TO THE SANCTUARY. ORIGEN: Because you are a priestly race you are able to approach the sanctuary of God. SERMONS ON LEVITICUS 9.9.[34]

THE ALTAR FIRE MAINTAINED. ORIGEN: If you want to exercise the priesthood of your soul, do not let the fire depart from your altar. SERMONS ON LEVITICUS 4.6.[35]

KING AND PRIEST TOGETHER. DIDYMUS THE BLIND: Under the old dispensation, the priesthood and the kingship were two different things. No one could be both a king and a priest. But afterwards came the gospel, which united these two offices in Christ. From this it follows that the people whom he has chosen will be both royal and priestly at the same time. Some people wonder how it is possible, seeing that we are called from all the nations on earth, for us to be regarded as one holy people. The answer to this is that although we are from many different nations, the fact that we have all repented of our sins and accepted a common will and a common mind gives those who have repented one doctrine and one faith. When there is a soul and heart common to all believers, then they are called one people. COMMENTARY ON 1 PETER.[36]

ALL BELIEVERS ANOINTED. AUGUSTINE: In ancient times only one high priest was anointed, but now all Christians are anointed. SERMONS 198A.[37]

ALL CHRISTIANS ARE MADE PRIESTS. LEO THE GREAT: All who have been born again in Christ are made kings by the sign of the cross and consecrated priests by the anointing of the Holy Spirit. SERMONS 4.[38]

---

[31]PG 39:1762-63. [32]PG 119:533. [33]FGNK 3:80-81. [34]FC 83:196. [35]FC 83:78. [36]PG 39:1763-64. [37]WSA 3/6:77. [38]FC 93:25.

A Holy People. Andreas: We are royal from the fact that Christ is a king, and we are a priesthood from the fact that he is a priest. Furthermore, we are also a holy people, so called by the one who is called holy in himself. Catena.[39]

A People Apart. Severus of Antioch: As believers in Christ we have received exactly the same things as he already has. Since he is of the royal tribe and became a high priest, so too have we been enriched by these gifts. Having them, we have become a holy nation and a people for safekeeping, that is, for being kept apart from the world; for we have entered into his rest. Catena.[40]

Believing Gentiles a Chosen Race. Bede: This title of honor, which God gave to his ancient people through Moses, the apostle Peter now applies to the Gentiles, and rightly so, because they have believed in Christ who was the true cornerstone of Israel's faith. The Gentiles are therefore a chosen race, in contradistinction to those who have been rejected because they themselves rejected the living stone. They are a royal priesthood because they are joined to the body of him who is both the king and the true high priest. As their king, Christ grants them a share in his kingdom, and as their priest he purifies them with the sacrifice of his own blood. On 1 Peter.[41]

2:10 You Are God's People

The New People of the Circumcision. Origen: O people of God, chosen to expound the virtues of the Lord: take up the circumcision worthy of the Word of God in your ears, on your lips, in your heart and in the foreskin of your flesh, as well as in every part of you. Sermons on Genesis 3.5.[42]

Believing Gentiles Now God's People. Didymus the Blind: This verse means that Gentiles who were not God's people before they believed have now been called by him and have come to him. Some people think that Peter is talking about a mixture of beings who are both good and bad by nature, but their interpretation comes up against many serious objections. You cannot say of spiritual beings that there was once a time when they were not a people and when they lacked mercy, nor can you say of earthly beings that they have been turned into a people or received mercy. Therefore I believe that that is the wrong interpretation of this verse. Commentary on 1 Peter.[43]

One Holy People. Andreas: When people from different races and nations are called to abandon all their differences and to take on one mind, drawing near to him by one faith and one teaching, by which the soul and the heart become one, they are one holy people. Catena.[44]

Brought Near by the Blood of Christ. Bede: These words are taken from the prophet Hosea[45] and confirm what Paul also said: "You were strangers to the covenants of promise, having no hope and without God in the world. But now you who were once far off have been brought near in the blood of Christ."[46] On 1 Peter.[47]

---

[39]CEC 53. [40]CEC 54. [41]PL 93:50. [42]FC 71:96. [43]PG 39:1764. [44]CEC 53. [45]Hos 1:9; 2:1. [46]Eph 2:12-13. [47]PL 93:51.

2:11-25 GOD'S PEOPLE IN A FOREIGN ENVIRONMENT

[11]*Beloved, I beseech you as aliens and exiles to abstain from the passions of the flesh that wage war against your soul.* [12]*Maintain good conduct among the Gentiles, so that in case they speak against you as wrongdoers, they may see your good deeds and glorify God on the day of visitation.*

[13]*Be subject for the Lord's sake to every human institution,*[f] *whether it be to the emperor as supreme,* [14]*or to governors as sent by him to punish those who do wrong and to praise those who do right.* [15]*For it is God's will that by doing right you should put to silence the ignorance of foolish men.* [16]*Live as free men, yet without using your freedom as a pretext for evil; but live as servants of God.* [17]*Honor all men. Love the brotherhood. Fear God. Honor the emperor.*

[18]*Servants, be submissive to your masters with all respect, not only to the kind and gentle but also to the overbearing.* [19]*For one is approved if, mindful of God, he endures pain while suffering unjustly.* [20]*For what credit is it, if when you do wrong and are beaten for it you take it patiently? But if when you do right and suffer for it you take it patiently, you have God's approval.* [21]*For to this you have been called, because Christ also suffered for you, leaving you an example, that you should follow in his steps.* [22]*He committed no sin; no guile was found on his lips.* [23]*When he was reviled, he did not revile in return; when he suffered, he did not threaten; but he trusted to him who judges justly.* [24]*He himself bore our sins in his body on the tree,*[g] *that we might die to sin and live to righteousness. By his wounds you have been healed.* [25]*For you were straying like sheep, but have now returned to the Shepherd and Guardian of your souls.*

f Or *every institution ordained for men* g Or *carried up . . . to the tree*

OVERVIEW: As citizens of the kingdom of heaven, God's people must regard themselves as resident aliens here on earth. God's people occupy the middle ground between heavenly and earthly delights (AUGUSTINE). When soul and body are joined together, the soul naturally feels the disordered passions of the flesh (DIDYMUS). Evil desires operate through the flesh yet involve the soul (HILARY OF ARLES).

Pagans who once reviled the faith of Christians, because they had abandoned their gods, stop doing so after they see what a holy life they lead in Christ (BEDE). When our lives are laid bare, it will become apparent that the truth is the opposite of what pagan critics suspect (OECUMENIUS).

Yet we must respect the customs of the countries in which we live and obey the civil authorities who have been instituted by God so that we will not bring the witness of the gospel into disrepute. When the government is shaken, all other institutions are shaken with it (Tertullian). We are to be subject to the governing authorities when it is clear that they are doing something in accordance with just laws (Didymus). But if they command something that is contrary to God's will, we must not obey them (Andreas). When they see us submitting to rulers because it is God's will, then they are stunned into silence (Andreas, Bede, Theophylact). It is as free people that we obey these rulers, honoring the one who has delivered us and who has told us to do this for his sake (Oecumenius). If we have really received so great a gift as forgiveness, we must not fall back into sin, because if we do so, we are falling back into the old slavery (Bede). We do not use our freedom as a pretext for rebellion (Hilary of Arles). Let no one say that we have already been set free from the orders of the world just because we have become citizens of heaven (Andreas). The respect the believer has for persons in authority is not based on abject fear but rational conscience (Andreas, Oecumenius). Do not split the unity of the worshiping community (Augustine).

It is possible that we shall be forced to suffer, not for doing things which are wrong but for living up to what we know to be right. Suffering for doing what is right may seem unfair, but it is what Christ did when he came to earth in order to die for our salvation. He was a perfect person who was made to suffer unjustly, but he did not try to retaliate. His death has made it possible for us to die to the old life of sin and to return to him like lost sheep who have come back to their spiritual shepherd. If Christ suffered unjust punishment, so must we be prepared to do so if nec-

essary (Hilary of Arles, Augustine, Bede, Andreas). Christ was nailed to the cross, paying the penalty not for his own sins (Augustine, Cyril of Alexandria) but paying for the debt of our nature (Theodoret). He bore our transgressions in himself and was made a sacrifice for them (Eusebius of Emesa, Basil, Severus). As physician (Theodoret) and guardian of our souls (Hilary of Arles), Jesus wanted to redeem us so much that he put our sins on his shoulder and bore them for us on the tree, in order to give us eternal life as well as blessings in this world (Bede).

2:11a As Aliens and Exiles

Distancing the Soul from Corrupted Passions. Didymus the Blind: Those who are worthy of love because of their godliness are called "beloved" not because they are that way by nature but because they have received love. The writer of this letter urges such people to abstain from carnal desires which attack the soul. The flesh and the soul have different natures. A soul which is uncorrupted and immortal will desire that kind of thing, whereas the flesh, which is both corrupt and dissolute, desires things which are wicked and vile. But when the two are joined together, the soul naturally feels the passions of the flesh. When it distances itself from bodily passions, it is preserved pure and glorious, with a saving understanding of the way it should act, with a will to behave in that way, with a love for God and with a desire to know him. Commentary on 1 Peter.[1]

Doctrine Points Toward Ethics.

---

[1]PG 39:1764-65.

Andreas: As always, the apostle turns to ethical matters after he has dealt with doctrine. After saying what good things are available because of Christ, he now calls us to lead the right kind of life. Catena.[2]

2:11b Abstain from the Passions of the Flesh

HEAVENLY AND EARTHLY DELIGHTS.
Augustine: God's people occupy the middle ground. They are to be compared neither with those who think that the only good is to enjoy earthly delights nor with those sublime inhabitants of heaven, whose sole delight is in the heavenly bread by which they were created. Between the people of heaven and those of earth, the apostle was suspended in the middle, heading toward heaven, though he was not yet there, but at the same time separated from others here below. Sermons 400.2.[3]

EVIL DESIRES. Hilary of Arles: Evil desires are called "carnal" because they operate through the flesh, but in reality they are spiritual, because they come from the soul. Introductory Commentary on 1 Peter.[4]

2:12a Maintain Good Conduct among the Gentiles

GOOD CONDUCT. Hilary of Arles: As the head of the church Peter lays down rules for everyday behavior, and by doing so he unites all the members of the church in one overall harmony. Introductory Commentary on 1 Peter.[5]

CONVERSION OF THE PAGANS. Bede: It often happens that pagans who once reviled the faith of Christians, because they had abandoned their gods, stop doing so after they see what a holy and pure life they lead in Christ. They begin instead to glorify and praise God, who is shown by acts of goodness and righteousness to be good and righteous himself. On 1 Peter.[6]

THE MARTYRDOM OF SANCTUS AND BLANDINA. Oecumenius: Peter presents the pagans as people who disparage us. Anyone who doubts the truth of this should read what Irenaeus wrote about the martyrs Sanctus and Blandina. Stated briefly, when the Gentiles discovered servants of these Christians, who were learned in the sacred mysteries, they tortured them in order to find out some secret evil about them. But since the servants had nothing to say which would please them, beyond the fact that they had heard their masters talk about the holy communion as the body and blood of Christ, which they took to mean real flesh and blood, they gave that answer to the inquisitors. The Gentiles seized on that apparent cannibalism as if it were something practiced by Christians and tortured Sanctus and Blandina as a result. Blandina replied to them freely and intelligently as follows: "How can people who do not touch meat because of their devotion to the study and contemplation of God do such things?" The day of visitation is the day on which worldly people like those Gentiles will be judged. For when our lives are laid bare, it will become apparent that the truth is the very opposite of what they suspected, and not only will they be ashamed, they will also be pun-

---

[2]CEC 54. [3]WSA 3/10:472. [4]PL Supp. 3:91. [5]PL Supp. 3:91. [6]PL 93:52.

ished, and God will be glorified. COMMENTARY ON 1 PETER.[7]

2:12b That Your Deeds May Glorify God

THE DAY OF VISITATION. HILARY OF ARLES: The day of visitation will be like the time when God visited Egypt through an angel and slew all the firstborn children. Similarly he will visit the lands of the earth and will cut off the firstfruits of all evil works. INTRODUCTORY COMMENTARY ON 1 PETER.[8]

2:13a Be Subject to Every Human Institution

RESPECT FOR HUMAN INSTITUTIONS. TERTULLIAN: Pray for kings, because when the kingdom is shaken, all its other members are shaken with it, and even if we stay aloof from tumults we shall have some part in the resulting misfortune. APOLOGY 1.31.[9]

BEHAVIOR TOWARD THOSE IN POWER. DIDYMUS THE BLIND: The proclaimers of the truth take all opportunity for wrongdoing away from us by describing how we should behave toward those who are in power in such a way that the gospel and its teaching will not be hindered by us through our unwillingness to do what they require of us and by telling us to be subject to them when it is clear that they are doing something in accordance with just laws. Nor should we be worried if they do not act in the way appointed by God, because he is in charge of them and will judge them accordingly. COMMENTARY ON 1 PETER.[10]

NO OBEDIENCE IF IT IS AGAINST GOD'S WILL. ANDREAS: By "every human authority" Peter means those which have been ordained by rulers. We are called to submit to them for the Lord's sake, because he himself said: "Render unto Caesar the things that are Caesar's,"[11] but if they command something which is not God's will we must not obey them. CATENA.[12]

2:13b Sent To Punish Those Who Do Wrong

ENDURE THE UNWORTHINESS OF RULERS. BEDE: It is not that every human ruler punishes those who do wrong and praises those who do right, since many obviously do not live up to what God expects of them. Nevertheless, Christians receive honor and praise from God if they endure the unworthiness of their rulers and stand up against their foolishness. ON 1 PETER.[13]

2:14a Governors Sent by the Emperor

APPOINTED MAGISTRATES. THEOPHYLACT: Peter calls those magistrates who are appointed by kings "human creatures." Sometimes Scripture describes appointments as creations [as in Ephesians 2:15]: "God's purpose was to create in himself one new man out of the two." COMMENTARY ON 1 PETER.[14]

2:14b Praise Those Who Do Right

PUTTING UP WITH IGNORANCE. BEDE: This therefore is the praise which good men receive, when they act properly and obey the king's servants, even when it means putting

---

[7]PG 119:536-37. [8]PL Supp. 3:91. [9]APT 72. [10]PG 39:1766. [11]Mt 22:21. [12]CEC 55. [13]PL 93:52. [14]PG 125:1213.

up with the ignorance of unwise governors. On 1 Peter.[15]

2:15 By Doing Right You Silence Their Ignorance

Christ Was No Anarchist. Andreas: Peter said this because there were some subversive people who were saying that Christ had come to overthrow the state, teaching us that we should despise every earthly power. But when they see us submitting to them because it is God's will, then they are silenced, because they realize that they were wrongly trying to tear the kingdom of Christ in two. Catena.[16]

2:16a Live as Free People

Do Not Return to Slavery. Bede: We are truly free if we have been cleansed of our sins through baptism and if we have been redeemed from slavery to the devil, because we have been made children of God. If we have really received so great a gift, we must not fall back into sin, because if we do so, we are falling right back into the old slavery again. On 1 Peter.[17]

Citizens of Heaven Freely Obey Earthly Rulers. Oecumenius: We have been set free from the world. We have become citizens of heaven. This verse does not imply, according to John Chrysostom, that the apostle now wants us to be subject once again to earthly powers and to obey them. No, we are to obey them as free people, honoring the one who has delivered us and who has told us to do this for his sake. Similarly you must not have any kind of evil in your mind, like disobedience or hardness of heart. You must not use your freedom as a pretext for refusing to obey. We might add that someone who is free according to the Lord would never do anything absurd or foolish. Commentary on 1 Peter.[18]

2:16b Freedom Not a Pretext for Evil

Pretext for Evil. Hilary of Arles: If we have a form of religion on the outside but inside we are opposed to the rulers of the church as well as to kings and princes, we are using our faith as a pretext for evil. Introductory Commentary on 1 Peter.[19]

2:17a Honor All

Love the Brotherhood. Augustine: How is it proved that we love the fellowship? Because we do not split unity; because we keep love. Tractates 2.3.2.[20]

2:17b Fear God

First Fear God. Didymus the Blind: The fear of God must come first and govern all the rest. Commentary on 1 Peter.[21]

2:17c Honor the Emperor

Not Optional. Augustine: Do not say to yourself: "What have I got to do with the emperor?" . . . The apostle intended that emperors should be served, and he wanted kings to be honored. Tractates 6.26.1.[22]

Heavenly Citizenship Does Not Imply

---

[15]PL 93:53. [16]CEC 55. [17]PL 93:53. [18]PG 119:540. [19]PL Supp. 3:91. [20]FC 92:147. [21]PG 39:1767. [22]FC 78:153.

Earthly Irresponsibility. Andreas: It is wrong to be insubordinate and disobedient to earthly authorities. Let no one say that we have been set free from the world because we have become citizens of heaven. Are you still insisting that we should obey earthly powers? Yes, says Peter, but obey them as free people, which is to say, in obedience to the one who has set you free and who has commanded you to do this. That way you will not glory in your freedom as if it were a cloak to cover up your evil thoughts, that is, of insubordination and disobedience. Catena.[23]

2:18 Submit to Your Superiors Out of Respect

Good Qualities for Those in Authority. Clement of Alexandria: Impartiality, patience and kindness are very appropriate qualities for a master to possess. The Teacher 3.11.74.[24]

Out of Respect. Andreas: The person who says that servants ought to obey their masters out of abject fear is mad and ought to be regarded as a dumb animal, for the fear which they ought to have is based on knowledge and reason and is properly known as respect. For the servant who fears his master for Christ's sake and because of his teaching will submit to him out of respect.... And there is another aspect to this, for Peter is also telling women to respect their husbands in godly fear, for that is fully consonant with the Holy Scriptures. Catena.[25]

Respect Based on Conscience. Oecumenius: The fear which is spoken of here is something which comes as the result of knowledge and conscience. It is not some wild emo-

tion produced by the unknown. It is the same kind of fear by which we come into the presence of God, the perfect fear with which we approach Christ. Commentary on 1 Peter.[26]

2:19 Enduring Unjust Suffering

God Too Suffered Unjustly. Hilary of Arles: You will be approved by God if you suffer unjustly, because you know that that is exactly what he did. Introductory Commentary on 1 Peter.[27]

2:20 Suffering for Doing Right

Not for Doing Wrong. Hilary of Arles: Peter shows here that those who deserve punishment receive no mercy or grace from God if they perish. Introductory Commentary on 1 Peter.[28]

Christ Too Was Beaten. Bede: Be sure to note carefully the extent to which Peter beholds glory even in the state of slavery, by saying that those who do well and are blameless but who are beaten by cruel and dishonest masters, are following in the footsteps of Christ, who suffered unjustly on our behalf. That is something to rejoice about! On 1 Peter.[29]

2:21a Christ Suffered for You

For Those Who Follow. Augustine: In this sentence the apostle Peter appears to have realized that Christ suffered for those who

---

[23]CEC 56. [24]FC 23:255. [25]CEC 56-57. [26]PG 119:541. [27]PL Supp. 3:92. [28]PL Supp. 3:92. [29]PL 93:54.

follow in his footsteps and that Christ's passion profits none but those who follow in his footsteps. SERMONS 304.2.[30]

2:21b Leaving You an Example

HIS GOODNESS BY NATURE, OURS BY GRACE. DIDYMUS THE BLIND: The praises referred to here are those of a person who is good, not by nature but by grace, and who invites us to join him in praising the One who is good by nature. COMMENTARY ON 1 PETER.[31]

BY SUFFERING HIMSELF. AUGUSTINE: Christ taught you to suffer, and he did so by suffering himself. Words would not be enough unless example were added. And how, precisely did he teach us, brothers and sisters? He was hanging on the cross, and the Jews were raging . . . he was hanging there, yet at the same time he was healing them. SERMONS 284.6.[32]

BEHOLD HIS EXAMPLE. ANDREAS: Having told servants to put up with unjust suffering, which was a bitter pill for them to swallow, Peter now comforts them by referring to Christ's longsuffering. It is as if he were saying: "I am not trying to persuade you to put up with injustice simply by arguments. Rather stand back and look at your master as freemen in Christ, and you will be comforted." CATENA.[33]

2:22 He Committed No Sin

NO SIN IN HIM. AUGUSTINE: Note that the apostle holds this statement that Christ did no sin sufficient to prove that there was no sin in him. He who did not sin could not have had

sin in him. . . . Certainly the adult man would have committed sin if there had been sin in the infant. Apart from him there is no one who has not committed sin after reaching his majority, and the reason for this is that there is no one who is without sin at the beginning of infancy. AGAINST JULIAN 5.15.57.[34]

NO GUILE ON HIS LIPS. CYRIL OF ALEXANDRIA: Since human flesh became that of the Word of God, its subjection to corruption has come to an end. He put an end to the sickness of loving pleasure. The only-begotten Word of God has not done this for himself, for his motive is not his own pleasure, but obviously he has done it for us. SERMONS 45.9.[35]

HE PAID FOR OUR SINS. THEODORET OF CYR: Christ was nailed to the cross, paying the penalty not for his own sins but paying the debt of our nature. For our nature was in debt after transgressing the laws of its maker. And since it was in debt and unable to pay, the creator himself in his wisdom devised a way of paying the debt. By taking a human body as capital, he invested it wisely and justly in paying the debt and thereby freeing human nature. ON DIVINE PROVIDENCE 10.26.[36]

2:23 When Reviled He Did Not Revile

CHRIST DID NOT ANSWER HIS ACCUSERS. DIDYMUS THE BLIND: Jesus did not curse those who insulted him but handed them over to God, who is a just judge. For although the divine union of God and man in Christ is holy and undivided, yet there is a distinction to be

---

[30]WSA 3/8:216. [31]PG 39:1767. [32]WSA 3/8:91. [33]CEC 57-58. [34]FC 35:297. [35]FC 76:195. [36]ACW 49:143.

made between the mind of the man assumed and the mind of the person assuming him.[37] COMMENTARY ON 1 PETER.[38]

2:24 He Bore Our Sins in His Body on the Tree

PENAL SUBSTITUTIONARY ATONEMENT. BASIL THE GREAT: By the blood of Christ, through faith, we have been cleansed from all sin, and by water we were baptized into the death of our Lord. We have sworn in effect that we are dead to sin and to the world but alive unto righteousness. ON BAPTISM 1.3.[39]

HE BORE OUR TRANSGRESSIONS. SEVERUS OF ANTIOCH: The one who offered himself for our sins had no sin of his own. Instead he bore our transgressions in himself and was made a sacrifice for them. This principle is set out in the law, for what sin did the lamb or the goat have, which were sacrificed for sins and which were even called "sin" for this reason? CATENA.[40]

2:24b By His Wounds You Have Been Healed

HIS WOUNDS ARE OUR SAVIORS. EUSEBIUS OF CAESAREA: He bore the blows and wounds in his body, he was beaten and scourged and thrashed, his head was bruised with a reed. But his wounds became our saviors, for "by his stripes we are healed."[41] For who are we, but those who were once deceived and who did not recognize him, nor were we aware of who he was? CATENA.[42]

A STRANGE KIND OF HEALING. THEODORET OF CYR: This is a new and strange kind of healing. For in this case it is the doctor who

receives the honor but the patient who is healed. CATENA.[43]

2:25 The Lost Sheep Have Returned

THE GUARDIAN OF YOUR SOULS. HILARY OF ARLES: Error has three causes—darkness, loneliness and ignorance. The Gentile sheep were wandering among idols because of their foolish ignorance, and they found themselves lost in the darkness of sin and in the loneliness of a strange nation. Peter goes on to add that now they have turned to the guardian [bishop] of their souls, because although there are many guardians around who care about the things of the flesh, there are few who can look deep into the soul and take care of it. INTRODUCTORY COMMENTARY ON 1 PETER.[44]

SHEPHERD AND GUARDIAN. BEDE: Here Peter alludes to the parable in the Gospels where the Good Shepherd leaves the ninety-nine sheep in the desert and goes after the one who has gone astray. For as it is said there, when he finds it he puts it on his shoulder and rejoices. Jesus wanted to redeem us so much that he put our sins on his shoulder and bore them for us on the tree, in order to give us eternal life as well as blessings in this world. He comes to us daily to visit the light which he has given us, in order to tend it and to help it grow. This is why he is called not only the shepherd but also the guardian of our souls. ON 1 PETER.[45]

---

[37]The mind of the divine person assuming humanity in a man. [38]PG 39:1768. [39]FC 9:386. [40]CEC 58. [41]Is 53:5. [42]CEC 58. [43]CEC 58. [44]PL Supp. 3:93. [45]PL 93:54.

3:1-7 CHRISTIAN WIVES AND HUSBANDS

¹*Likewise you wives, be submissive to your husbands, so that some, though they do not obey the word, may be won without a word by the behavior of their wives, ²when they see your reverent and chaste behavior. ³Let not yours be the outward adorning with braiding of hair, decoration of gold, and wearing of fine clothing, ⁴but let it be the hidden person of the heart with the imperishable jewel of a gentle and quiet spirit, which in God's sight is very precious. ⁵So once the holy women who hoped in God used to adorn themselves and were submissive to their husbands, ⁶as Sarah obeyed Abraham, calling him lord. And you are now her children if you do right and let nothing terrify you.*

⁷*Likewise you husbands, live considerately with your wives, bestowing honor on the woman as the weaker sex, since you are joint heirs of the grace of life, in order that your prayers may not be hindered.*

OVERVIEW: Christian women must respect their husbands and try to win them to Christ by their behavior. They must not dress up in the latest fashion but cultivate the inner virtues that are their true beauty. Peter and Paul agree on modest dress (TERTULLIAN). Peter wants wives to show their husbands the path of virtue through their actions (HILARY OF ARLES). Women's example is communicated to husbands by deeds (BEDE). There is nothing wrong with ornaments in themselves, but they are unnecessary extras for the faithful (HILARY OF ARLES). The proper beauty of women is not an outward matter but a matter of purity of heart (EUSEBIUS OF EMESA, HILARY OF ARLES). The adornment of women should be focused on the inner life of the heart, in the imperishableness of a quiet spirit, which is of great value in the sight of God (CLEMENT OF ALEXANDRIA). This applies equally to women and men (AMBROSE). Christ wants these invisible riches (AUGUSTINE) and desires to see the faithful clothed in this way (BEDE). Just as

Abraham is the father of all who believe, so his wife Sarah is the mother and example for Christian women today (DIDYMUS, BEDE).

Husbands also must respect their wives and treat them properly. Husbands owe the duty of protection to their wives (HILARY OF ARLES). Husbands are to bear patiently with wives, that their prayers may not be hindered (HILARY OF ARLES, BEDE). The pure and united marriage of a man and woman speeds them toward the gates of heaven. They bear the image of conjunction by which the church is mystically conjoined to Christ as his bride (SEVERUS).

3:1 *Wives Must Win Over Their Husbands*

SHOW HUSBANDS THE PATH OF VIRTUE.
HILARY OF ARLES: The husband is the head of the wife, and so she must be subject to him just as the other members of the body must be subject to the head. Peter wants wives to show

their husbands the path of virtue with just the same vitality as so many of them lead their husbands in the opposite direction. INTRODUCTORY COMMENTARY ON 1 PETER.[1]

3:2 When They See Your Reverent Behavior

THROUGH ACTIONS. HILARY OF ARLES: Actions speak louder than words, and the husbands will be persuaded by what they see, not by what they hear from their wives. INTRODUCTORY COMMENTARY ON 1 PETER.[2]

WOMEN'S EXAMPLE COMMUNICATED TO HUSBANDS. BEDE: Note how Peter wants good and honest women to be submissive to their husbands, so that not only will they not fail to heed their commands but also that they will be so firm in their pure behavior that their example will be communicated to their husbands as well. ON 1 PETER.[3]

3:3 Outward Adornment

ADORNMENT OF THE FAITHFUL. TERTULLIAN: But he who is both the head of the man and the beauty of the woman, the husband of the church, Christ Jesus, what sort of crown did he put on, for both male and female? A crown of thorns! ON THE CROWN 5.14.[4]

PETER AND PAUL AGREE ON MODEST DRESS. TERTULLIAN: Touching modesty of dress and ornament, the rule of Peter is also plain, because he speaks with the same spirit as Paul against the empty glory of apparel and the pride of gold. ON PRAYER 9.20.[5]

ORNAMENTATION UNNECESSARY. HILARY OF ARLES: There is nothing wrong with these ornaments in themselves, but they are unnecessary extras for the believer and should therefore be avoided. Most of them were invented by the daughters of Ham, which explains why the prohibition is directed to women rather than to men. INTRODUCTORY COMMENTARY ON 1 PETER.[6]

3:4 The Quiet Spirit Is Precious in God's Sight

INWARD ADORNMENT. CLEMENT OF ALEXANDRIA: Women should not indulge in the outward adornment of braiding the hair or of wearing gold, or of putting on robes. Their adornment should be in the inner life of the heart, in the imperishableness of a quiet and gentle spirit, which is of great price in the sight of God. THE TEACHER 3.11.66.[7]

WOMEN AND MEN. AMBROSE OF MILAN: When reading the apostle Peter I noticed that every wise man is rich. Note that Peter does not exclude women from this. Neither the wise man nor the rich one needs to hoard riches for himself. Peter has mentioned very beautifully the inner life of the heart, because the whole man of wisdom is invisible, just as wisdom itself is invisible, though understood. No one before the time of Peter used such an expression in speaking of the inner man. LETTERS TO PRIESTS 55.[8]

INVISIBLE RICHES. AUGUSTINE: God would not give riches to the outer man and leave the inner man in need; he has given invisible

---

[1]PL Supp. 3:93. [2]PL Supp. 3:93. [3]PL 93:55. [4]APT 183. [5]APT 313. [6]PL Supp. 3:94. In biblical typology Eve is cursed and Ham is cursed. The obsession toward ornamentation arises out of a cursed human condition. [7]FC 23:250. [8]FC 26:303.

riches to the invisible self and invisibly adorned it. SERMONS 161.11.[9]

PURITY OF SPIRIT. BEDE: Since the outer man is corrupt and you no longer possess the beauty of integrity which is proper to virgins, imitate the purity of your spirit by strict abstinence and do with your mind what you cannot achieve in your body. For Christ wants these inward riches. He desires to see you clothed in this way. ON 1 PETER.[10]

3:5 Holy Women Adorned with Piety

PROPER BEAUTY NOT OUTWARD. EUSEBIUS OF EMESA: Outward beauty is not the real thing but rather something quite superfluous. A woman's proper beauty is obedience to her husband. The truth of this statement is made manifest by the examples of the holy women of the past, like Sarah. CATENA.[11]

REMAIN HOLY. HILARY OF ARLES: Women must remain holy in every state of life, whether they are married, single or celibate. INTRODUCTORY COMMENTARY ON 1 PETER.[12]

3:6 You Are Sarah's Children

THE DAUGHTERS OF SARAH. DIDYMUS THE BLIND: Peter commands women to imitate their holy forebears, and in particular Sarah. He urges them to submit to their husbands just as she submitted to Abraham and says that they have become her children by their good behavior. For just as a man who does the works of Abraham and has his faith becomes his child, so also believing women who do good have Sarah as their mother. CATENA.[13]

THE MOTHER OF ALL RIGHTEOUSNESS.

BEDE: Since Sarah had become a companion to Abraham of such great faith, God called her the mother of all the righteous,[14] and when Peter was urging believing women among the Gentiles to practice the virtues of humility, chastity and modesty, he remembered our mother Sarah with due praise. HOMILIES ON THE GOSPELS 1.11.[15]

3:7 Husbands, Live Considerately with Your Wives

BESTOW HONOR UPON THE WOMAN. AUGUSTINE: Is it true that such spouses do not think about the things of the Lord, how they might please him? They are very rare. Who denies this? ON THE GOOD OF MARRIAGE 12.14.[16]

DOMESTIC TROUBLE HINDERS GOD'S WORK. SEVERUS OF ANTIOCH: The pure and united marriage of a man and woman speeds on toward the gates of heaven. For if they bear the image of conjunction by which the church is mystically conjoined to Christ as his bride, they can pray that they will be elevated to a position equal to that of the church. Peter enjoins obedience on wives and tells husbands to bear patiently with them. . . . He also shows that there is another reason for being patient, which is so that their prayers will not be hindered. For nothing hinders the work of God like trouble in the home. CATENA.[17]

THE HUSBAND'S DUTY TO PROTECT THE WIFE. HILARY OF ARLES: The head can easily corrupt the members of the body, but Peter

---

[9]WSA 3/5:143. [10]PL 93:55. [11]CEC 59. [12]PL Supp. 3:94. [13]CEC 59. [14]Gen 17:16. [15]HOG 1:107. [16]FC 27:28. [17]CEC 60.

addresses himself to the latter first, lest it be thought that the lesser might somehow despise the greater. But then he goes on to exhort the greater to treat the lesser members properly. This means, first, husbands must respect the times set aside for prayer and fasting and not demand their marital rights if these are going to be a distraction from other things. Second, men must accept that they are stronger than their wives and therefore have a duty to protect them. Third, both parties are heirs of eternal life which God gives by grace, not by any merit which we may possess, and we do well to remember that "It depends not on man's will or exertion, but on God's mercy."[18] INTRODUCTORY COMMENTARY ON 1 PETER.[19]

SEX AND PRAYER. BEDE: What Peter de-manded of wives he now demands of husbands as well, for husbands must find out what God wants and give honor to the weaker vessel. If we abstain from intercourse we honor one another, but if we do not abstain, it is obvious that the intercourse, which we have is contrary to the demands of honor. Sexual intercourse is a barrier to prayer, as Paul also implied.[20] This means that whenever I have intercourse I cannot pray. But if we are supposed to pray without ceasing, as Paul also said, it is obvious that I can never have sexual intercourse, because if I do so I shall have to interrupt my prayers. ON 1 PETER.[21]

---

[18]Rom 9:16. [19]PL Supp. 3:94-95. [20]1 Cor 7:5: "Do not refuse one another except perhaps by agreement for a season, that you may devote yourselves to prayer." [21]PL 93:55.

3:8-17 RETURNING GOOD FOR EVIL

[8]*Finally, all of you, have unity of spirit, sympathy, love of the brethren, a tender heart and a humble mind.* [9]*Do not return evil for evil or reviling for reviling; but on the contrary bless, for to this you have been called, that you may obtain a blessing.* [10]*For*
"He that would love life
and see good days,
let him keep his tongue from evil
and his lips from speaking guile;
[11]*let him turn away from evil and do right;*
let him seek peace and pursue it.
[12]*For the eyes of the Lord are upon the righteous,*
and his ears are open to their prayer.
But the face of the Lord is against those that do evil."

¹³*Now who is there to harm you if you are zealous for what is right? ¹⁴But even if you do suffer for righteousness' sake, you will be blessed. Have no fear of them, nor be troubled, ¹⁵but in your hearts reverence Christ as Lord. Always be prepared to make a defense to any one who calls you to account for the hope that is in you, yet do it with gentleness and reverence; ¹⁶and keep your conscience clear, so that, when you are abused, those who revile your good behavior in Christ may be put to shame. ¹⁷For it is better to suffer for doing right, if that should be God's will, than for doing wrong.*

OVERVIEW: The life of the church must be governed by mutual love, which will show itself in tenderness and kindness toward others, not least to those who try to do harm. The proper response to evil is to demonstrate the opposite, even if that means that we end up suffering unjustly. Do good in return for evil (HILARY OF ARLES). Bear insults (ANDREAS). Bless those who do you harm (BEDE). Make a habit of viewing the present always in relation to the future (CLEMENT OF ALEXANDRIA, HILARY OF ARLES). Guard your tongue (CHRYSOSTOM, CYRIL OF ALEXANDRIA). God sees and hears everything (CLEMENT OF ALEXANDRIA, ANDREAS). No harm can come to the faithful (HILARY OF ARLES, BEDE), who are blessed in suffering for righteousness' sake (CHRYSOSTOM, BEDE), who seek peace (BASIL), and who pursue profitable thoughts (CHRYSOSTOM). They will never lose God (AUGUSTINE). Unite in harmony of heart and mind (HILARY OF ARLES, BEDE). Every virtue is based on the law of love (ANDREAS, OECUMENIUS). God's own holiness shines forth from our hearts (ANDREAS, BEDE).

We must not be afraid of our enemies but always be ready to witness by our words and deeds that we have a living hope in Christ. Give clear reasons to those who ask what faith in Christ is all about (CYRIL OF ALEXANDRIA). Reason with meekness. For whoever says anything about God must do so as if God himself were present to hear him (DIDYMUS). Give reasons so that another person may see how absurd it is to ask a reason for things which one cannot grasp until one believes (AUGUSTINE). Your conscience is the part of you that embraces what is good and rejects evil, like a doorkeeper—open to friends, closed to enemies (HILARY OF ARLES). Act in such a way that those who revile you because they cannot see your faith may see your good works (BEDE). We may suffer unjustly for the specific purpose of being trained for what we are meant to be (ANDREAS, OECUMENIUS). Yet injustice is never of itself useful (AUGUSTINE). Christians who are faithful to their Lord will put their enemies to shame and thereby win a greater victory than any form of retaliation could hope to achieve.

3:8 Unity of Spirit, a Tender Heart and a Humble Mind

THE CALL TO SPIRITUAL UNITY. HILARY OF ARLES: Peter, as the head of the church, calls everyone to unite in harmony, whether they are secular rulers and peasants, princes of the church and monks, or husbands and wives. The same basic principles apply to them all. INTRODUCTORY COMMENTARY ON 1 PETER.[1]

---

[1]PL Supp. 3:95.

The Law of Love. Andreas: Here Peter moves on from husband and wife and sets out the law of love for everyone. Every virtue is based on it—compassion, mercy, humility, and so on. Catena.[2]

United in Heart and Mind. Bede: Peter has already taught that different persons, classes and sexes must live together. Here he exhorts them all to be united with one heart and mind in the cause of the faith of our Lord. On 1 Peter.[3]

This Advice Applies to All. Oecumenius: Peter now moves on to give general advice to everyone. There was no need for him to target specific groups, since what he says here applies equally to all. This is the law of love, from which every virtue derives. Commentary on 1 Peter.[4]

3:9 Do Not Return Reviling for Reviling

Do Good in Return for Evil. Hilary of Arles: Of course you should not return evil for good or cursing for blessing either, though some people do. A Christian is called to the exact opposite behavior! Introductory Commentary on 1 Peter.[5]

Bear Insults. Andreas: What is humility? It is to bear the insults of others, to accept sins against oneself, to bear punishments. Indeed this is not just humility, but prudence as well. Catena.[6]

Bless Those Who Do You Harm. Bede: Peter forbids us to return evil for evil and even commands us to bless those who harm us, but he also reminds us by quoting Psalm 34:12-16 that God keeps an eye on both the good and the bad and will reward us in eternity for the kindness which we show when we choose to do good to those who persecute us. Furthermore, he will also punish our persecutors if they do not repent, but if they do re-pent we shall also receive a crown of thanksgiving, because we have prayed to the Lord for their salvation. On 1 Peter.[7]

3:10 Guard the Tongue

To See Good Days. Clement of Alexandria: Peter is referring here to those who want to be eternal and incorruptible. Adumbrations.[8]

Keep Your Lips from Speaking Guile. Chrysostom: Guile elicits falsehood, deception, hypocrisy, and slanders which are untrue. It is the friend of the enemy of truth, that is, Satan, the father of lies. Believers are advised to avoid his influence and to prefer the things of God, who is truth. Catena.[9]

Keep Your Tongue from Evil. Cyril of Alexandria: James also said: "If anyone is never at fault in what he says, he is a perfect man, able to keep his whole body in check."[10] It is a great thing to be able to control the tongue, for failure to do so is the greatest of evils. Catena.[11]

View the Present in Relation to the Future. Hilary of Arles: The present is evil, but the future is bright. We should always remember that. Introductory Commentary on 1 Peter.[12]

---

[2]CEC 61. [3]PL 93:55. [4]PG 119:549. [5]PL Supp. 3:95. [6]CEC 61. [7]PL 93:56. [8]FGNK 3:81. [9]CEC 62. [10]Jas 3:2. [11]CEC 62. [12]PL Supp. 3:95.

3:11 *Turn Away from Evil*

SEEK PEACE AND PURSUE IT. BASIL THE GREAT: Exhortations and encouragements to godliness are of fundamental importance. It is essential to turn away from the tendency toward evil and from the evil path of acquiescence in wickedness, so as to reach out to what is good. We must first distance ourselves completely from everything evil if we want to enjoy genuine health, free from all disease. The person who seeks peace seeks Christ, for he is our peace, who made us both—Jew and Gentile—one new man, bringing peace by the blood of his cross. He will find it through faith, because our God and Father has called us to this inheritance. CATENA.[13]

CHOOSE PROFITABLE THOUGHTS. CHRYSOSTOM: These things do not come naturally to us, for bad thoughts are always entering our minds. But if a man is wise, he will put them aside and in their place choose thoughts which will be advantageous and profitable for him. This, I believe, is what it means to turn away from evil. CATENA.[14]

3:12 *God's Favor*

THE EYES OF THE LORD. CLEMENT OF ALEXANDRIA: Here Peter is referring to the many different ways in which the Holy Spirit observes us. ADUMBRATIONS.[15]

THE LORD IS TURNED AGAINST EVIL. HESYCHIUS: The Lord will accept those who repent but will punish those who remain in their sins. CATENA.[16]

GOD SEES AND HEARS EVERYTHING.

ANDREAS: It is not those who are still in their sins who are worthy of such divine oversight, but those who have been cleansed from them. The phrase "the eyes of God" is a metaphor for those divine powers which see everything. It is they who watch over the righteous, but his ears are also ready to hear their prayers. If you want to enjoy this experience, however, you must first turn your eyes away from evil. God never distances himself from the righteous. Whenever the hand of a righteous man does mercy, it has the eye of God watching over it. And whenever his tongue prays, it inclines the divine ear to hear, as for example the prayer of Cornelius was rewarded.[17]
CATENA.[18]

3:13 *Zealous for What Is Right*

YOU WILL NEVER LOSE GOD. AUGUSTINE: If you love the good, you will suffer no loss, because whatever you may be deprived of in this world, you will never lose God, who is the true Good. SERMONS 335C.5.[19]

WHO IS THERE TO HARM YOU? HILARY OF ARLES: Who can prevent you from being blessed, for the Scriptures say that no one can take our joy from us.[20] INTRODUCTORY COMMENTARY ON 1 PETER.[21]

NO HARM CAN COME. BEDE: Peter is speaking here of things like abuse, damage and bodily injury which come to us from our enemies. These and similar things are the common lot of believers, both because they are good imitators of Christ and because they

---

[13]CEC 62-63. [14]CEC 62. [15]FGNK 3:81. [16]CEC 64. [17]Acts 10:34. [18]CEC 63. [19]WSA 3/9:222. [20]Jn 16:22. [21]PL Supp. 3:96.

know that such things, far from doing them any harm, actually bring glory to those who endure them with patience. At the same time, harm does in fact come to those who do such things, because they are storing up eternal punishment for themselves. On 1 Peter.[22]

3:14 Suffer for Righteousness' Sake

Blessing Out of Suffering. Chrysostom: No one can harm a person who does not do evil himself. Peter shows that trials which come from the Gentiles cannot harm those who live according to virtue. On the contrary, they turn those who endure them into blessed people. Catena.[23]

You Will Be Blessed. Bede: Not only does Peter say that believers will not suffer any harm for being persecuted, but they will even be blessed. Here he repeats what Jesus said: "Blessed are those who are persecuted for righteousness' sake, for theirs is the kingdom of heaven."[24] On 1 Peter.[25]

3:15 Account for the Hope That Is in You

Reverence Christ as Lord. Clement of Alexandria: This is just what the Lord's Prayer says: "Hallowed be your name."[26] Adumbrations.[27]

With Gentleness and Reverence. Didymus the Blind: We must be so well instructed in the knowledge of our faith that whenever anyone asks us about it we may be able to give them a proper answer and to do so with meekness and in the fear of God. For whoever says anything about God must do so as if God himself were present to hear him. Catena.[28]

Be Prepared to Make a Defense. Augustine: The apostle tells us to be ready to give an answer to anyone who asks us for an explanation of our faith, because if an unbeliever asks me a reason for my faith and hope and I perceive that he cannot accept it unless he believes, I give him that very reason, so that he may see how absurd it is for him to ask a reason for things which he cannot grasp until he believes. Letters 120.[29]

Making Clear One's Faith. Cyril of Alexandria: The one who decides to do this is not doing anything new, nor is he making up some new explanation. Rather he is making clear to those who ask him what his faith in Christ is all about. Letters 40.8.[30]

Sanctify the Lord in Your Hearts. Andreas: Just as magnifying God cannot add anything to his greatness and glorifying him does not make him any more glorious, so sanctifying the Lord does not mean that there is any addition to his existing holiness. Rather we are called to sanctify him in our hearts, and if we form a clear understanding of his holiness, then we do not sanctify him on one occasion only, but rather by doing this we have a better understanding of what his holiness is and something of it is implanted in our hearts. Likewise someone who magnifies God receives a share of his greatness, and someone who glorifies him is glorified in turn. It is a prophetic voice which says that there should be no fear in you which might prevent you from confessing Christ in your hearts. You should sanctify him there also.

---

[22]PL 93:56. [23]CEC 64. [24]Mt 5:10. [25]PL 93:56-57. [26]Mt 6:9. [27]FGNK 3:81. [28]CEC 65. [29]FC 18:302. [30]FC 76:158.

For this confession is sanctification both for the soul and for the body. Some people wonder why the Savior said: "Do not worry about what you will say,"[31] but here the apostle writes: "Be ready to give an explanation." However, there is no contradiction. Jesus was speaking about bearing witness, whereas Peter is talking about teaching others the faith. CATENA.[32]

GOD'S HOLINESS SHINES FORTH. BEDE: What does it mean to sanctify God in your heart if not to love that holiness of his which is beyond understanding, in the innermost depths of your heart? Think what strength to overcome all enemies God gives to those from whose hearts his holiness shines forth. ON 1 PETER.[33]

3:16 Keep Your Conscience Clear

CONSCIENCE DEFINED. HILARY OF ARLES: Do not get angry or threaten anyone. Your conscience is the part of you which embraces what is good and which rejects evil. It is like the doorkeeper of a house which is open to friends and closed to enemies. INTRODUCTORY COMMENTARY ON 1 PETER.[34]

PUT TO SHAME THOSE WHO REVILE YOU. BEDE: Act in such a way that those who revile you because they cannot see your faith and your hope for a heavenly reward may see your good works and be put to shame by them, because they cannot deny that what you are doing is good. For it is quite certain, my brothers, that those who despise your good behavior will be put to shame when the last judgment comes and they see you crowned along with Christ, while they are condemned along with the devil. ON 1 PETER.[35]

3:17 Suffer for Doing Right, Not Wrong

WHETHER INJUSTICE IS SOMETIMES USEFUL. AUGUSTINE: Everyone who lies acts unjustly, and if lying ever seems to be useful to someone, it may be that injustice sometimes seems useful to him. But in fact injustice is never useful, and lying always does harm. ON CHRISTIAN DOCTRINE 1.40.[36]

UNJUST SUFFERING IS STILL MEANINGFUL. ANDREAS: Once again, Peter exhorts us not to grieve over unjust suffering, if that is God's will for us. He teaches us that we suffer for the specific purpose of being trained for what we are meant to be according to the mercy of God. CATENA.[37]

UNJUST SUFFERING HAS UNEXPECTED BENEFITS. OECUMENIUS: There are two benefits to be gained from unjust suffering. First, the righteous person who suffers grows in righteousness as a result of his patience. Second, the sinner who is spared in this way may be converted by seeing someone else suffer on his behalf. COMMENTARY ON 1 PETER.[38]

---

[31]Mk 13:11. [32]CEC 64-65. [33]PL 93:57. [34]PL Supp. 3:96-97. [35]PL 93:57. [36]FC 2:57. [37]CEC 66. [38]PG 119:553.

3:18-22 THE SAVING WORK OF CHRIST

[18]*For Christ also died[h] for sins once for all, the righteous for the unrighteous, that he might bring us to God, being put to death in the flesh but made alive in the spirit;* [19]*in which he went and preached to the spirits in prison,* [20]*who formerly did not obey, when God's patience waited in the days of Noah, during the building of the ark, in which a few, that is, eight persons, were saved through water.* [21]*Baptism, which corresponds to this, now saves you, not as a removal of dirt from the body but as an appeal to God for a clear conscience, through the resurrection of Jesus Christ,* [22]*who has gone into heaven and is at the right hand of God, with angels, authorities, and powers subject to him.*

h Other ancient authorities read *suffered*

OVERVIEW: Christ is brought to life in our spirits (CLEMENT OF ALEXANDRIA, ANDREAS). So great was his passion that, however often human beings may sin, his one act of suffering is sufficient to take away all our transgressions (OECUMENIUS). Going in his soul, Christ preached to those in hell that he might save all who would believe in him (CYRIL OF ALEXANDRIA, PRUDENTIUS). They did not see but heard him (CLEMENT OF ALEXANDRIA). His incarnation was made ever more complete by his breaking down the gates of hell (ORIGEN, TERTULLIAN). Only the few who believed were saved, as in the case of Noah, who was a type of the church (BEDE, THEOPHYLACT). Those who believed he brought back with him, but those who did not believe, he cast back again into their previous state (SEVERUS, AMMONIUS). Just as in that baptism of the world by which the ancient iniquity was purged, the one who was not in the ark could not be saved, so now anyone who has not been baptized into Christ and within the ark of the church cannot be saved (CYPRIAN). We are saved by this baptism (ANDREAS) even if we must pass through fire (AUGUSTINE). Jesus has risen from the dead and ascended into heaven, where he reigns in glory, and by sharing in his death we have also risen spiritually with him and become fellow heirs of his eternal kingdom. He now sits at the right hand of the Father, lest you imagine that when he suffered he lost something of his glory (LEO, ANDREAS), the angelic powers and authorities being subject to him (CLEMENT OF ALEXANDRIA, BEDE).

3:18 Christ Died for Sins Once for All

FOR OUR SINS. CLEMENT OF ALEXANDRIA: This is said in relation to our faith. In other words, Christ is brought to life in our spirits. ADUMBRATIONS.[1]

PUT TO DEATH IN THE FLESH BUT MADE ALIVE IN THE SPIRIT. ANDREAS: Again Peter expounds Christ's death and resurrection.

[1]FGNK 3:81.

Notice how he proclaims the mystery to us. For by saying that he died in the flesh and that he was made alive again in the Spirit, what he is really saying is that he died for the sake of our flesh, which is under the power of corruption, but that he rose again as God, for the word *spirit* means "God" in this instance. CATENA.[2]

THE RIGHTEOUS FOR THE UNRIGHTEOUS.

OECUMENIUS: The righteous person suffers for the salvation of others, just as Christ did. This is why Peter mentions our Lord's example, since Christ did not die for his own sins but for ours. This is the point he makes by adding "the righteous for the unrighteous." For as the prophet long ago foretold, Christ did not sin at all. Furthermore, in order to emphasize the effectiveness and completeness of Christ's sacrifice, Peter adds the key word *once*. So great was his passion that however often human beings may sin, that one act of suffering is sufficient to take away all our transgressions. COMMENTARY ON 1 PETER.[3]

3:19 He Preached to the Spirits in Prison

THE SPIRITS IN PRISON. CLEMENT OF ALEXANDRIA: They did not see his form, but they heard the sound of his voice. ADUMBRATIONS.[4]

TEACHING THE PATRIARCHS. TERTULLIAN: Christ descended into hell in order to acquaint the patriarchs and prophets with his redeeming mission. ON THE SOUL 55.2.[5]

DESCENT INTO HELL. ORIGEN: If the passage about John the Baptist not being worthy to untie Jesus' shoes[6] possesses a hidden meaning, we ought not to pass over it. I think

that the incarnation, when the Son of God takes on flesh and bones, is one of the shoes, and the descent into hell is the other. It is said in Psalm 16: "You will not leave my soul in hell." And Peter, in his general epistle, mentions Jesus' descent into hell. Therefore the one who can show the meaning of both sojourns in a worthy manner is able to unloose Jesus' shoes. COMMENTARY ON JOHN 6.174-76.[7]

SAVING ALL WHO WOULD BELIEVE. CYRIL OF ALEXANDRIA: Here Peter answers the question which some objectors have raised, namely, if the incarnation was so beneficial, why was Christ not incarnated for such a long time, given that he went to the spirits which were in prison and preached to them also? In order to deliver all those who would believe, Christ taught those who were alive on earth at the time of his incarnation, and these others acknowledged him when he appeared to them in the lower regions, and thus they too benefited from his coming. Going in his soul, he preached to those who were in hell, appearing to them as one soul to other souls. When the gatekeepers of hell saw him, they fled; the bronze gates were broken open, and the iron chains were undone. And the only-begotten Son shouted with authority to the suffering souls, according to the word of the new covenant, saying to those in chains: "Come out!" and to those in darkness: "Be enlightened." In other words, he preached to those who were in hell also, so that he might save all those who would believe in him. For both those who were

[2]CEC 66. [3]PG 119:556. [4]FGNK 3:81. [5]FC 10:298. [6]Jn 1:26. Shoes provide a metaphor of stepping, in this case from heaven to earth to hell. [7]FC 80:218.

alive on earth during the time of his incarnation and those who were in hell had a chance to acknowledge him. The greater part of the new covenant is beyond nature and tradition, so that while Christ was able to preach to all those who were alive at the time of his ap-pearing and those who believed in him were blessed, so too he was able to liberate those in hell who believed and acknowledged him, by his descent there. However, the souls of those who practiced idolatry and outrageous ungodliness, as well as those who were blinded by fleshly lusts, did not have the power to see him, and they were not delivered. CATENA.[8]

REVERSING THE MANDATE. PRUDENTIUS:
That the dead might know salvation,
    who in limbo long had dwelt,
Into hell with love he entered;
    to him yield the broken gates
As the bolts and massive hinges
    fall asunder at his word.
Now the door of ready entrance,
    but forbidding all return
Outward swings as bars are loosened
    and sends forth the prisoned souls
By reversal of the mandate,
    treading its threshold once more.
HYMNS 9.70-75.[9]

FORGIVENESS TO THOSE WHO BELIEVED.
SEVERUS OF ANTIOCH: Forgiveness was not granted to everyone in hell, but only to those who believed and acknowledged Christ. Those who cleansed themselves from evil by doing good works while they were alive recognized him, for until he appeared in the lower regions everyone, including those who had been educated in righteousness, was bound by the chains of death and was awaiting his arrival there, for the way to paradise was closed to them because

of Adam's sin. Nevertheless, not everyone who was in the lower regions responded to Christ when he went there, but only those who believed in him. CATENA.[10]

WHETHER JUDAS BELIEVED. AMMONIUS:
The academician Caesarius asked me whether the chains of all the souls in hell were cut off when Christ went down there or not. I said that they were. How can that be, he said. Was Judas also set free? Yes, I said. For when the king of all is present, it is not possible for the tyrant and his servant, I mean death, to retain their captives any longer. So what did the Lord do? He died. He preached the way which leads to eternal salvation on earth, and to all who were in hell, so that they might believe in the Father and in him, who became man and died for us and who went down into hell by the power of the Holy Spirit. And those who believed he brought back with him, but those who did not believe, he cast back again into their previous state. . . . Did he also preach to Judas and give him a chance to repent? I said that I did not think so, for it is superfluous to preach to someone who already knows the truth. Not only had Judas been instructed in the mystery and accepted it, but he had even preached it to others and been considered worthy to receive divine grace, so that he could drive out demons and heal the sick. Later on he fell away by his own choice. Do not tell me that he did evil unwillingly, for no Christian does that. Even Judas never blamed others for his betrayal but recognized that it was his own fault. CATENA.[11]

---

[8]CEC 66. [9]FC 43:65. [10]CEC 67-68. [11]CEC 68-69.

3:20 *In the Days of Noah*

God's Patience Waited. Clement of Alexandria: God is so good that he even works his salvation by means of patient instruction. Adumbrations.[12]

Noah Was a Type of the Church. Augustine: The question which you put to me about the spirits in hell is one which disturbs me profoundly.... What troubles me most is why only those who were imprisoned in the days of Noah should deserve this benefit. Think of all the others who have died since Noah's time and whom Jesus could have found in hell. The meaning must be that the ark of Noah is a picture of the church, and so those who were imprisoned in his days represent the entire human race. In hell Christ rebuked the wicked and consoled the good, so that some believed to their salvation and others disbelieved to their damnation. Letters 164.[13]

Eight Persons Were Saved Through Water. Bede: By pointing out that only eight people were saved from the flood, Peter reminds us that in comparison to the large numbers of Jews, heretics and unbelievers which there are in the world, the number of God's chosen ones is very small. As Jesus said: "The gate is narrow and the way is hard that leads to life, and those who find it are few."[14] On 1 Peter.[15]

Only a Few Who Believed Were Saved. Theophylact: Someone might easily ask: Who preached salvation before Christ, so that those who did not believe in him should be condemned? The answer to this, which Paul also adopted, is that those who lived before Christ had enough light given to them to enable

them to distinguish good from evil. Because of this, if they chose to do evil, they are worthy of condemnation. Therefore Peter reminds us that they were rebellious, not merely from the time of the prophets but long before that, virtually from the creation of the world in fact. As he demonstrates, the way of salvation was proclaimed to them from the beginning, but they spurned it and preferred to go after vanities of one kind or another. The result was that of all the millions of people who lived at that time, only eight were saved, because they alone believed the message which they heard. Commentary on 1 Peter.[16]

3:21 *Baptism Saves You as an Appeal to God*

The Meaning of Baptism. Cyprian: Peter showed and vindicated the unity of the church by commanding and warning that we can be saved only through the baptism of the one church. Just as in that baptism of the world by which the ancient iniquity was purged, the one who was not in the ark could not be saved through water, so now anyone who has not been baptized in the church cannot be saved, for the church has been founded in the unity of the Lord, as the sacrament of the one ark. Letters 74.11.[17]

A Clear Conscience. Augustine: If some people have the worst consciences, full of every fault and crime, unchanged by penance for their evil deeds, baptism nevertheless saves them, for on the basis of the foundation which is laid in baptism they will be saved, even if it is

---

[12]FGNK 3:81. [13]FC 11:382-84**. [14]Mt 7:14. [15]PL 93:59-60. [16]PG 125:1233. [17]FC 51:294.

through fire. EIGHT QUESTIONS OF DULCI-
TIUS I.[18]

SAVED THROUGH BAPTISM. ANDREAS: The
water of the flood is a type of baptism because
it both punished evil people and saved the
good, just as baptism expels evil spirits and
saves those who turn to Christ. This shows
the great power of baptism, and how much
we need it. CATENA.[19]

3:22 Christ Has Gone into Heaven

ANGELS AND AUTHORITIES. CLEMENT OF
ALEXANDRIA: The angels are the first rank in
the hierarchy of perfection, the authorities are
the second, and the powers are the third.
ADUMBRATIONS.[20]

**THE HOLINESS OF CREATURES IS BY
GRACE.** DIDYMUS THE BLIND: Just as all
rational creatures are made by the Son of
God, who is the Word, or Reason, so too is
their salvation brought about by him. For
those who possess holiness not by nature but
by grace, because they are creatures, must be
cleansed by him in order to obtain goodness.
COMMENTARY ON 1 PETER.[21]

TRANSFORMING AFFLICTION INTO TRI-

UMPH. LEO THE GREAT: While the strength of
the angelic legions that waited on Christ was
held in check, he drank the cup of sorrow and
death, thereby transforming the entire affliction into triumph. Deceptions were overcome,
and the powers of evil were suppressed. SER-
MONS 69.4.[22]

CHRIST SITS AT THE RIGHT HAND OF GOD.
ANDREAS: Look how clearly the dispensation
of grace is set out for us. Peter recalls Christ's
death and resurrection and then goes on to
mention his ascension as well, and the fact that
he sits at the right hand of the Father, lest you
imagine that when he suffered he lost something of his glory. CATENA.[23]

WITH ANGELIC POWERS SUBJECT TO HIM.
BEDE: There can be no doubt that the angels
and the powers of heaven were always subject
to the Son of God, but Peter wants to stress
that the humanity which that Son assumed has
also been taken up into that glory, so that now
it is greater than any angelic dignity or power.
ON 1 PETER.[24]

---

[18]FC 16:431. [19]CEC 70. [20]FGNK 3:81-82. [21]PG 39:1770. [22]FC 93:303. [23]CEC 70. [24]PL 93:60.

4:1-6 LIFE IN THE SPIRIT

[1]*Since therefore Christ suffered in the flesh,[i] arm yourselves with the same thought, for whoever has suffered in the flesh has ceased from sin,* [2]*so as to live for the rest of the time in the flesh no longer by human passions but by the will of God.* [3]*Let the time that is past suf-*

fice for doing what the Gentiles like to do, living in licentiousness, passions, drunkenness, rev-els, carousing, and lawless idolatry. ⁴They are surprised that you do not now join them in the same wild profligacy, and they abuse you; ⁵but they will give account to him who is ready to judge the living and the dead. ⁶For this is why the gospel was preached even to the dead, that though judged in the flesh like men, they might live in the spirit like God.

i Other ancient authorities add *for us;* some *for you*

OVERVIEW: Since Christ suffered in the flesh, we who follow him must also turn away from the desires of the flesh and live in the Spirit of God. Christ was passible in his flesh (CYRIL OF ALEXANDRIA) but impassible in his divinity (SEVERUS). Christ did not die in his divinity (ATHANASIUS) but in his flesh (NICETA). The saints who submitted their bodies to martyrdom at the hands of violent persecutors abstained from sin as far as they could, right up to the end of their lives (BEDE). So must we now depart from the evil deeds of pagan life and not imitate those who have relapsed into debauchery (SEVERUS, THEOPHYLACT), who are surprised when we do not join them (SEVERUS, OECUMENIUS).

After his death on the cross Christ preached in hell in the same way as he had preached to those who were alive on earth (OECUMENIUS). Christ went to hell to preach the gospel to the dead because he wanted to give those who had already been judged in the flesh a chance to live in the Spirit. The Fathers did not believe that by doing this Christ gave everyone in hell the chance to go to heaven. On the contrary, he went to hell to liberate only those Gentiles who had died before his coming but whom he had chosen to belong to his people. Whether "the dead" in this passage means unbelievers (AUGUSTINE) dead in their transgressions (ANDREAS) or those who having sinned stand before final judgment (SEVERUS)

was widely debated by the Fathers. That the gospel was preached "even to those dead" was variously interpreted to mean dead in sin (ISHO'DAD) or in hell (HILARY OF ARLES, OECU-MENIUS, THEOPHYLACT) or the Gentiles (ANDREAS) or to the worst of criminals (BEDE).

4:1 Christ Suffered in the Flesh

CHRIST DID NOT DIE IN HIS DIVINITY.
ATHANASIUS: The apostle did not say that Christ died in his divinity but in his flesh, so as to emphasize that it was not his divine nature which suffered but his human one. The sufferings are those of the one to whom the body belongs. Since the flesh belonged to the Word, the sufferings of the flesh must be attributed to the Word as well. CATENA.[1]

I GAVE MY BACK TO LASHES. CYRIL OF ALEXANDRIA: In order that Christ might be believed to be the Savior of all, according to their appropriation of his incarnation, he assumed the sufferings of his own flesh, as was foretold in Isaiah [50:6]: "I gave my back to lashes, my cheeks to those who plucked my beard; I did not turn away my face from the disgrace of their spittings." LETTERS 39.[2]

---

[1]CEC 70-71. [2]FC 76:151.

UNION OF TWO NATURES. SEVERUS OF ANTIOCH: By proclaiming that he would suffer and die in the flesh, Christ was indicating that he was passible in his flesh but impassible in his divinity. The ineffable union of the two natures did not cut him in two, for he remains one Lord, one Christ and one Son, one person and one hypostasis, that of the Word incarnate. By becoming man he became capable of suffering and death, but in the divine nature which he had from eternity he remained impassible and consubstantial with the Father and the Son. But insofar as he was consubstantial with us also, he was able to partake of our sufferings and did so willingly and in truth. CATENA.[3]

COMFORT TO SUFFERERS. BEDE: The apostle Peter gave this comfort to those of us who are bound by the chains of persecution. ON ACTS 12:7.[4]

ABSTAINING FROM SIN. BEDE: There can be no doubt that the saints who submitted their bodies to martyrdom at the hands of violent persecutors abstained from sin as far as they could, right up to the end of their lives. For who would have time to think about sinning if he were being crucified, stoned, thrown to the lions, burnt at the stake, buried alive with scorpions or whatever? Would such a person not be much more focused on obtaining an eternal crown of glory as soon as sufferings of that kind were over? Peter exhorts us all to have the same attitude. ON 1 PETER.[5]

FROM HIS WOUNDS FLOW SALVATION. NICETA OF REMESIANA: Christ did not suffer in his divinity but in his flesh. God can never suffer. Christ suffered in the flesh, as the apostle teaches, so that from his wounds might flow salvation to humanity. This was foretold by the prophet Isaiah:[6] Christ suffered for our sins so that grace might be given to us. EXPLANATION OF THE CREED 5.[7]

4:2 Live by the Will of God

WITNESS OF THE GOSPEL. HILARY OF ARLES: The will of God which we live by is the witness of the gospel, which kills any interest we may have in human glory. INTRODUCTORY COMMENTARY ON 1 PETER.[8]

DEAD TO SIN. THEOPHYLACT: Compare this with what Paul wrote: "If we are dead with Christ, we shall also live with him"[9] and "dead therefore to sin but alive to God."[10] COMMENTARY ON 1 PETER.[11]

4:3 Let the Time Past Suffice

LIVING IN LICENTIOUSNESS. SEVERUS OF ANTIOCH: What Peter is saying is this: We must depart from the evil deeds of pagan life and not go back to our old ways nor imitate those who have relapsed into debauchery and drunkenness. CATENA.[12]

DOING WHAT THE GENTILES LIKE TO DO. THEOPHYLACT: This is ironic, as if Peter were saying: "Have you not had enough of the pleasures which you once indulged in? Or do you still hanker after the Gentile life which you used to live?" It is in connection with this that he notes the various types of debauchery. COMMENTARY ON 1 PETER.[13]

---

[3]CEC 71. [4]CAA 112. [5]PL 93:61. [6]Is 53:5. [7]FC 7:46-47. [8]PL Supp. 3:100. [9]2 Tim 2:11. [10]Rom 6:11. [11]PG 125:1236. [12]CEC 73. [13]PG 125:1236.

4:4 You Do Not Now Join Them

GENTILES ARE SURPRISED BY CHRISTIANS.
SEVERUS OF ANTIOCH: These people are surprised and put off when they see us turning toward what is good rather than going along with them. And not only do they not seek the good, they fall away even into blasphemy.
CATENA.[14]

THE SAME WILD PROFLIGACY. OECUMENIUS: Not only do the Gentiles wonder at the change in you, not only does it make them ashamed, but they also attack you for it, for the worship of God is an abomination to sinners. COMMENTARY ON 1 PETER.[15]

4:5 They Will Have to Give Account to God

READY TO JUDGE THE LIVING AND THE DEAD. AUGUSTINE: It does not necessarily follow that we should here understand those who have departed from the body. For it could be that by "the dead" Peter means unbelievers, those who are dead in soul. Therefore we are not obliged to believe that he refers to hell when he mentions the dead in the next verse.
LETTERS 164.[16]

FINAL JUDGMENT. SEVERUS OF ANTIOCH: This will happen in the future, when everyone will have to be ready to give an account of himself, and no one will be able to stop him from doing so. For everything will be laid bare before God, who judges the righteous and the wicked. At that time he will judge and separate the ones from the others, as the Savior himself said: "He will put the sheep on his right and the goats on his left."[17]
CATENA.[18]

DEAD IN THEIR TRANSGRESSIONS.
ANDREAS: Some people say that the soul is living and the body dead, but it is impossible for a soul to come to judgment without its own body. Rather here Peter calls the righteous "living," because they do the works of the life to come, and the unrighteous he calls "dead," because they are dead in their transgressions and dead works. But the gospel has been preached to both the righteous and the unrighteous, even to those who are dead in their sins, so that they may judge themselves by casting their vote against themselves.
CATENA.[19]

4:6 Why the Gospel Was Preached Even to the Dead

THAT THEY MIGHT LIVE IN THE SPIRIT.
CLEMENT OF ALEXANDRIA: Those who abandon their faith in this life are judged according to the above judgments, so that they might repent. This is why Peter adds "so that in the spirit they might live as God lives." ADUMBRATIONS.[20]

EVEN TO THE DEAD. HILARY OF ARLES: The gospel is preached to the Gentiles who are dead in sin, but this may also refer to the fact that when the Lord was buried in the tomb he went to preach to those who live in hell. INTRODUCTORY COMMENTARY ON 1 PETER.[21]

THE GENTILES. ANDREAS: Here Peter uses "dead" to refer to the Gentiles, who are dead because of their insurmountable sins and whom he wants to see turn to Christ. Such

---

[14]CEC 73. [15]PG 119:561. [16]FC 20:396-97. [17]Mt 25:32-33. [18]CEC 73. [19]CEC 73. [20]FGNK 3:82. [21]PL Supp. 3:101.

sinners, after they accept his commandments, judge themselves in the flesh according to their human understanding, by mortifying it in fasting, prostrations, tears and other forms of suffering. They do this in order that they may live in the spirit as God wants them to, being inspired by the word of the apostle Paul, who said: "If our outer man is being destroyed, our inner man is being renewed day by day."[22] CATENA.[23]

PREACHED TO THE WORST OF CRIMINALS.

BEDE: So great is God's concern, so great is his love, so great is his desire that we should be dead to the flesh but alive in the Spirit, that he even decided to preach the message of faith to those who had committed major crimes and who deserved to be put to death for their licentiousness, their lust, their violence, their gluttony, their drunkenness and their illicit worship of idols. ON 1 PETER.[24]

PREACHING IN HELL. OECUMENIUS: This

means that those who are now attacking believers will have to give account of themselves to him who judges everyone, both living and dead, for the dead are also judged, as is clear from Christ's descent into hell. For when he went there after his death on the cross he preached in the same way as he had preached to those who were alive on earth. Moreover, he did this not in word but in deed. And just as when he came into the world in order to justify those who were ready to acknowledge him and to condemn those who refused to do so, so he did exactly the same in hell. For he

went to judge those who had lived according to the flesh, but those who had lived according to the Spirit, that is, who had lived an honest and spiritual life, he raised to glory and salvation. COMMENTARY ON 1 PETER.[25]

CHRIST PREACHED AFTER HIS DEATH.

THEOPHYLACT: It was the habit of the Fathers to take this verse completely out of context. They therefore said that the word *dead* has two different meanings in Scripture, referring either to those who are dead in their sins and who never lived at all or to those who have been made conformable to the death of Christ, as Paul said: "The life that I now live in the flesh, I live in the faith of the Son of God."[26] But if they had paid the slightest attention to the context, they would have seen that here the "dead" are those who have been shut up in hell, to whom Christ went to preach after his death on the cross. COMMENTARY ON 1 PETER.[27]

"THE DEAD" ARE SINNERS. ISHO'DAD OF

MERV: Christ was preached to many who rose again at his resurrection, something which is attested in Matthew [27:52-53]. In this life sinners bear sufferings in the body by means of repentance, in order to gain a constant and blessed life in that spiritual citizenship. It seems that by the "dead" Peter means sinners and that by life in the Spirit he means repentance. COMMENTARIES.[28]

---

[22]2 Cor 4:16. [23]CEC 74. [24]PL 93:62. [25]PG 119:561. [26]Gal 2:20. [27]PG 125:1237-40. [28]CIM 38

4:7-19 THE END IS NEAR

[7]*The end of all things is at hand; therefore keep sane and sober for your prayers.* [8]*Above all hold unfailing your love for one another, since love covers a multitude of sins.* [9]*Practice hospitality ungrudgingly to one another.* [10]*As each has received a gift, employ it for one another, as good stewards of God's varied grace:* [11]*whoever speaks, as one who utters oracles of God; whoever renders service, as one who renders it by the strength which God supplies; in order that in everything God may be glorified through Jesus Christ. To him belong glory and dominion for ever and ever. Amen.*

[12]*Beloved, do not be surprised at the fiery ordeal which comes upon you to prove you, as though something strange were happening to you.* [13]*But rejoice in so far as you share Christ's sufferings, that you may also rejoice and be glad when his glory is revealed.* [14]*If you are reproached for the name of Christ, you are blessed, because the spirit of glory[j] and of God rests upon you.* [15]*But let none of you suffer as a murderer, or a thief, or a wrongdoer, or a mischief-maker;* [16]*yet if one suffers as a Christian, let him not be ashamed, but under that name let him glorify God.* [17]*For the time has come for judgment to begin with the household of God; and if it begins with us, what will be the end of those who do not obey the gospel of God?* [18]*And*

> *"If the righteous man is scarcely saved,*
> *where will the impious and sinner appear?"*

[19]*Therefore let those who suffer according to God's will do right and entrust their souls to a faithful Creator.*

j Other ancient authorities insert *and of power*

OVERVIEW: The end of all prophecies is at hand (OECUMENIUS). The end will come when the gospel has been preached to the Gentiles (HILARY OF ARLES). Though its timing is uncertain, it is sure to come and should not be thought of as a long way off (BEDE). Meanwhile we must love one another and show hospitality, using the gifts that God has given us for the mutual benefit of the fellowship to which we belong. Nothing is stronger against sin than love (LEO, BEDE). Love cuts out the desire to sin, casts out fear (AMBROSE) and unites us to God (CLEMENT OF ROME). Receive your neighbor with hospitality, without grumbling (THEOPHYLACT), as if your neighbor were Christ himself (CHRYSOSTOM). Each one of us must use the varied gifts that we have received either by nature or by the Holy Spirit (AUGUSTINE, ANDREAS) for the benefit of others (BRAULIO OF SARAGOSSA).

Everything we do must be done to glorify God, because he is in control of all things. If we have to suffer for our beliefs, we should rejoice, because Christ also had to suffer. We shall be blessed for our faithfulness when he comes to judge the world. Our sufferings are part of that coming judgment, which begins with God's own people. This is not a cause for despair, because however severely we may be tested, it is nothing compared with what unbelievers will have to face. We should therefore be glad that we are not forced to suffer any more than we can bear, and we must remember that our endurance through that suffering is a sign and assurance that God has accepted and approved us. Fiery trials are nothing new (CASSIODORUS). The prophets suffered the same things. Such trials find their meaning and culmination in the cross of Christ (HILARY OF ARLES, THEOPHYLACT). The Spirit of God rests upon us when we suffer for the faith (OECUMENIUS). God's judgment is already beginning in the house of God, in the church, in that by undergoing our present sufferings we are being prepared for the joys of eternity (DIDYMUS, BEDE). Christ's glory is revealed in the church when it suffers (HILARY OF ARLES). Salvation is not to be taken for granted, either in the case of Moses or us (BASIL, BEDE). The righteous may flourish with many virtues, but they are scarcely saved because they stand nonetheless in need of the mercy of God (JEROME).

4:7 The End of All Things Is at Hand

AFTER THE GOSPEL PREACHED TO THE GENTILES. HILARY OF ARLES: Peter is saying that once the gospel has been preached to the Gentiles the end will have come. INTRODUCTORY COMMENTARY ON 1 PETER.[1]

TIMING UNCERTAIN BUT SURE TO COME. BEDE: Peter says this so that you will not be fooled into thinking that judgment is a long way off or even that it will never come. Its timing may be uncertain, as far as we are concerned, but it is sure to come sooner or later. ON 1 PETER.[2]

THE END OF ALL PROPHECIES IS NEAR. OECUMENIUS: The end of all things means their completion and consummation. Perhaps this means that the end of all the prophecies is near, for that refers to Christ who is in himself the consummation of all things. This is very different from Epicurus, who said that pleasure is the end of all things, or other Greeks, who said that the end is wisdom or contemplation or virtue. COMMENTARY ON 1 PETER.[3]

4:8 Love Covers a Multitude of Sins

LOVE UNITES US TO GOD. CLEMENT OF ROME: Love unites us to God. Love hides a multitude of sins. Love puts up with everything and is always patient. There is nothing vulgar about love, nothing arrogant.... Without love, nothing can please God. LETTER TO THE CORINTHIANS 49.[4]

LOVE CASTS OUT FEAR. AMBROSE OF MILAN: The one who sins does not love, for love covers a multitude of sins. Love cuts out the desire to sin, and since it also casts out fear, it is obviously full of perfect faith. LETTERS TO PRIESTS 48.[5]

---

[1]PL Supp. 3:101. [2]PL 93:62. [3]PG 119:565. [4]LCC 1:66. [5]FC 26:253.

LOVE CONQUERS SIN. LEO THE GREAT: Nothing is stronger against the wiles of the devil, dearly beloved, than the kindness, mercy and generosity of love, through which every sin is either avoided or conquered. SERMONS 74.5.[6]

HOLD UNFAILING YOUR LOVE FOR ONE ANOTHER. BEDE: There are many good works which alleviate sins, but Peter speaks especially of love, because it is by love that we forgive those who trespass against us, something which is righteous in the sight of God and in full agreement with the godliness which has been given to us. ON 1 PETER.[7]

4:9 Practice Hospitality Ungrudgingly

RECEIVE YOUR NEIGHBOR AS IF CHRIST. CHRYSOSTOM: If you receive your neighbor as though he were Christ, you will not complain or feel embarrassed but rather rejoice in your service. But if you do not receive him as if he were Christ, you will not receive Christ either, because he said: "Whoever receives you, receives me."[8] If you do not show hospitality in this way, you will have no reward. Abraham received passers-by and travelers just as they were. He did not leave them to his servants. On the contrary, he ordered his wife to bring flour, even though he had domestic help. But he and his wife wanted to earn the blessing, not only of hospitality but of service also. This is how we ought to show hospitality, by doing all the work ourselves, so that we may be sanctified. CATENA.[9]

WITHOUT GRUMBLING. THEOPHYLACT: Note that when Peter mentions love he immediately goes on to talk about offering hospitality without grumbling. That is a sure sign of what love is. COMMENTARY ON 1 PETER.[10]

4:10 Employ Gifts for Another

AS EACH HAS RECEIVED A GIFT. AUGUSTINE: God has granted to each of us the special graces needed for the upbuilding of his church, so that we will do what he has indicated should be done, not only without complaint but with joy. ON CHRISTIAN DOCTRINE 1.15.[11]

EMPLOY IT FOR ANOTHER. BRAULIO OF SARAGOSSA: Our creator and dispenser so orders all things that love is increased when the divine gifts which one does not see in himself are bestowed to be possessed by another. Thus the manifold grace of God is well dispensed when the gift received is believed to belong also to the one who does not have it and when it is believed to have been given for the sake of him with whom it is shared. LETTERS 5.[12]

AS GOOD STEWARDS OF GOD'S VARIED GRACE. ANDREAS: It is not merely that the rich man is obliged to meet the needs of those who are less well off than he is but also that each one of us must use the gifts which we have received either by nature or by the Holy Spirit, so that no one may say that we are keeping these things to ourselves and refusing to share them with our neighbors. CATENA.[13]

4:11 Whoever Renders Service

BY THE STRENGTH THAT GOD SUPPLIES.

---

[6]FC 93:329. [7]PL 93:62-63. [8]Mt 10:40. [9]CEC 77. [10]PG 125:1241. [11]FC 2:38. [12]FC 63:22. [13]CEC 77.

Cyril of Alexandria: Those who offer hospitality to others make themselves happy and content, not so much because they are giving of their own as because they are being helped by others. And this in two ways; first, because they enjoy the company of their guests, and second, because they earn a reward for their hospitality. But if you receive a brother, do not be distracted by too much serving, and do not attempt what is beyond your strength. Unnecessary effort is always tedious, and such exertions will only embarrass your guests. Do not let your guest become a cause for impoverishing yourself, but even in hard times be as generous as you can. Catena.[14]

That God May Be Glorified. Bede: It seems that Peter was afraid that he might say or teach something which goes against the will of God, or against what is written in Scripture, and be found to be a false witness to God or a blasphemer or a heretic who was introducing something which goes against the Lord's teaching. And what he practiced himself in this respect he enjoins on us all. On 1 Peter.[15]

4:12 Do Not Be Surprised at the Fiery Ordeal

Trials Nothing New. Hilary of Arles: The trials and temptations which come to Christians are nothing new. The prophets of the Old Testament suffered exactly the same things. All such trials find their meaning and culmination in the cross of Christ. The servant is not greater than his master. If Christ suffered, how can we expect to get off any more lightly? Introductory Commentary on 1 Peter.[16]

Remain Steadfast. Cassiodorus: Peter comforts believers here by telling them not to be upset when they face suffering, since Christ bore much more for our sakes than we could ever bear for his. We should therefore remain steadfast in such trials so that one day we may rejoice in his presence. Summary of 1 Peter.[17]

Do Not Be Surprised. Theophylact: Many Christians found afflictions hard to bear because they had read in the law that a prosperous and secure life was promised to those who serve God. Peter therefore approaches the subject by telling them that they are greatly beloved. He then goes on to warn them not to be surprised at their sufferings, which come to them as tests from God. Commentary on 1 Peter.[18]

4:13 Be Glad When His Glory Is Revealed

Sharing in Christ's Suffering. Clement of Alexandria: This means that if you are righteous you are suffering for righteousness's sake, just as Christ did. Adumbrations.[19]

4:14 Reproach for the Name of Christ

The Spirit of God Rests upon You. Oecumenius: How can it be that when the Spirit of God appears to be blasphemed among the ungodly he is glorified in you? This happens because when people accuse you falsely the shame of it rests on them, but you receive glory thereby. Commentary on 1 Peter.[20]

---

[14]CEC 78. [15]PL 93:63. [16]PL Supp. 3:102. [17]PL 70:1366-67. [18]PG 125:1241-44. [19]FGNK 3:82. [20]PG 119:568.

4:15 Do Not Commit Crimes

Not as a Murderer or Thief. Hilary of Arles: Our suffering must not be like that of the thief on the cross, who suffered because he was a murderer, even though he himself confessed that Christ had done no wrong. Nor should we be like Ananias and Sapphira, who tried to steal what belonged to God. Even less should we imitate Simon Magus, who denounced the apostles to Nero and who tried to buy their gifts with gold and silver. Introductory Commentary on 1 Peter.[21]

Or a Mischief Maker. Theophylact: A meddler is someone who loves to mind other people's business in order to find reasons for attacking them. This is the mentality of a wicked and treacherous person who is prepared to engage in any kind of evil. Commentary on 1 Peter.[22]

4:16 Glorify God in Your Suffering

Christ's Glory Revealed. Hilary of Arles: If you suffer as a Christian, you have nothing to be ashamed of. Think of James the son of Zebedee or Stephen. However awful the trials you suffer may be, learn to glory in them, not to be upset by them. Christ's glory is revealed in the church when it suffers. Introductory Commentary on 1 Peter.[23]

4:17 Judgment Begins with the Household of God

Persecution. Clement of Alexandria: This is the judgment which will occur in times of persecution. Adumbrations.[24]

The End of Those Who Do Not Obey.

Didymus the Blind: When the time comes for God's judgment to begin, it will start with the best and work its way downwards, that is to say, it will commence with those who believe and belong to the church of God. Just think— if the examination of our lives begins with those who belong to God's household, what will it be like by the time it gets to those who have rejected the gospel? God sends great suffering and fear on believers so that they may learn that he is the judge to whom they must answer, and on unbelievers he sends the same fear, saying that they will not escape the great punishments which are their lot. Catena.[25]

Hidden and Public Judgment. Bede: Scripture teaches us that there are two kinds of divine judgment—one which is hidden and one which is public. The hidden judgment is a punishment by which each one of us is moved to repentance, or to conversion, or if we despise the calling and discipline of God, to damnation. The public judgment is the one which will take place when Christ comes again to judge the living and the dead. This judgment is already beginning at the house of God, that is, in the church, in that by undergoing our present sufferings we are being prepared for the joys of eternity. The wicked are currently living securely in this present transitory life, but once that is over there will be nothing left for them but God's vengeance, which will be as great as the punishment which they deserve. On 1 Peter.[26]

4:18 The Righteous Person Is Scarcely Saved

---

[21]PL Supp. 3:103. [22]PG 125:1244. [23]PL Supp. 3:103. [24]FGNK 3:82. [25]CEC 79. [26]PL 93:64.

The Severity of God. Basil the Great: When I see Moses asking for forgiveness and not obtaining it, when I see him considered unworthy of pardon because of his few words, spoken against the rock in anger,[27] in spite of his many good deeds, I truly realize what the severity of God is like and am persuaded that these words of the apostle are true. On the Judgment of God.[28]

The Righteous Also Need God's Mercy. Jerome: It is the righteous man who is scarcely saved on the day of judgment. If he had no fault, he would easily be saved. As it is, he is righteous because he flourishes with many virtues, but he is scarcely saved because he stands in need of the mercy of God in some things. Against the Pelagians 2.5.[29]

Why Is a Righteous Person Scarcely Saved? Bede: The Pelagians do not want to believe that the entire human race has been corrupted by the sin of one person and condemned as a result. From that sin and damnation only the grace of Christ can cleanse and deliver us. Why is it therefore that a righteous man is scarcely saved? Is it difficult for God to deliver the righteous? Of course not! But in order to show that our nature has been justly condemned, even the Almighty does not want it to appear as if being delivered from it is something easy. On 1 Peter.[30]

4:19 Entrust Your Soul to the Creator

No One Tempted Beyond What One Can Bear. Oecumenius: Peter said "according to God's will" either because our afflictions are part of God's providence and are sent to us as a form of testing, or because although we are afflicted by God's will, we depend on him for the outcome. For he is faithful and sure and does not lie when he promises us that we shall never be tempted beyond what we are able to bear.[31] Commentary on 1 Peter.[32]

---

[27]Num 20:10. [28]FC 9:45. [29]FC 53:303. [30]PL 93:64. [31]1 Cor 10:13. [32]PG 119:569.

5:1-5 CHURCH ELDERSHIP

[1]So I exhort the elders among you, as a fellow elder and a witness of the sufferings of Christ as well as a partaker in the glory that is to be revealed. [2]Tend the flock of God that is your charge,[k] not by constraint but willingly,[l] not for shameful gain but eagerly, [3]not as domineering over those in your charge but being examples to the flock. [4]And when the chief Shepherd is manifested you will obtain the unfading crown of glory. [5]Likewise you that are younger be subject to the elders. Clothe yourselves, all of you, with humility toward one another, for "God opposes the proud, but gives grace to the humble."

k Other ancient authorities add *exercising the oversight* l Other ancient authorities add *as God would have you*

Overview: As an elder with pastoral responsibility for the church, Peter shares his commission with others in the local congregations to which he is writing. The Fathers saw this as a chain of delegation, beginning with Christ's gift to Peter and extending through him to all the leaders of the church. Elders possess God's authority to govern their churches, and the younger members must learn to obey them. But the elders must also exercise their responsibilities humbly and in a way that sets a good example for others. The pastor must give a good account to the prince of pastors (Augustine, Hilary of Arles). It is by constructive criticism that the flock of the Lord is to be set straight (Hilary of Arles) by those who have been witnesses to Christ's suffering (Bede). Let the demonic wolf look at the seal of Jesus Christ the chief shepherd (Augustine), and he will flee (Symeon). The elder will be opposed if he is proud but given grace if he is humble (Augustine, Bede).

5:1 One Elder to Another

I Exhort the Elders. Hilary of Arles: It is by exhortation and constructive criticism that the flock of the Lord is to be set straight. Introductory Commentary on 1 Peter.[1]

As a Witness. Bede: Here Peter reminds us both that he was present when Christ suffered and saw what happened, and also that he was there on the mountain of transfiguration, together with James and John. On 1 Peter.[2]

As a Fellow Elder. Oecumenius: As he is proposing to talk about modesty, the apostle refers to himself here as a fellow elder, by which he means that he is one among many other elders. In saying this he is either referring to his age or to the office of bishop, for bishops and elders were one and the same.[3] When he wants to reveal his dignity and point out that it is from modesty that he refers to himself as a fellow elder, he mentions that he was a witness of Christ's suffering. The point of this is to say that if he, who has so great an honor, does not mind referring to himself as a fellow elder among them, they too must not exalt themselves in the presence of those who serve in various offices. Commentary on 1 Peter.[4]

As a Partaker. Symeon the New Theologian: How will you be a partaker of Christ's glory if you refuse to be a partaker of his shameful death? It is in vain that you have left the world behind if you are unwilling to take up your cross, as he commanded you to. Discourses 27.11.[5]

5:2 Tend the Flock of God

Your Charge. Jerome: In the Greek the meaning is still plainer, for the word used is *episkopeuontes*, that is to say, "overseeing," and this is the origin of the word *bishop*. Letters 146.[6]

God's Power Can Turn Something into Its Opposite. Chrysostom: Christ said: "He who would be first among you, let him serve, for he who humbles himself will be exalted above all."[7] What do you mean? If I humble myself, will I then be exalted? Yes, says Jesus. For such is my power that I can turn something into its exact opposite. I am skilled and capable, do not doubt it. The

---

[1]PL Supp. 3:104. [2]PL 93:64. [3]Acts 20:17, 28. [4]PG 119:572. [5]CWS 293. [6]LCC 5:387. [7]Mt 20:27.

nature of things obeys my will, not the other way round. CATENA.[8]

GIVING ACCOUNT. AUGUSTINE: We are your guardians, and you are the flock of God. Reflect and see that our perils are greater than yours, and pray for us. This befits both us and you, that we may be able to give a good account of you to the prince of pastors and our universal head. LETTERS 231.[9]

FEED MY SHEEP. HILARY OF ARLES: Here Peter is telling the leaders of the church exactly what the Lord told him: "Feed my sheep."[10] INTRODUCTORY COMMENTARY ON 1 PETER.[11]

TEND THE FLOCK OF GOD. BEDE: Just as the Lord gave the entire church to Peter as his flock, so Peter subdelegates his responsibility to the pastors of the church and commands them to fulfill their task conscientiously. He himself looks after his flock even though he has nothing to live on. That is why he preaches the gospel, so that he might earn a living by it. But he preaches not for earthly rewards but rather for heavenly ones, and he does so eagerly, following the commandments of the Lord. ON 1 PETER.[12]

5:3 Be Good Examples

BEING EXAMPLES TO THE FLOCK. PASCHASIUS OF DUMIUM: Practice what you preach, so that you may offer your people not only advice but a model as well, that they may imitate your example. QUESTIONS AND ANSWERS OF THE GREEK FATHERS 43.1.[13]

NOT AS DOMINEERING. HILARY OF ARLES: Even though you may have authority over the church in what you say or in the office which you occupy, you should never have a superior attitude toward others. INTRODUCTORY COMMENTARY ON 1 PETER.[14]

IN HUMBLE MANNER. BEDE: Peter demonstrates in his own conduct the kind of humility which he wants his flock to show toward him and toward each other. This is in line with what Jesus said: "He who is greatest among you shall be called your servant; whoever exalts himself will be humbled, and whoever humbles himself will be exalted."[15] ON 1 PETER.[16]

5:4 The Glory of the Good Shepherd

WHEN THE CHIEF SHEPHERD IS MANIFESTED. AUGUSTINE: While thinking of himself as a martyr to be, Cyprian did not allow himself to forget that he was still a bishop and was more anxious about the account he was to give to the chief shepherd concerning the sheep committed to him than he was about the answer he would give to the unbelieving proconsul, concerning his own faith. SERMONS 309.4.[17]

LET THE WOLF LOOK AT THE SEAL. SYMEON THE NEW THEOLOGIAN: Can death have any power over the souls which have been sealed by the grace of the Holy Spirit and the blood of Christ? Dare the spiritual wolf look straight at the seal of Christ the good shepherd, which he places on his own sheep? By no means, faithful brothers of godly mind! DISCOURSES 2.5.[18]

---

[8]CEC 80. [9]FC 32:164. [10]Jn 21:17. [11]PL Supp. 3:104. [12]PL 93:65. [13]FC 62:165. [14]PL Supp. 3:104. [15]Mt 23:11-12. [16]PL 93:65. [17]WSA 3/9:64. [18]CWS 50.

5:5 Be Submissive to Your Elders

GOD OPPOSES THE PROUD. AUGUSTINE: I fear that you may presume to rely on your own spirit to mortify the doings of the flesh and so perish for pride and find yourselves opposed for being proud, not granted grace for being humble. SERMONS 156.10.[19]

THE YOUNGER SHALL BE SUBJECT TO THE ELDERS. HILARY OF ARLES: By "young men" Peter means everyone who occupies a subordinate role in the church. But note that those who are superiors must also act humbly, for humility is what should be common to both. INTRODUCTORY COMMENTARY ON 1 PETER.[20]

GOD GIVES GRACE TO THE HUMBLE. BEDE: After teaching the elders how to preside over the church, Peter turns his attention to the younger members of the congregation. They are to obey their parents. There is no need for them to do a lot of talking; all that is required is that they show an example of submission. For after teaching the elders how they should treat those under them, it is enough for the younger people to respect the good examples of their elders and imitate them carefully. But in order to avoid a situation in which the higher-ups will think that humility is owed to them by their inferiors but not the other way round, Peter goes on to add that we must all show humility to one another. ON 1 PETER.[21]

---

[19]WSA 3/5:102. [20]PL Supp. 3:105. [21]PL 93:65.

5:6-11 SPIRITUAL WARFARE

[6]*Humble yourselves therefore under the mighty hand of God, that in due time he may exalt you.* [7]*Cast all your anxieties on him, for he cares about you.* [8]*Be sober, be watchful. Your adversary the devil prowls around like a roaring lion, seeking some one to devour.* [9]*Resist him, firm in your faith, knowing that the same experience of suffering is required of your brotherhood throughout the world.* [10]*And after you have suffered a little while, the God of all grace, who has called you to his eternal glory in Christ, will himself restore, establish, and strengthen[m] you.* [11]*To him be the dominion for ever and ever. Amen.*

m Other ancient authorities read *restore, establish, strengthen and settle*

OVERVIEW: Humility is the essential preparation for those who want to receive God's blessing (CAESARIUS OF ARLES, BEDE, OECUMENIUS). We must learn to depend on God for everything and to be aware that our real enemy is the devil, who is always trying to get the better of us (BASIL, PRUDENTIUS, OECUMENIUS). We must at all costs resist him, even if that means that we shall be forced to suffer (HILARY OF ARLES, BEDE, OECUMENIUS). If that happens, we can take comfort from the knowledge that the whole church is suffering with us and that Christ will soon return to put everything right (CLEMENT OF ALEXANDRIA, CHRYSOSTOM, ANDREAS).

5:6 Humble Yourselves

EXALTATION TO COME. CHRYSOSTOM: Peter says that this will happen in due time, because he is teaching them that they will have to wait until the next life for this exaltation. CATENA.[1]

NO ONE GUILTLESS. CAESARIUS OF ARLES: Since no one is without sin, no one should be without penance, for by this very fact a man becomes guilty if he presumes that he is innocent. A man may be guilty of lesser sin, but no one is without guilt. SERMONS 144.4.[2]

GRACE TO THE HUMBLE. BEDE: God gives grace to the humble in such a way that the more they have been humiliated for his sake while here on earth, the more he will exalt them on the day of reckoning. The word *humiliation* can be understood in many different ways. It may be self-induced, as when someone who is starting out on the way of virtue humbles himself in repentance for the sins which he has committed. It may be what one sees in those who are closer to perfection when they voluntarily agree not to pursue their rights but to live in peace with their neighbors. And of course, it may be what we

see when a person is caught up in the whirlwinds of persecution and his spirit is unbowed thanks to the power of patience. ON 1 PETER.[3]

TRUE EXALTATION. OECUMENIUS: Peter puts exaltation off until the world to come, because the only true exaltation is the one which is immutable and eternal. Exaltation in this world is neither secure nor firm but leads rather to eternal humiliation, for it is easier to be humiliated than it is to be exalted. COMMENTARY ON 1 PETER.[4]

5:7 Cast Your Cares on God

ANDREAS: Peter tells us that we have a guide and leader and that if we act according to his instructions, we shall keep ourselves pure and spotless. CATENA.[5]

5:8 The Prowling Devil

THE STORY OF JOB. BASIL THE GREAT: That the devil wanders over all the earth under heaven and ranges about like a mad dog, seeking whom he may devour, we learn from the story of Job. ON RENUNCIATION OF THE WORLD 2.[6]

THE LION OF JUDAH. AUGUSTINE: Who could avoid encountering the teeth of this lion, if the lion from the tribe of Judah had not conquered? SERMONS 263.[7]

RAGING MADLY. PRUDENTIUS:
Who goes roaring around, raging madly

---

[1]CEC 81. [2]FC 47:303. [3]PL 93:66. [4]PG 119:573. [5]CEC 81. [6]FC 9:18. [7]WSA 3/7:220.

As he seeks to entrap and devour us,
When, O infinite God, we praise thee only!
HYMNS 4.79-81.[8]

THE WEIGHT OF PUNISHMENT. OECUME-
NIUS: Justin Martyr explains this by saying
that before the coming of Christ the devil did
not know what the weight of his punishment
would be, but that when the Lord came and
proclaimed that eternal fire was prepared for
him and his angels[9] he reacted by becoming
even more determined to ensnare believers, in
order to have as much company as possible in
his rebellion. COMMENTARY ON 1 PETER.[10]

5:9 Resist the Devil

A WORLD OF DIFFERENCE. HILARY OF
ARLES: There is a world of difference between
God and the devil. If you resist God, he will
destroy you, but if you resist the devil, you
will destroy him. INTRODUCTORY COMMEN-
TARY ON 1 PETER.[11]

STRONG FAITH, GREAT CONFIDENCE.
BEDE: The stronger you are in your faith, the
greater will be your confidence that you can
overcome the wiles of the devil. You will also
be aided in this endeavor by the knowledge
that what you are going through is something
common to the fellowship of all Christians
throughout the world. Ever since the beginning of time it has been the lot of the righteous to suffer, and what a shame it would be
if you were to be the only ones unable to
endure this. ON 1 PETER.[12]

SUFFERING FOR CHRIST. OECUMENIUS: It
seems likely that those to whom Peter was writing were undergoing many kinds of suffering
for the sake of Christ, and so he brings them
consolation, telling them that they are suffering
along with everyone else who professes the
name of Christ and that they will all be glorified
together. COMMENTARY ON 1 PETER.[13]

5:10 God Will Strengthen You

GIVER OF ALL GOOD. CLEMENT OF ALEXAN-
DRIA: He is called the God of all grace because
he is good and the giver of all good things.
ADUMBRATIONS.[14]

MERCY AND ETERNAL GLORY. ANDREAS: See
how the beginning and the end of the epistle
are the same. At the beginning Peter said that
the Father has mercy on us through the Son
and here he once again says that the Father
has called us into his eternal glory through
Jesus Christ. CATENA.[15]

5:11 Give God the Glory

ANDREAS: It is ultimately the role of the
Father and of the Son to proclaim the mystery
of faith, because the glory and power belong
to them, although they condescend to make
use of us and of our preaching. CATENA.[16]

---

[8]FC 43:28. [9]Mt 25:41. [10]PG 119:573. [11]PL Supp. 3:105. [12]PL
93:66-67. [13]PG 119:573-76. [14]FGNK 3:82. [15]CEC 82. [16]CEC
82.

5:12-14 FAREWELL GREETINGS

[12]*By Silvanus, a faithful brother as I regard him, I have written briefly to you, exhorting and declaring that this is the true grace of God; stand fast in it.* [13]*She who is at Babylon, who is likewise chosen, sends you greetings; and so does my son Mark.* [14]*Greet one another with the kiss of love.*

Peace to all of you that are in Christ.

OVERVIEW: The letter's ending reinforces the message that we must make the grace of Christ a reality in our lives. Silvanus is identified as Silas, the well-known companion of Paul (BEDE, OECUMENIUS). Mark is the Evangelist, and this text was regarded by the Fathers as proof that the second Gospel was commissioned by Peter. Babylon is regarded as a code name for Rome, since both cities were pagan capitals of great international empires that were hostile to God's people (EUSEBIUS OF CAESAREA, ANDREAS, BEDE, ISHO'DAD). Peter seals his letter with a prayer (CHRYSOSTOM) and a holy kiss of peace (BEDE, OECUMENIUS, THEOPHYLACT).

5:12 Silvanus

BEDE: What Peter writes here may refer to what has gone before, because in having written to these people only briefly he was exhorting them rather than ordering them to keep the faith. But it may also refer to what follows, not only because he is writing to bear witness to the truth of the grace which he is preaching to them, namely, that there is no other way in which we can be saved, but also to exhort them to make the grace which they have received in Christ a reality in their lives. For the grace of Christ is only real to those who receive it with a pure heart. ON 1 PETER.[1]

OECUMENIUS: This Sylvanus was a faithful man and a mighty warrior for the preaching of the gospel. Paul mentions him as one of his coworkers, along with Timothy.[2] COMMENTARY ON 1 PETER.[3]

5:13 Babylon and Mark

EUSEBIUS OF CAESAREA: Peter mentions Mark in his first epistle, which they say he composed in Rome itself, and they say that he indicates this by referring to the city metaphorically as Babylon. HISTORY OF THE CHURCH 2.15.[4]

ANDREAS: Peter calls Rome Babylon in a metaphorical sense. The woman who is chosen along with us is the church of Christ established in that city. He also mentions Mark the Evangelist, whom he calls his son in Christ and to whom he entrusted the task of writing the Gospel. CATENA.[5]

BEDE: Peter refers to Rome as Babylon, prob-

---

[1]PL 93:67. [2]1 Thess 1:1; 2 Thess 1:1. [3]PG 119:576. [4]FC 19:110. [5]CEC 82-83.

ably because of the enormous amount of idolatry which existed in both cities. In the midst of such confusion the church shone out in spite of its poor and primitive condition, following the example set by the people of Israel when they were in captivity in Babylon and found it so hard to sing the Lord's song in a strange land.[6] Peter therefore encourages his hearers by telling them that the church is in Babylon, that is, in a sea of troubles. He also uses this image to remind them that the church cannot escape being mixed up with the evils of this world. On 1 Peter.[7]

Isho'dad of Merv: Peter calls Rome Babylon [Babel] because of the many languages spoken there. Commentaries.[8]

5:14 The Kiss of Love

Peace a Seal. Chrysostom: See how when he has finished what he has to say, Peter seals it all with a prayer. Peace is the seal of everything he has written. Catena.[9]

The Holy Kiss. Bede: The holy kiss is the exact opposite of the kiss with which Judas betrayed the Savior. That is the sort of kiss used by those who speak peace to their neighbors, but their hearts are full of wickedness.[10] The holy kiss, in sharp contrast to this, is one which is given not in word only but in deed and in truth as well. On 1 Peter.[11]

Consecrated to God. Oecumenius: Paul says that there is a special kiss which is set apart and consecrated to God[12] which is similar to the kiss of love, a virtue which Paul also extols. Commentary on 1 Peter.[13]

The Peace of Christ. Theophylact: This is no ordinary peace, for it is the same peace that Christ left his disciples when he went to be crucified. "My peace I leave with you, not as the world gives,"[14] for you are not meant to pursue peace by natural affection for one another but by being joined in a holy fellowship, thereby avoiding the blows of enemies. Commentary on 1 Peter.[15]

---

[6]Ps 137:1. [7]PL 93:67. [8]CIM 39. [9]CEC 83. [10]Ps 28:3. [11]PL 93:68. [12]1 Thess 5:26. [13]PG 119:576. [14]Jn 14:27. [15]PG 125:1252.

THE SECOND EPISTLE
OF PETER

1:1-2 PETER INTRODUCES HIMSELF

¹*Simeon*ˣ *Peter, a servant and apostle of Jesus Christ,*
To those who have obtained a faith of equal standing with ours in the righteousness of our
*God and Savior Jesus Christ:*ᵃ
²*May grace and peace be multiplied to you in the knowledge of God and of Jesus our*
Lord.

x Other authorities read *Simon*   **a** Or *of our God and the Savior Jesus Christ*

OVERVIEW: The Fathers all recognized that there are great differences between the first and second letters attributed to Peter, but they explained these variations in different ways. Some of them rejected the authenticity of the second letter and refused to accept it as part of the canon, but the majority were unwilling to go that far. They recognized that although there were differences between the two letters, they were not as great as the differences between the letters, on the one hand, and other writings attributed to Peter that were known to be spurious, on the other. Perhaps the strongest argument in favor of this letter's authenticity was its remarkably personal style. In his opening salutation Peter reverts to his original name, Simon, in order to show those who preferred to forget his Jewish origins that he had not rejected them (HILARY OF ARLES). Whether Gentiles or Jews, all who are baptized share a faith of equal standing (ANDREAS, OECUMENIUS). Peter prays for the peace of the church, which comes from knowing God (OECUMENIUS). Peace is the mother of all good things and the foundation of our joy (CHRYSOSTOM).

1:1 A Servant and an Apostle of Jesus Christ

SIMON PETER. HILARY OF ARLES: In his second letter Peter describes himself both as Simon and as a servant, in order to show that he was humble and obedient. In his first letter he confined himself to the name *Peter*, which had been given to him by the Lord himself and signified that he was the chief of the apostles, but here he reverts to his original name *Simon* in order to show those who preferred to forget his Jewish origins that he had not rejected them. INTRODUCTORY COMMENTARY ON 2 PETER.[1]

THE GRACE OF BAPTISM THE SAME. ANDREAS: Notice how right from the start Peter encourages the souls of the believers by raising them up to the same spiritual level as that of the apostles. For the grace of baptism is the same in every believer. CATENA.[2]

A FAITH OF EQUAL STANDING. OECUMENIUS: Simon may also be written as "Simeon," of which it is the diminutive form. Compare Metras and Metrodorus, Menas and Menodorus, Theudas and Theodosius. Right from the beginning, Peter lifts up the hearts and minds of believers, encouraging us also to share in the apostles' zeal for preaching. For it would be unjust to suggest that those who have received this gift a little later in time are somehow inferior to them, when they have officially been declared to be their equals in honor. COMMENTARY ON 2 PETER.[3]

1:2 Grace and Peace in the Knowledge of God

PRAY FOR THE PEACE OF THE CHURCH. CHRYSOSTOM: There is nothing to equal this, which is why we pray and seek after the angel of peace. Everywhere we pray for peace in the churches—in the prayers, in the supplications and in the sermons. And the Guardian of the church gives it to us not once or twice but many times over: "Peace be unto you."[4] Why? Because peace is the mother of all good things and the foundation of our joy. For this reason Christ taught his disciples that when they entered people's houses they were to say: "Peace be unto you."[5] Without peace everything else is useless. CATENA.[6]

IN THE KNOWLEDGE OF GOD. OECUMENIUS: This is not the peace of the world but the peace which comes from knowing God. For the only true peace is the one which delivers us from our transgression and enmity against God. It is the same peace which Christ gave his disciples when he was about to go to the Father, and when he rose again from the dead.[7] COMMENTARY ON 2 PETER.[8]

---

[1]PL Supp. 3:106 [2]CEC 85. [3]PG 119:580. [4]Lk 24:36. [5]Lk 10:5. [6]CEC 85. [7]Jn 14:27; 20:19, 21, 26. [8]PG 119:580.

1:3-11 GOD'S GREAT GIFTS

[3]His divine power has granted to us all things that pertain to life and godliness, through the knowledge of him who called us to[b] his own glory and excellence, [4]by which he has granted to us his precious and very great promises, that through these you may escape from the corruption that is in the world because of passion, and become partakers of the divine nature. [5]For this very reason make every effort to supplement your faith with virtue, and virtue with knowledge, [6]and knowledge with self-control, and self-control with steadfast-

ness, and steadfastness with godliness, [7]and godliness with brotherly affection, and brotherly affection with love. [8]For if these things are yours and abound, they keep you from being ineffective or unfruitful in the knowledge of our Lord Jesus Christ. [9]For whoever lacks these things is blind and shortsighted and has forgotten that he was cleansed from his old sins. [10]Therefore, brethren, be the more zealous to confirm your call and election, for if you do this you will never fall; [11]so there will be richly provided for you an entrance into the eternal kingdom of our Lord and Savior Jesus Christ.

b Or by

OVERVIEW: It is by knowing our Lord and Savior by faith that we come to understand the mysteries of his divinity (HILARY OF ARLES, BEDE). God gives us everything we need in order to live godly lives (THEOPHYLACT). To have fellowship with the Holy Spirit is to participate in the divine nature (ORIGEN). In becoming Christ-bearers (CYRIL OF JERUSALEM) and in sharing by faith in God's nature, we measure divine truths in accordance with the magnificence of God's own testimony of himself (HILARY OF POITIERS). He granted us a relationship with himself, and we have a rational nature that makes us able to seek what is divine, which is not far from each one of us, in whom we live and move (AMBROSE). So realize your dignity (LEO). Step out of your former nature (HILARY OF ARLES). When God blesses us, he changes our very being, so that whatever we were by nature is transformed by the gift of his Holy Spirit (BEDE, ANDREAS). God's power has rescued us from a life of sin and self-destruction and made it possible for us to share in his divine nature. This means that we must go on from our initial profession of faith and by grace ascend the ladder of spiritual perfection, which will bring us to a deep, personal experience of the love of God at work in our lives.

Insofar as we have the spiritual gifts, we shall be effective workers for Christ, but if we lack them we are in much the same impotent state as we were before our conversion. The purpose of the Christian life is to confirm the calling that we have received from God and to prepare our entrance into his eternal kingdom. Those who bring faith into fulfillment with virtue (BEDE) must make sure that in running away from the appetitive desires they do not give birth to vices that are much worse (GREGORY THE GREAT, BEDE, THEOPHYLACT). Godliness takes on concrete meaning through brotherly love (BEDE). The more we are like God, the more we are compelled by that likeness to love (THEOPHYLACT). The Christian life begins with simple faith (CYRIL OF ALEXANDRIA). The discernible qualities of the Christian life—virtue, knowledge, temperance, patience, godliness, brotherly love and charity—are found in abundance among the lives of the faithful (CHRYSOSTOM, OECUMENIUS). Where these virtues are present, we can see God; where they are absent, we are blind (HILARY OF ARLES, BEDE). Therefore it is necessary that once one has been cleansed and has partaken of holiness, he or she hold on to it through thick and thin (CHRYSOSTOM, OECUMENIUS). Those who consistently practice virtue to avoid falling (OECUMENIUS) make their calling and election certain

(Hilary of Arles, Bede, Andreas). The same person who was once led into the narrow way of the judge's courtroom is now welcomed into the eternal kingdom (Hilary of Arles, Oecumenius).

1:3 All Things That Pertain to Life and Godliness

Granted All Things. Hilary of Arles: Here Peter is talking about the Scriptures, the miracles which Christ did in the flesh, the work of baptism and the doctrine which was preached, all of which bring us into the enjoyment of eternal life. Introductory Commentary on 2 Peter.[1]

Through the Knowledge of Him Who Called Us. Bede: This verse follows on what has gone before, because it is by the knowledge of our Lord and Savior that we come to understand all the mysteries of his divinity, by which we have been saved. For he did not send an angel or an archangel to save us, nor did he find anything in us which might allow us to contribute to our own salvation, but when he saw that we were weak and had nothing to boast of, he came in his own glory and power and redeemed us. On 2 Peter.[2]

Pertaining to Life and Godliness. Theophylact: Grace and peace are the means by which God gives us everything we need in order to live godly lives. Commentary on 2 Peter.[3]

1:4 Participating in the Divine Nature

Fellowship with the Holy Spirit. Origen: What is the fellowship of the Holy Spirit?[4] Peter describes this by calling it "shar-ing in the divine nature." Sermons on Leviticus 4.4.2.[5]

Escape from Corruption. Novatian: The word of Christ bestows immortality.[6] But immortality is the companion of divinity, because divinity is immortal, and so immortality is the result of partaking in the divine nature. On the Trinity 15.7.[7]

We Become Christ-Bearers. Cyril of Jerusalem: When Christ's body and blood become the tissue of our members, we become Christ-bearers and "partakers of the divine nature," as the blessed Peter said. Mystagogical Lectures 4.3.[8]

The Measure of God's Nature. Hilary of Poitiers: Since the Christian is conscious of having been made a partaker of the divine nature, as blessed Peter says in his second epistle, he must measure the nature of God not by the laws of our own nature, but evaluate the divine truths in accordance with the magnificence of God's testimony concerning himself. On the Trinity 1.18.[9]

A Relationship with Himself. Ambrose of Milan: The fact is that God made humankind a partaker of the divine nature, as we read in the second epistle of Peter. He granted us a relationship with himself, and we have a rational nature which makes us able to seek what is divine, which is not far from each one of us, in whom we live and are and move. Letters to Priests 49.[10]

---

[1]PL Supp. 3:107. [2]PL 93:69. [3]PG 125:1257. [4]Cf. 2 Cor 13:14. [5]FC 83:73. [6]Jn 8:51. [7]FC 67:59. [8]FC 64:182. [9]FC 25:18. [10]FC 26:259.

Realize Your Dignity! Leo the Great: Realize your dignity, O Christian! Once you have been made a partaker of the divine nature, do not return to your former baseness by a life unworthy of that dignity. Remember whose head it is and whose body of which you constitute a member! Sermons 21.3.[11]

Step Out of Your Former Nature. Hilary of Arles: Just as God stepped out of his nature to become a partaker of our humanity, so we are called to step out of our nature to become partakers of his divinity. Introductory Commentary on 2 Peter.[12]

Become Partakers. Bede: The greater your knowledge of God becomes, the more you will realize the magnitude of his promises. When God blesses us, he changes our very being so that whatever we were by nature is transformed by the gift of his Holy Spirit, so that we may truly become partakers of his nature. On 2 Peter.[13]

Grace Enables Participation. Andreas: God has blessed us abundantly—that is the meaning of this passage. We have received thousands of good things as a result of Christ's coming, and through them we can become partakers of the divine nature and be turned toward life and godliness. Therefore we must behave in such a way as to add virtue to faith, and in virtue walk along the way which leads to godliness until we come to the perfection of all good things, which is love. Catena.[14]

1:5 Beginning the Christian Life

Supplement Faith with Virtue. Bede: When Peter talks about virtue here, he does not mean the power to perform miracles but the strength to lead a good life, which means putting our faith into practice. If we fail to do this, our faith is dead and we become aiders and abettors of those who want to destroy any good works we may have done. On 2 Peter.[15]

Steps to Complete Responsiveness to Grace. Theophylact: Peter lays out here the order which we are to follow to come into full maturity. First of all comes faith, which is the foundation and source of all good works. Next comes virtue, by which he means good works, for without them faith is dead, as Saint James said.[16] Next comes knowledge. What is that? It is an understanding of the secret things hidden in God which are not revealed to everyone, but only to those who continue faithfully in the works already mentioned. Commentary on 2 Peter.[17]

1:6 Going On in the Christian Life

Supplement Knowledge with Self-Control. Gregory the Great: Those who fast must be very careful to make sure that in running away from the desires of the stomach they do not give birth to vices which are much worse, almost as if their virtue were producing them. For it is easy to mortify the flesh but at the same time to become very impatient in spirit, and this impatience upsets the minds of many who abstain from the desires of the world. Commentary on 2 Peter.[18]

Self-Control with Steadfastness. Bede: As people learn to do good, so they will

---

[11]FC 93:79. [12]PL Supp. 3:107. [13]PL 93:69. [14]CEC 85-86. [15]PL 93:70. [16]Jas 2:26. [17]PG 125:1257. [18]PL 79:1387.

soon stop doing evil. If anyone does not do so his knowledge of heavenly things disappears as if in a vacuum. Self-control requires steadfastness, because whoever has learned to stay away from the pleasures of this world needs the willpower to go on doing so. The person who reaches that point of self-discipline may truly be called godly. On 2 Peter.[19]

Temperance and Patience. Theophylact: Next in the list comes abstinence, or temperance. This is necessary in order to ensure that those who get this far are not carried away by the magnitude of the gift they have received and become haughty as a result. Patience follows next, because it takes time to acquire temperance, and without patience a person is liable to give up and fall into something even worse than what he has been delivered from. Patience increases our trust in God, which is why godliness comes next. Commentary on 2 Peter.[20]

1:7 Mature Love

Supplement Godliness with Brotherly Affection. Bede: The only context in which godliness has any meaning is that of brotherly love. You cannot win people to Christ merely by arguing them into the kingdom. It is necessary to practice godliness by prayer and good works. Charity here means the love of God, because we cannot love God without loving our neighbor, nor can we love our neighbor without loving God. The love of God is greater than the love of our neighbor, which is why we have to practice it with all our heart, mind and strength. On 2 Peter.[21]

Supplement Brotherly Affection with Love. Theophylact: The more we are like

God, the more we are compelled by that likeness to love others, which is why brotherly love is next in the list. Finally, there is charity, the perfection of all virtues, as Paul also confirms.[22] Commentary on 2 Peter.[23]

1:8 Gracious Virtues Keep You from Being Ineffective

The Overflowing Life of the Virtues. Chrysostom: These things, as well as those already mentioned, namely, virtue, knowledge, continence, patience, godliness, brotherly love and charity, must not only be present in us, they must be present to overflowing. For if their presence is a good thing, how much more their abundance! What advantage do these things have, and what will it mean to have assurance on the day of our Lord Jesus Christ? Peter is speaking here of his second coming, when Christ will come to judge the living and the dead. Before the great and terrible judgment seat of God, what a good and wonderful thing it will be to have assurance of being acquitted! Catena.[24]

The Christian Life Begins with Simple Faith. Cyril of Alexandria: Those who have chosen to live the glorious and beloved way of life devised by Christ must first be adorned with simple and unblemished faith, and then add virtue to their faith. When this has been done, they must strive to enrich their knowledge of the mystery of Christ and ascend to the most complete understanding of him. Letters 1.3.[25]

---

[19]PL 93:70. [20]PG 125:1257. [21]PL 93:70-71. [22]Cf. 1 Cor 13. [23]PG 125:1257. [24]CEC 86. [25]FC 76:14.

QUALITIES OF THE CHRISTIAN LIFE. OECU-
MENIUS: What are the qualities which we possess? They are faith, virtue, knowledge, temperance, patience, godliness, brotherly love
and charity, all of which must not only be
present in us but present in abundance. COM-
MENTARY ON 2 PETER.[26]

1:9 Not Forgetting You Were Cleansed from Your Old Sins

ONE WHO HAS FORGOTTEN. CHRYSOSTOM:
When we hear these things, we must fortify
ourselves and obey what is said, and cleanse
ourselves from earthly things. If we do that,
we shall share in his blessings, and we shall
not need anything else. But if we do not obey,
we shall be destroyed. What difference does it
make whether we are destroyed through
wealth or through laziness? Or if not through
laziness, through cowardice? For when a
farmer destroys his crop, it hardly matters
how he does it. On the other hand, he will
raise us up to do all the good works which he
has predicted we shall do. Therefore it is necessary that once someone has been cleansed
and has partaken of holiness, that he hold on
to it through thick and thin, for without it he
will not see the Lord. CATENA.[27]

BEHOLDING GOD THROUGH THE VIRTUES.
HILARY OF ARLES: If these virtues are present, we can see God, but if they are absent, we
are blind. INTRODUCTORY COMMENTARY ON
2 PETER.[28]

THE EYE AND THE HAND. BEDE: The eye
stands for knowledge and the hand for action.
A blind man who tries to act is someone who
does not know what he should be doing. Lacking the light of truth, he puts his hand to

something which he cannot understand and
goes down a road which he cannot see, with
the result that he ends up in a complete wreck.
The person who lacks the things which Peter
mentions here is just like that. ON 2 PETER.[29]

PURSUE HOLINESS. OECUMENIUS: This person ought to realize that he has been cleansed
by holy baptism and that now he is expected
to pursue holiness, without which no one will
see the Lord.[30] COMMENTARY ON 2 PETER.[31]

1:10 Confirming Your Call and Election

GROW IN FAITH. HILARY OF ARLES: Peter is
telling us that we should not be content with
our baptism but should go on and grow in our
faith. INTRODUCTORY COMMENTARY ON
2 PETER.[32]

STAND FAST. ANDREAS: Lest you be judged
unmindful of God's gift, you must stand fast,
having a sure calling. CATENA.[33]

MAKE YOUR CALLING CERTAIN. BEDE: Jesus
said: "Many are called but few are chosen."[34]
The calling of all those who come to faith is
certain, but those who consistently add good
works to the sacraments of faith which they
have received are the ones who make their
calling and election certain in the eyes of those
who observe them. The opposite is also true,
for those who go back to their crimes after
they have been called and who die in their sins
make it clear to everyone that they are
damned. ON 2 PETER.[35]

---

[26]PG 119:584. [27]CEC 86. [28]PL Supp. 3:108. [29]PL 93:71. [30]Heb
12:14. [31]PG 119:584. [32]PL Supp. 3:108. [33]CEC 87. [34]Mt 22:14.
[35]PL 93:71.

PRACTICE VIRTUE TO AVOID FALLING.
OECUMENIUS: What are we supposed to do in order to avoid falling? The answer is clear from what is written above—we are to practice virtue, knowledge, temperance and so on. COMMENTARY ON 2 PETER.[36]

1:11 An Entrance into Our Lord's Eternal Kingdom

THE NARROW WAY. HILARY OF ARLES: Here Peter reminds us that the entrance into heaven is the narrow way of following God's commandments. INTRODUCTORY COMMENTARY ON 2 PETER.[37]

THE STEPS OF VIRTUE. BEDE: This verse reminds us of Ezekiel [40:31], which says: "Its stairway had eight steps." The reason for this connection is that here Peter lists the eight steps of virtue by which those of us who are fleeing the corruption of worldly lust must ascend if we are to enter the heavenly kingdom. ON 2 PETER.[38]

FROM CONDEMNATION TO WELCOME.
OECUMENIUS: Notice that the person who was once led by his terrible deeds straight into the judge's courtroom is now welcomed because of his good deeds into the eternal kingdom of the Lord. COMMENTARY ON 2 PETER.[39]

---

[36]PG 119:585. [37]PL Supp. 3:108. [38]PL 93:71. [39]PG 119:584.

1:12-21 PETER'S CALLING

[12]*Therefore I intend always to remind you of these things, though you know them and are established in the truth that you have. [13]I think it right, as long as I am in this body,[c] to arouse you by way of reminder, [14]since I know that the putting off of my body[c] will be soon, as our Lord Jesus Christ showed me. [15]And I will see to it that after my departure you may be able at any time to recall these things.*

[16]*For we did not follow cleverly devised myths when we made known to you the power and coming of our Lord Jesus Christ, but we were eyewitnesses of his majesty. [17]For when he received honor and glory from God the Father and the voice was borne to him by the Majestic Glory, "This is my beloved Son,[d] with whom I am well pleased," [18]we heard this voice borne from heaven, for we were with him on the holy mountain. [19]And we have the prophetic word made more sure. You will do well to pay attention to this as to a lamp shining in a dark place, until the day dawns and the morning star rises in your hearts. [20]First of all you must understand this, that no prophecy of scripture is a matter of one's own interpreta-*

tion, ²¹because no prophecy ever came by the impulse of man, but men moved by the Holy Spirit spoke from God.^e

c Greek *tent*   d Or *my Son, my (or the) Beloved*   e Other authorities read *moved by the Holy Spirit holy men of God spoke*

OVERVIEW: Peter saw his primary responsibility as his duty to warn the churches of the dangers that they would face after his departure from this life. He knew that the time left to him on earth was short, and therefore he felt that it was right to use it in this way, even at the risk of appearing to be repetitive. Peter grounds his faith and his calling in his experience of the transfiguration, which he portrays as the meeting point of heaven and earth, when the meaning of prophecy was fully revealed. He wrote to people who knew the truth already and exhorted them to live up to it (BEDE). The truth is the gospel (HILARY OF ARLES), of which the faithful need a constant reminder (OECUMENIUS). On three occasions the same Peter who wrote both the first and the second letter (GREGORY THE GREAT) would have known that the voice from heaven had confirmed Jesus' sonship—at his baptism, transfiguration and on the cross (THEOPHYLACT, ANDREAS). In this confirmation the Son in the flesh revealed his glory in the Father (HILARY OF ARLES).

Peter concludes by reminding his hearers that the Bible cannot be interpreted by individuals relying on their own fantasies, because it is not the word of humans. Scripture was given to holy people who were moved by the Spirit of God and therefore is approached as a divine revelation that brings the light of Christ's transfiguration to us. The lamp of the prophetic word is necessary until the daylight comes (BEDE), until the light of truth shines upon all (AUGUSTINE, CYRIL OF ALEXANDRIA). Even Balaam was empowered to attest this

word (ANDREAS). No prophecy comes from humans but by the Holy Spirit (SYMEON). The urge to interpret is constrained (BEDE), and no attempt is made by the prophet to slant the meaning of the divine word (OECUMENIUS). Faith will recognize its meaning (ANDREAS). Prophecy is focused on the delivery of God's message, whether it is fully understood or not (BEDE, OECUMENIUS).

1:12 A Constant Reminder

THOUGH YOU KNOW THEM. HILARY OF ARLES: The people to whom Peter is writing already know what he has to say because they have read his first letter. The truth which he has to share with them is the New Testament, for as Paul said: "The old has passed away, and all things are made new in Christ."[1] INTRODUCTORY COMMENTARY ON 2 PETER.[2]

WHAT TO FEAR, WHAT TO SEEK. ANDREAS: Peter repeats what he has already said about virtue and the commandments consequent on it, through which we shall enter the kingdom of heaven with great assurance. Notice how, when speaking of the kingdom of heaven, Peter first goes over the things we should be afraid of and then over the good things, ending up with the judgment seat. CATENA.[3]

I INTEND ALWAYS TO REMIND YOU. BEDE: Why did Peter want to go on reminding peo-

---

[1]2 Cor 5:17. [2]PL Supp. 3:108-9. [3]CEC 87.

ple of these things, when he says that they know them and are already established in the presence of the truth? Perhaps the reason was that he wanted them to turn their head knowledge into practical action and maintain the truth which they knew they had, in order to escape being led away from the purity and simplicity of their faith by teachers of heresy, of whom he has a good deal to say in the course of his letter. Compare what Peter says to John's statement in his first epistle: "I write to you, not because you do not know the truth, but because you know it."[4] The apostles wrote to people who knew the truth already and exhorted them to live up to what they knew. As John added a little further on: "Let what you heard from the beginning abide in you."[5] ON 2 PETER.[6]

BEING CONSTANTLY REMINDED. OECUMENIUS: Peter tells his hearers that they already know what he is talking about, so that they will not think that it is because they are lazy that they have to be constantly reminded of these things and get upset as a result. COMMENTARY ON 2 PETER.[7]

1:13 Arousing by Way of Reminder

CALLING GENTILES TO FAITH. HILARY OF ARLES: Peter thought that it was right to call Gentiles to faith, but the Jews did not. This is why he expresses himself like this here. INTRODUCTORY COMMENTARY ON 2 PETER.[8]

THIS BODILY TENT. BEDE: Peter calls his body a tent because we normally use tents when we are on a journey or in combat. Those who believe are rightly said to be dwelling in tents as long as they are in the body and distant from the Lord, because it is in this bodily tent

that they are journeying through life and fighting the enemies of the truth. ON 2 PETER.[9]

IN THIS BODY. OECUMENIUS: Some think that Peter was saying this in order to ensure that even after his death his hearers would still remember what he was saying to them and go on practicing it. Others say that Peter's intention was simply to leave a record behind him, so that it could be referred to after his death, for he was not condemning their inadequacy in matters of faith but merely confirming them in the way which they were already pursuing. COMMENTARY ON 2 PETER.[10]

1:14 Peter Is Near the End of His Life on Earth

AS THE LORD SHOWED HIM. HILARY OF ARLES: The Lord Jesus showed Peter that his end was near either by a revelation through the Holy Spirit or by his response to Peter when he said: "Get behind me, Satan"[11] or perhaps by dreams and visions in the night. INTRODUCTORY COMMENTARY ON 2 PETER.[12]

PUTTING OFF THIS EARTHLY TENT. BEDE: Peter has a wonderful way of describing his death, not as the end but as a putting off of this earthly tent, because going to be with the Lord is like coming home from a journey and exchanging the tent for the comforts of home. The only home a believer has is in heaven. ON 2 PETER.[13]

---

[4]1 Jn 2:21. [5]1 Jn 2:24. [6]PL 93:72. [7]PG 119:585. [8]PL Supp. 3:109. [9]PL 93:72. [10]PG 119:585. [11]Mk 8:33. [12]PL Supp. 3:109. [13]PL 93:72.

His End Coming Quickly. Theophylact: Peter explains that he keeps repeating the same things to his hearers because he knows that his end is coming quickly and that he will soon be delivered from his body. Commentary on 2 Peter.[14]

1:15 After His Departure

Able to Recall These Things. Hilary of Arles: By writing to them often Peter hoped to leave something behind him after his death. Introductory Commentary on 2 Peter.[15]

The Hope of Christ's Return. Andreas: The reason why we have to remember these things is that we hope that Christ will soon come back and transform our present life. Catena.[16]

1:16 An Eyewitness of Christ's Majesty

Seeing the Truth. Cyril of Alexandria: The constructions of the heretics are myths and human fantasies, which Paul wants us to avoid, as he writes: "Warn a heretic once or twice, and after that have nothing to do with him."[17] Peter is here already starting to do battle against the heretics. To the extent that they do not possess the truth, heretics are obliged to concoct a lie by using flowery words. But we are not like that, he says, because we saw the truth with our eyes when we were with him on the mountain. Therefore we have the prophets who have proclaimed the same truth to us, and even better, as we came to behold ourselves, the Word came to us. What the prophets foretold, Christ fulfilled when he appeared. We were witnesses of this, and we heard the

Father's testimony also. Catena.[18]

The Power and Coming of Our Lord. Bede: In this verse Peter strikes out at pagans and at heretics as well. Pagans were not afraid to divinize anything they happened to like, whereas heretics, although they received the mysteries of the true God, paid no attention to the teaching of Scripture but by wrongly interpreting it did their best to twist it to suit their own falsehoods. On 2 Peter.[19]

No Cleverly Devised Myths. Oecumenius: Peter says that he has not invented stories like those of the Valentinians[20] but merely handed on the teaching of Christ in simple and humble words, as Paul also told the Corinthians he was doing.[21] Commentary on 2 Peter.[22]

1:17 The Voice Borne by the Majestic Glory

The Son Received Glory. Hilary of Arles: The one who received glory and honor was not inferior to the one who bestowed these things, because it was in his human flesh that the Son received them, not in his eternal divinity. Introductory Commentary on 2 Peter.[23]

The Second Epistle Written by Peter. Gregory the Great: There used to be many people who thought that this letter was not written by Peter. But it is enough to read this verse, and you will soon see that it was Peter

---

[14]PG 125:1261. [15]PL Supp. 3:109. [16]CEC 88. [17]Tit 3:10. [18]CEC 88. [19]PL 93:72. [20]Gnostics. [21]1 Cor 2:1. [22]PG 119:588. [23]PL Supp. 3:109.

who stood with Jesus on the mount of transfiguration. It is therefore the same Peter who heard the voice testifying to the Lord who wrote this letter. SERMONS ON EZEKIEL 2.6.11.[24]

THREE TIMES CONFIRMED. THEOPHYLACT: Peter knew that Jesus received the Father's confirmation from heaven on three different occasions, in his baptism, at his passion and on the mountain. However, this was the one which he himself witnessed. COMMENTARY ON 2 PETER.[25]

1:18 With Christ on the Mountain

ON THE HOLY MOUNTAIN. HILARY OF ARLES: Tradition says that the transfiguration took place on Mt. Tabor. INTRODUCTORY COMMENTARY ON 2 PETER.[26]

THE TRANSFIGURATION. ANDREAS: This was the third time this happened. The first was at Jesus' baptism, and the second was when the Son cried to the Father: "Father, glorify me with the glory which I had with you before the foundation of the world."[27] The transfiguration was therefore the third time. CATENA.[28]

WE HEARD THIS VOICE. BEDE: Those who doubt that Peter wrote this letter need to pay careful attention to this verse and to the one which follows, because the eyewitness testimony makes it clear that no one else could have written it. ON 2 PETER.[29]

1:19 The Prophetic Word Made More Sure

MY BELOVED SON. AUGUSTINE: The blessed apostle Peter, with two other disciples of Christ the Lord, James and John, was up the

mountain with the Lord himself and heard a voice coming down from heaven saying "This is my beloved Son in whom I am well pleased. Listen to him"[30] To remind us of this and draw it to our attention, the same apostle referred to it in his letter and went on to add that all this confirmed the message of the prophets. The voice echoed from heaven, and the prophetic word was thus made more certain. SERMONS 43.5.[31]

THE LIGHT OF TRUTH. CYRIL OF ALEXANDRIA: For those who have died in the faith, the light-bearing lamp has risen and the day dawns, according to the Scriptures, and to them the light of truth is sent, which is the face of the Holy Spirit. LETTERS 55.6.[32]

THE LIGHT OF SCRIPTURE. HILARY OF ARLES: The light which shone on them was the light of Scripture. INTRODUCTORY COMMENTARY ON 2 PETER.[33]

EVEN BALAAM SPOKE. ANDREAS: The prophets of the New and of the Old Testament spoke in the same Spirit. If it is true that some things were saved to be revealed in the New Testament, it is also true that the prophets of the Old Testament were commanded to be silent about them. For prophets are not what they are merely because of what they say. Their whole being proclaims their calling. Willingly and knowingly they ministered to the word which came to them, for no such word ever came by the will of man. Rather it was conveyed by God to men, and the men

---

[24]PL 79:1099. [25]PG 125:1264. [26]PL Supp. 3:109. [27]Jn 17:5. [28]CEC 88. [29]PL 93:72. [30]Mt 17:5. [31]WSA 3/2:240. [32]FC 77:17. [33]PL Supp. 3:109.

who received it ministered to it. Thus even Balaam was commanded to speak what had been given to him, even though he had the power not to say anything if he did not want to. Jonah is another example of the same phenomenon. CATENA.[34]

UNTIL THE MORNING STAR RISES IN YOUR HEARTS. BEDE: In the night of this world, so full of dark temptations, where there is hardly anyone who does not sin, what would become of us if we did not have the lamp of the prophetic word? Will this word always be necessary? No. It is only necessary until the daylight comes. Right now we have a night lamp because we are children of God, and in comparison with the ungodly, we are the very daylight itself. But if we compare what we are now with what we shall be in the future, then we are still in darkness and need this lamp. ON 2 PETER.[35]

1:20 Not One's Own Interpretation

NO PROPHECY BY THE IMPULSE OF HUMANS. HILARY OF ARLES: You must take care when interpreting the Scriptures not to be too greatly fixated upon the places, times and people who wrote them down, as if they were merely human compositions. Rather you ought to rely on the clarity and sufficiency of the Spirit. INTRODUCTORY COMMENTARY ON 2 PETER.[36]

NO SCRIPTURE IS A MATTER OF ONE'S OWN INTERPRETATION. BEDE: The prophets heard God speaking to them in the secret recesses of their own hearts. They simply conveyed that message by their preaching and writing to God's people. They were not like pagan oracles, which distorted the divine mes-

sage in their own interest, for they did not write their own words but the words of God. For this reason the reader cannot interpret them by himself, because he is liable to depart from the true meaning, but rather he must wait to hear how the One who wrote the words wants them to be understood. ON 2 PETER.[37]

NO ATTEMPT TO TILT ITS MEANING. OECUMENIUS: This means that the prophets received their prophecies from God and transmitted what he wanted to say, not what they wanted. They were fully aware that the message had been given to them, and they made no attempt to put their own interpretation on it. If they could not bring themselves to accept what the Spirit had said to them, then they kept their mouths shut, as Jonah did, for example, when he refused to preach to Nineveh,[38] and Balaam also did when he was commanded to say what had been communicated to him.[39] COMMENTARY ON 2 PETER.[40]

1:21 Men Moved by the Holy Spirit

FAITH WILL RECOGNIZE THE MEANING. ANDREAS: Peter does not say that the prophets interpreted their own sayings. They were not speaking to themselves but serving the Holy Spirit. What is the interpretation of their words if not the works which Christ revealed when he came? So if anyone wants to understand the words of the prophets properly, let him obtain faith in Jesus Christ, through which he will recognize the divine message. John bore witness before we did. Christ came

---

[34]CEC 89. [35]PL 93:73. [36]PL Supp. 3:110. [37]PL 93:73. [38]Jon 1:3. [39]Num 22:13. [40]PG 119:589.

from heaven, enlightening everyone. Likewise he showed that the power to prophesy is of the Holy Spirit, as did the apostle Paul when he said: "To another [the gift of] prophecy, etc."[41] So the one who prophesies is undoubtedly speaking with a tongue inspired by the Holy Spirit. CATENA.[42]

THE URGE TO INTERPRET CONSTRAINED. BEDE: Theoretically it is always possible to predict the future, but the Holy Spirit filled the hearts of the prophets when he wanted to. It was not in their power to teach whatever they wished; rather they taught by the illumination of the Holy Spirit and said only what he told them to. We say this just in case there might be someone who feels the urge to interpret Scripture for himself. Some interpret Peter's words to mean that the Spirit inspired the prophets in much the same way as the flutist blows into his flute, so that the latter were no more than mechanical instruments in God's hands, saying what the Spirit told them to say without necessarily understanding or believing it themselves. This is ridiculous. For how could the prophets have given such good counsel to people if they did not know what they were saying? Are prophets not also called seers? How could a prophet possibly have communicated what he saw in secret heavenly visions to a wider audience if he did not fully grasp what it was that he had seen? ON 2 PETER.[43]

INSPIRED BY THE HOLY SPIRIT. OECUMENIUS: The prophets knew that they were inspired by the Holy Spirit, even if they did not always understand the full significance of what they were told. But they were eager to see the outcome of what they did understand, as the Lord himself pointed out. COMMENTARY ON 2 PETER.[44]

THE SPIRIT SPEAKS IN US. SYMEON THE NEW THEOLOGIAN: You see that it is not I who speak great and extraordinary things to your charity, but the Spirit of God who speaks in us. To this Peter, the chief apostle, bears witness when he says that no prophecy ever came by man, but holy men of God spoke, moved by the Holy Spirit. For though we are insignificant and unworthy, far from all holiness and from the holy men of God, yet we cannot deny the power that has been given to us by God. DISCOURSES 34.5.[45]

---

[41]1 Cor 12:10. [42]CEC 89. [43]PL 93:73-74. [44]PG 119:592. [45]CWS 351.

2:1-22 EVIL PEOPLE AND THEIR FATE

[1]But false prophets also arose among the people, just as there will be false teachers among you, who will secretly bring in destructive heresies, even denying the Master who bought them, bringing upon themselves swift destruction. [2]And many will follow their licentiousness, and because of them the way of truth will be reviled. [3]And in their greed they will

exploit you with false words; from of old their condemnation has not been idle, and their destruction has not been asleep.

⁴For if God did not spare the angels when they sinned, but cast them into hell^f and committed them to pits of nether gloom to be kept until the judgment; ⁵if he did not spare the ancient world, but preserved Noah, a herald of righteousness, with seven other persons, when he brought a flood upon the world of the ungodly; ⁶if by turning the cities of Sodom and Gomorrah to ashes he condemned them to extinction and made them an example to those who were to be ungodly; ⁷and if he rescued righteous Lot, greatly distressed by the licentiousness of the wicked ⁸(for by what that righteous man saw and heard as he lived among them, he was vexed in his righteous soul day after day with their lawless deeds), ⁹then the Lord knows how to rescue the godly from trial, and to keep the unrighteous under punishment until the day of judgment, ¹⁰and especially those who indulge in the lust of defiling passion and despise authority.

Bold and wilful, they are not afraid to revile the glorious ones, ¹¹whereas angels, though greater in might and power, do not pronounce a reviling judgment upon them before the Lord. ¹²But these, like irrational animals, creatures of instinct, born to be caught and killed, reviling in matters of which they are ignorant, will be destroyed in the same destruction with them, ¹³suffering wrong for their wrongdoing. They count it pleasure to revel in the daytime. They are blots and blemishes, reveling in their dissipation,^g carousing with you. ¹⁴They have eyes full of adultery, insatiable for sin. They entice unsteady souls. They have hearts trained in greed. Accursed children! ¹⁵Forsaking the right way they have gone astray; they have followed the way of Balaam, the son of Beor, who loved gain from wrongdoing, ¹⁶but was rebuked for his own transgression; a dumb ass spoke with human voice and restrained the prophet's madness.

¹⁷These are waterless springs and mists driven by a storm; for them the nether gloom of darkness has been reserved. ¹⁸For, uttering loud boasts of folly, they entice with licentious passions of the flesh men who have barely escaped from those who live in error. ¹⁹They promise them freedom, but they themselves are slaves of corruption; for whatever overcomes a man, to that he is enslaved. ²⁰For if, after they have escaped the defilements of the world through the knowledge of our Lord and Savior Jesus Christ, they are again entangled in them and overpowered, the last state has become worse for them than the first. ²¹For it would have been better for them never to have known the way of righteousness than after knowing it to turn back from the holy commandment delivered to them. ²²It has happened to them according to the true proverb, The dog turns back to his own vomit, and the sow is washed only to wallow in the mire.

f Greek *Tartarus* g Other ancient authorities read *love feasts*

Overview: This chapter and the next are reminiscent of Jude and deal with the same problem of false prophets, who were teaching heresy and trying to lead church members astray. Peter condemns them not only for their false doctrine but also for their immoral life, a combination that is almost always found whenever heretics are mentioned in the New Testament. Many are led astray by those who reject the rule given them at their baptism (Hilary of Arles). The way of truth is reviled (Bede), especially by the Nicolaitans, who are both wrong in doctrine and wicked in behavior (Andreas, Oecumenius), whose condemnation has long been hanging over them (Hilary of Arles, Bede). God foreknew their wickedness (Andreas). God did not spare the angels when they sinned by their pride, envy and lust (Hilary of Arles) but cast them into the abyss (Pachomius). They will be kept in custody until final judgment (Augustine). If God did not spare the angels, who had once stood in honor before him because of the immortality of their nature, how much less will he spare mere human beings, whom he has created out of perishable matter (Oecumenius)? Remember that the wicked angels were not created that way by God but became evil by their own sins (Bede).

Using examples of how God punished wickedness in the Old Testament, Peter compares the heretics of his day to the people of Sodom and Gomorrah and says that they have nothing to offer but immorality and lies. The ungodliness of people from Adam to Noah was what caused the flood (Hilary of Arles). Noah's godliness spared him (Oecumenius). The physical shape of the planet was forever changed by the flood (Bede). Sodom and Gomorrah were condemned to extinction (Salvian) as an example to the ungodly

(Hesychius), because they committed the sin more disgusting than any other (Chrysostom). They were first reduced to ashes and then covered by the Dead Sea (Bede). By rescuing Lot the Lord made clear that he does not abandon those who hope in him (Hesychius), even if Lot was unable to put things right in Sodom (Bede). Though vexed in his soul, Lot refused to collude with Sodom's lawlessness (Severus, Oecumenius). Even then, human history did not fall away from God so as to be absolutely nothing, but insofar as humans turned toward themselves they became less than they were when they were loving the supreme Being (Augustine).

Heresy was a universal problem in the early church, and the Fathers felt a special kinship with Peter when he denounced false teachers. They frequently tried to identify who Peter was attacking, but they usually ended up focusing on heretics who arose after Peter's day. In practice this made little difference, since the spiritual state of these men was the same, as was the condemnation they received from the leaders of the church. Although the Fathers variously interpreted those who blatantly indulge lust as the Simonians (Andreas), the Nicolaitans or the Gnostics (Oecumenius), they agreed that they would be punished for their offenses (Bede). These moral permissivists were compared with animals (Cyril of Alexandria) who live only by their bodily instincts (Bede), not with their mind or rational soul. This is why they are so easily ensnared by their own corruption, and in turn they corrupt everything they touch (Oecumenius), reveling in their dissipations (Bede). They have received knowledge of salvation but not lived by it (Augustine). They are like Balaam, who was hindered by God. In his greed Balaam attempted to live off his prophetic spirit. Only after Balaam was corrected by the terrors he met along the way was he able to get the word of blessing right (ANDREAS). If an ass can become a teacher of a prophet, and if the grace of God could work through the ass, it is clear that God is prepared to work in us (CHRYSOSTOM). This shows that a dumb animal can be wiser than a madman (HILARY OF ARLES).

These false teachers are like empty wells that animals fall into and die (HILARY OF ARLES). They are not clear-sighted but obscure (ANDREAS). Although they promise freedom, they themselves are slaves of corruption (AUGUSTINE, HILARY OF ARLES, ANDREAS). So take care not to become entangled once more in the very errors you have already renounced (LEO, CAESARIUS OF ARLES). That puts you in a worse state than before (HILARY OF ARLES, OECUMENIUS). The evil awaiting those who turn away from their faith is so great that it would have been better if they had never accepted it (HILARY OF ARLES, THEOPHYLACT). The fact that they once knew Christ but have now turned away from him makes their condemnation worse, though the Fathers were keen to point out that such people had never really been part of God's flock.

2:1 False Teachers and Their Heresies

KNOWN FROM THEIR CONDUCT. DIDACHE: Not everyone who speaks in the spirit is a prophet, but only if he follows behaviorally in the path of the Lord. Accordingly, from their conduct the false prophet and the true prophet will be known. DIDACHE 11.8.[1]

DENYING THE MASTER WHO BOUGHT THEM. HILARY OF ARLES: It is typical of false teachers that they cannot accept the full equality of the persons of the Trinity. INTRODUCTORY COMMENTARY ON 2 PETER.[2]

FALSE PROPHETS AROSE. ANDREAS: Peter says this so that people will not just listen to everyone who claims to be a prophet, without discerning whether they really are or not. He tells them to be careful not to listen to false prophets instead of the true ones. CATENA.[3]

2:2 Many Will Be Led Astray

THEY REJECTED THE BAPTISMAL RULE. HILARY OF ARLES: They revile the way of truth because they have turned orthodox doctrine into heresy, or because they have rejected the rule given to them at their baptism, or because they have abandoned the way of truth. INTRODUCTORY COMMENTARY ON 2 PETER.[4]

THE NICOLAITANS. ANDREAS: The heresy of the Nicolaitans[5] had already appeared at that time. Peter says that it was evil in two ways. The Nicolaitans were wrong in their doctrine, and they were also wicked in their behavior. It reminds us of what was said about the Jews: "Because of you my name is blasphemed among the Gentiles."[6] CATENA.[7]

THE WAY OF TRUTH WILL BE REVILED. BEDE: The way of truth will be blasphemed by the heretics not only in those people whom they manage to win over to their errors but also in those who reject Christianity by the wicked things which they see these heretics

---

[1]FC 1:181. [2]PL Supp. 3:110. [3]CEC 90. [4]PL Supp. 3:110. [5]Cf. Rev 2:6, 14-15, an early dualistic heresy reported in Revelation, claiming prophetic inspiration yet tending toward antinomian license. [6]Is 52:5; Ezek 36:22; quoted in Rom 4:24. [7]CEC 90.

doing, and because they know no better, imagine that all Christians must be caught up in the same depravity. On 2 Peter.[8]

Avoid Heresy. Oecumenius: Peter says this in order to persuade his hearers to avoid the heresy of the Nicolaitans, who were guilty of a double sin. For not only was their doctrine most ungodly, their lives also were totally obscene. Commentary on 2 Peter.[9]

2:3 False Teaching Brings Its Own Condemnation

Their Destruction. Hilary of Arles: The destruction of these people comes from none other than the God of Israel, who is never idle or asleep. Introductory Commentary on 2 Peter.[10]

God Foreknew Their Wickedness. Andreas: They were doing this for money. Excess is sometimes geared toward wickedness and sometimes toward profit, but here the addition of the word *exploit* makes the meaning clear. They will indeed have their reward, which is death. The phrase "of old" indicates God's foreknowledge of what they would do. For just as God foresaw who would be good and prepared good things for them in heaven, so he also foresaw who would be evil and prepared the other place for them. Catena.[11]

Their Condemnation. Bede: If the condemnation of these people started such a long time ago, we can be sure that it will not end any time soon. On 2 Peter.[12]

2:4 God Did Not Spare the Angels When They Sinned

God Cast Them into Hell. Pachomius: The angels were in heaven and were thrown into the abyss. But on the other hand, Elijah[13] and Enoch[14] were raised into the kingdom of heaven. Communion 3.25.[15]

To Be Kept Until the Judgment. Augustine: It is a fixed and unchanging religious truth that the devil and his angels are never to return to the life and holiness of the saints. From Scripture we know that God's sentence implies that he dragged them down by infernal ropes to Tartarus and delivered them to be tortured and kept in custody for judgment. They will be received into everlasting fire and there tortured forever and ever. The City of God 21.23.[16]

Committed to Pits of Nether Gloom. Cyril of Alexandria: When Christ came from heaven, he bound the leaders of the demons in hell. This is clear from the way in which he commanded the spirits, lest they be thrown into the abyss. For he bound some and ordered others to depart, as we can see from sayings like "Look, I have given you power over unclean spirits";[17] "Cast out demons,"[18] and so on. Afterwards, in order to perfect the punishment of those whom he had earlier bound, he cast them into eternal fire.[19] Catena.[20]

God Did Not Spare the Angels. Hilary of Arles: The angels sinned in three ways, by their pride, by their envy and by their lust. In this verse it is made clear that sin can occur even if it is not done overtly in the flesh. It is

---

[8]PL 93:74. [9]PG 119:592. [10]PL Supp. 3:110. [11]CEC 90-91. [12]PL 93:74. [13]2 Kings 2:11. [14]Gen 5:24. [15]CS 47:24. [16]FC 24:386. [17]Mt 10:1. [18]Mk 3:15. [19]Rev 20:10. [20]CEC 91.

obvious that the essence of sin is consent to do evil. Introductory Commentary on 2 Peter.[21]

Evil Angels Were Created Good. Bede: It is to be remembered that the wicked angels were not created that way by God. They became evil by their own sins. Therefore they too will have to undergo the last judgment, even though they have already been cast into the fiery prison of the lower depths. Hell is referred to in this way in order to emphasize that it is as far away from the heights of heaven as it can possibly be. On 2 Peter.[22]

Comparing the Rebellion of Angels and Humans. Oecumenius: If God did not spare the rebellious angels, who had stood in honor before him because of the immortality of their nature, how much less will he spare mere humans, whom he has created out of perishable matter! Commentary on 2 Peter.[23]

2:5 God Preserved Noah

A Flood on the Ungodly. Hilary of Arles: The ungodliness of those who lived in the time from Adam to Noah was what caused the flood. Introductory Commentary on 2 Peter.[24]

The Earth's Surface Changed. Bede: Here Peter means the world as it was before the flood, when people lived in it just as they do now. Basically it was the same planet that we live on, but there were some differences. For example, the earth changed its shape when the waters overflowed it during the flood, and there were fewer mountains and valleys than there are now. This would be easy

to deny if it were not for the fact that every year we see how the shape of the land is altered by periodic flooding. It is bad enough now, so think how much worse it must have been after the great flood. On 2 Peter.[25]

God Preserved Noah. Oecumenius: Noah was spared because he was not led astray by the ungodliness of those who lived before the flood. God honored him because he did what was right. Commentary on 2 Peter.[26]

2:6 Sodom and Gomorrah

One Sin More Disgusting Than Any Other. Chrysostom: Do you want to know why these things happened? There was one sin which was more wicked and disgusting than any other which those people were committing. It was because of that that God gave them this judgment. Catena.[27]

Condemned to Extinction. Salvian the Presbyter: God wished to proclaim the judgment that is to come when he sent fiery death from heaven upon a wicked people, setting an example for those who desire to lead wicked lives. On the Governance of God 1.8.[28]

An Example to the Ungodly. Hesychius: Here is proof that all the ungodly will be punished. For Peter goes over the examples of Sodom and Gomorrah so that anyone who sees this will not behave wickedly, knowing that if he does so he will suffer the same kind of punishment as they did. Catena.[29]

---

[21]PL Supp. 3:110. [22]PL 93:75. [23]PG 119:593-96. [24]PL Supp. 3:111. [25]PL 93:75-76. [26]PG 119:597. [27]CEC 92. [28]FC 3:44. [29]CEC 91-92.

Reduced to Ashes, Then Covered by the Dead Sea. Bede: The destruction of Sodom and Gomorrah has two sides to it. First of all, the cities were reduced to ashes, and then the Dead Sea was made to go over the ruins, in which nothing can live. If God did that to visible cities, so that they would stand forever afterwards as an example of how he punishes the ungodly, it is clear that fire awaits the wicked in the spiritual realm and that the smoke of their torment will ascend forever. On 2 Peter.[30]

2:7 Righteous Lot

God Rescued Lot. Clement of Rome: By rescuing Lot the Lord made clear that he does not abandon those who hope in him but that he hands those who turn away over to punishment and torture. Letter to the Corinthians 11.1.[31]

It Is Possible to Avoid Doing Evil. Hesychius: Peter adds the story of Lot to his other examples in order to teach us that it is possible to avoid doing evil and thus to escape from the punishment which they will receive. Catena.[32]

Lot Unable to Put Right the Sodomites. Bede: The evil words and deeds of the Sodomites were a daily agony for this righteous man, who saw what they were doing but was unable to put it right, though in spite of everything, he was able to keep himself pure. On 2 Peter.[33]

2:8 Lot's Distress

Vexed in His Soul. Severus of Antioch: We need to be clearly convinced that our dis-

tress at such evil deeds and our compassion for those who suffer earns the greatest reward with God and guarantees acceptance with him. All the more so, because in the face of what often appears to be an overwhelming, threatening wrath, the mental equilibrium of those who are overcome with grief is lost. This is why Peter wrote about Lot in this way. Catena.[34]

Lot Refused to Collude. Oecumenius: Like us, Lot saw and heard many unrighteous things which might have tempted him into doing evil, but when he gave hospitality to the angels and the men of Sodom wanted to take them away and abuse them, Lot refused to give in, in spite of what he would suffer at their hands because of that refusal. Commentary on 2 Peter.[35]

2:9 The Lord Will Rescue the Godly

The Unrighteous under Punishment. Bede: Peter says that the punishment of the wicked is kept in reserve until the day of judgment, not because they are not already receiving punishment for their sins, even before that day, but because then their punishment will be much greater. The reason for this is that at the last judgment they will be punished in their resurrected bodies, whereas now they are suffering only in their souls. On 2 Peter.[36]

Until the Day of Judgment. Oecumenius: Peter knows that God will deliver the godly from their trials and afflictions and that

---

[30]PL 93:76. [31]FC 1:18. [32]CEC 92. [33]PL 93:76-77. [34]CEC 93. [35]PG 119:597. [36]PL 93:77.

the ungodly are being preserved only to face their punishment on the day of judgment. Notice how all along he has been using the examples of wicked people in order to reinforce the message that the deliverance of the righteous is foreordained and thereby to comfort those who emulate the righteous by showing that they are much better off than the ungodly. COMMENTARY ON 2 PETER.[37]

2:10 Despising Authority

BECOMING LESS THAN ONE WAS. AUGUSTINE: Man did not fall away from the supreme Being as to be absolutely nothing, but insofar as he turned himself toward himself he became less than he was when he was adhering to him who is the supreme Being. To be no longer in God but in oneself is not to be nothing, but rather to be heading in that direction. For this reason, Holy Scripture gives another name to the proud, calling them "rash" and "self-willed." THE CITY OF GOD 14.13.[38]

BAD DOCTRINE, BAD BEHAVIOR. ANDREAS: This refers to the Simonians,[39] who combined wicked behavior with false doctrine. CATENA.[40]

GRAVE OFFENSES. BEDE: Peter says that fornicators will suffer even more serious punishments than ordinary sinners, because of the gravity of their offense. ON 2 PETER.[41]

REJECTING THE TEACHINGS OF CREATION AND PROVIDENCE. OECUMENIUS: These are the Nicolaitans and Gnostics, whose wickedness has appeared under different names, a confusion which reflects their evil deeds. For by inventing their own fabulous stories about the origin of the world they rejected the biblical teaching about God's creation and providential ordering of all things. The end result was that they fell into all kinds of moral depravity. COMMENTARY ON 2 PETER.[42]

THEY SCOFF AT DIGNITARIES. OECUMENIUS: What Peter is saying here is that the evil spirits are quite prepared to curse the angels as much as they can, but these curses are not returned in kind. Rather, the angels reserve any judgment against them to the Lord, even though they are more powerful than the demons. COMMENTARY ON 2 PETER.[43]

2:11 Angels Greater in Power

THE ANGELS TEND TO HOLY PEOPLE. DIDYMUS THE BLIND: The angels who dwell in holiness are stronger than human beings, even if it is true that we are more blessed than they are. Angels look after holy people who are helped by them, since human beings cannot offer consolation to angels. COMMENTARY ON 2 PETER.[44]

2:12 Irrational Animals

DESTROYED IN THE SAME DESTRUCTION. CYRIL OF ALEXANDRIA: The inspired psalmist said this when he sang: "Man, when honored, had no understanding. He is like the beasts that perish."[45] Although human beings had laws, their morals were irrational, and they soon degenerated into animals whose only end was destruction. CATENA.[46]

THE CORRUPT APPETITES OF THE HERE-

---

[37]PG 119:593. [38]FC 14:381. [39]Followers of Simon Magus. [40]CEC 93. [41]PL 93:77. [42]PG 119:597-600. [43]PG 119:600. [44]PG 39:1772-73. [45]Ps 49:12. [46]CEC 93.

tics. Bede: Just as it is natural for dumb animals to be led into a trap in their search for food, so the heretics, like such animals, have spurned the pure and holy doctrine of the whole church in order to satisfy their corrupt appetites. Church history tells us that there were many such groups in apostolic times, like the Simonians, the Menandrians, the Basilidians, the Nicolaitans, the Ebionites, the Marcionites, the Cerdonians, and so on. On 2 Peter.[47]

Creatures of Instinct. Oecumenius: These men are compared to animals because they live only by their bodily instincts and not with their mind or rational soul. For this reason they are easily ensnared by corruption and are so far gone in depravity that they do not even know when they are being cursed. Commentary on 2 Peter.[48]

2:13 Blots and Blemishes

Suffering for Their Wrongdoing. Andreas: Peter means that after they went astray they were able to lead others astray after them, but that in the end they will have to pay the price of their wickedness. Catena.[49]

They Revel in Their Dissipations. Bede: Peter calls their punishment the just reward for their unrighteousness, since they not only live in wickedness themselves but they also blaspheme the lifestyle of those who try to live righteously. Bound up in their own wicked errors, they never stop trying to seduce others as well. On 2 Peter.[50]

They Corrupt All They Touch. Oecumenius: These people have nothing pure about them. Rather, like stains on clothing

they pervade everyday life and corrupt everything they touch. If they are taken to a social gathering and are able to turn it into an orgy, they are delighted because they have won others over to their lusts. Their social life is not rooted in love but in filth. Commentary on 2 Peter.[51]

2:14 Insatiable for Sin

They Entice Unsteady Souls. Hilary of Arles: These people even greeted one another with kisses which were full of lust. What was meant to be a sign of peace was transformed into adultery by those who had turned away from God. Introductory Commentary on 2 Peter.[52]

Eyes Full of Adultery. Andreas: Peter says that these people are not motivated by love. Their only interest is to find the right moment when they can seduce women. Catena.[53]

2:15 The Way of Balaam

Forsaking the Right Way. Hilary of Arles: The right way is the way of Christ, who said: "I am the way, the truth and the life."[54] Introductory Commentary on 2 Peter.[55]

The Way of Balaam. Andreas: As we know from the Old Testament,[56] Balaam was hindered by God for his greed in trying to obtain a living off his prophetic spirit. He

---

[47]PL 93:77-78. [48]PG 119:601. [49]CEC 95. [50]PL 93:78. [51]PG 119:604. [52]PL Supp. 3:112. [53]CEC 95. [54]Jn 14:6. [55]PL Supp. 3:112. [56]Num 23—24.

obstinately tried to run to Balak a second time, and only after he was corrected by the fear of God and the terrors which he met along the way was he able to get the word of blessing right, so that what he said was from God and not his own wicked preference. For even his tongue was not totally given over to the service of a lie. CATENA.[57]

WHO LOVED GAIN FROM WRONGDOING. BEDE: There is nothing quite like the love of money to tempt the licentious into corrupting the word of truth. ON 2 PETER.[58]

2:16 An Ass Spoke with Human Voice

THE PROPHET'S MADNESS RESTRAINED. CHRYSOSTOM: If the grace of God could work through the animal without affecting the animal—for the ass was not saved—but only as a means of helping the Israelites, it is perfectly clear that he is prepared to work in us, which is why this story is so poignant. CATENA.[59]

WITH HUMAN VOICE. HILARY OF ARLES: The ass spoke with a human voice so that Balaam would understand what God was saying to him. He had become a madman because of his disobedience to the commandments of God, and dumb animals are wiser than that, since they observe the law of nature. INTRODUCTORY COMMENTARY ON 2 PETER.[60]

THE ASS BECAME BALAAM'S TEACHER. ANDREAS: The common interpretation of this is that Balaam's ass condemned him because it obeyed the angel and submitted to him, whereas Balaam, although he heard God, did not go and warn the people, nor did he obey

God's will. Thus the ass became Balaam's teacher. CATENA.[61]

2:17 Darkness Has Been Reserved

LIKE WATERLESS SPRINGS. AUGUSTINE: Peter calls these people dry springs—springs, because they have received knowledge of the Lord Christ, but dry, because they do not live in accordance with that knowledge. ON FAITH AND WORKS 25 (46).[62]

LIKE EMPTY WELLS. HILARY OF ARLES: These people are empty wells of the kind that animals fall into and die in, because there is no water at the bottom. INTRODUCTORY COMMENTARY ON 2 PETER.[63]

LIKE MISTS DRIVEN BY A STORM. ANDREAS: They did not have the living word of the Spirit, the channel of delights which overflows to the glory of the nations. They were not clear-sighted like the saints. They were in some sense like clouds but more like "mists" covered in darkness and ignorance, for they were governed by an evil spirit. CATENA.[64]

2:18 The Boasters

PRIDE YIELDS STUPIDITY. HILARY OF ARLES: Pride is always vain because it makes people stupid, as they are without God insofar as they are proud. INTRODUCTORY COMMENTARY ON 2 PETER.[65]

---

[57]CEC 95. [58]PL 93:79. [59]CEC 96. [60]PL Supp. 3:112. [61]CEC 96. [62]FC 27:276. [63]PL Supp. 3:113. [64]CEC 96. [65]PL Supp. 3:113.

Enormity of Ungodliness. Andreas: They are not punished merely for their ungodliness but for the enormity of it as well. Catena.[66]

2:19 Slaves of Corruption

Whatever Overcomes One, Enslaves One. Augustine: When a man is said to be given up to his desires, he derives guilt from them, because, deserted by God, he yields and consents to them, is conquered, seized, attracted and possessed by them. Against Julian 5.3.12.[67]

A Slave to Vice. Hilary of Arles: A man is the slave of whatever vice controls him. Introductory Commentary on 2 Peter.[68]

They Promised Freedom. Andreas: These men promised people freedom from deception when in fact they were encouraging others to lapse back into it. Catena.[69]

Enslaved to Passion. Symeon the New Theologian: The one who is enslaved to any single passion is also dominated by it and is unable to obey the commandments of the Lord. Discourses 27.1.[70]

2:20 The Last State Is Worse Than the First

They Are Again Entangled. Leo the Great: We cannot fathom the depths of God's mercy toward us. Yet we must take care not to be ensnared again by the devil's traps and become entangled once more in the very errors which we have renounced. For the ancient enemy does not stop laying down traps everywhere and doing whatever it takes to corrupt the faith of believers. Sermons 27.3.[71]

Having Been Set Free. Caesarius of Arles: Since we have been set free from the power of the devil through the grace of Christ and without any preceding merits of our own, dearest brothers, let us try as hard as we can, with his help, always to engage in good works, fearing what the apostle Peter proclaims in these terrible words. Sermons 175.5.[72]

Dwelling in Dirt. Salvian the Presbyter: Look what the apostle Peter has to say about Christians who live in the mire and impurities of this world. On the Governance of God 4.19.[73]

They Sin Knowingly. Hilary of Arles: It is always worse to sin knowingly than to sin in ignorance. Introductory Commentary on 2 Peter.[74]

Worse State Than Before. Oecumenius: From this we learn two things. First, a person must serve the one who has overcome him, whoever that may be. Second, those who go back to their former ways after knowing the truth find themselves in an even worse state than the one from which they were originally rescued. Commentary on 2 Peter.[75]

2:21 Ignorance Is Better Than Rejection

Better Never to Have Known. Hilary of Arles: To know the way of righteousness is to know Christ and the holy gospel. Peter is

---

[66]CEC 96. [67]FC 35:253. [68]PL Supp. 3:113. [69]CEC 97. [70]CWS 284. [71]FC 93:112. [72]FC 47:436. [73]FC 3:124. [74]PL Supp. 3:113. [75]PG 119:605.

talking here about people who have been baptized after professing faith in Jesus but who have then turned away from him. INTRODUCTORY COMMENTARY ON 2 PETER.[76]

MAKING DECEPTION WORSE. ANDREAS: Peter shows by this that these men were not liberating those who followed them from their deception but merely making that deception worse. CATENA.[77]

LIKE A DOG RETURNING TO ITS OWN VOMIT. THEOPHYLACT: Peter is saying that the evil awaiting those who turn away from their faith is so great that it would have been better if they had never accepted it in the first place. At least that way their wickedness would seem natural, instead of being as bizarre as a dog returning to its own vomit. COMMENTARY ON 2 PETER.[78]

2:22 The Truth of a Proverb

REVERTING TO THE SAME SINS. CHRYSOS-

TOM: Repentance consists in no longer doing the same things, for he who reverts to the same sins is like a dog returning to his vomit. COMMENTARY ON JOHN 34.[79]

THE PROVERB. BEDE: This verse refers to what Solomon said in his Proverbs: "Like a dog that returns to his vomit is a fool that repeats his folly."[80] ON 2 PETER.[81]

THE SOW LOOKS WORSE IN MUD. OECUMENIUS: What is going on here is that we have people who take delight even in things which nature has rejected and who are prepared to indulge in the very things which they themselves have corrupted. People like that are even more abominable than they were before, just as a sow looks even worse after she has covered herself in mud. COMMENTARY ON 2 PETER.[82]

---

[76]PL Supp. 3:113. [77]CEC 97. [78]PG 125:1277. [79]FC 33:339. [80]Prov 26:11. [81]PL 93:79. [82]PG 119:605.

3:1-18 THE SECRET OF CHRISTIAN LIVING

[1]*This is now the second letter that I have written to you, beloved, and in both of them I have aroused your sincere mind by way of reminder;* [2]*that you should remember the predictions of the holy prophets and the commandment of the Lord and Savior through your apostles.* [3]*First of all you must understand this, that scoffers will come in the last days with scoffing, following their own passions* [4]*and saying, "Where is the promise of his coming? For ever since the fathers fell asleep, all things have continued as they were from the beginning of creation."* [5]*They deliberately ignore this fact, that by the word of God heavens existed long ago, and an earth formed out of water and by means of water,* [6]*through which the world*

that then existed was deluged with water and perished. [7]But by the same word the heavens and earth that now exist have been stored up for fire, being kept until the day of judgment and destruction of ungodly men.

[8]But do not ignore this one fact, beloved, that with the Lord one day is as a thousand years, and a thousand years as one day. [9]The Lord is not slow about his promise as some count slowness, but is forbearing toward you,[h] not wishing that any should perish, but that all should reach repentance. [10]But the day of the Lord will come like a thief, and then the heavens will pass away with a loud noise, and the elements will be dissolved with fire, and the earth and the works that are upon it will be burned up.

[11]Since all these things are thus to be dissolved, what sort of persons ought you to be in lives of holiness and godliness, [12]waiting for and hastening[i] the coming of the day of God, because of which the heavens will be kindled and dissolved, and the elements will melt with fire! [13]But according to his promise we wait for new heavens and a new earth in which righteousness dwells.

[14]Therefore, beloved, since you wait for these, be zealous to be found by him without spot or blemish, and at peace. [15]And count the forbearance of our Lord as salvation. So also our beloved brother Paul wrote to you according to the wisdom given him, [16]speaking of this as he does in all his letters. There are some things in them hard to understand, which the ignorant and unstable twist to their own destruction, as they do the other scriptures. [17]You therefore, beloved, knowing this beforehand, beware lest you be carried away with the error of lawless men and lose your own stability. [18]But grow in the grace and knowledge of our Lord and Savior Jesus Christ. To him be the glory both now and to the day of eternity. Amen.

h Other ancient authorities read *on your account*   i Or *earnestly desiring*

OVERVIEW: Peter marks the transition from his denunciation of the heretics to his counsels for Christian living by reminding his hearers that this is his second letter to them. The Fathers who accepted the authenticity of this letter used this assertion to justify their belief that 1 and 2 Peter were both the work of the apostle (HILARY OF ARLES, OECUMENIUS), even though he may have used a different secretary for drafting purposes. Others denied that this letter is a part of the canon (DIDYMUS).

Peter is again stirring up the sincere mind of a person who has heard and received the message of salvation (HILARY OF ARLES, OECUMENIUS). They are urged to make sure that, whether Christ comes sooner or later, he will find them ready (BEDE). The heavens are made of destructible matter and did not exist at all until God made them by his will and power (EUSEBIUS OF EMESA). The earth is made of water and would not exist without water (HILARY OF ARLES, BEDE). After the deluge of the lower part of the world (BEDE), the world was refounded through Noah and those who were with him in the ark, along with the animals and seeds required to make a new beginning (Oecumenius). What had been the world up to then perished in water, and what are now the heavens and the earth are based on the Word but are being kept for destruction by fire (Didymus, Bede), only to be finally renewed in the end (Oecumenius).

The bulk of the chapter is again reminiscent of Jude and begins with a reminder that Jesus and the apostles had both predicted that scoffers would come into the church, denying Christ's promise that he would soon return. Peter counters this attack by telling his people that God does not measure time in the same way that we do and that the day of judgment would come suddenly and without warning. To him this was all the more reason for being prepared for it at all times. At the judgment the present world will be destroyed, but there will be a new heaven and a new earth, something that is also foretold in the book of Revelation. God's relation with time is quite different from ours (Athanasius, Augustine, Hilary of Arles, Caesarius of Arles). What we regard as long or short is all the same to God (Bede). A thousand years is as a day. It may be a long time before God punishes sinners, but when he does so he uses his power in a single instant (Hilary of Arles). God would rather wait for repentance than to punish sins (Fastidius). God is taking time to gather the elect (Bede). Soon this will all be clear (Augustine). The heavens will be changed into something better, in the same way that our bodies are not destroyed in order to disappear altogether but in order to be renewed in an indestructible state (Eusebius of Emesa). Everything that has been made in the creation will be remade along with us

(Andreas). We watch in peace for Christ's coming (Bede). He wants to find you spotless in faith and chastity (Hilary of Arles).

Peter concludes by saying that Paul had also written about these matters, though there were some in the church who found him hard to understand and who distorted his teaching accordingly. The Fathers were particularly intrigued by the way in which Peter commended Paul, because they were aware that the two men had once disagreed about the place of the Jewish law in the Christian church. Generally speaking, they held up this passage as a wonderful example of humility and reconciliation, brought about by the power of God in their lives (Augustine). They recommended that all Christians should try to follow their example by growing in the faith, which would protect them from being swept away by false teachings. Peter, the friend of truth, was able to praise even the fact that he had been criticized by Paul and was happy to do so because he realized that he had been wrong (Gregory the Great). It is a characteristic of the elect that they admire the virtues of others more than their own and that those virtues encourage them to grow more deeply in their own faith (Bede). Those who try to corrupt the holy Scriptures and pervert the catholic faith do nothing other than condemn themselves (Bede). They make the most wicked confident of obtaining salvation (Augustine). Scripture itself is not corrupted by its corrupted interpreters (Symeon, John of Damascus). The heretics are bringing in many errors—denying that there will be a future judgment, giving themselves over to their lusts, deceiving the hearts of the innocent. So be on guard that you are not taken away from the firm foundation of your faith (Cyril of Alexandria, Bede).

3:1 Peter's Second Letter

BY WAY OF REMINDER. HILARY OF ARLES: Peter makes a point of mentioning that this is his second letter, so that the recipients will not doubt its authenticity. INTRODUCTORY COMMENTARY ON 2 PETER.[1]

AROUSING YOUR SINCERE MIND. OECUMENIUS: We learn from this verse that this is Peter's second letter. What he is saying is that in both of them he has tried to stir up the sincere mind which he knows is latent in his readers. COMMENTARY ON 2 PETER.[2]

3:2 Remember the Commandments

REMEMBER THE PREDICTIONS OF THE HOLY PROPHETS. OECUMENIUS: Here Peter tells us what the content of a sincere and pure mind is. It is the mind of a person who has heard and received the message of salvation which was preached by the prophets and the apostles. This is precisely what Paul meant when he said: "Built upon the foundation of the prophets and apostles."[3] COMMENTARY ON 2 PETER.[4]

3:3 Scoffers Will Come in the Last Days

IN THE LAST DAYS. HILARY OF ARLES: Here Peter prophesies what will happen in the future, for we must always remember that there are prophets in the New Testament too. INTRODUCTORY COMMENTARY ON 2 PETER.[5]

GNOSTIC SCOFFERS. THEOPHYLACT: These scoffers were the Gnostics and other similar heretics who appeared at that time. COMMENTARY ON 2 PETER.[6]

3:4 When Is Christ Coming Back?

THINGS HAVE CONTINUED. HILARY OF ARLES: People were talking this way as if the flood had never occurred and as if fire had never come down from heaven in the past. INTRODUCTORY COMMENTARY ON 2 PETER.[7]

WHERE IS THE PROMISE OF HIS COMING? BEDE: All those who love our Lord's return must have a balanced approach to the whole question. We must not think that it is so near that it will come before time, but neither must we think that it will not come until much later. Rather we must be careful to make sure that, whether Christ comes sooner or later, he will find us ready and waiting for him when he appears. ON 2 PETER.[8]

THE SCOFFER'S IMPATIENCE. OECUMENIUS: These scoffers will start with the failure of Christ to return immediately. From there they will go on to corrupt all the saving commandments of the Lord, in order to destroy our faith completely. COMMENTARY ON 2 PETER.[9]

3:5 The Earth Was Formed by God Out of Water

GOD LAID THE FOUNDATION OF THE EARTH. EUSEBIUS OF CAESAREA: "In the beginning you, O Lord, laid the foundation of the earth, and the heavens are the works of your hands," said the psalmist.[10] If you did not know from the beginning, O Lord, who laid the foundation of the earth, and if the heavens were not the

---

[1]PL Supp. 3:113. [2]PG 119:608. [3]Eph 2:20. [4]PG 119:608. [5]PL Supp. 3:114. [6]PG 125:1280. [7]PL Supp. 3:114. [8]PL 93:80. [9]PG 119:608. [10]Ps 102:25.

work of your hands, it would be impossible for them to be changed or to be transformed into anything else. If they had not been created, they would have to remain incomplete forever. But since you were their maker, you can do whatever you want to with them. They are made of destructible matter and did not exist at all until you made them by your will and power. There is only one that is eternal and can never be removed and that is you, the only maker of everything that exists. CATENA.[11]

EARTH FORMED OUT OF WATER. HILARY OF ARLES: The whole creation is basically formed out of water, even if it is solidified in the form of earth or elevated in the way that heaven is. INTRODUCTORY COMMENTARY ON 2 PETER.[12]

WITHOUT WATER, NO WORLD. BEDE: The world is penetrated by water just as the body is by blood and would not be able to exist without it since then it would dry up completely. ON 2 PETER.[13]

3:6 The Earth Was Destroyed by Water

THE LOWER PART OF THE WORLD DELUGED. BEDE: Peter means that the lower part of the universe was destroyed, because the higher part was not touched by the flood at all. More specifically, the earth perished, not just because it was submerged and therefore lost the ability to bear fruit, but also because when the floodwaters receded its shape was different, as we have already mentioned. The heavens also perished, or at least the earth's atmosphere did, because the Bible also talks about the birds being affected by the flood. ON 2 PETER.[14]

THE NEW BEGINNING WITH NOAH. OECU-MENIUS: When God originally made it, creation was good, and this was not by accident but by his design. However, human beings sinned and subjected the creation to their own vanity, which is why it is no longer firm but subject to many ups and downs. Then during the flood, because there were a few people who had maintained the pure worship of God, the world was refounded through Noah and those who were with him in the ark, along with the animals and seeds required to make a new beginning. COMMENTARY ON 2 PETER.[15]

3:7 Heaven and Earth Will Be Destroyed by Fire

DESTRUCTION BY WATER AND FIRE. DIDYMUS THE BLIND: Many people think that these words refer to changes and revolutions which will take place here on earth. They say that heaven and earth were once both water and that they were formed out of water by the Word of God. What had been the world up to then perished in water, and what are now the heavens and the earth are based on the Word but are being kept for destruction by fire. By these words the preacher is saying that what we now see before us will be consumed by fire. For he says that the day of judgment will come as a thief in the night, and that on that day the heavens will implode, and the elements will be burnt by the resulting fire. Afterward there will be new heavens and a new earth, in which the righteous will possess righteousness and the promises of God in their own dwellings. However, it must not be forgotten that this

---

[11]CEC 99. [12]PL Supp. 3:114. [13]PL 93:80. [14]PL 93:80. [15]PG 119:609.

letter is counterfeit, and although it may be published, it does not form part of the earliest list of recieved writings. COMMENTARY ON 2 PETER.[16]

HEAVENS AND EARTH THAT NOW EXIST.

BEDE: Beyond the present heaven and earth there is also an outer universe, but whether it too will perish by fire, or only those parts which once perished in the flood, is a topic much debated among specialists. ON 2 PETER.[17]

KEPT UNTIL THE DAY OF JUDGMENT. OECU-
MENIUS: If someone asks why God created the world if all he intends to do is to destroy it, the answer is that the world will be renewed at the end of time. COMMENTARY ON 2 PETER.[18]

3:8 One Day Is Like a Thousand Years to God

A THOUSAND YEARS AS ONE DAY. EUSEBIUS
OF EMESA: Scripture says that human life is short and full of trouble, but you belong to the unseen and eternal one. And a thousand years are like a single day, or even like a watch of the night. It is during the fourth watch that those who are entrusted to guard it are divided, and it was during that watch that the Lord came to the holy apostles. If he has spoken this way about a thousand years, it is clear that the lifespan of a man is extremely short. The day of the Lord is like a thousand years, and yet it is undivided. No one lives for a thousand years, but no one has known a full day of the Lord either. CATENA.[19]

ALL WAS NIGHT BEFORE THE COMING OF
THE LORD. ATHANASIUS: A thousand years is the time that the temple worship lasted. For from the completion of the temple by Solomon, who built the Lord's house until it became redundant when Christ died on the cross is a thousand years. This thousand years is compared to a day, or to a watch in the night, because everything appeared to be night before the coming of the Savior. For until the sun of righteousness arose, everyone dwelt in ignorance and confusion. CATENA.[20]

CONSIDERING THE MILLENNIUM AS THE
LAST DAY. AUGUSTINE: If we take the millennium and think of the end of that time as being the end of the world, we could say that it was the end of time in general, for a thousand years in God's sight are like a single day. Because of this, anything that was done during the millennium could be spoken of as done at the end of time or on the last day. LETTERS 199.17.[21]

WHO CAN TELL? CAESARIUS OF ARLES:
Since it is written concerning the day of judgment that a thousand years will be like one day, who can tell whether we shall spend days, months or even years in that fire? SERMONS 179.5.[22]

GOD REMEMBERS. HILARY OF ARLES: Just as
a man works for a day and afterwards remembers what he has done, so God does not forget even after a thousand years. It may be a long time before he gets round to punishing sinners, but when he does so he uses his power in a single instant. INTRODUCTORY COMMENTARY ON 2 PETER.[23]

WHETHER JUDGMENT DAY WILL LAST A

---

[16]PG 39:1773-74. [17]PL 93:80. [18]PG 119:609. [19]CEC 99-100. [20]CEC 100. [21]FC 30:368-69. [22]FC 47:453. [23]PL Supp. 3:114.

Thousand Years. Bede: There are some people who think that this means that the day of judgment will last for a thousand years, but the context from which it is taken makes such an interpretation impossible. Psalm 90:4 says clearly that the thousand years refer to what is already past and that it is a way of describing the shortness of our life here on earth. What we regard as long or short is all the same to God. On 2 Peter.[24]

3:9 The Lord Is Waiting for People to Repent

His Promises Not Delayed. Augustine: The Lord does not delay the promise. A little while and we shall see him, where we shall no more ask anything. We will no more ask anything because nothing will remain to be desired, nothing will be hidden to be inquired about. Tractates 101.6.2.[25]

God Is Forbearing Toward You. Fastidius: In his fatherly love, his kindness and his clemency, God does not punish immediately, so that you may recognize the extent of his loving regard for you and of his compassion. He would rather wait for you than punish you in your sin. On the Christian Life 21.[26]

As Some Count Slowness. Pachomius: Let us not look upon God's patience as ignorance. He holds back and delays so that, when we have been converted to a better state, we may not be handed over to torments. Book of Our Father Horsiesios 3.[27]

Time to Gather the Elect. Bede: Given that in God's eyes all time is the same, it is impossible for him to delay his promise, for in any case he already predestined it before the foundation of the world. The only reason it has not yet arrived is that he needs time to gather in all the elect, whom he also predestined before time began. Hence we read in the Apocalypse that the souls of the martyrs long day and night for the coming of the day of judgment and resurrection and have heard that they must wait yet a little while until the full complement of their fellow servants and brothers is reached. On 2 Peter.[28]

3:10 The Day of the Lord

Changed into Something Better. Eusebius of Emesa: Like a cloak, every body grows old with time. But although it grows old, it will be renewed again by your divine will, O Lord. The heavens will not be destroyed, but rather they will be changed into something better. In the same way our bodies are not destroyed in order to disappear altogether but in order to be renewed in an indestructible state. Catena.[29]

Which Elements Will Be Dissolved with Fire? Bede: There are four elements, earth, air, fire and water, all of which will be swept away by a great fire. Yet that fire will not devour them all but only two of them (fire and water), for there will be a new heaven and a new earth[30] after this destruction has passed. On 2 Peter.[31]

Will Come Like a Thief. Oecumenius: The day of the Lord will come without notice and unexpectedly, just as the flood did in the

---

[24]PL 93:81. [25]FC 90:239. [26]MFC 17:99. [27]CS 47:172. [28]PL 93:81. [29]CEC 100. [30]Cf. Rev 21:1. [31]PL 93:82.

days of Noah. People will be eating and drinking and will not realize what is happening to them until the flood overtakes them. COMMENTARY ON 2 PETER.[32]

3:11 What Sort of Persons Ought You to Be

HOLY AND GODLY. HILARY OF ARLES: As you wait for the end of all things, you must live holy lives according to the three laws—the Old Testament, the New Testament and the law of nature—and you must keep faith in the Trinity, which is the law of godliness. INTRODUCTORY COMMENTARY ON 2 PETER.[33]

3:12 Waiting for the Day of the Lord

HILARY OF ARLES: You are waiting for the end as the virgins waited for the bridegroom.[34] INTRODUCTORY COMMENTARY ON 2 PETER.[35]

3:13 New Heavens and a New Earth

CREATION WILL SHARE IN OUR GLORY. ANDREAS: It is not just we, says Peter, but the whole creation around us also, which will be changed for the better. For the creation will share in our glory just as it has been subjected to destruction and corruption because of us. Either way it shares our fate. CATENA.[36]

3:14 Be Found by Him Without Spot or Blemish

SPOTLESS IN FAITH. HILARY OF ARLES: When he returns, Christ wants to find you spotless in your faith and uncorrupted in the chastity of your body. INTRODUCTORY COMMENTARY ON 2 PETER.[37]

YOU WAIT FOR THESE. ANDREAS: Everything in creation was made for our enjoyment, and it will be remade along with us.... This new life is for all who believe, and not just for Israel, for the Lord has exalted the Gentiles, lifting us up by the cross toward himself. Has he not provided for believers? Indeed he has. He has lifted them up and carried them and placed them in the many mansions which there are in the Father's presence. CATENA.[38]

WATCHING IN PEACE. BEDE: Peter is talking here about those holy vigils which Jesus referred to when he said: "Blessed are those servants whom the Master finds awake when he comes."[39] The person who keeps himself pure from all evil may be said to be watching, as may the one who does his utmost to live in peace with everyone. ON 2 PETER.[40]

3:15 Count the Forbearance of Our Lord as Salvation

SO PAUL WROTE. AUGUSTINE: Peter, in his second epistle, urged us to holiness in living and character, declaring that this world would pass. New heavens and a new earth are expected which will be given to the just to inhabit.... Some people had used certain obscure passages from Paul's writings in order to excuse their lack of concern to live well, on the ground that they were secure in their salvation. Peter was saying that some of the things which Paul said are hard to understand and that these people were twisting them to their own ruin. ON FAITH AND WORKS 14.22.[41]

---

[32]PG 119:616-17. [33]PL Supp. 3:115. [34]Mt 25:6. [35]PL Supp. 3:115. [36]CEC 101. [37]PL Supp. 3:115. [38]CEC 102-3. [39]Lk 12:37. [40]PL 93:83. [41]FC 27:248.

THE WISDOM GIVEN HIM. HILARY OF ARLES: Note that Paul wrote to them not according to the wisdom which he possessed but according to the wisdom which was given to him specifically for that purpose. INTRODUCTORY COMMENTARY ON 2 PETER.[42]

THE FRIEND OF TRUTH. GREGORY THE GREAT: Look how Peter says that there is much to be admired in Paul's writings. Yet in his letters, Paul criticized Peter. Peter could hardly have said what he did if he had not read Paul, but when he read him he would have discovered criticism of himself in them. Thus the friend of truth was able to praise even the fact that he had been criticized, and he was happy to do so because he realized that he had been wrong. SERMONS ON EZEKIEL 2.6.9.[43]

THE FORBEARANCE OF OUR LORD. ANDREAS: This is a reference to what Paul said when he wrote: "Do you not know that the kindness of God leads you to repentance?"[44] CATENA.[45]

GRATEFUL FOR THE WISDOM GIVEN TO PAUL. BEDE: Peter records that Paul wrote to them, because even if Paul addressed his letters to specific churches, he nevertheless intended them to circulate among them all, because there is only one universal church. Note too that although Peter here praises Paul's wisdom, Paul said of himself: "I am the least of the apostles, who am not worthy to be called an apostle, because I persecuted the church of God."[46] Paul humbled himself because he remembered his early unbelief, and he put the other apostles ahead of himself. Peter, on the other hand, the first of the apostles, almost forgets his primacy and the fact that the keys of the kingdom were

given to him and instead marvels at the wisdom which was given to Paul. The reason for this is that it is a characteristic of the elect that they admire the virtues of others more than their own and that those virtues encourage them to grow more deeply in their faith. ON 2 PETER.[47]

THE LORD'S PATIENCE IS OUR SALVATION. OECUMENIUS: If the patience and kindness of God calls us to repentance, this is because repentance is the way of salvation for us. God's patience always works toward our benefit and salvation. COMMENTARY ON 2 PETER.[48]

3:16 Some Things in Paul Hard to Understand

DO NOT MAKE THE WICKED CONFIDENT OF SALVATION. AUGUSTINE: If it is both true and clear that those lacking in good works will be thrown into the fire,[49] without doubt another interpretation of Paul's sayings must be sought and his teaching must be adapted in those matters which the apostle Peter says are difficult to understand but ought not to turn people to their own destruction, so that, contrary to the most obvious testimony of Scripture, they make the most wicked confident of obtaining salvation, although they most stubbornly cling to their sin and are not changed by correction or penance. EIGHT QUESTIONS OF DULCITIUS 1.[50]

WISDOM FROM ABOVE. CYRIL OF ALEXANDRIA: It seems that some people find Paul hard to understand, no doubt because he

---

[42]PL Supp. 3:115. [43]PL 79:1100. [44]Rom 2:4. [45]CEC 103. [46]1 Cor 15:9. [47]PL 93:83. [48]PG 119:616. [49]1 Cor 3:11-15 [50]FC 16:432-33.

speaks about the wisdom which comes from above, for in him Christ himself is speaking. CATENA.[51]

PETER AWED BY PAUL'S BRILLIANCE. HILARY OF ARLES: Peter says this because he himself was overwhelmed by Paul's brilliance. INTRODUCTORY COMMENTARY ON 2 PETER.[52]

EVERY PART OF SCRIPTURE CORRUPTED BY HERETICS. BEDE: The heretics corrupt every part of Scripture. There is no book in either the Old or the New Testament which they have not perverted according to their own fantasies, by adding to it, subtracting from it or altering something which it says to make it mean something else. Those whom Peter calls unlearned and unstable are the people who have neither the light of knowledge nor the steadfastness of mind to stay in the company of the learned until they are properly instructed. For the only cure for the unlearned is to listen in all humility to the words of those who know better. The heretics do not have this humility, with the result that they are tossed about by the wind like chaff and are swept right out of the church. But those who try to corrupt the holy Scriptures and pervert the catholic faith do nothing other than condemn themselves. ON 2 PETER.[53]

THEY TWIST SCRIPTURE. JOHN OF DAMASCUS: The enemy of our souls has made some people turn away from the straight road and divided them by strange teachings and taught them to interpret certain sayings of the Scriptures falsely. But the truth is one, and it is that which was preached by the glorious apostles and inspired Fathers and which shines in the universal church. BARLAAM AND IOASAPH 16.134.[54]

SCRIPTURE NOT UNSTABLE. SYMEON THE NEW THEOLOGIAN: It is not divine Scripture which suffers from those who twist it according to their own desires and who corrupt themselves in their own passions but rather those who disfigure it. DISCOURSES 15.2.[55]

3:17 Do Not Be Carried Away by Error

BEWARE LEST YOU BE CARRIED AWAY. CYRIL OF ALEXANDRIA: Peter has to warn his people so that they will not be deceived. Our Lord Jesus Christ himself warned us for our safety, that we should "beware of those who come to us in sheep's clothing, but inside they are ravenous wolves."[56] And again: "Take care that you are not deceived. For many shall come in my name, saying, I am the Christ, and they will deceive many."[57] And Paul cries: "Beware of dogs, beware of evil workers claiming to believe in the Lord Jesus."[58] For those who deform the truth by their doctrines of ungodliness and works of evil are like those who killed the prophets and apostles. Indeed, they are worse, because they have killed not only the living but those who have been saved as well. CATENA.[59]

THE ERROR OF THE LAWLESS. BEDE: Since you already know that the heretics are bringing in many crazy errors—that some deny that there will be a future judgment, some pervert the words of God, some interpret Scripture wrongly, some give themselves over to their lusts, and some deceive the hearts of the innocent by their frauds—you must be on guard so that you are not taken away from the

---

[51]CEC 103. [52]PL Supp. 3:116. [53]PL 93:84. [54]LCL 227. [55]CWS 194. [56]Mt 7:15. [57]Lk 21:8. [58]Phil 3:2. [59]CEC 103-4.

firm foundation of your faith by their cleverness. On 2 Peter.[60]

3:18 To Him Be the Glory Now and to Eternity

Grow in Faith and Knowledge. Hilary of Arles: Grow in the faith which is yours by baptism and in the knowledge which comes from putting that faith into practice. Introductory Commentary on 2 Peter.[61]

To Him Be the Glory. Bede: May glory always be given to God our Lord and Savior, both now when we are still in the flesh and far from him, wandering through the daily pressures of our adversaries, and especially at that

future time when he who has been long desired shall come to all the nations and deign to illuminate us by his presence. Meanwhile, as we await that glorious day, let us go on singing: "One day in your courts is better than a thousand."[62] On 2 Peter.[63]

The Letter Ends in Prayer. Oecumenius: Just as the other New Testament letters end with prayers, so too does this one, by praying that its recipients might grow in the faith of the Lord. Commentary on 2 Peter.[64]

---

[60]PL 93:85. [61]PL Supp. 3:116. [62]Ps 84:10. [63]PL 93:86. [64]PG 119:617.

THE FIRST EPISTLE
OF JOHN

1:1-4 ETERNAL LIFE

¹*That which was from the beginning, which we have heard, which we have seen with our eyes, which we have looked upon and touched with our hands, concerning the word of life—* ²*the life was made manifest, and we saw it, and testify to it, and proclaim to you the eternal life which was with the Father and was made manifest to us—*³*that which we have seen and heard we proclaim also to you, so that you may have fellowship with us; and our fellowship is with the Father and with his Son Jesus Christ.* ⁴*And we are writing this that our*ᵃ *joy may be complete.*

a *Other ancient authorities read* your

OVERVIEW: Uniquely among these letters, 1 John does not have an opening salutation. Instead it begins in much the same way as the Fourth Gospel, a fact that for most of the Fathers confirmed their belief that the apostle John was the author of both, though this was challenged by some on literary grounds (ISHO'DAD). The emphasis is placed firmly on the incarnation of the Son of God and the witness to that incarnation that was the hallmark of a true apostle. The central theme of the epistle is love (AUGUSTINE). The Word of life was manifest in the flesh (AUGUSTINE). He rose in the same flesh in which he died (ANDREAS). The disciples now testify to what they saw (DIDYMUS, BEDE). It was in his incarnate and human form that he became visible and touchable (BEDE, SEVERUS). What always existed had an incarnate beginning in time

(PETER CHRYSOLOGUS). With their own eyes the original disciples had seen the resurrected Lord, the same who was in the beginning (DIDYMUS). We proclaim what we have heard and seen that you may have fellowship with us in the worshiping community, where our fellowship is with the Father and the Son (HILARY OF ARLES, ANDREAS, BEDE). Those who have heard but not seen—the later generations of disciples—share in the same joy as the first generation (AUGUSTINE, ANDREAS, BEDE, THEOPHYLACT).

1:1 We Have Seen the Word of Life

THE GENERATION OF THE SON HAS NO BEGINNING. CLEMENT OF ALEXANDRIA: When the elder wrote this, he was explaining that the principle of generation is not separate from the principle of creation. For when he says "which was from the beginning" he is referring to the generation of the Son which has no beginning, because he exists coeternally with the Father. Therefore the word *was* signifies eternity, just as the Word himself, that is, the Son, which is one with the Father in equality of substance, is eternal and unmade. When he says that "our hands touched the Word of life," he means not merely the Son's flesh but his power as well. One tradition has it that when the disciple touched Christ's physical body he put his hand right inside and was not stopped by the hardness of the flesh from doing so, because the flesh made way for the disciple's hand. Adumbrations.[1]

Various Hypotheses. Didymus the Blind: Many think that these words apply to the postresurrection appearances of Jesus and say that John is speaking of himself and the other disciples who first of all heard that the Lord had risen and afterwards saw him with their own eyes, to the point where they touched his feet, his hands and his side and felt the imprint of the nails. For even if Thomas was the only one who actually made physical contact with him, he was representative of the others, for the Savior told them all to touch him and see for themselves.[2] But others take these words in a deeper sense, noting that they do not simply speak about touching but also about handling the "word of life which was from the beginning." Who can this refer to, other than to the one who said: "I am that I am"?[3] Another interpretation is that we have now seen openly with our own eyes the one who was in the beginning, of whom the law and the prophets spoke, saying that he would come. He has

indeed come and was seen in the flesh, and after much handling of the scriptural texts which bear witness to him, this is what we believe about the Word of life. Commentary on 1 John.[4]

The Central Theme—Love. Augustine: This book is very sweet to every healthy Christian heart that savors the bread of God, and it should constantly be in the mind of God's holy church. But I choose it more particularly because what it specially commends to us is love. The person who possesses the thing which he hears about in this epistle must rejoice when he hears it. His reading will be like oil to a flame. . . . For others, the epistle should be like flame set to firewood; if it was not already burning, the touch of the word may kindle it. Ten Homilies on 1 John, Prologue.[5]

What Always Existed. Peter Chrysologus: How can you believe that what always existed took a beginning later on? Sermons 57.[6]

Seen and Touched. Severus of Antioch: Given that this same John also said, "No one has ever seen God,"[7] how can he assure us that the living Word of life has been seen and touched? It is clear that it was in his incarnate and human form that he was visible and touchable. What was not true of him by nature became true of him in that way, for he is one and the same indivisible Word, both visible and invisible, and without diminishing in either respect he became touchable in both his

---

[1]FGNK 3:87. [2]Lk 24:39. [3]Ex 3:14. [4]PG 39:1775-76. [5]LCC 8:259. [6]FC 17:106. [7]Jn 1:18; 1 Jn 4:12.

divine-human nature. For he worked his miracles in his divinity and suffered for us in his humanity. Catena.[8]

With Him from the Beginning. Bede: The disciples were with Jesus from the beginning, and so they could preach what they had seen and heard in his presence without any ambiguity. Homilies on the Gospels 2.16.[9]

Written Against Heresies. Bede: It was against heretics like Cerinthus and Marcion that John wrote his Gospel, stating both in his own words and in those of the Lord that the Son is consubstantial with the Father. Here in his letter he does the same thing again by conveying the Lord's teaching in his own words and confounding the foolishness of the heretics with his apostolic authority. On 1 John.[10]

What Has Been from the Beginning. Oecumenius: John writes this against both the Jews and the Greeks, because they were protesting that the mystery which has appeared among us is too new to be taken seriously. He therefore answers them by saying that in fact it is very old and has been there from the beginning. It is higher than the law and even higher than the creation itself, because while creation has a beginning this was there already. Commentary on 1 John.[11]

We Have Touched the Word of Life. Theophylact: When John talks about having seen this life, he means that the disciples understood its meaning, and when he says that they touched it, he means that they had investigated it thoroughly. Commentary on 1 John.[12]

This Letter Not by the Apostle John. Isho'dad of Merv: About this epistle many have erred, supposing that it was written by the apostle John, yet if they had investigated the matter they would have seen that the thought, shape and authority of this letter are greatly inferior to the sound words of the Evangelist. Commentaries.[13]

1:2 We Proclaim to You Eternal Life

We Saw It. Didymus the Blind: Note that there is an important difference between seeing and contemplating. For what is seen can be told to others, which is not always possible with things which are contemplated. For there are many things which may be perfectly well contemplated but which cannot be expressed in words because they are known by some ineffable understanding. In this verse it should be noticed that those who are bearing witness are not validating the life of Jesus but improving themselves by their confession. Commentary on 1 John.[14]

The Life Was Made Manifest. Augustine: The life itself has been manifested in flesh, so that what can be seen by the heart alone might be seen also by the eyes, in order that hearts might be healed. Ten Homilies on 1 John 1.1.[15]

The Same Flesh Crucified. Andreas: John says this with reference to the close union of the Word with the flesh. Or perhaps he says

---

[8]CEC 106. [9]HOG 1:151. [10]PL 93:85. [11]PG 119:621. [12]PG 126:13. [13]CIM 40. [14]PG 39:1777. The main purpose is not simply to validate historical events but to confess their meaning. [15]LCC 8:260.

this with reference to the resurrection, considering the way in which it was made known to the apostles by the action of Thomas. That proved that Christ rose again with the same flesh in which he had been crucified. CATENA.[16]

WE TESTIFY TO IT. BEDE: The life of which John is speaking here was the same as that of which we read in his Gospel, when Jesus said: "I am the resurrection and the life."[17] It was manifested and declared in the flesh by the divine miracles, and the disciples who were present saw and later testified to them with undoubted authority. ON 1 JOHN.[18]

1:3 We Also Proclaim to You

FELLOWSHIP WITH US. HILARY OF ARLES: Our fellowship is in the unity of our faith here on earth and in the eternal dwelling place of God in heaven. INTRODUCTORY COMMENTARY ON 1 JOHN.[19]

WITH THE FATHER AND HIS SON. ANDREAS: What did they proclaim, but that eternal life has appeared to us and that we have become witnesses of it? What you gain from this proclamation is the right to share this experience with us. For the one who is in fellowship with us has fellowship with the Father and with his Son, Jesus Christ, and since you share in the same fellowship, we shall all have joy together, in that we have been united to God. CATENA.[20]

THAT WHICH WE HAVE SEEN AND HEARD. BEDE: John shows quite clearly that those who want to have fellowship with God must first of all be joined to the church and there learn that faith and be blessed with its sacraments, which the disciples truly received during the time of Christ's incarnation. Nor do those who believe the apostles' testimony belong any less to the Lord than those who believed him when they heard him preaching in the flesh do, although there might be some distinction in the quality of the works of faith which they perform. ON 1 JOHN.[21]

1:4 Bringing Our Joy to Perfection

SHARING IN THIS JOY. AUGUSTINE: The disciples saw the Lord in the flesh, and they heard his words, which they made known to us. We have also heard but have not seen. Are we less happy than they, who both saw and heard? No, for John goes on to say that the reason for his preaching is that we might share in their fellowship. TEN HOMILIES ON 1 JOHN 1.3.[22]

THAT OUR JOY MAY BE COMPLETE. HILARY OF ARLES: The fullness of joy comes when we are in fellowship with the apostles, as well as of the Father, Son and Holy Spirit. INTRODUCTORY COMMENTARY ON 1 JOHN.[23]

JOY IN FELLOWSHIP. BEDE: The joy of all teachers is complete when by their preaching they bring many into the fellowship of the holy church and also into the fellowship of God the Father and his Son Jesus Christ, through whom the church is strengthened and grows. ON 1 JOHN.[24]

THE SOWER IS HAPPY TO HAVE REAPERS. THEOPHYLACT: John says that having his hearers as fellow participants in the grace of

---

[16]CEC 107. [17]Jn 11:25. [18]PL 93:86. [19]PL Supp. 3:117. [20]CEC 107-8. [21]PL 93:86. [22]LCC 8:261. [23]PL Supp. 3:117. [24]PL 93:87.

eternal life will make him and the other disciples happy in the same way that a sower is happy to have the reapers alongside him on the day of harvest. COMMENTARY ON 1 JOHN.[25]

[25]PG 126:16.

1:5-10 THE TRUE LIGHT

[5]*This is the message we have heard from him and proclaim to you, that God is light and in him is no darkness at all. [6]If we say we have fellowship with him while we walk in darkness, we lie and do not live according to the truth; [7]but if we walk in the light, as he is in the light, we have fellowship with one another, and the blood of Jesus his Son cleanses us from all sin. [8]If we say we have no sin, we deceive ourselves, and the truth is not in us. [9]If we confess our sins, he is faithful and just, and will forgive our sins and cleanse us from all unrighteousness. [10]If we say we have not sinned, we make him a liar, and his word is not in us.*

OVERVIEW: Those who want to have fellowship with God must walk in his light, something which we cannot do in our own strength. God is light (ORIGEN, DIDYMUS), but light unapproachable with our bodily eyes (CLEMENT OF ALEXANDRIA, AUGUSTINE). God imparts his own brightness to us (SYMEON). The Manichaean idea of the prince of darkness overcoming is an absurdity (BEDE). The truth is light, so if we do not walk according to it, we are in the dark (IRENAEUS, HILARY OF ARLES, ANDREAS, SYMEON). Light resembles God to some extent in its nature and can be used to describe him by analogy (SYMEON). The mere confession of one's faith is not enough for salvation if there is no sign of active good works confirming that faith; but the goodness of the works is of no value either if they are not done in the simplicity of faith and love (BEDE). Though small lapses are distinguishable from mortal sins (JOHN CASSIAN), no one is without sin (AUGUSTINE, ANDREAS, BEDE).

But God in his mercy has sent his Son to die for our sins, and his blood cleanses us, making it possible for us to walk hand in hand with God. Those like Pelagius who believe that it is possible for us to reach perfection by our own efforts and to live in this world without sin of any kind, are deceiving themselves, and we must not fall into that trap (BEDE). Only a repentant sinner can claim to have God's word dwelling within. We humbly confess our wrongdoings to him every day when we receive the sacrament of his blood, when we forgive those who have trespassed against us and ask him to forgive us, remembering what Christ did for our sake (HILARY OF ARLES, BEDE). God is faithful (OECUMENIUS) and will forgive our sins (CYPRIAN, ANDREAS). He who has taught us to pray for our sins and trespasses has also promised the Father's mercy (BEDE).

1:5 God Is Light

The Essence of God. Clement of Alexandria: John is not defining the essence of God, but desiring to declare his majesty, God has adapted something belonging to divinity and used it to suit his purpose. Paul also calls God "unapproachable light."[1] Adumbrations.[2]

The Son Is the Brightness of That Light. Origen: God is light, according to John. The only-begotten Son therefore is the brightness of that light, proceeding from God without separation, as brightness from light, and lightening the whole creation. On First Principles 1.2.7.[3]

This Message Proclaimed to You. Didymus the Blind: John wrote that the proclamation, by which it was stated that God is light, with no shadows in him at all, was made by the Savior himself to his disciples. Now he is sharing it with his readers so that they too might believe the same thing about God. Commentary on 1 John.[4]

In Him Is No Darkness. Jerome: When John says that there is no darkness in the light of God, he proves that all the lights of others are stained by some blemish. Against the Pelagians 2.7.[5]

Not Seen by Bodily Eyes. Augustine: God is the light of purified minds, not of these bodily eyes. For then[6] the mind will be able to see that light, which right now it is not yet able to do. Letters 92.[7]

The Heart of the Message. Andreas: What is this message? It is that eternal life has appeared to us. For the Father so loved the world that he gave his only-begotten Son, and this is what we proclaim to you—that the Word of God who has come into the world and become a man is both God and light. Catena.[8]

The Prince of Darkness Does Not Overcome. Bede: In this verse John shows the excellence of God's purity, which we are also called to imitate, as the Lord himself said: "Be holy, for I the Lord your God am holy."[9] He also proves that the Manichaean belief that the nature of God was overcome by the prince of darkness and corrupted is an absurdity. On 1 John.[10]

Imparting Brightness to You. Symeon the New Theologian: Let no one deceive you. God is light, and to those who have entered into union with him, he imparts of his own brightness to the extent that they have been purified. Discourses 15.3.[11]

1:6 Light and Darkness Do Not Mix

We Lie. Irenaeus: A lie has no fellowship with the truth, any more than light with darkness. The presence of one excludes the other. Against Heresies 3.5.1.[12]

Walking According to Truth. Hilary of Arles: The truth is light, so if we do not walk according to it, we are in the dark. Introductory Commentary on 1 John.[13]

---

[1]1 Tim 6:16. [2]FGNK 3:87-88. [3]OFP 20. [4]PG 39:1777. [5]FC 53:305. [6]In heaven. [7]FC 18:51. [8]CEC 108. [9]Lev 19:1. [10]PL 93:87. [11]CWS 195. [12]LCC 1:376. [13]PL Supp. 3:118.

While We Walk in Darkness. Andreas: John says that if we sin we have no fellowship with God, but if we do the works of light, then we have fellowship with one another. Catena.[14]

Those Surrounded by Darkness. Bede: John calls sin heresies, and hatred darkness. Therefore the mere confession of one's faith is not enough for salvation if there is no sign of good works confirming that faith. But at the same time, the goodness of the works is of no value either, if they are not done in the simplicity of faith and love. Anyone who is in any way surrounded by darkness is totally unable to have fellowship with the One in whom there is no sign of wickedness at all. On 1 John.[15]

Seeming to Be in God. Symeon the New Theologian: See to it, brothers, that while we seem to be in God and think that we have communion with him, we should not be found excluded and separated from him, since we do not now see his light. Discourses 33.2.[16]

1:7 Walking in the Light

The Blood of Jesus Cleanses. Clement of Alexandria: God's teaching is here called blood. Adumbrations.[17]

Cleansing from All Sin. Hilary of Arles: The blood of animal sacrifices was enough to cleanse people from whatever particular sin they had committed, but the blood of Christ is sufficient to cleanse those who walk in love from all sin. Introductory Commentary on 1 John.[18]

Walking and Dwelling. Bede: Note the different verbs which John uses. God dwells in the light, but we are told that we must walk in it. The righteous walk in the light when they do good works and thereby go on to better things. God does not need to improve because he is already the perfection of all goodness, which is why he is said to dwell in the light. John also gives us an indication of how we can know that we are on the right track, and that is whether we rejoice in the link of brotherly fellowship which we have with those who are journeying along with us toward the pure light. However, even if we are shown to be doing the works of light, and even if we are seen to be maintaining the bonds of mutual love, we must never think that we can be cleansed from our sins by our own progress and effort, as the last part of the verse reminds us. For the sacrament of our Lord's passion has both cleansed us in baptism from all our previous sins and forgives us by the grace of our Redeemer for whatever we have done in our human weakness after baptism. For along with all the works of light which we do, we also humbly confess our wrongdoings to him every day, whenever we receive the sacraments of his blood, when we forgive those who have trespassed against us and ask him to forgive our trespasses against him, and when we cheerfully endure all adversity, remembering what he did for our sake. On 1 John.[19]

1:8 We Are All Sinners

Enlightened by God. Didymus the Blind: Since God is light, there is no dark-

---

[14]CEC 109. [15]PL 93:87. [16]CWS 341. [17]FGNK 3:88. [18]PL Supp. 3:118. In the old covenant the blood of animals sufficed in a partial way, whereas in the new covenant the blood of Christ suffices in a complete way, to reconcile God and humanity. [19]PL 93:87.

ness in him at all, and he has nothing to do with darkness. The person who is enlightened by his light walks in the light, according to the words of the Savior himself: "While you have the light, walk in the light, lest the darkness take hold of you."[20] Anyone who walks in the darkness of sin but claims that his mind is not darkened and that he has a relationship with God is lying. COMMENTARY ON 1 JOHN.[21]

PRIDEFUL PRESUMPTION. LEO THE GREAT: It is pride to presume that it is easy not to sin, since the presumption itself is sin. SERMONS 41.1.[22]

THE WORST KIND OF SIN. CAESARIUS OF ARLES: Let no one deceive you, brothers. Not to know your sin is the worst kind of sin. SERMONS 144.4.[23]

DECEIVING YOURSELF. HILARY OF ARLES: If you say that you are not a sinner but act otherwise, you are deceiving yourself. INTRODUCTORY COMMENTARY ON 1 JOHN.[24]

CRUCIFYING CHRIST. ANDREAS: This is how John describes the Jews who dared to say: "Let his blood be upon us and upon our children,"[25] as if they could crucify Christ without being sinners. If we say such things, we deceive ourselves. CATENA.[26]

CLEANSING IN CHRIST. BEDE: This verse refutes the teachings of the Pelagians, who say that babies are born without sin and that the elect can make such progress in this life that it becomes possible for them to attain perfection. We cannot live in the world without guilt, since we brought it with us when we came into the world. As David said: "I was brought forth in iniquity, and in sin did my

mother conceive me."[27] But the blood of Jesus Christ cleanses us from all sin, so that our guilt does not keep us in the power of the enemy, because the man Jesus Christ, the Mediator between God and man, has freely paid the price on our behalf, even though he did not owe anything himself. He surrendered himself to the death of the flesh, which he did not deserve, in order to deliver us from the richly deserved death of our souls. ON 1 JOHN.[28]

1:9 God Forgives Those Who Confess Their Sins

IF WE CONFESS. CYPRIAN: In his epistle John has combined the fact that we should entreat God for our sins and that we should obtain mercy when we do so. THE LORD'S PRAYER 22.[29]

HE WILL FORGIVE AND CLEANSE US. ANDREAS: If we acknowledge our sin and confess it, he will forgive it, and not only that one but all our sins. For when a person repents and is baptized into the name of Jesus Christ, God forgives all his sins which he has committed both against himself and against heaven. CATENA.[30]

CONFESSION AND LOVE. BEDE: Since we cannot live in this world without sin, the first hope we have of salvation is through confession, nor should anyone be proud enough to claim that he is righteous in God's sight. The next step is love, which John often commends to us in this letter, because love covers a multi-

---

[20]Jn 12:35-36. [21]PG 39:1778-79. [22]FC 93:177. [23]FC 47:302. [24]PL Supp. 3:118. [25]Mt 27:25. [26]CEC 110. [27]Ps 51:5. [28]PL 93:88. [29]FC 36:146. [30]CEC 110.

tude of sins.[31] Each of these things encourages us to pray for our sins and to ask God's forgiveness when we do so. This is why John says that God is faithful and will forgive our sins, pointing to the reliability of his promise, for he who has taught us to pray for our sins and trespasses has also promised the Father's mercy and the forgiveness which flows from that. John also says that God is just, because he will rightly forgive anyone who truly confesses his sins. In this life God forgives the everyday, trivial sins of the elect, which we cannot avoid as long as we are here on earth, and after our death he cleanses us from all sin and brings us into that life in which no one wants or is able to sin. Now he forgives those who pray their greater temptations, so that they will not be overcome by them, and he forgives the least as well, so that they will not suffer any harm. But in the life to come he will cleanse us from every sin, so that there will no longer be any sign of wickedness in the eternal kingdom of the blessed. ON 1 JOHN.[32]

GOD IS FAITHFUL AND JUST. OECUMENIUS: To say that God is faithful means that he is reliable, for faithful is a word which is not just applied to those who believe but also to those who can be relied upon. It is in this second sense that it is applied to God. He is also just in that he does not refuse anyone who comes to him, however seriously they may have sinned. COMMENTARY ON 1 JOHN.[33]

1:10 If We Say We Have Not Sinned

DISTINGUISHING SMALL LAPSES FROM MORTAL SINS. JOHN CASSIAN: Among holy men it is impossible not to fall into those small lapses which occur because of something said, some thought, some surreptitious act. These sins are quite different from those which are called mortal, but they are not without blame or reproach. CONFERENCE 11.9.[34]

NONE SINLESS. AUGUSTINE: Who is there on earth without sin? Even a baby has contracted it from its parents. SERMONS 181.1.[35]

WE MAKE HIM A LIAR. ANDREAS: If we say that we have not sinned, we reject his word, which is spirit and life.[36] CATENA.[37]

ASKING FORGIVENESS. BEDE: God's word says: "Surely there is not a righteous man on earth who does good and never sins."[38] He himself has taught us not only that we cannot escape sin but also that we should pray: "Forgive us our debts, as we forgive our debtors."[39] Therefore when we see even the apostles praying for their sins to be forgiven, as the Lord taught them, no one should think, as Pelagius taught, that it is possible to lead a sinless life here on earth. ON 1 JOHN.[40]

---

[31]1 Pet 4:8. [32]PL 93:88. [33]PG 119:629. [34]CWS 148. [35]WSA 3/5:324. [36]Jn 6:63. [37]CEC 110. [38]Eccles 7:20. [39]Mt 6:12. [40]PL 93:88-89.

2:1-17 THE CHRISTIAN LIFE

^{1}*My little children, I am writing this to you so that you may not sin; but if any one does sin, we have an advocate with the Father, Jesus Christ the righteous;* ^{2}*and he is the expiation for our sins, and not for ours only but also for the sins of the whole world.* ^{3}*And by this we may be sure that we know him, if we keep his commandments.* ^{4}*He who says "I know him" but disobeys his commandments is a liar, and the truth is not in him;* ^{5}*but whoever keeps his word, in him truly love for God is perfected. By this we may be sure that we are in him:* ^{6}*he who says he abides in him ought to walk in the same way in which he walked.*

^{7}*Beloved, I am writing you no new commandment, but an old commandment which you had from the beginning; the old commandment is the word which you have heard.* ^{8}*Yet I am writing you a new commandment, which is true in him and in you, because^b the darkness is passing away and the true light is already shining.* ^{9}*He who says he is in the light and hates his brother is in the darkness still.* ^{10}*He who loves his brother abides in the light, and in it^c there is no cause for stumbling.* ^{11}*But he who hates his brother is in the darkness and walks in the darkness, and does not know where he is going, because the darkness has blinded his eyes.*

^{12}*I am writing to you, little children, because your sins are forgiven for his sake.* ^{13}*I am writing to you, fathers, because you know him who is from the beginning. I am writing to you, young men, because you have overcome the evil one. I write to you, children, because you know the Father.* ^{14}*I write to you, fathers, because you know him who is from the beginning. I write to you, young men, because you are strong, and the word of God abides in you, and you have overcome the evil one.*

^{15}*Do not love the world or the things in the world. If any one loves the world, love for the Father is not in him.* ^{16}*For all that is in the world, the lust of the flesh and the lust of the eyes and the pride of life, is not of the Father but is of the world.* ^{17}*And the world passes away, and the lust of it; but he who does the will of God abides for ever.*

b Or that   c Or him

OVERVIEW: Sin is to be avoided as far as possible, but when it occurs we have someone who will plead our case with the Father, Jesus Christ, who has paid the price for our sins. The way to be sure that we know him is to keep his commandments, an injunction that the Fathers interpreted as having two dimensions. At one level it meant holding the orthodox belief that the Son of God had become incarnate. In practice it meant loving others and fighting against the power of evil. As the Lord is an advocate (GREGORY OF NAZIANZUS) on our behalf before the Father (AMBROSE), so also the Spirit is an advocate whom he sent after his ascension (CLEMENT OF ALEXANDRIA, ORIGEN). Our judge himself becomes our advocate (AUGUSTINE, MAXIMUS OF TURIN). The Lord intercedes for us not only by words but also by his active compassion in taking our sins upon himself. While Christ's humanity pleads for sinners, his divinity propitiates their sin (BEDE).

Those who say that they know God must also keep his commandments (CLEMENT OF ALEXANDRIA, DIDYMUS, ANDREAS). Love is the sure sign that we know God (DIDYMUS, HILARY OF ARLES, BEDE). We dwell in God by faith, hope and love (LEO, HILARY OF ARLES) and by following in his footsteps (BEDE). The darkness of perversion is passing, and the light of faith is working in us according to God's foreordained plan (CLEMENT OF ALEXANDRIA). God's commandment cannot be called new with respect to God, but from the human point of view it was a mystery hidden in the Creator from the beginning (ISHO'DAD), bringing the new person into the light of love (BEDE, ANDREAS, HILARY OF ARLES). God's commandment to love is old because it had been around since the beginning of time (CLEMENT OF ALEXANDRIA, DIDYMUS, ANDREAS), but it is also new, because it poured the desire for new light into our hearts (BEDE). When John wrote to different age groups in the church, the Fathers invariably interpreted this in spiritual terms. The children were new converts, the young people were those still battling against sin in their lives, and the fathers were the mature believers—there was no correlation to physical age (CLEMENT OF ALEXANDRIA, BEDE, ANDREAS, OECUMENIUS).

One who comes to baptism or to the Lord's Supper with hatred toward another believer is still imprisoned (CAESARIUS OF ARLES) in the darkness, even if one thinks oneself enlightened (BEDE, ANDREAS), until one turns and repents and loves (HILARY OF ARLES). It is a law derived from nature that we should do good to those who are of the same nature as we are (THEOPHYLACT). Whoever hates a brother has already extinguished the lamp of love and therefore walks in darkness (ORIGEN). This path leads finally to hell, because such a person voluntarily withdraws from the light of Christ (CAESARIUS OF ARLES). The devil has blinded such a person's inner vision (BEDE, ANDREAS).

The forces ranged against God and his people are variously referred to as the "evil one" and as the "world," but there is little practical difference, since the devil is the prince of this world, and these terms refer to his temptations and the means that he uses to persuade us to fall into his power. The Christian life is a spiritual battle against everything the devil is and does to subvert us from the service of God. If one wants to be a friend of God, one must turn away from love of the world and the things that are in the world (DIDYMUS, CYRIL OF ALEXANDRIA, SEVERUS, SYMEON). Learn to use the world as needed, but do not love it inordinately (BEDE), for it is soon to vanish (HILARY OF ARLES). Let the power of the eyes be focused on the light, not given over to error. That power is available for the enjoyment of life, so it must turn away from what causes death (EUCHERIUS). The lust of the flesh is what pertains to our physical appetites, whereas the lust of the eye and the pride of life are what pertain to the vices of the soul, such as inordinate self-love, which does not come from the Father but from the devil (HILARY OF ARLES). Every sort of wickedness is described in these brief phrases (BEDE). By sinning habitually against one's own body, one is left marooned by the Creator of the body (AUGUSTINE). The lust of the world is destined to disappear. There will be no place for it in the new creation (BEDE, ANDREAS, OECUMENIUS).

2:1 An Advocate with the Father

SON AND SPIRIT. CLEMENT OF ALEXANDRIA: For just as the Lord is an advocate on our behalf before the Father, so also there is an advocate whom he deigned to send after his ascension. ADUMBRATIONS.[1]

GOD'S POWER FLOWS. ORIGEN: How could Jesus have become an advocate and propitiation without the power of God which completely destroys our weakness, a power furnished by Jesus which flows in the souls of believers? COMMENTARY ON JOHN 1.241.[2]

COMFORTER AND INTERCESSOR. ORIGEN: Let us consider whether the title advocate ("paraclete") means one thing when applied to the Savior and another when applied to the Holy Spirit.[3] In regard to the Savior "paraclete" seems to mean intercessor, for in Greek it bears both meanings, comforter and intercessor, but according to the phrase which follows, in which it is said that he is the propitiation for our sins, it seems that it must mean intercessor, because he intercedes with the Father for our sins. When used of the Holy Spirit, however, the word paraclete ought to be understood as comforter, because he provides comfort for the souls to whom he opens and reveals a consciousness of spiritual knowledge. ON FIRST PRINCIPLES 2.7.4.[4]

THE MEANING OF HIS ADVOCACY. GREGORY OF NAZIANZUS: We have an advocate, Jesus Christ, not indeed someone who prostrates himself before the Father on our behalf—such an idea is slavish and unworthy of the Spirit! It would be unworthy of the Father to require this, as also for the Son to submit to it, nor is it right to think such things of God. But by what he suffered as man, he as the Word and counselor persuades the Father to be patient with us. I think this is the meaning of his advocacy. THEOLOGICAL ORATIONS 30.14.[5]

GLORY IN HIS ADVOCACY. AMBROSE OF MILAN: I will not glory because I have been redeemed. I will not glory because I am free of sins but because sins have been forgiven me. I will not glory because I am profitable or because anyone is profitable to me but because Christ is an advocate on my behalf before the Father, because the blood of Christ has been poured out on my behalf. ON JACOB AND THE HAPPY LIFE 6.21.[6]

YOUR ADVOCATE BECOMES THE JUDGE. AUGUSTINE: If you should have a case to be tried before a judge and should procure an advocate, you would be accepted by the lawyer and he would plead your case to the best of his ability. If, before he has finished his plea, you should hear that he is to be the judge, how you would rejoice, because he could be your judge, who shortly before was your lawyer. SERMONS 213.5.[7]

---

[1]FGNK 3:88. [2]FC 80:82. [3]Jn 14:26-27. [4]OFP 119. [5]FGFR 272; LCC 3:187. [6]FC 65:133. [7]FC 38:125.

Judge and Advocate. Maximus of Turin: Christ is a judge when he sits and an advocate when he rises. It is clear that he was a judge to Jews[8] but arises as an advocate for Christians. On the one hand, standing before the Father of the Christians, even though they are sinners, he pleads their cause, while on the other he sits with the Father of the Pharisees, who are persecutors, condemning their sins. Angry with the ones, he wreaks harsh vengeance on them, while he gently has mercy on the others, interceding on their behalf. Sermons 40.3.[9]

Accusing Oneself. Gregory the Great: There is a problem here. A righteous advocate never takes unrighteous cases, which ours of course are. What can we do, dear brothers? The only way to get around this is to follow what Scripture says: "The righteous man accuses himself first of all."[10] Therefore a sinner who weeps over his sins and accuses himself is set on the path of righteousness, and Jesus can take up his case. Sermons on Ezekiel 1.7.24.[11]

That You May Not Sin. Andreas: John knows that those who have been enlightened have not been given an impassible nature, but neither have they been let out of prison in order that they might sin. Catena.[12]

He Took Our Sins upon Himself. Bede: There is no contradiction between what John is saying here and what he has just said in the first chapter, namely, that it is impossible to live without sin. There he warned us with great foresight and concern for our welfare that we must be aware of our human frailty and not think that we are somehow innocent. Here, following on from that, he tells us that if we want to avoid all blame for our sinful state, we must do our utmost to live in such a way that we are not bound by it, but rather put it away from us as firmly and as conscientiously as we can, so that we can overcome at least the greater and more obvious faults that we have. . . . The Lord intercedes for us not by words but by his dying compassion, because he took upon himself the sins which he was unwilling to condemn his elect for. On 1 John.[13]

The Power to Forgive Sins. Oecumenius: John calls Jesus our advocate because it is he who prays to the Father for us. In saying this he is speaking in a human way and within a human context, just as elsewhere he says: "The Son can do nothing by himself."[14] He puts it this way so that the Son will not appear to be the Father's opponent. For that the Son has the power to forgive sins is clear from the case of the paralytic,[15] and by giving his disciples the power to forgive sins, he shows that he can also share his power with others.[16] Commentary on 1 John.[17]

2:2 The Expiation for Our Sins

Not for Ours Only. Clement of Alexandria: Christ saves from all sin. He converts some by punishing them and others by their own free will and with the dignity of honor. Adumbrations.[18]

For the Whole World. Hilary of Arles: When John says that Christ died for the sins of the "whole world," what he means is that he died for the whole church. Intro-

---

[8]To those who seek to become righteous under the law, as typified by the Pharisees. [9]ACW 50:100. [10]Prov 18:47 (LXX). [11]PL 79:1101. [12]CEC 110. [13]PL 93:89. [14]Jn 5:19. [15]Mt 9:2-8. [16]Jn 20:23. [17]PG 119:629-32. [18]FGNK 3:89.

ductory Commentary on 1 John.[19]

Do Not Remain in Sin. Andreas: John is saying: "I am writing these things to you, not so that you may say that you no longer sin at all, but so that when you do sin, you will not remain in that state, for Jesus propitiates your sins in the Father's presence." Catena.[20]

His Humanity Pleads, His Divinity Propitiates. Bede: In his humanity Christ pleads for our sins before the Father, but in his divinity he has propitiated them for us with the Father. Furthermore, he has not done this only for those who were alive at the time of his death, but also for the whole church which is scattered over the full compass of the world, and it will be valid for everyone, from the very first among the elect until the last one who will be born at the end of time. This verse is therefore a rebuke to the Donatists, who thought that the true church was to be found only in Africa. The Lord pleads for the sins of the whole world, because the church which he has bought with his blood exists in every corner of the globe.[21] On 1 John.[22]

2:3 Assurance Through Obedience

Knowing and Doing. Clement of Alexandria: The one who understands will also do the works which pertain to the duty of virtue, but someone who does the works is not necessarily among those who understand. For he may just be someone who understands the difference between right and wrong but who has no knowledge of the heavenly mysteries. Furthermore, knowing that some people do the right thing out of fear of punishment or for some kind of reward, John teaches that a man of perfect understanding does these

things out of love. Adumbrations.[23]

By This We Know Him. Didymus the Blind: Often in the Scriptures the word *know* means not just being aware of something but having personal experience of it. Jesus did not know sin, not because he was unaware of what it is but because he never committed it himself. For although he is like us in every other way, he never sinned.[24] Given this meaning of the word *know,* it is clear that anyone who says that he knows God must also keep his commandments, for the two things go together. Commentary on 1 John.[25]

If We Keep His Commandments. Andreas: John shows here that true knowledge means demonstrating that one is faithful to Christ by obeying his commandments. Catena.[26]

2:4 You Cannot Claim to Know God If You Disobey Him

"I Have Never Known You." Hilary of Arles: Those who are perishing do not know God, and God will deny that he has even known them, as he himself said: "Depart from me, for I have never known you."[27] Introductory Commentary on 1 John.[28]

A Liar. Gregory the Great: We can be said to be loving God only to the extent that

---

[19]PL Supp. 3:118. [20]CEC 111. [21]Bede was not ignorant of the fact that John wrote before the Donatists were in Africa. Rather, the point is that anyone, whether in the first or fourth century, who imagines that catholic faith is to be found in only one continent or location stands rebuked already in an anticipatory way by this text. [22]PL 93:90. [23]FGNK 3:89. [24]Cf. Heb 4:15. [25]PG 39:1779. [26]CEC 111. [27]Mt 7:23. [28]PL Supp. 3:118.

we are keeping his commandments. HOMI-
LIES ON THE GOSPELS 30.1.[29]

THE TRUTH LACKING. ANDREAS: It is obvious that the person who does not keep God's
commandments has no knowledge of him.
CATENA.[30]

2:5 Whoever Keeps His Word

WE MAY BE SURE. DIDYMUS THE BLIND:
The person who really loves God keeps his
commandments and by so doing realizes that
he knows the love of God. Our obedience
results in his love. COMMENTARY ON 1 JOHN.[31]

LOVE FOR GOD PERFECTED. HILARY OF
ARLES: Love sustains all those who try to put
God's commandments into practice. INTRO-
DUCTORY COMMENTARY ON 1 JOHN.[32]

KEEPING GOD'S COMMANDMENTS. BEDE:
The person who really knows God is the one
who proves that he lives in his love by keeping
his commandments. Love is the sure sign that
we know God. We know that we are truly
children of God when his love in us persuades
us to pray even for our enemies, as he himself
did when he said: "Father, forgive them."[33] ON
1 JOHN.[34]

2:6 Abiding in Christ

THE SAME WAY IN WHICH HE WALKED.
LEO THE GREAT: Our hope of eternal life is in
him. He is the pattern of our patience. Otherwise we are using the likeness of a false profession if we do not follow the commands of him
in whose name we glory. And these would not
be burdensome to us and would free us from
all dangers, if we would love only what he

commands us to love. SERMONS 90.2.[35]

DWELLING IN GOD. HILARY OF ARLES:
There are three ways that we dwell in God—
by faith, by hope and by love. God dwells in us
by patience and humility. INTRODUCTORY
COMMENTARY ON 1 JOHN.[36]

FOLLOW CHRIST'S FOOTSTEPS. BEDE: Let us
follow Christ's footsteps with the entire effort
of our minds. And so that we may deserve to
come to the gate of his heavenly kingdom, let
us seriously consider entering it by that
course of action by which he proceeded when
he was spending his life on earth. HOMILIES
ON THE GOSPELS 2.11.[37]

2:7 The Commandment You Had from the Beginning

THE WORD YOU HAVE HEARD. CLEMENT OF
ALEXANDRIA: You had the commandment
through the law and the prophets. ADUMBRA-
TIONS.[38]

NO NEW COMMANDMENT. DIDYMUS THE
BLIND: Some people were apparently object-
ing that the Evangelist's teaching was a new
thing, and so he had to insist that this was not
so. COMMENTARY ON 1 JOHN.[39]

THE COMMAND. CYRIL OF ALEXANDRIA:
John is talking here about love. The commandment was not new, because long before
that time it had been proclaimed by the
prophets. CATENA.[40]

---

[29]PL 79:1101. [30]CEC 111. [31]PG 39:1780. [32]PL Supp. 3:119.
[33]Lk 23:34. [34]PL 93:90. [35]FC 93:380. [36]PL Supp. 3:119. [37]HOG
2:105. [38]FGNK 3:90. [39]PG 39:1781. [40]CEC 112.

FROM THE BEGINNING. ANDREAS: Someone may ask how it was possible for the hearers of this letter to have known the commandment from the beginning, since they were not Jews (as appears from the end of the letter, where they are told to keep themselves from idols). But is there not a commandment which is old, which has existed from the beginning and which all people everywhere have heard? For everybody, even domestic animals, naturally loves those who are close to them. CATENA.[41]

BOTH OLD AND NEW. BEDE: God's commandment to love was old because it had been around since the beginning of time, but it was also new, because once the darkness was taken away, it poured the desire for new light into our hearts. ON 1 JOHN.[42]

2:8 The Darkness Is Passing

THE DARKNESS OF PERVERSION. CLEMENT OF ALEXANDRIA: The darkness is the darkness of perversion, and the light is the light of faith, working in us according to God's foreordained plan. ADUMBRATIONS.[43]

A NEW COMMANDMENT. HILARY OF ARLES: The commandment is true *in him* because he loved us so much that he died for us, and it will be true *in us* also if we love one another. INTRODUCTORY COMMENTARY ON 1 JOHN.[44]

THE TRUE LIGHT. ANDREAS: The new dimension to the commandment is that now the light has come into the world, our Lord Jesus, because of whom the power of the devil has passed away. CATENA.[45]

THE NEW NATURE. BEDE: The commandment is new in the sense that the old man

lived in darkness, whereas the light belongs to the new man. The apostle Paul said the same thing when he wrote: "Put off your old nature . . . and be renewed in the Spirit."[46] ON 1 JOHN.[47]

LOVING ENEMIES. OECUMENIUS: The commandment is new in that it is no longer restricted to Israel as it was under the law of Moses. Under that law it was normal to love one's friends and to hate one's enemies, as Jesus himself testified.[48] But he then turned that around by saying that we should love our enemies and do good to those who hate us, concentrating on the fact that these people are human beings like ourselves and not worrying about how they feel toward us. COMMENTARY ON 1 JOHN.[49]

NEW IN WHAT SENSE? ISHO'DAD OF MERV: By "commandment" John means the revelation of the dispensation. It cannot be called new with respect to God, but from the human point of view it was a mystery hidden in the Creator from the beginning. COMMENTARIES.[50]

2:9 Saying One Is in the Light

LIVING IN THE LIGHT. CLEMENT OF ALEXANDRIA: The light is the truth, and a brother is not just our neighbor but the Lord [Jesus] as well. ADUMBRATIONS.[51]

LOCKED IN DARKNESS. CAESARIUS OF ARLES: Perhaps you think that such darkness

---

[41]CEC 112. [42]PL 93:90. [43]FGNK 3:90. [44]PL Supp. 3:119. [45]CEC 112-13. [46]Eph 4:22-23. [47]PL 93:90. [48]Mt 5:43. [49]PG 119:636. [50]CIM 40. [51]FGNK 3:90.

is like that which people suffer when they are locked in prison. If only it were as easy as that! SERMONS 185.2.[52]

ONE WHO HATES. HILARY OF ARLES: The person who hates is in darkness until he repents or until he discovers love. INTRODUCTORY COMMENTARY ON 1 JOHN.[53]

HATE AND LOVE. ANDREAS: How can someone say that he belongs to Christ and at the same time hate his brother for whom Christ died? Or if someone says he belongs to God and yet hates Christ, who has become our brother by becoming a man, he is not of God but of the devil. For if he were of God, he would love the brother who had been sent to him and anointed by grace. CATENA.[54]

LIVING IN DARKNESS STILL. BEDE: The Lord told us to love our enemies, so if someone claims to be a Christian and hates his brother, he is still dead in his sins. It is good that John added the word *still* here, because everyone is born in the darkness of sin and remains there until he is enlightened through Christ by the grace of baptism. But the person who comes to the font or to the Lord's Supper with hatred towards his brother is still in the darkness, even if he thinks that he has been enlightened by God, nor can he get rid of the shadows of sin unless he begins to love. ON 1 JOHN.[55]

2:10 Brotherly Love

NO CAUSE FOR STUMBLING. HILARY OF ARLES: Someone who loves his brothers is in no danger of stumbling. INTRODUCTORY COMMENTARY ON 1 JOHN.[56]

ONE WHO LOVES HIS BROTHER. BEDE: The person who loves his brother puts up with everything for the sake of unity. Such an attitude keeps us from hurting anyone unduly. ON 1 JOHN.[57]

LOVING THOSE OF THE SAME NATURE AS YOURSELF. THEOPHYLACT: Even the Gentiles have always accepted the law or command which appears to derive from nature, that we should do good to those who are of the same nature as we are. The reason for this is that man is a rational and social animal who cannot exist without mutual love. Ancient tales even relate that there were many people who were prepared to sacrifice themselves on behalf of others, and the Savior himself calls this the highest form of love: "Greater love has no man than this, that a man should lay down his life for his friends."[58] COMMENTARY ON 1 JOHN.[59]

2:11 Walking in Darkness

EXTINGUISHING LOVE. ORIGEN: Whoever does evil and hates his brother has extinguished the lamp of love, and therefore he walks in darkness. SERMONS ON LEVITICUS 13.2.4.[60]

WALKING IN DARKNESS. CAESARIUS OF ARLES: If a man hates his brother, he walks in darkness and does not know where he is going. In his ignorance he goes down to hell, and in his blindness he is thrown headlong into punishment, because he withdraws from the light of Christ. SERMONS 90.6.[61]

---

[52]FC 47:485. [53]PL Supp. 3:119. [54]CEC 113. [55]PL 93:91. [56]PL Supp. 3:119. [57]PL 93:91. [58]Jn 15:13. [59]PG 126:21-24. [60]FC 83:235. [61]FC 47:47.

Losing Sight of Love. Hilary of Arles: The person who loses sight of love will not know which way to turn when it comes to doing good works. Introductory Commentary on 1 John.[62]

Blinded by Darkness. Andreas: Those who hate Christ do not realize that they have become the inheritors of eternal fire. This is what the devil makes them suffer, because he has blinded their inner vision. Catena.[63]

Turning from the Light. Bede: The person who has turned away from the light of Christ goes ignorantly into hell, blind and unaware of the punishment which awaits him. On 1 John.[64]

2:12 Your Sins Are Forgiven for His Sake

Little Children. Clement of Alexandria: "Little children" means those whose sins have been forgiven. Adumbrations.[65]

Born Again. Bede: John calls all those who have come after him in the faith of Christ his children, because they have been born again of water and the Spirit and have received the forgiveness of their sins. On 1 John.[66]

In Need of Instruction. Oecumenius: John knew that not everyone would receive the gospel message with the same understanding or commitment. Some would respond like children in need of further instruction, and to them he expounds the forgiveness of sins through faith in Christ. Commentary on 1 John.[67]

2:13 Fathers and Young People

You Have Overcome the Evil One. Clement of Alexandria: By "fathers" John means those perfect people who understood everything from the very beginning and readily perceived that the Son had always existed. Adumbrations.[68]

Maturity and Immaturity in Faith. Andreas: The different ages here are to be understood in spiritual terms; they refer to our maturity in faith. First you must become a child and be weaned off evil. It is in this state that you must put off the weight of your old sins. Once you have done this, you can progress to the status of adolescents, when you must struggle against evil. Finally you will be deemed worthy of the deep knowledge of God which characterizes parents. This is the best and truest order of growth toward acceptance by the Father. Catena.[69]

Humble in Spirit. Bede: John calls those who are humble in spirit children. The more they humble themselves under the powerful hand of God, the more they will discover of the hidden things of his sublime eternity, as the Lord said: "You have hidden these things from the wise and understanding, and revealed them to babes."[70] On 1 John.[71]

2:14 Young Men, You Are Strong

The Word Abides in You. Origen: In my opinion, if someone is a child inside, then he will appear to be a child on the outside as well,

---

[62]PL Supp. 3:119. [63]CEC 113. [64]PL 93:91. [65]FGNK 3:90. [66]PL 93:91. [67]PG 119:636-37. [68]FGNK 3:90. [69]CEC 114. [70]Lk 10:21. [71]PL 93:92.

however old he is. The same is true of someone who is an overgrown teenager. But it also follows from this that anyone can be an adult and parent on the inside, whatever age they may be. CATENA.[72]

YOU HAVE OVERCOME. CLEMENT OF ALEXANDRIA: By strong "young men" John means those who have overcome their lusts. ADUMBRATIONS.[73]

THE MODEL OF COURAGE. CYRIL OF ALEXANDRIA: The young men are a model of courage, the elders are a model of understanding, and the sons and daughters are a model of what it means to be children in Christ. CATENA.[74]

YOU KNOW HIM WHO IS FROM THE BEGINNING. BEDE: Remember that you are fathers, says John. If you forget him who is from the beginning, then you will lose that status. Never forget that you are still young men, which means that you must go on fighting until you win the battle and receive the crown of victory. Be humble, so as not to be killed in battle. ON 1 JOHN.[75]

2:15 Do Not Love the World

FRIENDSHIP WITH GOD. DIDYMUS THE BLIND: Since the nature of friendship with God is such that if anyone loves this world he is an enemy of God, it follows that if someone wants to be a friend of God and dwell in God's love, he must turn away from love of the world and the things which are in the world. COMMENTARY ON 1 JOHN.[76]

THE VANITY OF THE WORLD. CYRIL OF ALEXANDRIA: What is there in the world but vanity, which is of no use to anybody? The distractions of the present life are unnecessary and pointless, as is the excessive abundance of worldly passions. CATENA.[77]

THE THINGS OF THE WORLD. EUCHERIUS: Do not love the world or the things in it, says the apostle, for all these things flatter our gaze with their deceptive show. Let the power of the eyes be focused on the light, not given over to error, and since that power is available for the enjoyment of life, let it not receive what causes death. EXHORTATION TO HIS KINSMAN VALERIAN.[78]

THE DESIRES OF THE WORLD. SEVERUS OF ANTIOCH: John means the lusts and desires of the world, which are ruled by the devil. CATENA.[79]

LOVING THAT WHICH VANISHES. HILARY OF ARLES: A wise father warns his children not to love things which quickly vanish away. This wisdom is the crowning glory of the supreme Maker of all things, and it is well-suited to everyone who is righteous. INTRODUCTORY COMMENTARY ON 1 JOHN.[80]

AT WAR WITHIN THE SOUL. ANDREAS: Lest anyone think that he has completely broken with the system of this world, John here reminds us that something of it remains inside us and that we are attracted by it because of the desires of our flesh, which are at war with our soul. From this it may be seen that the visible world is no longer loved by those who have risen above it, who no longer contemplate

---

[72]CEC 115. [73]FGNK 3:90. [74]CEC 115. [75]PL 93:92. [76]PG 39:1782. [77]CEC 116. [78]MFC 17:192-93. [79]CEC 116. [80]PL Supp. 3:120.

temporal things but gaze on eternity instead. Catena.[81]

Use the World As Needed. Bede: John addresses these remarks to everyone indiscriminately, whether they are fathers, mature in their faith, whether they are just humble children or whether they are young people who are busily engaged in fighting spiritual battles. Whatever their situation, they must all learn to use the world when they have to but not to love it inordinately. On 1 John.[82]

Flee the World. Symeon the New Theologian: Let us flee the world. For what have we got in common with it? Let us run and pursue until we have laid hold of something which is permanent and does not pass away, for all things perish and pass away like a dream, and nothing is lasting or certain among the things which are seen. Discourses 2.14.[83]

2:16 The Lust of the Flesh

Vehement Lust. Augustine: The stronger and more vehement the lust which is not from the Father but from the world, the more each one becomes willing to accept all annoyances and griefs in pursuing the object of his desires. On Patience 17.[84]

Enslaved to Bodily Desires. Augustine: This love of the world, which contains in itself the universal lust of the world, is the general kind of fornication by which one sins against one's own body, in that the human mind is unceasingly enslaved to all bodily and visible desires and pleasures, left marooned and abandoned by the very Creator of all things. Sermons 162.4.[85]

The Pride of Life. Hilary of Arles: The lust of the flesh is what pertains to our physical appetites, whereas the lust of the eye and the pride of life are what pertains to the vices of the soul, such as inordinate self-love, which does not come from the Father but from the devil. Introductory Commentary on 1 John.[86]

Corruption Fades Away. Andreas: None of the vain pleasures of corruption will last. They are temporal and will fade away and in fact are flimsier than any cobweb. Catena.[87]

Every Wickedness Described. Bede: Those who love the world have nothing but the lust of the flesh, the lust of the eyes and the pride of life. These few words describe every kind of wickedness which exists. On 1 John.[88]

2:17 Time and Eternity

Abiding Forever. Andreas: In discussing with the Jews, Christ explained: "This is the will of the Father, that you should believe in the one whom he has sent."[89] The one who keeps his commandments will gain eternal life. Catena.[90]

The World Passes Away. Bede: The world will pass away on the day of judgment when it will be transformed by fire into something better, for then there will be a new heaven and a new earth. The lust of the world will also disappear, because there will be no place for it in

---

[81]CEC 116. [82]PL 93:92. [83]CWS 57. [84]FC 16:252. [85]WSA 3/5:149. [86]PL Supp. 3:120. [87]CEC 117. [88]PL 93:92. [89]Jn 6:39. [90]CEC 117.

the new creation. But the person who does God's will does not have to worry about this because the things which he desires are heavenly and eternal, so that they do not and cannot change, whatever happens to the world. ON 1 JOHN.[91]

CLINGING TO PERISHABLE THINGS. OECU-MENIUS: Wise people do not go on despising the gospel and clinging to the perishable things of this world, for that is just like trying to build a house on sand. COMMENTARY ON 1 JOHN.[92]

[91]PL 93:93. [92]PG 119:640.

2:18-29 FIGHTING THE ANTICHRIST

[18]*Children, it is the last hour; and as you have heard that antichrist is coming, so now many antichrists have come; therefore we know that it is the last hour.* [19]*They went out from us, but they were not of us; for if they had been of us, they would have continued with us; but they went out, that it might be plain that they all are not of us.* [20]*But you have been anointed by the Holy One, and you all know.*[d] [21]*I write to you, not because you do not know the truth, but because you know it, and know that no lie is of the truth.* [22]*Who is the liar but he who denies that Jesus is the Christ? This is the antichrist, he who denies the Father and the Son.* [23]*No one who denies the Son has the Father. He who confesses the Son has the Father also.* [24]*Let what you heard from the beginning abide in you. If what you heard from the beginning abides in you, then you will abide in the Son and in the Father.* [25]*And this is what he has promised us,*[e] *eternal life.*

[26]*I write this to you about those who would deceive you;* [27]*but the anointing which you received from him abides in you, and you have no need that any one should teach you; as his anointing teaches you about everything, and is true, and is no lie, just as it has taught you, abide in him.*

[28]*And now, little children, abide in him, so that when he appears we may have confidence and not shrink from him in shame at his coming.* [29]*If you know that he is righteous, you may be sure that every one who does right is born of him.*

d *Other ancient authorities read* you know everything e *Other ancient authorities read* you

OVERVIEW: We are now living in the last times, which are characterized by the coming of the antichrist. Here John uses this word in the plural, as well as in the singular, and it is clear that he has heretics primarily in view. Antichrists are people who once belonged to the church in formal terms but who never shared its spirit and who eventually went off to proclaim their own beliefs. The most common of these was that Jesus was not the Messiah come from God to save us from our sins. The Fathers recognized that this denial of Christian orthodoxy could come in many forms, ranging from Judaism to the heresies of the fourth and fifth centuries, but the precise details were secondary. It was only to be expected that heretics would have confused and contradictory beliefs. All that mattered is that whatever they were, they were a departure from the faith once delivered by the apostles.

As the lamb is sacrificed in the evening, the Lord will return at the end of time (JEROME, ANDREAS). Then the world will reach the limits of what evil can do (OECUMENIUS). Blasphemies of those who have once been Christian (DIDYMUS) will precede his coming (ANDREAS). Some will not persevere (AUGUSTINE). The antichrists were never really a part of us (BEDE, OECUMENIUS). Had they been truly faithful, they would have continued with us (ANDREAS). All who have withdrawn from the love and the unity of the universal church are adversaries, antichrists (CYPRIAN).

By contrast, the faithful received the sacred anointing (SEVERUS) by their baptism (ANDREAS) and by the same Holy Spirit (BEDE) who led them into all truth (OECUMENIUS). You all know the same truth because you received it in the rule of faith that you professed at your baptism (HILARY OF ARLES). Never lie (AUGUSTINE). Any lie is foreign to Christ (BEDE). To deny that Jesus is the Christ (ANDREAS) is the supreme lie (BEDE). It is a lie to say that the Christ is

merely another human being and not truly God (OECUMENIUS). No one comes to the Father except through the Son (HILARY OF ARLES, ANDREAS). Only by confessing him in heart, word and deed by the Spirit (BEDE) will you have fellowship with both the Father and the Son (ANDREAS). To have eternal life is to know the one true God, and Jesus Christ whom he has sent (THEOPHYLACT). Insofar as you have been taught by the indwelling Holy Spirit, you do not need innovative teachers. The anointing of which John speaks is the love of God itself, which has been poured into our hearts by the Holy Spirit (BEDE). Those in the church who were filled with the Holy Spirit came to know what that teaching was. They did not require further instruction about it, though they did need exhortation and encouragement to live up to it, in spite of every temptation and inducement to do otherwise. Perfect righteousness is possible for those who trust God's righteousness by faith, who have not succumbed to pride but who have remained attentive to the Word of God and accepted no lord other than the One who created them (BEDE). When the Lord appears at his second coming, the one who knows the Son and the Father will have confidence and will not shrink in shame or be confounded (CLEMENT OF ALEXANDRIA, ANDREAS, BEDE, OECUMENIUS).

2:18 Many Antichrists Have Come

ANTICHRISTS WERE ONCE CHRISTIANS. DIDYMUS THE BLIND: These things are not said of all who teach false doctrine but only of those who join a false sect after they have heard the truth. It is because they were once Christians that they are now called antichrists. COMMENTARY ON 1 JOHN.[1]

IT IS THE LAST HOUR. AUGUSTINE: Let us recall how long ago it was that John said that it is the last hour. If we had been alive then and had heard this, how could we have believed that so many years would pass after it, and would we not rather have hoped that the Lord would come while John was still present in the body? LETTERS 199.7.[2]

THE CLOSE OF THE AGES. JEROME: Why is the lamb offered up in the evening and not during the day? The reason is plain enough, for our Lord and Savior suffered his passion at the close of the ages, which is why John called it the last hour. SERMONS 91.[3]

HIS COMING ANNOUNCED. ANDREAS: The antichrist will come at the end of the world, and the heresies have already announced his coming, for they are his friends and brothers, since they both blaspheme Christ. CATENA.[4]

THE ELEVENTH HOUR. BEDE: As Jesus indicated in the parable of the vineyard, this is the last hour. The laborers who were in the vineyard from the first hour cultivated the Lord's vine, which means that by teaching and living righteous lives they served the will of their Creator. The laborers who entered at the third hour are those who came in after the time of Noah. The sixth hour was the time of Abraham. The ninth hour was the time at which the law was given. The eleventh hour is the time from the incarnation of our Lord until the end of time, which is described by divine revelation as follows. During the eleventh hour the Savior will return in the flesh, and the plague of the antichrist, who will attack the messengers of salvation, will follow. ON 1 JOHN.[5]

THE LIMITS OF WHAT EVIL CAN DO. OECUMENIUS: It is possible that John calls this the last hour because in it we have reached the limits of what evil can do. For since the coming of the Savior the world has been upset by great evils caused by the devil, either as a way of testing the good or as a way of confusing those who are better still, so that they will no longer know the difference between good and evil. Therefore he calls this the last hour, because things cannot get any worse than they are now. This interpretation is supported by what he goes on to say about the antichrist. COMMENTARY ON 1 JOHN.[6]

2:19 They Were Never Part of Us

PLAIN TO ALL. CYPRIAN: This verse makes it plain that all who are known to have withdrawn from the love and the unity of the universal church are adversaries of the Lord and antichrists. LETTERS 69.1.[7]

SOME WILL NOT PERSEVERE. AUGUSTINE: It seems to us that all who appear to be good and faithful ought to receive the gift of final perseverance. God, however, has judged it better to mingle some who will not persevere with the certain number of his saints, so that those for whom security in the temptations of this life is not helpful cannot be secure. ON THE GIFT OF PERSEVERANCE 8.19.[8]

THEY WERE NEVER REALLY WITH US. ANDREAS: John says this because there were some people who had become teachers but had subsequently departed from the truth in

---

[1]PG 39:1783. [2]FC 30:369. [3]FC 57:237. [4]CEC 117. [5]PL 93:94. [6]PG 119:641. [7]LCC 5:150. [8]FC 86:285.

order to follow the blasphemies of their own minds. But even if they were once among us, John adds, they were never really part of us, since if they had been, they would have stayed with us. CATENA.[9]

THE BENEFIT OF REMOVING A TUMOR.
BEDE: John says that the antichrists have gone out from us but then adds the comforting words that they were never really with us beforehand. In fact, he is saying that no one except an antichrist would even leave us, for those who are not against Christ will cling to his body. In the body of Christ there are those who are still being healed and who will not be fully well again until the resurrection of the dead. But there are also others who are malignant tumors, and when they are removed the body is spared. Thus it is that the departure of such people is of great benefit to the church. ON 1 JOHN.[10]

THEY WENT OUT FROM US.
OECUMENIUS: Some people will ask where the antichrists have come from, and the sad answer is that they have come from our midst. That way they can pretend to have all the credibility of true disciples and stand a better chance of seducing the unwary. They became disciples themselves at first but then departed from the truth and invented their own blasphemies to replace it. COMMENTARY ON 1 JOHN.[11]

2:20 Anointed by the Holy One

YOU HAVE BEEN ANOINTED.
SEVERUS OF ANTIOCH: All have been anointed, not only the prophets and holy men who lived in their days but also and especially all those who later believed in the great and only true anointed

one (Christ), our God and Savior, along with those who continue to believe in him. For in the divine washing of regeneration and baptism when we are symbolically anointed with myrrh, we receive his inheritance by the Holy Spirit and his rich gifts, by which we know that we are heirs of God and fellow heirs with Christ. CATENA.[12]

ANOINTED AT BAPTISM.
ANDREAS: This is what each of us has received at baptism. CATENA.[13]

SPIRITUAL ANOINTING.
BEDE: The spiritual anointing is the Holy Spirit himself, who is given in the sacrament of anointing. John says that they all have this anointing and can distinguish good people from evil ones, so that he has no need to teach them what they already know because of their anointing. Because he is talking about heretics in this passage, he points out that they have received their anointing from the Holy One in order to underline the fact that the heretics and all antichrists are deprived of that gift and do not belong to the Lord but rather are servants of Satan. ON 1 JOHN.[14]

YOU ALL KNOW.
OECUMENIUS: They had all received the sacred anointing by their baptism and by the same Holy Spirit who led them into all truth. Because of this John was not writing to the ignorant but to people who knew what he was talking about. COMMENTARY ON 1 JOHN.[15]

2:21 No Lie Is of the Truth

---

[9]CEC 118. [10]PL 93:94. [11]PG 119:641. [12]CEC 119. [13]CEC 119. [14]PL 93:94-95. [15]PG 119:644.

We Ought Not to Lie. Augustine:
Therefore it is not true that sometimes we
ought to lie. What is not true we should never
try to persuade anyone to believe. Against
Lying 18 (37).[16]

You Know the Truth. Hilary of Arles:
You all know the truth because you received it
in the rule of faith which you professed at
your baptism. Introductory Commentary
on 1 John.[17]

Lies Foreign to Christ. Bede: You know
the truth of faith and life because you have
been anointed by the Spirit, and you have no
need to be taught anything other than that
you should continue along the path you have
already embarked upon. . . . We have been
warned how to recognize the antichrist, for
Christ said: "I am the truth."[18] Therefore
every lie is foreign to Christ, and those who
tell lies do not belong to him. On 1 John.[19]

2:22 Denying Christ Is Lying

Denying That Jesus Is the Christ.
Andreas: This was the heresy of Simon,
which said that Jesus and the Christ were two
different people. According to them, Jesus was
a man, the son of Mary, but Christ descended
from heaven in the form of a dove at the Jordan. John therefore condemns those who
think like that and brands their belief with the
name of the devil. There were still others who
made a distinction between the Father and
some nameless deity beyond him, whom they
called the Father of Christ. These too denied
Jesus, saying that he was a mere man and did
not have the nature of God. Catena.[20]

The Supreme Lie. Bede: John has already

said that every lie is a departure from the
truth, but as there are many different kinds of
lies, here he is more specific. Denial of Christ
is the supreme lie, a lie so great that it is hard
to think of anything which can be compared
with it. It is a lie which is evident among the
Jews, of course, but the heretics, who do not
believe in Christ in the right way, are guilty of
it as well. It is also the case that orthodox people who do not follow Christ's commands are
guilty of denying that Jesus is the Christ, not
because they refuse to give Christ the love and
devotion which is his due as the Son of God
but because they treat him as if he were a man
of no account and are not afraid to contradict
what he says. On 1 John.[21]

Denying the Father and the Son. Oecumenius: In addition to the Simonians there
were other heretics who followed Valentinus,
who said that there was another being who
was called the "father" apart from the Father
of Christ. They also denied the Son, claiming
that he was just a human being and did not
possess the nature of God. Commentary on
1 John.[22]

2:23 The Son Is the Way to the Father

Through the Son. Hilary of Arles: You
cannot know the Father if you deny the Son,
because no one comes to the Father except
through him.[23] Introductory Commentary
on 1 John.[24]

**No One Who Denies the Son Has the
Father.** Andreas: There were other heretics

---

[16]FC 16:174. [17]PL Supp. 3:121. [18]Jn 14:6. [19]PL 93:95. [20]CEC 119. [21]PL 93:95. [22]PG 119:645. [23]Jn 14:6. [24]PL Supp. 3:121.

who denied the Son but claimed to know the Father. In fact of course they did not know the Father either, because if they had known him they would have known that he is the Father of the only-begotten Son. These people were similar to the Jews, who say that they know the Father but do not accept the Son. They are also like the Simonians, who share the same ungodly confusion. CATENA.[25]

CONFESSION BY HEART, WORD AND DEED. BEDE: John is looking for a confession of faith which involves the heart, as well as confessing in both word and deed. He is saying the same thing as the apostle Paul when he wrote: "No one can say that Jesus is Lord, except by the Holy Spirit,"[26] which means that unless the Holy Spirit gives us the power to do so, we cannot serve Christ with perfect faith and action. ON 1 JOHN.[27]

2:24 What You Heard from the Beginning

YOU WILL ABIDE. ANDREAS: Rejecting ungodliness, John goes on to teach the doctrine of godliness and to encourage his listeners to accept it, saying that by it they will have fellowship with both the Father and the Son, as well as the promise of eternal life. CATENA.[28]

FROM THE BEGINNING. BEDE: Follow with all your heart that faith and that teaching which you have received from the apostles at the beginning of the church, for only this will make you partakers of divine grace. ON 1 JOHN.[29]

FELLOWSHIP WITH GOD. OECUMENIUS: This means that if you do these things you will have fellowship with God. COMMENTARY ON 1 JOHN.[30]

2:25 The Promise of Eternal Life

WHAT HE PROMISED US. HILARY OF ARLES: Christ's promise is that we shall receive a hundred times over in this life,[31] and eternal life in the next. INTRODUCTORY COMMENTARY ON 1 JOHN.[32]

WHY FOLLOW CHRIST? BEDE: John adds this as if to answer those who want to know what point there is in following Christ. What are we going to get out of it? The answer is that we have been promised eternal life. ON 1 JOHN.[33]

ETERNAL LIFE. THEOPHYLACT: What is eternal life? It is that we should know the one true God and Jesus Christ whom he has sent.[34] COMMENTARY ON 1 JOHN.[35]

2:26 Those Who Would Deceive You

A WARNING AGAINST HERESIES. HILARY OF ARLES: People want to deceive us in order to teach you some heresy or other. John has written in order to warn us about this. INTRODUCTORY COMMENTARY ON 1 JOHN.[36]

THE DECEIVERS. BEDE: The deceivers about whom John is writing are not only the heretics who try to turn us away by their false doctrine but all those who divert weak minds from the promise of eternal life, either by charming them with the lusts of the flesh or by threatening them with the world's disapproval. ON 1 JOHN.[37]

---

[25]CEC 119. [26]1 Cor 12:3. [27]PL 93:96. [28]CEC 120. [29]PL 93:96. [30]PG 119:645. [31]Mt 19:29. [32]PL Supp. 3:121. [33]PL 93:96. [34]Jn 17:3. [35]PG 126:32. [36]PL Supp. 3:121. [37]PL 93:96.

2:27 Your Anointing Teaches You Everything

AWAITING IN FAITH. AUGUSTINE: All who await him in faith will rejoice when he comes. Those who are without faith will be ashamed when what they do not now see has indeed come. TEN HOMILIES ON 1 JOHN 4.2.[38]

THE OIL UNMIXED. ANDREAS: Do not mix anything earthly with the oil of anointing with which you have been anointed, and the devil will not get hold of you. CATENA.[39]

HIS ANOINTING TEACHES YOU. BEDE: Since you have been taught by the indwelling presence of the Holy Spirit, you do not need contrary teachers to teach you. The anointing of which John speaks may be understood as the love of God itself, which has been poured into our hearts by the Holy Spirit, who has been given to us.[40] ON 1 JOHN.[41]

2:28 Confidence When Christ Returns

WHEN HE APPEARS. CLEMENT OF ALEXANDRIA: When the Lord appears at his second coming, the one who knows the Son and the Father according to knowledge will have confidence and will not be confounded, for confusion is a great punishment. ADUMBRATIONS.[42]

THE HOLY SPIRIT AS TEACHER. ANDREAS: Having the Holy Spirit as your teacher of godly knowledge, do not go after deceiving spirits, but think in the way that he has taught you, so that at his appearing in glory we may stand with confidence before him. CATENA.[43]

NOT SHRINKING FROM HIM IN SHAME. BEDE: Those who stand firm against the per-secutions of unbelievers and the ridicule which comes from worldly people around them will have complete confidence when Christ comes again, because they know that the patience of the poor will not perish at the end. But anyone who is ashamed to stand up for Christ in this life or to do anything else which the Lord commands, or who in time of persecution is afraid to be known as a believer, will have no confidence at all when Christ returns, because he has not stuck to his profession of faith in this life. ON 1 JOHN.[44]

CONFIDENCE WHEN CHRIST APPEARS. OECUMENIUS: Why does John tell us to remain in Christ? So that we may have confidence in him when he appears. For what could be better or more desirable than to have confidence with which to show Christ the works we have done in this life and to do this with full assurance, not being ashamed of anything? COMMENTARY ON 1 JOHN.[45]

2:29 Everyone Who Does Right Is Born of Christ

BORN BY FAITH. CLEMENT OF ALEXANDRIA: To be born of him means to be born again by faith. ADUMBRATIONS.[46]

YOU MAY BE SURE. BEDE: Our righteousness is based exclusively on faith. Perfect righteousness exists only in the angels, and not even in them if they are compared to God. Nevertheless, to the extent that the righteousness of angels and the saints whom God created can be perfect, perfect righteousness is

---

[38]LCC 8:287. [39]CEC 120. [40]Rom 5:5. [41]PL 93:96. [42]FGNK 3:91. [43]CEC 120. [44]PL 93:97. [45]PG 119:648. [46]FGNK 3:91.

also possible for the righteous and the good, who have not fallen away or succumbed to pride but who have remained faithful and attentive to the Word of God and accepted no lord other than the One who created them. On 1 John.[47]

The One Who Is Righteous. Oecumenius: It is obvious that the One who is righteous produces offspring who are also righteous. Commentary on 1 John.[48]

[47]PL 93:97. [48]PG 119:648.

3:1-24 BEING CHILDREN OF GOD

[1]See what love the Father has given us, that we should be called children of God; and so we are. The reason why the world does not know us is that it did not know him. [2]Beloved, we are God's children now; it does not yet appear what we shall be, but we know that when he appears we shall be like him, for we shall see him as he is. [3]And every one who thus hopes in him purifies himself as he is pure.

[4]Every one who commits sin is guilty of lawlessness; sin is lawlessness. [5]You know that he appeared to take away sins, and in him there is no sin. [6]No one who abides in him sins; no one who sins has either seen him or known him. [7]Little children, let no one deceive you. He who does right is righteous, as he is righteous. [8]He who commits sin is of the devil; for the devil has sinned from the beginning. The reason the Son of God appeared was to destroy the works of the devil. [9]No one born of God commits sin; for God's[f] nature abides in him, and he cannot sin because he is[g] born of God. [10]By this it may be seen who are the children of God, and who are the children of the devil: whoever does not do right is not of God, nor he who does not love his brother.

[11]For this is the message which you have heard from the beginning, that we should love one another, [12]and not be like Cain who was of the evil one and murdered his brother. And why did he murder him? Because his own deeds were evil and his brother's righteous. [13]Do not wonder, brethren, that the world hates you. [14]We know that we have passed out of death into life, because we love the brethren. He who does not love abides in death. [15]Any one who hates his brother is a murderer, and you know that no murderer has eternal life abiding in him. [16]By this we know love, that he laid down his life for us; and we ought to lay down our lives for the brethren. [17]But if any one has the world's goods and sees his brother in need, yet closes his heart against him, how does God's love abide in him? [18]Little children, let us not

love in word or speech but in deed and in truth.

¹⁹*By this we shall know that we are of the truth, and reassure our hearts before him* ²⁰*whenever our hearts condemn us; for God is greater than our hearts, and he knows everything.* ²¹*Beloved, if our hearts do not condemn us, we have confidence before God;* ²²*and we receive from him whatever we ask, because we keep his commandments and do what pleases him.* ²³*And this is his commandment, that we should believe in the name of his Son Jesus Christ and love one another, just as he has commanded us.* ²⁴*All who keep his commandments abide in him, and he in them. And by this we know that he abides in us, by the Spirit which he has given us.*

f *Greek his*　g *Or for the offspring of God abide in him, and they cannot sin because they are*

OVERVIEW: Christians are God's children, not yet fully mature but born again to a new hope that the unconverted world cannot understand. The basic demand placed on us is that we must live up to this new birth by purifying ourselves of evil and by doing all we can to avoid falling into sin. The grace of our Creator is so great that he has allowed us both to know him and to love him, and moreover, to love him as children love a father (BEDE, ANDREAS, OECUMENIUS). The faithful are now made ready to be loved as children of God, even in this world (SEVERUS), where now knowing in part, we have received the first fruits of the Spirit. Already having received the adoption of heirs, we can see what the fullness of eternal sonship will be like when it comes eternally (DIDYMUS). We are already blessed in God while remaining unlike him in our limitations and creatureliness (AUGUSTINE, BEDE, MAXIMUS THE CONFESSOR). We are commanded to imitate the purity of God's holiness to the extent that we are capable of doing so, just as we are taught to hope for the glory of the divine likeness (ANDREAS) according to our capacity for receiving it (BEDE, THEOPHYLACT). One who remains steadily in Christ, who is our righteousness and sanctification, does not choose to sin (DIDYMUS, HILARY OF ARLES, BEDE). The difference between God's righteousness and ours is the difference between beholding the face of a person and its image in a mirror (BEDE).

As often as we sin, we are born of the devil (ANDREAS). The Bible does not say that whoever is born of God is sinless but that such a person will not sin as long as he or she walks according to the way of righteousness (DIDYMUS). Committing sin and making room for the devil amount to the same thing (CHRYSOSTOM). To sin is to accept the lordship of the devil, whom the Son of God has come to destroy. Sin is not inherent in the human race, since if it were it could not have been eradicated by a sinless human being (DIDYMUS, BEDE). By faith we are born again in principle, but God still has to work on us in order to refashion us according to his likeness (MAXIMUS THE CONFESSOR). Insofar as persons who are born of God retain the grace of their new birth, they cannot sin in the way they behave (SEVERUS). The teaching or seed of God remains in the faithful (ANDREAS, ISHO'DAD, BEDE).

The ultimate test of whether we are God's children or not can be seen in the way that we love one another. The love in us that is increasing and being perfected also belongs to the new birth from God, but it continues to fight against the law of our mind (AUGUSTINE). Love is the great divide between the children of God and the children of the devil. Those who have love are children of God, and those who do not are children of the devil (BEDE, CYRIL OF JERUSALEM). One who is born of God will love the brothers, whereas one who does not have this new birth will not do so (DIDYMUS, ANDREAS). Whoever loves the brothers in God's way has passed from death to life (BEDE, ANDREAS), but whoever does not have this love remains in death (DIDYMUS). *Brother* is a generic term applying to women also (AUGUSTINE, CAESARIUS OF ARLES).

The prototype of the rebel against God's love is Cain, who murdered his own brother. Anyone who harbors hatred in his heart is regarded by God already as a murderer because of his intent (BEDE). True love is not seen in murder but in self-sacrifice, both of our lives and of our possessions. To hate another one is to kill oneself (AUGUSTINE). One who hates a brother will envy even that person's righteous works (BEDE). By the world, John is not referring to the heavens or the earth or to anything that God has made but to the lovers of the world (AUGUSTINE, BEDE). Be ready to lay down your life for others, as Christ laid down his life for you (TERTULLIAN, AUGUSTINE, BEDE). Do not close your heart against your brother in need (CYPRIAN, CHRYSOSTOM). If you are not yet ready to die for your brother, at least you should be ready to share some of your resources with him (AUGUSTINE, BEDE). It is not enough to have good words or intentions (BEDE). You must also put them into effect with genuine willingness and a happy heart

(CHRYSOSTOM, HILARY OF ARLES).

If we do this, we shall have no reason to fear any pangs of conscience, because we shall have confidence before God that we are walking in the way he has laid out for us. When we love our neighbors in deed and in truth, we find our hearts reassured in the light of the supreme truth (BEDE, OECUMENIUS). If we practice what we preach, our hearts and consciences will be persuaded that we are on the right track (BEDE, OECUMENIUS, AUGUSTINE, CYRIL OF ALEXANDRIA). If we are to get what we ask for from God, we have to obey his commands (GREGORY THE GREAT, THEOPHYLACT). If our hearts do not condemn us, then we have confidence toward God, who is greater than our hearts (BEDE). It is impossible to love one another in the right way if we do not have faith in Christ, just as it is impossible to believe in the name of Christ if we do not love one another (BEDE, THEOPHYLACT).

3:1 See What Love the Father Has Given Us

THE WORLD. CLEMENT OF ALEXANDRIA: The "world" means those who live in pleasure. ADUMBRATIONS.[1]

THE INHERITANCE GIVEN US. ANDREAS: God shows us the necessary patience because of the inheritance which he has given us. Here the "world" refers to wicked people. CATENA.[2]

AS CHILDREN LOVE A FATHER. BEDE: The grace of our Creator is so great that he has allowed us both to know him and to love him,

---

[1]FGNK 3:91. [2]CEC 121.

and moreover, to love him as children love a wonderful father. It would be no small thing if we were able to love God in the way that a servant loves his master or a worker his employer. But loving God as father is much greater still. ON 1 JOHN.[3]

CHILDREN OF GOD. OECUMENIUS: John is telling us that we know from all that has been said above that we have been taken up by God as his children. Even if that is not immediately apparent, we should not be disturbed, for it will be fully revealed when he comes again. COMMENTARY ON 1 JOHN.[4]

3:2 We Shall Be Like God

GOD'S CHILDREN NOW. DIDYMUS THE BLIND: By writing these things John is exhorting his readers to recognize what it means to be born again of God. He tells them that they are now worthy to be loved as children of God, even in this world, and that the adoption of sons is a reality here and now. For since we now know in part and have the first fruits of the Spirit, we already have something of the adoption of sons and can see what the fullness of it will be like when it arrives. COMMENTARY ON 1 JOHN.[5]

WE SHALL BE LIKE HIM. AUGUSTINE: Despite the measure of likeness which we find in God's Word, we also recognize a great unlikeness to God and his Word in this enigma. We must admit that even when we are like him and shall see him as he is (words which clearly imply an awareness of our present unlikeness), we shall still have no natural equality with him. For the created nature must always be less than the Creator. ON THE TRINITY 15.16.26.[6]

WE SHALL SEE HIM AS HE IS. SEVERUS OF ANTIOCH: Therefore we live as children of God even in this present life, sanctifying ourselves by virtue and striving toward the likeness of something even better. Encouraged by this, we shall be fashioned according to the brightness of the resurrection, when we shall see him, insofar as that is possible, as he is. CATENA.[7]

IT DOES NOT YET APPEAR WHAT WE SHALL BE. BEDE: The believer in Christ has already died to his old life and has been born again by faith, but it is not yet clear what the full extent of that new life will be. However, we do at least know that we shall be immortal and unchanging, because we shall enjoy the contemplation of God's eternity. Because we shall be blessed we shall be like Christ, yet at the same time we shall be unlike him because he is our Creator and we are only creatures. It seems that this verse applies most obviously to our resurrection body, which will be immortal. In that case we shall be like God after the likeness of his Son, who alone among the persons of the Trinity took a human body in which he died and rose again and which he then took with him into heaven. We shall see God as he is, but this does not mean that we shall fully understand him. For it is one thing to see and another thing to see in such a way as to understand everything. ON 1 JOHN.[8]

JOHN DOES NOT CONTRADICT PAUL. MAXIMUS THE CONFESSOR: Is there any connection between what John says here and what Paul says when he writes: "God has revealed it

---

[3]PL 93:98. [4]PG 119:648. [5]PG 39:1785. [6]LCC 8:156. [7]CEC 121. [8]PL 93:98-99.

to us by his Spirit. For the Spirit searches everything, even the deep things of God"?[9] What then shall we be like? The answer is that here John says that he does not know what form the coming deification through the virtues of faith will take for those who are children of God here on earth now. The independently existing nature of the good things to come has not yet been revealed in detail. Here on earth we walk by faith, not by sight. Paul on the other hand says that through revelation we have received the divine promise concerning the good things which are to come but does not claim to know what these are in any detail. Thus he says quite clearly that he examines himself and pursues the higher calling as far as he understands what it is.[10] Any contradiction between the two apostles is merely apparent, not real, because they are both inspired by the same Spirit. CATENA.[11]

3:3 Purify Yourselves as God Is Pure

FAITH PAST AND PRESENT. HILARY OF ARLES: We shall see him as he is because we shall be like him. This is our hope for the future, our love in the present and our faith in both the past and the present. INTRODUCTORY COMMENTARY ON 1 JOHN.[12]

THE IMAGE AND LIKENESS OF GOD IN HUMANITY. ANDREAS: Some people argue from this that God made man according to his image but not according to his likeness, which he will give us later on. We have supposedly believed in him according to the likeness which we have, and if that is worthy enough, then we shall receive God's likeness as well. But if you have believed according to the likeness and then turn away from it and destroy it, who will give you what belongs to the like-

ness? You will not be able to acquire the likeness unless you have fully perfected the image first. This is supposed to be why John adds the words: "Everyone who thus hopes in him purifies himself, as he is pure." But my bishop, in his letter to Conon, has shown on the basis of the recognized Fathers of the church that the image and the likeness are one and the same thing and that John was speaking here of something which has already taken place. CATENA.[13]

IMITATING GOD'S PURITY. BEDE: There are many who say they have faith in Christ but somehow seem to forget about this pure aspect of it. It is clear that anyone who has real faith will demonstrate that fact by living a life of good works . . . by rejecting ungodliness and worldly desires and by imitating Christ's sober, righteous and godly life. We are commanded to imitate the purity of God's holiness to the extent that we are capable of doing so, just as we are taught to hope for the glory of the divine likeness according to our capacity for receiving it. INTRODUCTORY COMMENTARY ON 1 JOHN.[14]

PURIFY YOURSELVES. THEOPHYLACT: Note that John uses the present tense when he talks about our need to purify ourselves. The practice of virtue is an ongoing thing and has its own inner dynamic. If we stop living this way or put it off until some future time, there is nothing virtuous about that at all. COMMENTARY ON 1 JOHN.[15]

3:4 Sin Is Lawlessness

---

[9]1 Cor 2:10. [10]Cf. Phil 3:14. [11]CEC 121-22. [12]PL Supp. 3:122. [13]CEC 122-23. [14]PL 93:99. [15]PG 126:33.

Everyone Who Commits Sin. Hilary of
Arles: John says that sin and iniquity are the
same thing, though there were heretics who
denied this. According to some of them, iniquity was a crime deliberately committed, but
sin was a fact of nature and therefore not a
crime. Introductory Commentary on
1 John.[16]

Sin Is Lawlessness. Bede: Let no one say
that sin is one thing and wickedness another.
Let no one claim to be a sinner but not
wicked. Sin and wickedness are the same
thing. Actually, the true meaning of this verse
is clearer when we look at the Greek, because
the word which in Latin is rendered "wickedness" (iniquitas) in Greek is "lawlessness" (ano-
mia). So what John really means is that sin is
lawlessness. On 1 John.[17]

Clinging to Evil. Oecumenius: John's
message is that those of us who have been
adopted into Christ must do the works of
righteousness and not show ourselves to be
lazy in that respect. However, the person who
has sinned or will sin is not called wicked or a
sinner merely on that account. What John is
talking about here is the person who clings to
evil and becomes a worker of evil on an ongoing basis. Commentary on 1 John.[18]

Sin Is Against Nature. Theophylact:
Sin is a falling away from what is good,
whereas iniquity is transgression of the law.
The first is a rejection of good as a general
principle, the second is a particular violation
of a law. The sinner therefore is someone who
goes against nature, and it is the nature of
human beings to live rationally. Sin is therefore something which must be regarded as
absurd. Commentary on 1 John.[19]

3:5 In Christ There Is No Sin

No Sin in Christ. Hilary of Arles: There
is no sin in Christ because he was not conceived in sin as we are. Introductory Commentary on 1 John.[20]

He Takes Away the Sins of the World.
Bede: John the Baptist testified of Jesus that
he was the Lamb of God who takes away the
sins of the world.[21] He could do this because
there was no sin in him. There are many great
people in the world who are respected as if
they were perfect, but none of them could
take away the sins of the world because none
of them could live in the world entirely free of
sin. For there is no one who can take away sin
apart from the One who has no sin at all himself. On 1 John.[22]

No Excuse to Sin. Oecumenius: Since
Christ, in whom there was no sin, came to
take away your sins, now you have no excuse
to go on sinning. Commentary on 1 John.[23]

3:6 Sinners Have Not Known Christ

One Who Sins Is Outside Christ. Didymus the Blind: Just as the person who dwells
in virtue and true doctrine does not sin and is
not ignorant, so the one who remains in
Christ, who is his righteousness and sanctification, does not sin. For how can someone act
unrighteously when he is in the company of
righteousness, and how can he be content to
place corruption alongside holiness? Therefore anyone who sins is outside Christ and has

---

[16]PL Supp. 3:122. [17]PL 93:100. [18]PG 119:649. [19]PG 126:36.
[20]PL Supp. 3:122. [21]Jn 1:29. [22]PL 93:100. [23]PG 119:649.

no part or fellowship in him. COMMENTARY ON 1 JOHN.[24]

SINNERS DO NOT SEE CHRIST. HILARY OF ARLES: Sinners have not seen Christ with the eye of faith, nor have they known him by putting that faith into practice in the right way. INTRODUCTORY COMMENTARY ON 1 JOHN.[25]

NO ONE WHO ABIDES IN HIM SINS. ANDREAS: How can someone sin if he is not cut off from God in any way? CATENA.[26]

NO ONE WHO SINS HAS SEEN HIM OR KNOWN HIM. BEDE: We cannot sin to the extent that we remain in Christ. John is speaking here about the vision and knowledge by which the righteous are able to enjoy God in this life, until they come to that perfect vision of him which will be revealed to them at the end of time. ON 1 JOHN.[27]

3:7 Do Right and Be Righteous

LET NO ONE DECEIVE YOU. HILARY OF ARLES: Let no one deceive you by saying that there is nothing wrong with sin. The devil has sinned all along because there is no truth in him. He is the ultimate deceiver. INTRODUCTORY COMMENTARY ON 1 JOHN.[28]

FACE AND MIRROR IMAGE. BEDE: It goes without saying that we can never be righteous in the same full way that God is righteous. The difference between God's righteousness and ours is the difference between the face of a man and its image in a mirror. There is a certain resemblance, but the two substances are completely different. The comparison is not at all the same as the vague resemblance between the Father and the Son, because they share a

common substance. ON 1 JOHN.[29]

RIGHTEOUS OR WICKED. OECUMENIUS: Do not be confused about this. The person who does what is right is righteous, and the person who does what is wrong is wicked. It is as simple as that. COMMENTARY ON 1 JOHN.[30]

3:8 To Destroy the Works of the Devil

ONE WHO COMMITS SIN. ORIGEN: Insofar as we commit sins, we have not yet put off the generation of the devil, even if we are thought to believe in Jesus. Everyone who is not of the devil does not commit sin. COMMENTARY ON JOHN 20.103-4.[31]

THE DEVIL HAS SINNED FROM THE BEGINNING. DIDYMUS THE BLIND: Since the devil was first and foremost sent into the world in order to lead people astray, that is where his name comes from.[32] Thus anyone who sins can be called a devil. Sin is not inherent in the human race, since if it were it could not have been eradicated by a sinless human being. But this is exactly what happened when the Son of God appeared in human flesh, and so sin must be regarded as accidental to human nature, not as intrinsic to human nature. COMMENTARY ON 1 JOHN.[33]

FIRST TO SIN. CHRYSOSTOM: Because the devil was the first to be locked into sin, everyone who now sins acts according to his bidding. For the devil rules in the sinner by a mass of evil thoughts, as in the case of Judas.

---

[24]PG 39:1788. [25]PL Supp. 3:122. [26]CEC 123. [27]PL 93:100. [28]PL Supp. 3:122. [29]PL 93:101. [30]PG 119:648. [31]FC 89:228. [32]The Greek word *diabolos* means "seducer" or "accuser." [33]PG 39:1789-90.

Someone might say that the devil is present in sinners even before they sin because they have made room for him. The answer to this is that committing sin and making room for the devil amount to one and the same thing—sin. CATENA.[34]

AS OFTEN AS WE SIN. ANDREAS: As often as we sin, we are born of the devil. But we are of God once again, as often as we pursue virtue. CATENA.[35]

WE WERE NOT CREATED DEMONIC. BEDE: We do not resemble the devil because of the way we were created, as the Manichaeans blasphemously assert, but because we have followed him into his sinful ways. . . . John describes the devil's sinfulness in the present tense, because he is just the same now as he was in the beginning, when he first fell into sin. This verse also implies that the devil was created before anything else. There is no reason to doubt that the angels were made before any of the other creatures or that the one who was the highest among them became proud and rebelled against his Maker. It was by pride that he sinned from the beginning and was transformed from being an archangel into being a devil. ON 1 JOHN.[36]

3:9 No One Born of God Commits Sin

RECEIVING BAD SEED. ORIGEN: When we are persuaded by the devil to sin, we receive his seed. But when we go on to complete the work which he urged, then he has begotten us, for through sin we are born to him as children. SERMONS ON EXODUS 8.6.[37]

BORN OF GOD. DIDYMUS THE BLIND: Heretics,[38] who are deceived in everything by everything, like to object that any birth which is produced by the creator of this world is automatically sinful, whereas any birth which comes from the God of the New Testament is not so. They base this idea on the supposition that sinners and the righteous must have different creators, but this notion is based on a misunderstanding of the teaching of Scripture. The Bible does not say that whoever is born of God is sinless but that such a person will not sin as long as he walks according to the way of righteousness. If he turns aside from that he will sin, and indeed those who do sin have turned away from their Creator. The ability not to sin is guaranteed by the presence of God's seed in us. This seed is either his power or the spirit of adoption, which cannot sin. COMMENTARY ON 1 JOHN.[39]

LUST EXTINGUISHED IN THE NEXT LIFE. AUGUSTINE: If our circumstances are such that we make some progress in this life by the grace of the Savior, when lust declines and love increases, it is in the next life that we reach perfection, when lust is finally extinguished and love is made perfect. That saying, that whoever is born of God does not sin, is undoubtedly meant to apply to that pure love which alone does not sin. The love in us which is increasing and being perfected also belongs to the new birth from God, but as long as lust continues to exist in us it fights against the law of our mind. As a result, the one who is born of God and who does not obey his own lusts can say that it is no longer he who sins but the sin which dwells in him.[40] LETTERS 177.[41]

---

[34]CEC 123-24. [35]CEC 123. [36]PL 93:101. [37]FC 71:329. [38]Such as the Manichaens. [39]PG 39:1791. [40]Rom 7:20 [41]FC 30:107.

Sin Is Undone by Love. Augustine: How can we avoid sin? By keeping the commandment of Christ. And what is that commandment? It is that we should love. Love, and sin is undone. Ten Homilies on 1 John 5.2.[42]

Retaining Grace. Severus of Antioch: John did not say this with respect to the existence of sin in our lives, as if our nature were covered with impassibility. Rather he means that insofar as someone who is born of God retains the grace of his new birth he cannot sin in the way he behaves. And the reason for this is that God's seed dwells in him. What is this seed of God which dwells in believers? What else but the indwelling of the Holy Spirit, by which we have been born again? This presence never leaves us. Catena.[43]

Two Meanings of "Born of God." Maximus the Confessor: If someone who is born of God does not sin, how is it that we who have been born of water and the Spirit, and thus of God, do in fact commit sins? The answer is that the phrase "born of God" has two different meanings. According to the first of these, God has given the grace of sonship with all power to those who have been born again. According to the second, the God who has thus given birth is working in us to bring us to perfection. By faith we are born again in principle, but God still has to get to work on us in order to refashion us according to his likeness. Catena.[44]

The Seed Dwells in Believers. Andreas: The divine seed is Christ, who dwells in believers and makes them become sons of God. Likewise, when it is said that in Abraham's seed all the nations will be blessed, this too is a reference to Christ. John says that the Spirit is the seed which we receive through the blessing of our mind. For he dwells in us, making the mind of sin no longer welcome. Catena.[45]

Having God's Nature in Us. Bede: This does not mean that there is no sin in us at all, since John has already said that that is not the case. Rather what he is saying here is that if we have God's nature, that is, his Word, in us we shall not go against the law of love. On 1 John.[46]

The Seed of God Remains. Isho'dad of Merv: The person who has once denied Satan and confessed God, and who has been born again and discarded all the oldness of Adam, is not guilty of sin, because he is the seed of God. The teaching of God remains in him, for he calls this teaching "seed." Commentaries.[47]

3:10 Children of God and Children of the Devil

By This It May Be Seen. Didymus the Blind: Since a person who walks in righteousness is born of God, it follows that someone who is so born will love his brothers. Someone who lacks righteousness because he does not practice it, but instead hates his brother, is not born of God. Commentary on 1 John.[48]

Children of the Devil. Cyril of Jerusalem: The chief author of sin is the devil, the

---

[42]FC 92:187. [43]CEC 124. [44]CEC 125. [45]CEC 126. [46]PL 93:102. [47]CIM 40-41. [48]PG 39:1792.

begetter of all sin. Before him, no one sinned. Nor did he sin because he was by nature prone to sin (since in that case the responsibility for his sin would lie with his Creator). Rather, being created good he became a devil by his own free choice, receiving that name from his willed action. Though he was originally an archangel, he became a slanderer (*diabolos*), because of his slandering. CATECHETICAL LECTURES 2.4.[49]

NOT OF GOD. ANDREAS: Love is the mark of sinlessness, and hate is the mark of sin. Since the person who walks in righteousness is born of God, it follows that someone who is so born will love the brothers, whereas someone who does not have this new birth will not do so. Rather he who hates his brother is not of God. CATENA.[50]

ONE WHO DOES NOT LOVE A BROTHER. BEDE: Love is the great divide between the children of God and the children of the devil. Those who have love are children of God, and those who do not are children of the devil. Have anything else you like, but if you lack this one thing, then all the rest is of no use to you whatsoever. On the other hand, you may lack almost anything else, but if you have this one thing, you have fulfilled the law. ON 1 JOHN.[51]

3:11 The Message You Have Heard

LOVE DEMONSTRATED. GREGORY THE GREAT: Our love must always be demonstrated both in respectful speech and in generous service to others. LESSONS IN JOB 21.29.[52]

LOVE ONE ANOTHER. BEDE: John is just repeating what Jesus said: "This is my com-

mandment, that you love one another as I have loved you."[53] ON 1 JOHN.[54]

3:12 Cain's Wickedness

NOT LIKE CAIN. DIDYMUS THE BLIND: We have had the commandment to love one another from the beginning, so that we should not fall into evil as Cain did, who murdered his brother. COMMENTARY ON 1 JOHN.[55]

HE MURDERED HIS BROTHER. ANDREAS: Cain became unrighteous and turned into the very first person who killed a member of his family, thereby teaching human nature the way of murder. CATENA.[56]

OF THE EVIL ONE. BEDE: John explains in what way Cain was of the evil one. Wherever there is jealousy, brotherly love is impossible. Rather the sin of the evil one, that is, the devil, is in that man's heart, because the devil also rejected man because of his envy. The works of righteous Abel are works of love, whereas the works of Cain amount to hatred for his brother. It is only to be expected that someone who hates his brother will envy his works. ON 1 JOHN.[57]

3:13 The World Hates You

LEAVING THE DARKENED HOUSE OF DEATH. ORIGEN: If we have passed from death to life by passing from unbelief to faith, let us not be surprised if the world hates us. For no one who has failed to pass from death to life, but has remained in death, can love those who

---

[49]FC 61:98. [50]CEC 127. [51]PL 93:102. [52]PL 79:1103. [53]Jn 15:12. [54]PL 93:102. [55]PG 39:1792. [56]CEC 127. [57]PL 93:102.

have left the darkened house of death. Exhortation to Martyrdom 41.[58]

Do Not Wonder. Didymus the Blind: It is not to be wondered at if evil people, who are here called the "world," hate those who live godly lives according to the commands of Christ. It would be much more surprising if such people loved us instead! Commentary on 1 John.[59]

The World Distinguished from Creation. Augustine: How often do you have to be told what the world is? John is not referring to the heavens or the earth or to anything which God has made but to the lovers of the world. Ten Homilies on 1 John 5.9.[60]

Those Who Love the World. Bede: By "world" John means those who love the world. It is hardly surprising that those who love the world will be incapable of loving a brother who has separated himself from the world and whose only concern is to acquire heavenly things. Religion is an abomination to the sinner, as Scripture testifies. On 1 John.[61]

3:14 We Have Passed from Death into Life

Because We Love. Didymus the Blind: Whoever loves his brothers in God's way has passed from death to life, but whoever does not have this love remains in death. In the same way the widow who enjoyed herself was dead, even if technically she was alive.[62] For anyone who lives like that has obviously forgotten God. Commentary on 1 John.[63]

Passed from Death to Life. Andreas: God says: "He who hears my words and does

them will not see death but will be changed from death into life."[64] Catena.[65]

Haters Should Not Approach the Holy Mysteries. Bede: Let no one who is preparing death traps for the members of Christ, no one who is still abiding in death, presume to approach the holy mysteries[66] of life, as if prepared to receive them. Homilies on the Gospels 2.4.[67]

We Have Passed Out of Death. Bede: By death, John means the death of the soul, for the soul which sins will surely die. The soul is the life of the flesh, but the life of the soul is God. Therefore when the body dies, the soul leaves it, but when the soul dies, it is God who abandons it. Thus we can say that all of us who are born into this world are dead in soul, since we have inherited original sin from Adam, but the grace of Christ works in believers by giving a new life, so that our souls may live once again. On 1 John.[68]

3:15 No Murderer Has Eternal Life

Eternal Life Abiding. Clement of Alexandria: Christ lives in a believing mind. Adumbrations.[69]

Brother a Generic Term. Augustine: Whoever hates his brother is a murderer. But this text of Scripture does not apply to males only; it is equally valid for females. Any woman who has injured someone else must make amends as quickly as possible, and the

---

[58]CWS 72. [59]PG 39:1793. [60]FC 92:194. [61]PL 93:102. [62]Cf. 1 Tim 5:6. [63]PG 93:1793. [64]See Jn 8:51. [65]CEC 128. [66]Sacraments. [67]HOG 2:34. [68]PL 93:102. [69]FGNK 3:91.

injured sister must forgive without reserve. Letters 211.[70]

Killing Yourself with Hatred. Augustine: Whoever hates is a murderer. You may not have prepared any poison or committed a crime. You have only hated, and in doing so, you have killed yourself first of all. Sermons 49.7.[71]

All Christians Are Brothers. Caesarius of Arles: In this passage, every person should be regarded as a brother, for we are all brothers in Christ. Sermons 219.2.[72]

Already as a Murderer. Bede: If someone has failed to take fraternal hatred seriously, will he not also disregard murder in his heart? His hand does not move to kill anyone, but he is already regarded by God as a murderer. The victim is alive, but the slayer has already been judged a murderer. On 1 John.[73]

3:16 *Laying Down One's Life for Others*

Be Ready to Lay Down Your Life. Tertullian: John tells us that we must be ready to lay down our lives for our friends. If that is true, how much more should we be ready to lay them down for Christ? On Flight in Time of Persecution 9.3.[74]

Readiness to Die for Christ. Augustine: We have been given the privilege of being able to lay down our lives for our brothers. But are you prepared to die for Christ? Tractates on the Gospel of John 47.11.[75]

He Laid Down His Life for Us. Bede: Christ has taught us by the example of his own passion what kind of love we ought to have in

us. "For greater love has no man than this, than a man should lay down his life for his friends."[76] On 1 John.[77]

3:17 *Closing One's Heart to Another in Need*

To the Least of These. Cyprian: If alms given to the least are given to Christ, there is no reason for anyone to prefer earthly things to heavenly ones or to place human things before divine ones. Works and Almsgiving 16.[78]

Closing One's Heart. Chrysostom: When you see someone in need, do not run away, but think to yourself, if that were you, would you want to be treated like that? Catena.[79]

Be Ready at Least to Give Goods. Augustine: If you are not yet able to die for your brother, at least show him your ability to give him of your goods. Let love be stirring your inmost heart to do it, not for display but out of the very marrow of compassion, thinking only of the brother and his need. Ten Homilies on 1 John 5.12.[80]

Have Sympathy for Another's Plight. Bede: Look where charity begins. If you are not yet ready to die for your brother, at least you should be ready to share some of your wealth with him. For if you are not prepared to show sympathy for your brother's plight, then the love of the Father, who has given

---

[70]FC 32:49. [71]WSA 3/2:338. [72]FC 66:130. [73]PL 93:103. [74]FC 40:293. [75]FC 88:223. [76]Jn 15:13. [77]PL 93:103. [78]FC 36:242. [79]CEC 128. [80]LCC 8:301.

birth to both of you, is not in you. ON
1 JOHN.[81]

3:18 Love in Deed and in Truth

PUT LOVE INTO PRACTICE. CHRYSOSTOM: It
is not enough to have good intentions. You
must also put them into effect with genuine
willingness and a happy heart. CATENA.[82]

LOVE IS ACTIVE. HILARY OF ARLES: Actions
speak louder than words. INTRODUCTORY
COMMENTARY ON 1 JOHN.[83]

OFFERING BASIC NECESSITIES. BEDE: If a
brother or sister has nothing and cannot even
find enough to eat, we ought to give them the
basic necessities of life. Likewise if we notice
that they are deficient in spiritual things, we
ought to guide them in whatever way we can.
Of course we must be sincere in doing this,
not looking for praise from other people, not
boasting, and not pointing out that others
who are richer than we are have not done
nearly as much. For someone who thinks like
that is full of wickedness, and the gift of truth
does not dwell in him, even if it appears on the
surface that he is showing love to others. ON 1
JOHN.[84]

3:19 Knowing That We Are of the Truth

BY THIS WE SHALL KNOW. OECUMENIUS:
We know that we belong to the truth if we
love in deed as well as in word. Anyone who
says one thing but does another is a liar and a
stranger to the truth. COMMENTARY ON
1 JOHN.[85]

WE REASSURE OUR HEARTS BEFORE GOD.
BEDE: When we do the works of godliness, it
becomes apparent that we are of the truth
which is God, because we are copying his perfect love to the best of our ability. When we
love our neighbors in deed and in truth, we
see clearly that we are reassuring our hearts in
the light of the supreme truth. For whenever
we want to do something, we think it over
long enough to persuade ourselves to do it.
Those who want to do something wicked also
want to hide it from God as much as they can,
but those who want to do good have no hesitation about reassuring themselves that they
want to do this good in the sight of God. ON
1 JOHN.[86]

3:20 God Is Greater Than Our Hearts

GOD KNOWS EVERYTHING. CLEMENT OF
ALEXANDRIA: This means that God's power is
greater than the conscience which belongs to
the soul, because God's love knows everything.
ADUMBRATIONS.[87]

PERSUADING OUR HEARTS. OECUMENIUS: If
we practice what we preach, we shall persuade
our hearts, that is to say, our consciences, that
we are on the right track. For then God will
bear witness that we have listened to what he
says. COMMENTARY ON 1 JOHN.[88]

WHENEVER OUR HEARTS CONDEMN US.
BEDE: If our conscience accuses us inside because it does not see the good works which we
ought to be doing, how can we set aside the
knowledge of him to whom is sung: "Even the
darkness is not dark to you . . . for darkness is
as light with you."[89] ON 1 JOHN.[90]

---

[81]PL 93:103. [82]CEC 128. [83]PL Supp. 3:123. [84]PL 93:103-4.
[85]PG 119:657. [86]PL 93:104. [87]FGNK 3:92. [88]PG 119:657.
[89]Ps 139:12. [90]PL 93:104.

3:21 We Have Confidence Before God

If Our Hearts Do Not Condemn Us.
Augustine: Our conscience gives us a true
answer, that we love and that genuine love is
in us, not feigned but sincere, seeking our
brother's salvation and expecting nothing
from him except his salvation. Ten Homilies on 1 John 6.4.[91]

**Attend to the Warnings of Con-
science.** Cyril of Alexandria: As long as
you are in this life (for this life is nothing
other than the way which we all take), do not
ignore or reject the warnings of your conscience. For if you do so, when you have run
your course, your conscience will rise up
against you and accuse you before your judge,
and thrust you in front of the judge's sentence
and turn you over to eternal punishment. You
will not have to endure this if along the way
you show yourself kind toward this adversary
and accept his well-intended rebukes with
gratitude. Catena.[92]

We Can Have Confidence. Bede: If the
truth is that we love, and love is second nature
to us, not feigned but sincere, seeking the welfare of others and asking for nothing in return
except the salvation of a brother, we have
confidence. If, in other words, our heart does
not condemn us, then we have confidence
toward God, not in the sight of other people
but where God alone can see it—in our
hearts. On 1 John.[93]

3:22 Ask and You Will Receive

Because We Keep His Commandments.
Gregory the Great: It must be understood
that if we are to get what we ask for from God

we have to obey his commands. The two things
go indissolubly together. Lessons in Job
28.9.[94]

Listen to the Divine Promise. Bede:
This is a great promise to believers, and one
which is highly desirable. For if someone is so
stupid and absurd that he does not rejoice in
the heavenly promises, he ought to listen to
what wisdom says: "If one turns away from
hearing the law, even his prayer is an abomination."[95] On 1 John.[96]

Whatever We Ask. Theophylact: If we
obey God's commands, then our obedience will
bear fruit, for we shall receive whatever we ask
for. Commentary on 1 John.[97]

3:23 Love One Another

This Is His Commandment. Bede: Note
that here John gives us only one commandment, though he goes on in the next verse to
speak about commandments in the plural, adding love to faith, since these can hardly be separated from each other. For in truth it is
impossible to love one another in the right way
if we do not have faith in Christ, just as it is
impossible to believe in the name of Christ if
we do not love one another. On 1 John.[98]

Believe in the Name of the Son. Theophylact: The first point to be made here is
that we must love one another according to the
faith which we have in the name of Jesus
Christ, for it is by this that we know that the
grace of the Holy Spirit given to us will be

---

[91]FC 92:202. [92]CEC 129. [93]PL 93:104. [94]PL 79:1104. [95]Prov
28:9. [96]PL 93:104. [97]PG 126:41. [98]PL 93:105.

firmly planted in us. The second thing to notice is the use of the word *name*, which is quite frequent in Scripture. It includes the will, the glory and the honor of the one who bears it, and his will is that everyone everywhere should be baptized in the name of the Father, and of the Son and of the Holy Spirit.[99] COMMENTARY ON 1 JOHN.[100]

3:24 God Abides in Us by His Spirit

GOD'S CARE. CLEMENT OF ALEXANDRIA: Our assurance comes from his care for us and his provision for the future. ADUMBRATIONS.[101]

ABIDE IN HIM. BEDE: Let God become a home to you, and he will dwell in you. Remain in him, and he will remain in you. God remains in you in order to hold you up. You remain in God in order not to fall. . . . In earlier times the Holy Spirit fell on believers, and they spoke in tongues which they had not learned. But nowadays the church has no lack of external signs, and anyone who believes in the name of Jesus Christ can have brotherly love, which John holds out to us as the sign that the Holy Spirit is dwelling in us. For the Spirit works in us to give us love. ON 1 JOHN.[102]

DO UNTO OTHERS. OECUMENIUS: What does John mean by this? It is exactly what Jesus said: "Whatever you want others to do to you, do the same to them."[103] Therefore if we want our neighbors to be well-disposed toward us, we must be equally well-disposed toward them. If this is God's command, how much more ought we to obey it if we dwell in him and are sealed by him? He cannot deny himself, and it must surely be the case that whatever he has asked us to do he has already done or become in himself. Therefore if we do what he says, we know that he will give us whatever we ask and that his gift will be sealed in us. COMMENTARY ON 1 JOHN.[104]

---

[99]Mt 28:19. [100]PG 126:44. [101]FGNK 3:92. [102]PL 93:105. [103]Mt 7:12. [104]PG 119:660.

4:1-21 PERFECT LOVE

[1]*Beloved, do not believe every spirit, but test the spirits to see whether they are of God; for many false prophets have gone out into the world.* [2]*By this you know the Spirit of God: every spirit which confesses that Jesus Christ has come in the flesh is of God,* [3]*and every spirit which does not confess Jesus is not of God. This is the spirit of antichrist, of which you heard that it was coming, and now it is in the world already.* [4]*Little children, you are of God, and have overcome them; for he who is in you is greater than he who is in the world.*

⁵They are of the world, therefore what they say is of the world, and the world listens to them. ⁶We are of God. Whoever knows God listens to us, and he who is not of God does not listen to us. By this we know the spirit of truth and the spirit of error.

⁷Beloved, let us love one another; for love is of God, and he who loves is born of God and knows God. ⁸He who does not love does not know God; for God is love. ⁹In this the love of God was made manifest among us, that God sent his only Son into the world, so that we might live through him. ¹⁰In this is love, not that we loved God but that he loved us and sent his Son to be the expiation for our sins. ¹¹Beloved, if God so loved us, we also ought to love one another. ¹²No man has ever seen God; if we love one another, God abides in us and his love is perfected in us.

¹³By this we know that we abide in him and he in us, because he has given us of his own Spirit. ¹⁴And we have seen and testify that the Father has sent his Son as the Savior of the world. ¹⁵Whoever confesses that Jesus is the Son of God, God abides in him, and he in God. ¹⁶So we know and believe the love God has for us. God is love, and he who abides in love abides in God, and God abides in him. ¹⁷In this is love perfected with us, that we may have confidence for the day of judgment, because as he is so are we in this world. ¹⁸There is no fear in love, but perfect love casts out fear. For fear has to do with punishment, and he who fears is not perfected in love. ¹⁹We love, because he first loved us. ²⁰If any one says, "I love God," and hates his brother, he is a liar; for he who does not love his brother whom he has seen, cannotʰ love God whom he has not seen. ²¹And this commandment we have from him, that he who loves God should love his brother also.

ʰ Other ancient authorities read how can he

OVERVIEW: There are many spirits in the world, but only the Spirit that confesses that the Son of God was incarnate in Jesus Christ is to be believed. Christians must not be afraid of those who deny this, because the Spirit in us has already overcome all denials. Instead, we should concentrate on loving one another, because it is by that love that we shall know God's presence at work in us and refute the arguments of our opponents. Since false prophets abound (BEDE), it is essential to have that gift of the Holy Spirit that is called the discernment of spirits in order to have the ability to test the spirits thoroughly (JOHN CASSIAN). By this we will see which ones are to be believed and which ones are to be rejected (DIDYMUS). Any one who comes from God (OECUMENIUS) will confess through his or her behavior (BEDE) that Jesus Christ, although in the form of God, took upon himself the form of a servant and came in the flesh (DIDYMUS). The denial of this is evidence of antichrist (POLYCARP, AUGUSTINE, ANDREAS). If anyone dissolves the divine-human unity of Christ and thinks that the pure Word of God cannot really be a man, that person is not from God (DIDYMUS, OECUMENIUS).

The antichrist will be a man who bears

Satan inside him and who exalts himself above everything that is called God (THEOPHYLACT). God's power to save is always much greater than the devil's power to do us harm (HILARY OF ARLES). We have already overcome the demonic by believing (BEDE) in the triune God (ANDREAS). False prophets make believers sad (THEOPHYLACT). Those who teach only what the world wants to hear will always find followers in it (AUGUSTINE, THEOPHYLACT, ANDREAS). The world listens to them, but they are unable to win spiritually minded hearts away from the simplicity of faith (BEDE). The carnal person does not hear (DIDYMUS) or accept the things that are of the Spirit of God, for they are foolishness to him (BEDE).

Each of us is loved and is called to love (ANDREAS) as God loves us (DIDYMUS, AUGUSTINE). God is love (BEDE). Love is so much the gift of God that it is called God (CHRYSOSTOM, AUGUSTINE). We breathe the air of resurrection when we love (ISAAC THE SYRIAN). One who does not love does not know God (BEDE). Christ proved his love for us by dying for us (OECUMENIUS, BEDE). When we were not yet able to seek him because of our many sins, he sent his Son to us to be the expiation of our sins (JOHN CASSIAN), so that he might grant forgiveness to all who believe in him and call us back into the fellowship of his fatherly glory (BEDE). The love we show to one another ought to be like the love that God has shown to us (OECUMENIUS, BEDE). No one has ever seen the invisible God (DIDYMUS, ANDREAS) because no one has ever comprehended the fullness of the divinity that dwells in him (AUGUSTINE, BEDE). Examine your own heart and you will know whether or not God has given his Spirit to you. If you are full of love, you have the Spirit of God (BEDE, OECU-

MENIUS). To confess the one Lord Jesus Christ is to confess him as God and man, not as a man only (DIDYMUS, BEDE). The Trinity is revealed in the relation of the Lover, the Beloved and Love (AUGUSTINE). One who has love has God (CYPRIAN, BASIL), for God is love (AUGUSTINE, PSEUDO-DIONYSIUS). If love is God, there can be no progress or regress; love is said to make progress in you only inasmuch as you progress in love (AUGUSTINE), imitating God (HILARY OF ARLES, ANDREAS), and so have confidence in the last day (BEDE). If God dwells in us, we dwell in him and shall have no reason to be afraid when the day of judgment comes. God's love is perfect, and it takes away all fear. If you do not want to have any fear, first of all see whether you have that perfect love that turns fear out of the door (AUGUSTINE, LEO, BEDE). The perfect expression of the faithful person is love (CLEMENT OF ALEXANDRIA).

We love God for no other reason than that he first loved us (AUGUSTINE) and gave himself for us (BEDE), understanding us exactly (ANDREAS). This is why the incarnation and the atonement of Christ are so central, since without them we would not know what God's love is like. The heart's eye must be continually strengthened by love, in order to see that changeless being in whose presence the lover may always delight (AUGUSTINE).

4:1 *Test the Spirits*

MANY FALSE PROPHETS. DIDYMUS THE BLIND: Just as in ancient Israel there were some prophets who spoke the word of God and others who did not, so also, as soon as the apostles appeared, speaking in Christ and having the Holy Spirit whom the Lord had given to them, many false apostles were sent by the devil to counterfeit the teaching of the gospel. It is essential to have that gift of the Holy Spirit which is called the discernment of spirits in order to have the ability to test the spirits, to see which ones are to be believed and which ones are to be rejected. CATENA.[1]

DO NOT BELIEVE EVERY SPIRIT. JOHN CASSIAN: First we must scrutinize thoroughly anything that appears in our hearts, as well as anything that is said to us. Has it come purified by the divine and heavenly fire of the Holy Spirit? Or does it lean toward Jewish superstition? Is its surface piety something which has come down from bloated worldly philosophy? We must examine all this most carefully, doing as the apostle bids us. CONFERENCE 1.20.[2]

DISCERN FALSE PROPHETS. BEDE: Who is it who tests the spirits, and how they can be tested? Our Lord shows this in the Gospels, where he predicted that evil spirits of the kind of which John had experienced would come. Jesus said: "Beware of false prophets, who come to you in sheep's clothing but inwardly are ravenous wolves. You will know them by their fruits. Are grapes gathered from thorns, or figs from thistles?"[3] These therefore are the fruits by which the evil spirits who speak by false prophets can be discerned: the thorns of schisms and the terrible thistles of heresy which sting all those who go anywhere near them. ON 1 JOHN.[4]

4:2 Jesus Has Come in the Flesh

THE SPIRIT OF GOD TESTIFIES. POLYCARP OF SMYRNA: Everyone who shall not confess that Jesus Christ has come in the flesh is antichrist. Whoever shall not confess the testimony of the cross is of the devil. Whoever shall pervert the oracles of the Lord to his own lusts and say that there is neither resurrection or judgment, that man is the firstborn of Satan. So let us forsake the vanity of many and their false teachings, and turn to the word which was delivered to us from the beginning. LETTER TO THE PHILIPPIANS 7.[5]

IN THE FORM OF A SERVANT. DIDYMUS THE BLIND: A spirit which comes from God will confess that Jesus Christ, although he was in the form of God, took upon himself the form of a servant and came in the flesh. COMMENTARY ON 1 JOHN.[6]

MANICHAEAN DENIAL. AUGUSTINE: The Manichaean denies that Christ has come in the flesh. There is no need to labor the point or to persuade you any further that this error is not from God. SERMONS 183.[7]

ANTICHRIST DENIES CHRIST IN THE FLESH. ANDREAS: It is characteristic of the antichrist, who is coming into the world and has indeed already come, to deny Christ through false prophets and spirits by saying that he never came in the flesh. There are many different heretics, but on this point they all speak with the same voice. To confess that Jesus Christ has come in the flesh does not just mean that he has come in his own flesh but that he enters my flesh as well. CATENA.[8]

CONFESSION THROUGH BEHAVIOR. BEDE: It is to be understood that the word *confesses* here includes not merely the profession of an

---

[1]CEC 129-30. [2]CWS 54. [3]Mt 7:15-16. [4]PL 93:105-6. [5]AF 97. [6]PG 39:1795. [7]WSA 3/5:337. [8]CEC 130.

orthodox faith but also the practice of the good works which ought to accompany faith. If it were not so, then there would be some heretics, many schismatics and many pseudo-orthodox who would confess that Jesus Christ has come in the flesh but who would deny that confession by their behavior, for they have no love. For it was the love of God toward us which induced his Son to come in the flesh. God showed his love to us not in words but in deeds, not by talking but by loving. ON 1 JOHN.[9]

SUCH A ONE IS OF GOD. OECUMENIUS: The confession that the Lord has come is not made in words but in deeds. Paul said: "Always bearing about in the body the death of Jesus, so that the life of Jesus might also appear in our body."[10] Therefore whoever has Jesus at work inside him and is dead to the world, and who no longer lives for it but for Christ, and who carries him about in his body—this person is of God. COMMENTARY ON 1 JOHN.[11]

4:3 The Spirit of Antichrist

SPIRITS NOT OF GOD. DIDYMUS THE BLIND: If a spirit dissolves the divine-human unity of Christ and thinks that the pure Word of God is outside all flesh, and cannot really be a man, and states that everything done in his incarnation is a fantasy, then that spirit is not from God. But someone will say that there are many heretics who do accept the incarnation, the Montanists for instance. The answer to them is that just as no one says that Jesus is Lord except by the Holy Spirit, so the Montanists do not accept all the implications of incarnational belief. For those who say that Jesus is Lord but who do not follow his commandments do not have the Holy Spirit.

Although they honor him with their lips, their hearts are far from him. COMMENTARY ON 1 JOHN.[12]

EVERY SPIRIT THAT DOES NOT CONFESS JESUS. BEDE: John is talking here about people who deny the divinity of Christ or who say that he did not have a human soul or did not take on human flesh. But the person who misinterprets the commands and sayings of Jesus in a perverse way also denies him. So, too, does the person who upsets the unity of the church, which Jesus came to gather to himself. . . . The antichrist will come on the eve of the day of judgment. He will be a man born in the world but much more wicked than others, in fact the very son of iniquity. He is already in the world, dwelling in the minds of those who have rejected Christ either in word or in deed, to the point that there is no longer any hope for them. ON 1 JOHN.[13]

LACKING THE SPIRIT OF CHRIST. OECUMENIUS: Paul said, "For while there is jealousy and strife among you, are you not of the flesh, and behaving like ordinary men?"[14] Whoever walks in an ordinary human way does not have the Spirit of Christ and does not live according to his teaching, so clearly he is not of Christ. COMMENTARY ON 1 JOHN.[15]

THE SPIRIT OF ANTICHRIST. THEOPHYLACT: The antichrist will be a man who bears Satan inside him and who exalts himself above everything which is called God or which is worshiped. For that reason he

---

[9]PL 93:106. [10]2 Cor 4:10. [11]PG 119:661. [12]PG 39:1795. [13]PL 93:106. [14]1 Cor 3:3. [15]PG 119:661.

will spurn idolatry and demand that people worship him instead. COMMENTARY ON 1 JOHN.[16]

4:4 Greater Than He Who Is in the World

GOD'S POWER. HILARY OF ARLES: God's power to save is always much greater than the devil's power to do harm. INTRODUCTORY COMMENTARY ON 1 JOHN.[17]

HE WHO IS IN YOU. ANDREAS: The one who is in you is God the Father, through the Son and the Paraclete. The one in the world is Satan, for "world" here refers to evil people. CATENA.[18]

YOU HAVE OVERCOME BY BELIEVING. BEDE: By believing that Jesus Christ has come in the flesh you have already overcome the antichrist. "For greater love has no man than this, that a man should lay down his life for his friends."[19] But how could the Son of God have laid down his life for us if he had not taken on human flesh, which made it possible for him to die? Anyone who violates the law of love denies by the way he lives that Christ has come in the flesh, whatever his tongue might say, and this person is the antichrist. ON 1 JOHN.[20]

FALSE PROPHETS MAKE BELIEVERS SAD. THEOPHYLACT: You have overcome the false prophets because the God who is in you is greater than the one by whom the false prophets have chosen to live. There is another sign of false prophets, which is that they make simple believers sad. There must be many who react very badly when they see the so-called prophets being given the highest honors while they themselves are treated with disrespect by the world. COMMENTARY ON 1 JOHN.[21]

4:5 The World Listens to Its Own People

WHAT THEY SAY. AUGUSTINE: Those who speak for the world, you must observe, speak against love. TEN HOMILIES ON 1 JOHN 7.3.[22]

THEY SPEAK EVIL. ANDREAS: Who are these but the heretics and Manichaeans? For they blaspheme, speaking evil words out of their evil minds. CATENA.[23]

THE ANTICHRISTS ARE OF THE WORLD. BEDE: The antichrists are of the world, that is, they belong to those who are familiar with worldly things, who look for the lowest of the low and who turn their backs on heavenly realities. Therefore they talk like men of the world, using human reason to oppose the Christian faith, saying for example that the Son of God cannot be coeternal with the Father; that a virgin cannot give birth; that flesh cannot rise again from the dust, immortal; that a man born of the earth cannot inherit a heavenly home; that a newborn baby cannot be tainted with the guilt of original sin. . . . The world listens to them because they are unable to win spiritually minded hearts away from the simplicity of their faith and call them back to carnal desires. ON 1 JOHN.[24]

THE WORLD LISTENS. THEOPHYLACT: Those who teach what the world wants to hear will always find followers in it, for the perverted love each other. We on the other hand will never

---

[16]PG 126:45-48. [17]PL Supp. 3:123. [18]CEC 132. [19]Jn 15:13. [20]PL 93:106-7. [21]PG 126:48. [22]LCC 8:313. [23]CEC 132. [24]PL 93:107.

be accepted by them. COMMENTARY ON 1 JOHN.[25]

4:6 Whoever Knows God Listens to Us

TO HEAR TRULY IS TO DO. DIDYMUS THE BLIND: If we take the word *hear* literally, it is clear that this cannot be true, since everybody can pick up the sounds of the words. It is therefore clear that the word means something more than that—it means that we should do what we hear. If someone does not know that he is supposed to act, he has not really heard. COMMENTARY ON 1 JOHN.[26]

DISTINGUISHING TRUTH AND ERROR. BEDE: The carnal man does not accept the things which are of the Spirit of God, for they are foolishness to him. Therefore, those who do not want to listen to the preachers of love are soon recognized as not knowing God or coming from him, because they have done nothing to imitate the love which God has toward us. ON 1 JOHN.[27]

4:7 The Person Who Loves

LET US LOVE ONE ANOTHER. DIDYMUS THE BLIND: Just as the person who does not choose what he ought to choose has done wrong and does not love what he ought to love, so those who love only those who are worthy of love receive only that level of praise due to them. COMMENTARY ON 1 JOHN.[28]

BASING LIFE ON LOVE. AUGUSTINE: To practice righteousness and judgment means to live virtuously, and to live virtuously means to obey God's law, the purpose of which is to help us to base our lives on the principle of love. This is the love which comes from God,

as John says. THE CITY OF GOD 17.4.[29]

LOVE IS FROM GOD. AUGUSTINE: Love is from God, as have declared those whom he has made not only his great lovers but also his great preachers. ON THE GIFT OF PERSEVERANCE 21.56.[30]

LOVED AND CALLED TO LOVE. ANDREAS: What does it mean to say that love is from God? Surely this refers to the man who came from God, who was revealed according to the image and likeness of the one who made him? For when this man appeared, he was revealed as the beloved and as worthy of being loved. Now since this Savior has been sent into the world because of the Father's great love for the things which he has made, those who have received this blessing and who are thus beloved ought to love one another. For each of us is loved and is called to love, having the command that we should love our neighbor. CATENA.[31]

PRAISING LOVE. BEDE: John often praised love, which he said came from God, which is why we read that "he who loves is born of God." What more need be said? God is love, and therefore to go against love is to go against God. ON 1 JOHN.[32]

4:8 God Is Love

WHAT KIND OF LOVE? CHRYSOSTOM: What kind of love are we talking about here? It is the true love and not simply what people use this word to mean. It comes from our attitude and

---

[25]PG 126:48. [26]PG 39:1796-97. [27]PL 93:107. [28]PG 39:1797. [29]FC 24:31**. [30]FC 86:327. [31]CEC 132-33. [32]PL 93:107-8.

knowledge and must proceed from a pure heart. For there is also a love of evil things. Robbers love other robbers, and murderers love each other too, not out of love which comes from a good conscience but from a bad one. CATENA.[33]

THE INCREASE OF LOVE. AUGUSTINE: If God is love, it follows that the more companions and partners in the faith whom we see being born, in addition to ourselves, the more effusive will be the love in which we rejoice, since it is the possession of this love which is being set before us. SERMONS 260C.1.[34]

THE GIFT OF GOD. AUGUSTINE: Love is so much the gift of God that it is called God. LETTERS 186.[35]

OUR COMMON LOVE. AUGUSTINE: Although your course of action is different from ours, our common love has made both courses necessary for the salvation of our brother, for one God has done it all, and God is love. LETTERS 219.[36]

BREATHING THE AIR OF RESURRECTION. ISAAC THE SYRIAN: "God is love." Wherefore, the man who lives in love reaps the fruit of life from God, and while yet in this world, he even now breathes the air of the resurrection. ASCETICAL HOMILIES 46.[37]

ONE WHO DOES NOT LOVE. BEDE: Let no one say that when he sins he sins against other people but not against God, for how can you not be sinning against God when you are sinning against love? ON 1 JOHN.[38]

4:9 So That We Might Live

GOD'S LOVE MADE MANIFEST. BEDE: Christ proved his love for us by dying for us. Thus it follows that the Father's love for us is also proved in this way, because it was he who sent his Son to die for us. ON 1 JOHN.[39]

GOD SENT HIS ONLY SON. OECUMENIUS: God is love because he sent his only-begotten Son to die for us. COMMENTARY ON 1 JOHN.[40]

4:10 To Pay the Price for Our Sins

IN THIS IS LOVE. JOHN CASSIAN: The perfect love with which God first loved us will come into our hearts, for our faith tells us that this prayer of our Savior will not be in vain. CONFERENCE 10.7.[41]

NOT THAT WE LOVED GOD. BEDE: We come to God not by our own merits but by the bestowal of his grace alone, as John bears witness when he says that we did not love God but rather he loved us. HOMILIES ON THE GOSPELS 2.3.[42]

THE EXPIATION FOR OUR SINS. BEDE: This is the greatest sign of God's love for us: when we were not yet able to seek him because of our many sins, he sent his Son to us, so that he might grant forgiveness to all who believe in him and call us back into the fellowship of his fatherly glory. ON 1 JOHN.[43]

4:11 Love One Another as God Has Loved Us

IF GOD SO LOVED US. BEDE: This is pre-

---

[33]CEC 133. [34]WSA 3/7:194. [35]FC 30:196. [36]FC 32:101. [37]AHSIS 224. [38]PL 93:108. [39]PL 93:108. [40]PG 119:665. [41]CWS 129. [42]HOG 2:25. [43]PL 93:107.

cisely what the apostle Paul meant when he wrote: "Therefore be imitators of God, as beloved children. And walk in love, as Christ loved us and gave himself up for us, a fragrant offering and sacrifice to God."[44] On 1 John.[45]

We Ought to Love One Another. Oecumenius: The love we show to one another ought to be like the love which God has shown to us. I mean by that it should be sincere and pure, without ulterior motives or other hidden thoughts of the kind we normally associate with robbers and other evildoers. Commentary on 1 John.[46]

4:12 God's Love Is Perfected

God Is Invisible. Didymus the Blind: Since God is invisible, nobody has ever seen him, since bodily sight cannot see things which have no bodies. But there are some heretics who say that the Old Testament speaks of a visible God, because occasionally people are said to have seen him, whereas the New Testament makes him completely invisible. So we have to ask what substance he is supposed to have which would make him visible. They would have to answer, unless they are out of their minds, that God is a body, even though it is not made of any perceivable substance. If that is what they think, they ought to consider how incongruous and full of ungodliness their beliefs are. For how can there be a body if there is no way of defining what it is? Commentary on 1 John.[47]

If We Love One Another. Augustine: Why does John say so much about loving our brothers, but nothing at all about loving our enemies? Reaching out to our enemies does not exclude loving our brothers. Our love, like a

fire, must first take hold of what is nearest and then spread to what is further off. Ten Homilies on 1 John 8.1.[48]

God Abides in Us. Andreas: This is how God's love works. God comes to dwell in us, though no one has ever seen him. Catena.[49]

No One Has Ever Seen God Physically. Bede: This verse causes a problem when we remember that the Lord promises that those who are pure in heart will see God and tells the saints that their angels are constantly gazing at the face of God in heaven. John repeats this phrase in his Gospel, where he adds that the only-begotten Son has seen the Father and has made him known to us.[50] Our blessed father Ambrose expounded this as follows: "No one has ever seen God because no one has ever comprehended the fullness of the divinity which dwells in him, either with his mind or with his eye. For the verb *see* implies both physical and mental perception." It is therefore clear that here we are not talking about physical sight so much as about mental perception, and our minds are incapable of ever grasping the fullness of God's being. On 1 John.[51]

4:13 God Has Given Us His Own Spirit

We Know We Abide in Him. Bede: Examine your own heart and you will know whether or not God has given his Spirit to you, for if you are full of love, you have the Spirit of God. On 1 John.[52]

---

[44]Eph 5:1-2. [45]PL 93:108. [46]PG 119:665. [47]PG 39:1798-99. [48]LCC 8:320. [49]CEC 133. [50]Jn 1:18. [51]PL 93:108-9. [52]PL 93:110.

GOD'S LOVE AT WORK. OECUMENIUS: Many things which are invisible in themselves we discover by the way in which they work inside us. Just as nobody has ever seen a soul, but we know it from the way it behaves in us, so we detect God's love from the fact that it is at work and bears fruit in us. COMMENTARY ON 1 JOHN.[53]

4:14 The Father Has Sent His Son to Be Our Savior

OUR SAVIOR, OUR JUDGE. BEDE: Let no one despair of being saved. For if the diseases of wickedness which oppress us are great, there is an almighty doctor coming who can deliver us. But all of us should remember that the same Son of God who comes in meekness to save us will come again in severity to judge us. ON 1 JOHN.[54]

WE HAVE SEEN AND TESTIFY. OECUMENIUS: Therefore since we have fellowship with him in pure love, it is also by love that we who saw him in the flesh have acknowledged him and bear witness that the Father sent him to be the Savior of the world. But above and beyond our testimony he has also taught us about this, leading us thereby to a more perfect understanding of him, as when he said: "I went out from the Father and came into the world."[55] COMMENTARY ON 1 JOHN.[56]

4:15 Confessing That Christ Is His Son

CONFESSING HIS HUMANITY AND DIVINITY. DIDYMUS THE BLIND: This needs to be properly understood. God will not dwell in anyone who does not obey his commandments, however much he may confess him with his lips. Some people are confused by the various names of Jesus, because they do not interpret the Scriptures correctly. They think that because he came out of the womb of Mary according to the flesh and was given the name Jesus at that time, he is not to be identified with the eternal Son of God, who did not think it robbery to be considered equal with God. They restrict themselves to the human form which the Word of God assumed, even though the being of the Word was never changed into humanity. To confess the one Lord Jesus Christ is to confess him as God and man, not as a man only. COMMENTARY ON 1 JOHN.[57]

WHOEVER CONFESSES. BEDE: John says that the perfect confession of the heart is one which cannot be corrupted by the wicked persuasion of the heretics. It cannot be overcome by the tortures inflicted by pagans in persecution or slacken under the pressure of the example of worldly brothers or the weakness of our own frailty. ON 1 JOHN.[58]

4:16 The Person Who Abides in Love

OF ONE MIND. CYPRIAN: Those who have refused to be of one mind in the church of God cannot abide with God. ON THE UNITY OF THE CATHOLIC CHURCH 14.[59]

ONE WHO HAS LOVE. BASIL THE GREAT: If God is love, as John says, then it must be that the devil is hatred. As he who has love has God, so he who has hatred has the devil dwelling in him. ASCETICAL DISCOURSES 2.[60]

---

[53]PG 119:668. [54]PL 93:110. [55]Jn 16:28. [56]PG 119:668. [57]PG 39:1800-1801. [58]PL 93:110. [59]LCC 5:134. [60]FC 9:220.

TRINITARIAN COMMUNION. AUGUSTINE: The Holy Spirit is commonly shared in some way between the Father and the Son. But this communion is itself consubstantial and coeternal. If it can appropriately be described as friendship, let it be so called—but it is better to call it love. It is a substance, because God is a substance, and God is love. ON THE TRINITY 6.5.7.[61]

THE LOVER, THE BELOVED AND LOVE. AUGUSTINE: When we come to the subject of love, which is what God is called in Scripture, the Trinity begins to dawn a little, for there is the Lover, the Beloved and Love. ON THE TRINITY 15.10.[62]

GOD AS LOVE AND BELOVED. PSEUDO-DIONYSIUS: Why is it that theologians sometimes refer to God as Yearning or Love and sometimes as the Yearned-for or the Beloved? On the one hand, he causes, produces and generates what is being referred to, and on the other hand, he is the thing itself. ON THE DIVINE NAMES 4.14.[63]

THE LOVE GOD HAS FOR US. BEDE: We know that Jesus is the Son of God and that the Father has sent him to be the Savior of the world. And we believe in the love which God has for us, the same love which he has for his only-begotten Son, because God did not want his Son to be an only child. He wanted him to have brothers and sisters, and so he adopted us in order that we might share his eternal life. ON 1 JOHN.[64]

SEEK ONE WHO IS LOVE. ISHO'DAD OF MERV: There is no Scripture which calls God only love,[65] but John says this in order that we might seek him who is love, from whom the commandment to show mercy came. COMMENTARIES.[66]

4:17 Confidence for the Day of Judgment

HOW TO TEST THE PROGRESS OF LOVE. AUGUSTINE: This is how everyone ought to test the progress of love in himself, or rather his own progress in love, for if love is God there can be no progress or regress, and love is only said to make progress in you inasmuch as you make progress in love. TEN HOMILIES ON 1 JOHN 9.2.[67]

LOVE PERFECTED IN US. HILARY OF ARLES: In this world we must do our best to be generous, godly, merciful and patient, imitating God as closely as we can. INTRODUCTORY COMMENTARY ON 1 JOHN.[68]

AS HE IS. ANDREAS: Jesus said: "The ruler of this world is coming, and he shall find nothing in me."[69] We ought to be the same, so that nothing of this world may be found in us either. CATENA.[70]

HAVING CONFIDENCE. BEDE: John tells us how we can know where we stand in God's eyes. Everyone who has assurance on the day of judgment has perfect love in him. What does it mean to have assurance? It means that we are not afraid of the coming of judgment. When someone is newly converted, he starts by being afraid of the day of judgment, because he thinks that when the righteous Judge appears, he will be condemned as

---

[61]FC 45:207. [62]FC 45:462-63. [63]CWS 82. [64]PL 93:110. [65]As if love were the only language we could fittingly use of God. [66]CIM 41. [67]LCC 8:330. [68]PL Supp. 3:124. [69]Jn 14:30. [70]CEC 134.

unrighteous. But as he grows in the faith and his life starts to change, he learns not to be afraid anymore but to look forward eagerly for the coming of the One who is the desire of the nations, hoping that on the strength of his good life he will be crowned among the saints. ON 1 JOHN.[71]

4:18 One Who Fears Is Not Perfected in Love

PERFECT LOVE CASTS OUT FEAR. CLEMENT OF ALEXANDRIA: The perfection of a faithful man is love. ADUMBRATIONS.[72]

NO FEAR IN LOVE. AUGUSTINE: What John said is true. So if you do not want to have any fear, first of all see whether you have that perfect love which turns fear out of the door. But if fear is pushed out before such perfection is achieved, it is a matter of pride puffing up, not of charity building up. SERMONS 348.1.[73]

CONSTANT LOVE DRIVES OUT FEAR OF PERSECUTION. LEO THE GREAT: The apostles had to ensure that no other truth would creep in and that no other doctrine would be taught. To do this, it was necessary to increase the capacity of those who were being taught and to multiply the constancy of that love which drives out all fear, not dreading the rage of persecutors. SERMONS 76.5.[74]

FEAR HAS TO DO WITH PUNISHMENT. BEDE: The love of God is such that it makes it possible to imitate God's goodness to the point where we start to do good toward our enemies and even to love them. The fear which love casts out is that spoken of in the psalm: "The fear of the Lord is the beginning of wis-

dom."[75] The new convert is afraid that the strictness of the righteous Judge will condemn him, but love casts this kind of fear out and gives him assurance on the day of judgment. ON 1 JOHN.[76]

4:19 We Love Because God Loved Us First

WHY WE LOVE GOD. AUGUSTINE: By God's grace we love him who first loved us, in order to believe in him, and by loving him we perform good works, but we have not performed the good works in order to love him. LETTERS 186.[77]

GOD EXACTLY UNDERSTANDS US. ANDREAS: God loves us so much that even the hairs of our head are numbered, as it says in the Gospels.[78] It is not that God goes around numbering hairs but rather that he has exact understanding and complete foreknowledge of everything to do with us. CATENA.[79]

HE FIRST LOVED US. BEDE: From where would we get the power to love God if he had not loved us first of all? Jesus says in the Gospel: "You have not chosen me, but I have chosen you."[80] We shall therefore be perfect in love if, following his example, we love him for no other reason than that he first loved us and gave himself for us. ON 1 JOHN.[81]

4:20 No One Can Hate His Brother and Still Love God

NOT IN LOVE, NOT IN GOD. AUGUSTINE: He

---

[71]PL 93:111. [72]FGNK 3:92. [73]WSA 3/10:91. [74]FC 93:338. [75]Ps 111:10. [76]PL 93:111. [77]FC 30:196. [78]Mt 10:30. [79]CEC 137. [80]Jn 15:16. [81]PL 93:112.

who does not love his brother is not in love, and he who is not in love is not in God, for God is love. On the Trinity 8.11.[82]

Seeing with the Heart's Eye. Augustine: Why does a man not see God? Because he has not love. He has not love because he does not love his brother, and it follows that the reason for his not seeing God is that he does not love. The heart's eye must be continually cleansed and strengthened by love, in order to see that changeless being in whose presence the lover may always delight and enjoy it in the company of the angels for all eternity. Ten Homilies on 1 John 9.10.[83]

Loving Those Whom God Loves. Bede: Anyone who loves God must love his brother also, for the simple reason that loving God means loving those whom God loves. On 1 John.[84]

4:21 Love God and Love Your Brother

Also

Fulfilling God's Commandments. Andreas: The person who loves God keeps his commandments, and loving one's brother is the fulfillment of those commandments. The person who does not love his brother has not kept the commandments and by not keeping them has not loved God. The one who says he loves but does not do so is a liar. Catena.[85]

This Commandment from God. Bede: How can you love someone if you hate what he asks you to do? Who is there who would say that he loves the emperor but cannot abide his laws? The true lover of God is one who loves his commandments also, as Psalm 119 makes perfectly clear. On 1 John.[86]

---

[82]LCC 8:53. [83]LCC 8:337. [84]PL 93:112. [85]CEC 138. [86]PL 93:112.

5:1-21 ASSURANCE OF SALVATION

[1]Every one who believes that Jesus is the Christ is a child of God, and every one who loves the parent loves the child. [2]By this we know that we love the children of God, when we love God and obey his commandments. [3]For this is the love of God, that we keep his commandments. And his commandments are not burdensome. [4]For whatever is born of God overcomes the world; and this is the victory that overcomes the world, our faith. [5]Who is it that overcomes the world but he who believes that Jesus is the Son of God?

[6]This is he who came by water and blood, Jesus Christ, not with the water only but with the water and the blood. [7]And the Spirit is the witness, because the Spirit is the truth. [8]There are three witnesses, the Spirit, the water, and the blood; and these three agree. [9]If we receive

the testimony of men, the testimony of God is greater; for this is the testimony of God that he has borne witness to his Son. [10]He who believes in the Son of God has the testimony in himself. He who does not believe God has made him a liar, because he has not believed in the testimony that God has borne to his Son. [11]And this is the testimony, that God gave us eternal life, and this life is in his Son. [12]He who has the Son has life; he who has not the Son of God has not life.

[13]I write this to you who believe in the name of the Son of God, that you may know that you have eternal life. [14]And this is the confidence which we have in him, that if we ask anything according to his will he hears us. [15]And if we know that he hears us in whatever we ask, we know that we have obtained the requests made of him. [16]If any one sees his brother committing what is not a mortal sin, he will ask, and God[i] will give him life for those whose sin is not mortal. There is sin which is mortal; I do not say that one is to pray for that. [17]All wrongdoing is sin, but there is sin which is not mortal.

[18]We know that any one born of God does not sin, but He who was born of God keeps him, and the evil one does not touch him.

[19]We know that we are of God, and the whole world is in the power of the evil one.

[20]And we know that the Son of God has come and has given us understanding, to know him who is true; and we are in him who is true, in his Son Jesus Christ. This is the true God and eternal life. [21]Little children, keep yourselves from idols.

i Greek he

OVERVIEW: If we love God, we must also love all those who believe with us that his Son became a man in Jesus Christ. The practical outworking of this is that we must obey his commandments, which are easy for those who are filled with the Holy Spirit. John immediately joined love to faith, because without love faith is useless (CAESARIUS OF ARLES). By practicing virtue, those who believe that Jesus is the Christ (BEDE) are born of God. They have become his children and friends, just as Abraham was (ANDREAS). To love God, the parent, is to love the neighbor, the child (CYRIL OF JERUSALEM, THEOPHYLACT). Only someone who is on fire with the love of his Maker can be said to love other people in the right way

(BEDE, OECUMENIUS). To love the children of God is to love the Son of God; to love the Son of God is to love the Father. And if you love, you cannot but do well (AUGUSTINE). The commandments of God are not burdensome (ANDREAS, BEDE) to those who have expelled every kind of unbelief (THEOPHYLACT).

There are three witnesses to the coming of Christ: the water of baptism, the blood of atonement and the indwelling presence of the Holy Spirit who bears witness to the power of these things. Anyone who believes has this testimony within and therefore has the full assurance of salvation by faith. The Son of God came not by water only, in order to cleanse us from our sins, but also with the blood of his passion (ANDREAS, OECUMENIUS). By this he consecrates the sacrament of our baptism, giving his blood for us, redeeming us by his suffering, that we might be made fit for salvation (BEDE) through the Spirit (ISHO'DAD). These three are one: the Spirit of sanctification and life, the blood of redemption and the water of regeneration in baptism (LEO, CLEMENT OF ALEXANDRIA). The Spirit makes us children of God by adoption, the water of the sacred font cleanses us, and the blood of the Lord redeems us (BEDE). In this way everything is accomplished in unity by the one Christ (ISHO'DAD). If the testimony of the prophets is great (HILARY OF ARLES) and worthy to be received, the testimony of God to his beloved Son is much greater still (BEDE, ANDREAS). God can never be a liar, because he is the essence of truth. But an unbelieving person always ends up lying because he or she does not believe in the truth of God (HILARY OF ARLES). Whoever refuses to honor the Son does not honor the Father who sent him (BEDE).

Right now we live on earth in the hope of his promise, which we shall receive in its fullness after we die and go to be with God. John does not simply say that there is life in the Son; he says that the Son is life itself (BEDE). God will grant the requests of those who ask according to his will (DIDYMUS, BEDE). If he hears us in everything that we ask of him, we know that we are praying according to his will (OECUMENIUS). We are expected to ask for the things that he wants us to ask for and to come to understand what those things are (BEDE). We can know now that we have eternal life, and we can also be certain that whatever we ask for in prayer, he will hear and answer. We have already received the answer if we have prayed in the Spirit according to God's will.

Armed with this assurance, we have a duty to seek the rescue of others from their sins, as long as such rescue is possible. There are two kinds of sin, one that is unavoidable because we are living in a sinful world, and one that is deliberate. Mortal sin occurs when a believer opposes the fellowship after having come to acknowledge God. That person starts to fight against that grace by which he or she has been reconciled to God. A nonmortal sin is one that does not infringe on brotherly love but fails to show it adequately because of some weakness (BEDE, OECUMENIUS). One who has fully given himself over to Christ will not commit mortal sin, even though the old sin nature remains, yet that person may still commit nonmortal sins (OECUMENIUS). It would be self-contradictory to pray that some sins be forgiven (ORIGEN), especially at the end of a perverse life (AUGUSTINE) or in cases of blasphemy (ANDREAS).

Because the ability to avoid sin is given by grace and is not by nature (ANDREAS), John adds that the righteous person must watch out, that evil will not touch him or her (DIDYMUS). Though David sinned, he was born of God and hence he did not sin up to his death, for when he repented he received forgiveness (BEDE). We know that we are of God because we have been born again by grace and baptism through faith, and we know that we shall persevere in that faith to the very end (BEDE). But those who love the world are subjected to the enemy (CLEMENT OF ALEXANDRIA, DIDYMUS, ISHO'DAD). We have been given understanding to the extent that we have known the Son of God (BEDE), who really has come into the world. The person who has this mind and understanding knows what is really true and is united with him because he shares the same mind (DIDYMUS, ANDREAS). We must recognize that we live in a hostile environment and that in Jesus Christ we have been given a knowledge of the truth sufficient to enable us to escape from its clutches, especially from the temptations of idolatry. Many former idolaters are in the church (DIDYMUS). It is wrong for one created in the image of the living God to worship the image of an idol (TERTULLIAN, HILARY OF ARLES).

5:1 Those Who Love God Love His Children Too

ONE WHO LOVES THE PARENT LOVES THE CHILD. CYRIL OF JERUSALEM: We can turn this around and say that anyone who despises the Begotten also despises the One who begat him. CATECHETICAL LECTURES 11.7.[1]

EVERYONE WHO BELIEVES. DIDYMUS THE BLIND: This describes everyone who is born of God and does what God wants him to do. COMMENTARY ON 1 JOHN.[2]

JOINING LOVE TO FAITH. CAESARIUS OF ARLES: John immediately joined love to faith, because without love faith is useless. According to charity, faith belongs to Christians, but without love it belongs to the demons. Moreover, those who do not believe are even worse than the demons. SERMONS 186.1.[3]

A CHILD OF GOD. ANDREAS: By practicing virtue, those who are born of God have become his children, his friends, just as Abraham was. Once again John touches on the doctrine of truth, revealing the depths of the unbelief of the heretics. CATENA.[4]

BELIEVING THAT JESUS IS THE CHRIST. BEDE: Who is it who believes that Jesus is the

Christ? It is the person who lives according to Christ's commandments. Let no heretic or schismatic say that he believes that Jesus is the Christ, for even the devils believe and tremble, because they too know that much. But those who do not have his love or the works of truth are not of God. ON 1 JOHN.[5]

5:2 Obedience Is the Test of Love

WHEN WE LOVE GOD. AUGUSTINE: To love the children of God is to love the Son of God; to love the Son of God is to love the Father. Nobody can love the Father without loving the Son, and anyone who loves the Son will love the other children as well. TEN HOMILIES ON 1 JOHN 10.3.[6]

ON FIRE WITH LOVE. BEDE: Only someone who is on fire with the love of his Maker can be said to love his fellow humans in the right way. For if a person's love for his Creator starts to flag, his words of love for his fellows lose all their power. ON 1 JOHN.[7]

WE LOVE THE CHILDREN OF GOD. THEOPHYLACT: If we love God, then we must also love those whom God has brought to birth and who have become our brothers and sisters. Loving one another is a sign of how much we love God. COMMENTARY ON 1 JOHN.[8]

5:3 Keep God's Commandments

THE SUBSTANCE OF LOVE. DIDYMUS THE BLIND: The substance and ground of the love

---

[1]FC 61:214. [2]PG 39:1081. [3]FC 47:490. [4]CEC 138. [5]PL 93:112. [6]LCC 8:341. [7]PL 93:113. [8]PG 126:57.

we ought to have for God is obedience to his commandments. COMMENTARY ON 1 JOHN.[9]

LOVE, AND YOU DO WELL. AUGUSTINE: The commandments of which John speaks are the two given by Jesus: Love God and love one another. Hold fast to this love and set your minds at rest. You need not be afraid of doing harm to anyone, for how can you harm the person you love? Love, and you cannot but do well. TEN HOMILIES ON 1 JOHN 10.7.[10]

THEY ARE NOT BURDENSOME. ANDREAS: Keeping the commandments is both the form and substance of our love for God. Those who obey them are brought close to God by them. If someone looks at them in the wrong way and says that they are heavy to bear, he is merely revealing his own weakness. CATENA.[11]

THE EASY YOKE. BEDE: The proof of love is found in the works that we do. We truly love God if we bend our wills to his commandments, for whoever runs after his own illicit desires does not love God, because he contradicts that love in his own will. God's commands are not onerous, for Christ himself said: "My yoke is easy and my burden is light."[12] ON 1 JOHN.[13]

5:4 Whatever Is Born of God Overcomes the World

VICTORY THROUGH FAITH. CYRIL OF ALEXANDRIA: Neither a Jew nor a pagan nor a heretic can do anything in the face of this victory which is ours through faith. CATENA.[14]

THIS IS THE VICTORY. ANDREAS: This means that such a person has overcome all evil and ungodliness. For our faith has destroyed all ignorance and driven out all darkness. CATENA.[15]

OVERCOMING NOT BY OUR EFFORTS. BEDE: The commandments of God are not burdensome. All those who are bound to keep them with true devotion, despite the adversities of this world, regard its temptations with equanimity, even to the point of looking forward to death, because it is the gateway to the heavenly country. And lest anyone should think that we can somehow achieve all this by our own efforts, John adds that the substance of our victory is our faith, not our works. ON 1 JOHN.[16]

FAITH OVERCOMES THE WORLD. THEOPHYLACT: Once you have become brothers and sisters in love, you must go on to the next stage, which is to overcome the world. For those who have been born again in God must expel every kind of unbelief from their midst. COMMENTARY ON 1 JOHN.[17]

5:5 Believe and Overcome the World

WHO OVERCOMES? BEDE: The person who believes that Jesus is the Son of God overcomes the world by adding works worthy of that faith to it. If you think that faith in his divinity and a profession of that faith are enough by themselves, read on! ON 1 JOHN.[18]

ONE WHO BELIEVES IN JESUS. OECUMENIUS: It is not faith in the abstract that

---

[9]PG 39:1802. [10]LCC 8:343. [11]CEC 139. [12]Mt 11:30. [13]PL 93:113. [14]CEC 140. [15]CEC 139. [16]PL 93:113. [17]PG 126:57. [18]PL 93:113.

overcomes the world. It must be faith in Jesus Christ, as John makes plain. COMMENTARY ON 1 JOHN.[19]

5:6 Jesus Christ Came by Water and Blood

WITH CLEANSING BLOOD. ANDREAS: What flowed from his side was also the blood which cleanses us from sin and sanctifies the people of God.... It was not a mere man who appeared at the Jordan[20] but the incarnate Word of God, to whom the Father also bore witness: "This is my beloved Son in whom I am well pleased."[21] Similarly, when he was hanging on the cross, what sounded to the people like thunder was the voice of God speaking at the moment that his blood fell to the ground. CATENA.[22]

NOT WITH WATER ONLY. BEDE: The Son of God came not by water only, in order to cleanse us from our sins, but also with the blood of his passion, by which he consecrates the sacrament of our baptism, giving his blood for us, redeeming us by his suffering and nourishing us with his sacraments so that we might be made fit for salvation. ON 1 JOHN.[23]

BY WATER AND BLOOD. OECUMENIUS: Why did Jesus come? To give us new birth and to make us children of God. How are we born? Through water and blood. The Jesus who came gives us new birth by water and by blood. The water stands for his baptism, when Jesus was revealed as the Son of God. The blood, of course, stands for his crucifixion, when he prayed that the Father would glorify him and a voice answered from heaven: "I have glorified and I will glorify."[24] COMMENTARY ON 1 JOHN.[25]

BY BAPTISM, PASSION AND THE SPIRIT.

ISHO'DAD OF MERV: John calls Christ's baptism "water" and his passion "blood." He fulfilled all the dispensations for our sake, by means of his baptism, his passion and by the Holy Spirit. COMMENTARIES.[26]

5:7 The Spirit Is the Truth

THE SAVING POWERS. CLEMENT OF ALEXANDRIA: The spirit is life, the water is regeneration and faith, the blood is knowledge, and these three are one. In the Savior these are the saving powers, and life itself is found in the Son. ADUMBRATIONS.[27]

WHAT THE SPIRIT ATTESTS. BEDE: When the Lord was baptized in the Jordan, the Spirit descended on him in the form of a dove, bearing witness that he is the truth, that he is the true Son of God, that he is the true Mediator between God and humanity, that he is the true Redeemer and Reconciler of the human race, that he is truly free from any contamination of sin, that he is truly able to take away the sins of the world. ON 1 JOHN.[28]

5:8 The Three Witnesses Agree

THE SPIRIT, THE WATER AND THE BLOOD. AUGUSTINE: What was it that flowed from Jesus' side if not the sacrament which believers receive? The Spirit, the blood and the water— the Spirit which he gave up, the blood and water which flowed from his side. The church is signified as being born from this blood and water. SERMONS 5.3.[29]

---

[19]PG 119:676. [20]To be baptized. [21]Mt 3:17. [22]CEC 140. [23]PL 93:114. [24]Jn 12:28. [25]PG 119:677. [26]CIM 40. [27]FGNK 3:92. [28]PL 93:114. [29]WSA 3/1:218.

The Witnesses Distinct Yet Not Separated. Leo the Great: This means the Spirit of sanctification, the blood of redemption and the water of baptism, which three are one and remain distinct, and none of them is separated from union with the others. This is the faith by which the church lives and moves. Letters 28.[30]

How the Spirit Bore Witness. Bede: The Spirit bore witness that Jesus is the truth when he descended on him at his baptism. If Jesus were not the truth, the Spirit would not have done that. The water and the blood bore witness that Jesus is the truth when they both flowed from his side at the time he was crucified. That would not have been possible if he had not had a genuine human nature. All three are independent of each other, but their testimony is one and the same, because Christ's divinity is not to be believed in apart from his humanity, nor is his humanity to be accepted apart from his divinity. And all three are present also in us, not in their natural form but by the mystical union of our souls with him. The Spirit makes us children of God by adoption, the water of the sacred font cleanses us, and the blood of the Lord redeems us. They are invisible in themselves, but in the sacraments they are made visible for our benefit. On 1 John.[31]

All Accomplished in Unity. Isho'dad of Merv: The three things are one because everything was accomplished by the one Christ. Commentaries.[32]

5:9 The Testimony of God

The Testimony of Humans. Hilary of Arles: The testimony of men refers to the testimony of people like Moses and the prophets, who were all men of God. Introductory Commentary on 1 John.[33]

The Testimony of God. Bede: There are many great testimonies to the Son of God, for example: "The Lord said to my Lord, Sit at my right hand,"[34] and "The Lord said to me, You are my Son."[35] This testimony is great and true and worthy to be received by everyone, but the testimony of God to his beloved Son is much greater still. For the Father himself spoke from heaven, saying: "You are my beloved Son, in whom I am well pleased."[36] On 1 John.[37]

5:10 Unbelief Makes God Out to Be a Liar

Does Unbelief Make God a Liar? Hilary of Arles: God can never turn himself into a liar, because he is the essence of truth. But an unbelieving man is a liar, because he does not believe in the truth of God. Introductory Commentary on 1 John.[38]

The Testimony God Has Borne. Andreas: After giving us one testimony about his Son, God gave us another, which is eternal life. Catena.[39]

One Who Believes in God Believes in the Son. Bede: This means that whoever believes in the Son in such a way as to do what the Son commands has the witness of God in him and may be counted among the

---

[30]FC 34:103. [31]PL 93:114-15. [32]CIM 41. [33]PL Supp. 3:125. [34]Ps 110:1. [35]Ps 2:7. [36]Lk 3:22. [37]PL 93:115. [38]PL Supp. 3:125. [39]CEC 141.

children of God. Jews and heretics are wasting their time when they claim to believe in God,[40] because they reject Christ and refuse to believe in him. For whoever refuses to honor the Son does not honor the Father who sent him. ON 1 JOHN.[41]

5:11 God Gave Us Eternal Life in the Son

ETERNAL LIFE. BEDE: John says that God has given us eternal life, and remember that he was saying this at a time when he was still in the flesh and subject to physical death. But God gave us eternal life in exactly the same way as he has given us the power to become his children. Right now we live on earth in the hope of his promise, which we shall receive in its fullness after we die and go to be with him. ON 1 JOHN.[42]

THIS LIFE IS IN HIS SON. OECUMENIUS: God has promised to give us eternal life because we have been adopted into him through his Son, of whom Scripture says: "In him was life."[43] Therefore whoever has the Son by holy baptism also has life. COMMENTARY ON 1 JOHN.[44]

5:12 One Who Has the Son Has Life

LIFE ONLY IN CHRIST. AUGUSTINE: Here John testifies that no one has life unless he has Christ. AGAINST JULIAN 6.9.27.[45]

THE SON IS OUR LIFE. BEDE: John does not simply say that there is life in the Son; he says that the Son is life itself. The Son in his turn glorified the Father by saying: "Just as the Father has life in himself, so he has given the Son also life in himself."[46] He goes on to show how this life is common to both Father and

Son, when he says: "And this is eternal life, that they know you the only true God, and Jesus Christ whom you have sent."[47] ON 1 JOHN.[48]

5:13 That You May Know That You Have Eternal Life

REASSURED OF FUTURE BLESSEDNESS. BEDE: John writes these things so that those who believe in Christ will be reassured about their future blessedness. They will not be led astray by the deception of those who say that Jesus was not the Son of God and therefore has nothing to offer to those who have believed in him. ON 1 JOHN.[49]

TO YOU WHO BELIEVE. OECUMENIUS: John says that he has written to those who are inheritors of eternal life, for such things would never be written to people who are not. After all, it is not right to give holy things to dogs or to scatter pearls before swine.[50] COMMENTARY ON 1 JOHN.[51]

5:14 God Hears Us If We Ask According to His Will

THE CONFIDENCE WE HAVE IN HIM. DIDYMUS THE BLIND: Those who possess technical skills and know how to repair things are fully confident that when the need arises they will be able to do so. Similarly these holy men, John and the other apostles, knew from their own experience that if they asked God for what was pleasing and acceptable to him, they would

---

[40]While they yet reject the Son. [41]PL 93:115. [42]PL 93:116. [43]Jn 1:4. [44]PG 119:680. [45]FC 35:336. [46]Jn 5:26. [47]Jn 17:3. [48]PL 93:116. [49]PL 93:116. [50]Mt 7:6. [51]PG 119:680.

obtain it. For God is most generous to those who have this knowledge and will grant the requests of those who ask according to his will. COMMENTARY ON 1 JOHN.[52]

IF WE ASK IN THE RIGHT WAY. BEDE: John holds out to us the great assurance that we can expect to receive heavenly blessings from the Lord and that whatever we ask for here on earth will be given to us as long as we ask for it in the right way. This is in full agreement with what Jesus said in the Gospels: "I say to you, whatever you ask in prayer, believe that you receive it and you will."[53] ON 1 JOHN.[54]

5:15 We Know He Hears Us

UNDERSTANDING WHAT TO ASK. BEDE: John repeats what he has already said many times over, in order to stir us up to more vibrant prayer. But the condition which he imposed at the beginning remains valid, which is that we must ask according to our Maker's will. There are two sides to this, because on the one hand we are expected to ask for the things which he wants us to ask for, and at the same time we are expected to come to understand what those things are. This is what it means to have the kind of faith which works through love. ON 1 JOHN.[55]

HE HEARS US. OECUMENIUS: What this means is that if we ask according to his will, he hears us, and if he hears us in everything that we ask of him, we know that we are praying according to his will. Therefore we already have inside us the things which we have asked for. For these are the kingdom and righteousness of God, which he has asked us to pray for. COMMENTARY ON 1 JOHN.[56]

5:16 Mortal and Nonmortal Sins

SOME SINS ARE UNTO DEATH. ORIGEN: Since there are sins "unto death," it follows that anyone who commits one of them will die as a result. SERMONS ON LEVITICUS 11.2.6.[57]

SELF-CONTRADICTORY TO PRAY THAT SOME SIN BE FORGIVEN. AUGUSTINE: Even though the Lord commands us to pray for our very persecutors, this passage clearly shows that there are some brothers for whom we are not commanded to pray. We therefore must acknowledge that there are some sins among the brothers which are worse than persecution by enemies. I think that the sin of a brother is unto death when anyone who has attained a knowledge of God through the grace of our Lord Jesus Christ opposes the brotherhood and is aroused by the fires of envy against that very grace by which he was reconciled to God. COMMENTARY ON THE SERMON ON THE MOUNT 1.22.73.[58]

ESPECIALLY SINS AT THE END OF LIFE. AUGUSTINE: In another place I defined the sin of a brother unto death [see above], but I should have added: "if he ends this life in a perversity of mind as wicked as this." For surely we must not despair of anyone, no matter how wicked he is, while he lives, and we should pray with confidence for him of whom we should not despair. RETRACTATIONS 1.18.7.[59]

WHO CAN PRAY AGAINST GOD? ANDREAS: It is the sin of heresy, or of blasphemy against the

---

[52]PG 39:1804. [53]Mk 11:24. [54]PL 93:116. [55]PL 93:117. [56]PG 119:680-81. [57]FC 83:214. [58]FC 11:99-100. Note the qualifying phrase in the next selection. [59]FC 60:83.

Holy Spirit, which leads to death. If one man sins against another, pray for him. But if he sins against God, who is there who can pray on his behalf? Catena.[60]

Some Sin Not unto Death. Bede: Just as Christ washes us from our sins by interceding with the Father on our behalf, so also should we, if we know that our brother is committing a sin which is "not unto death." Homilies on the Gospels 2.5.[61]

Distinguishing Sins Mortal and Non-mortal. Bede: These are things which are asked for according to God's will, because they are part of what it means to love our brothers. John is talking here about trivial, everyday sins which are hard to avoid but which are easy to put right. The question of what constitutes a mortal sin is very difficult, and it is hard to accept that there are people whom John tells us not to pray for, when our Lord tells us that we should pray for those who persecute us. The only answer to this is that there must be sins committed within the fellowship of the brothers which are even more serious than persecution from outside enemies. Mortal sin therefore occurs when a brother opposes the fellowship after he has come to acknowledge God by the grace of our Lord Jesus Christ given to him and when he starts to fight against that grace, by which he has been reconciled to God, with the weapons of hatred. A nonmortal sin is one which does not infringe on brotherly love but merely fails to show it adequately because of some weakness of the mind. On 1 John.[62]

5:17 Not Every Sin Is Mortal

Minor Infractions versus Sins Lead-

ing to Death. Bede: The variety of sins is such that everything which fails to agree with the law of fairness is a sin, although minor infractions of the kind which are almost impossible to avoid in this life can be forgiven the righteous without too much difficulty. But there are other sins which are so contrary to any kind of righteousness that they will lead the one who does them into eternal punishment without any doubt whatsoever, unless he happens to put them right. On 1 John.[63]

Sins That Lead to Death. Oecumenius: Only those sins which are not repented of lead to death. Judas, for example, although he showed remorse, did not repent and was led off to his death. But whoever has given himself over to Christ cannot commit mortal sin, even though his nature[64] remains unchanged and he still sins. Commentary on 1 John.[65]

5:18 Anyone Born of God Does Not Sin

The Evil One Cannot Touch God's Children. Didymus the Blind: If it is true that when someone does what is righteous his power to do so comes from God, and if it is also true that righteousness and evil cannot live together, then it is perfectly clear that as long as a person does such things he is righteous and does not sin. But because this ability is given by grace and is not natural, John adds that the righteous person must watch out, so that evil will not touch him. Commentary on 1 John.[66]

No One Is a Child of God by Nature.

---

[60]CEC 142. [61]HOG 2:48. [62]PL 93:117. [63]PL 93:118. [64]Fleshly nature in tune with grace. [65]PG 119:681-84. [66]PG 39:1804-5.

ANDREAS: It may be true that the righteous person does not sin, but no one is a child of God by nature. This is why we avoid sin, not by the way in which we were made, which would make sin impossible for us,[67] but by watching out that we do not fall into it. CATENA.[68]

DAVID'S CASE. BEDE: Anyone born of God does not commit mortal sin, which we have defined earlier on. But mortal sin can also be understood to mean sin which retains its force right up to the moment of death, and those who are born of God do not commit that kind of error. David, for, example, confessed to having committed mortal sin, for how else can we regard such things as adultery and murder? But David was also born of God and because he belonged to that fellowship he did not sin up to his death, because when he repented he was regarded as worthy to receive forgiveness. ON 1 JOHN.[69]

5:19 The World Is in the Power of the Evil One

IN THE POWER OF THE EVIL ONE. CLEMENT OF ALEXANDRIA: "World" does not mean creation as a whole but rather worldly people and those who live according to their lusts. ADUMBRATIONS.[70]

THE WORLD SUBJECTED TO EVIL. DIDYMUS THE BLIND: The "world," that is, those who love the world, are subjected to evil. This includes everybody, because we are all born under sin, which traces its origin to the disobedience of Adam. Many heretics claim that there is a creator god who made the world evil to begin with, but this is not so. The word refers to people, not to the material substance of creation. COMMENTARY ON 1 JOHN.[71]

WE ARE OF GOD. BEDE: We know that we are of God because we have been born again by grace and baptism through faith, and we know too that we shall persevere in that faith to the very end. But those who love the world are subjected to the enemy, and there is no water of regeneration which can deliver them from that subjection, especially if they sin again after their baptism. Nor is it just the lovers of the world who are in this state, because it applies also to those who are newly born and who have inherited the guilt of original sin, although they cannot yet tell the difference between good and evil. Such people are in the power of the enemy, unless by the power of a loving Creator they are taken out of the power of darkness and placed in the kingdom of the Son of his love. ON 1 JOHN.[72]

PERVERSION GENERATES SIN. ISHO'DAD OF MERV: The world is subjected to the perversion which gives birth to sin, and because of that it is prone to the cultivation of evil things. COMMENTARIES.[73]

5:20 We Are in Him Who Is True

TO KNOW HIM WHO IS TRUE. DIDYMUS THE BLIND: The understanding which God gave, by which it is known that the true Son of God is coming, is the same as the mind of Christ. COMMENTARY ON 1 JOHN.[74]

THE SON HAS GIVEN US UNDERSTANDING.

---

[67]Insofar as we lived according to our prefallen creaturely nature, we would not be sinning, as Adam did not sin before the Fall. [68]CEC 143. [69]PL 93:118-19. [70]FGNK 3:92. [71]PG 39:1805-6. [72]PL 93:119. [73]CIM 41. [74]PG 39:1807.

ANDREAS: Even at the end of his letter, John never stops insisting on the need for right doctrine. We have been given understanding to the extent that we have known the Son of God, who really has come into the world. This is what it means to say that "we have the mind of Christ."[75] The person who has this mind and understanding knows what is really true and is united with him because he shares the same mind. CATENA.[76]

THE TRUE GOD AND ETERNAL LIFE. BEDE:

What could be clearer than these words? What could be sweeter to the ear? What could be a more powerful weapon to use against the heretics? Christ is the true Son of God. The Father of our Lord Jesus Christ is the true God. The eternal Son of God has come into the world of time, and he came only in order to save us, so that we might come to know the true God. For no one can come to eternal life without a knowledge of the true God. All these things John just keeps repeating over and over again. ON 1 JOHN.[77]

5:21 *Stay Away from Idols*

AVOID IMAGES. TERTULLIAN: John did not tell us to keep away from worship, but from idols, that is, from their very likeness. For it is wrong for you, who are created in the image of the living God, to become the image of an idol and a dead man. ON THE CROWN 5.10.[78]

MANY FORMER IDOLATERS IN THE CHURCH. DIDYMUS THE BLIND: Why is it that after everything else which he has said to his hearers during the course of his letter, John should keep this warning about idols to the very end? In my opinion it is because here he is addressing the church in general. There must have been many in that assembly who were former idolaters, and he adds this caution for their benefit. CATENA.[79]

WORSHIP THE ONE TRUE GOD. HILARY OF ARLES: The letter ends as it began, with an admonition to worship the one true God alone. Everything else that John says is contained in this one golden rule. INTRODUCTORY COMMENTARY ON 1 JOHN.[80]

KEEP AWAY FROM FALSE TEACHERS. BEDE: You who know the true God, in whom you have eternal life, must keep yourselves away from the teachings of the heretics which lead only to eternal death. In the manner of those who made idols in the place of God, the heretics have corrupted the glory of the incorruptible God by their wicked doctrines which bear the stamp of corruptible things. ON 1 JOHN.[81]

---

[75]1 Cor 2:16. [76]CEC 144-45. [77]PL 93:120. [78]APT 176. [79]CEC 145. [80]PL Supp. 3:126. [81]PL 93:120.

The Second Epistle of John

1-3 THE ELDER GREETS THE ELECT LADY

¹*The elder to the elect lady and her children, whom I love in the truth, and not only I but also all who know the truth, ²because of the truth which abides in us and will be with us for ever:*

³*Grace, mercy, and peace will be with us, from God the Father and from Jesus Christ the Father's Son, in truth and love.*

OVERVIEW: The identity of both the elder and of the elect lady were matters of controversy in the early church. If it is true that majority opinion eventually decided that the elder was John, the Evangelist and beloved disciple of Jesus (THEOPHYLACT), and that the elect lady was a church (CLEMENT OF ALEXANDRIA, HILARY OF ARLES), neither view can be regarded as settled in ancient times. Some thought that there was another John, distinguished here as the elder (OECUMENIUS), and quite a number were prepared to believe that the elect lady was a particular individual who had a church in her house (ANDREAS). Of special interest to us is the recognition that originally there was no difference between elders (*presbyteroi*) and bishops (*episcopoi*) and that John was therefore writing in his capacity as a bishop (JEROME). Because the heretics of that time denied that our Lord Jesus Christ was the true Son of God and claimed that he was born in a merely human way, John rightly recalls that he is the Father's Son (BEDE).

1 The Elder to the Elect Lady and Her Children

TO THE ELECT CHURCH. CLEMENT OF ALEXANDRIA: John's second letter, which is written to virgins, is extremely straightforward. It was written to a certain Babylonian woman called Electa, whose name stands for the election of the holy church. ADUMBRATIONS.[1]

TO THE ELECT LADY. HILARY OF ARLES: The elect lady is clearly a church to which the letter is written. It is elect in faith and mistress of all virtues. INTRODUCTORY COMMENTARY ON 2 JOHN.[2]

THE ELDER. JEROME: Originally "presbyters"

---

[1]FGNK 3:92. [2]PL Supp. 3:126.

and "bishops" were the same. When later on one was chosen to preside over the rest, this was done to avoid schism. For apart from ordination, what function is there which belongs to a bishop which does not also belong to a presbyter? LETTERS 146.[3]

TO A PARTICULAR LADY. ANDREAS: John is either writing to a church, or else to a particular woman who has ordered her household spiritually, according to the commandments of God. He writes this letter to one of the women who has accepted the proclamation and exhorts her to do two things. The first of these is to walk in love, and the second is to avoid welcoming false teachers. John also tells us that the overall purpose of his letter is to keep her informed until he is able to come to her in person. CATENA.[4]

TO ALL WHO KNOW THE TRUTH. BEDE: John is writing against the heretics who have departed from the truth. He rightly recalls that there is a love in the Holy Spirit which is common to all who know the truth. By mentioning the unanimity and the large number of catholic Christians he frightens those few who have separated themselves from their number. Look how all catholic Christians everywhere follow a single rule of truth, whereas heretics and unbelievers do not all agree on what they reject and attack each other just as much as they attack the truth. ON 2 JOHN.[5]

JOHN THE ELDER. OECUMENIUS: There are some people who think that this and the following letter are not by John the beloved disciple but by someone else of the same name. The reasons they give for this are that in both letters he describes himself as the elder and addresses a single correspondent (either the

elect lady as here, or Gaius), which is not the case in the Catholic Epistle (1 John). Moreover, he starts with a personal introduction in both these letters, which is missing from 1 John. In answer to these points we would say that he did not put an introduction in his first letter because he was writing neither to a particular church nor to a specific individual. The fact that he calls himself an elder rather than an apostle may be due to the fact that he was not the first missionary to preach the gospel in Asia Minor. There he followed Paul, but unlike his predecessor, who merely passed through, John remained in the province and ministered directly to the local people. Nor did he refer to himself as a slave of Christ[6] because as the beloved disciple he had the confidence that he had gone beyond the fear of slavery. COMMENTARY ON 2 JOHN.[7]

THE AUTHOR. THEOPHYLACT: The most convincing argument in favor of the belief that John wrote this and the following letter is that the themes found in the first letter recur whenever the opportunity presents itself. COMMENTARY ON 2 JOHN.[8]

2 Truth Is with Us Forever

THE TRUTH ABIDES IN US. HILARY OF ARLES: By "truth" John is referring to the Holy Spirit, because love is always the work of the Spirit. INTRODUCTORY COMMENTARY ON 2 JOHN.[9]

PERSEVERANCE. OECUMENIUS: Here John

---

[3]LCC 5:387. [4]CEC 146-47. [5]PL 93:120-21. [6]As did both Peter (2 Pet 1:1) and James (Jas 1:1). [7]PG 119:685-88. [8]PG 126:69-72. [9]PL Supp. 3:126.

states that our faith is firm and sure, and he alludes to the divine gift of perseverance. He had to do this because the people to whom he was writing were not properly established and confirmed in their faith. COMMENTARY ON 2 JOHN.[10]

3 Grace, Mercy and Peace

FROM JESUS CHRIST THE FATHER'S SON. BEDE: Because the heretics of that time, people like Marcion and Cerinthus, denied that our Lord Jesus Christ was the true Son of God and claimed that he was born in a merely human way, John rightly recalls that he is the Son of God the Father in order to refute these blasphemers. He also bears witness that grace, mercy and peace come from the Son in exactly the same way as they come from the Father,

thereby demonstrating that the Father and the Son are equal and consubstantial with each other. ON 2 JOHN.[11]

IN TRUTH AND LOVE. OECUMENIUS: Here John is saying that good things arise out of perfect love. His choice of words here gives solidity to what he is saying and provide real evidence of his charity, or love, toward those to whom he is writing. COMMENTARY ON 2 JOHN.[12]

---

[10]PG 119:688. [11]PL 93:121. Since Marcion and Cerinthus come after John, and it is probable that Bede understood this sequence, the meaning here may be that John anticipated critics like Marcion and Cerinthus who were to develop later but whose views may have been embryonically present during the time of John's writing. [12]PG 119:688.

4-6 TRUTH AND LOVE

[4]I rejoiced greatly to find some of your children following the truth, just as we have been commanded by the Father. [5]And now I beg you, lady, not as though I were writing you a new commandment, but the one we have had from the beginning, that we love one another. [6]And this is love, that we follow his commandments; this is the commandment, as you have heard from the beginning, that you follow love.

OVERVIEW: One of the hallmarks of John is that truth and love always go together and that in combination they are the best defense against the attacks of heretics. The Fathers assumed that the letter had certain potential heresies in mind, such as Marcionism, although it was written too early

for that particular one. Nevertheless, it is quite likely that there were other serious divisions in the church that needed to be confronted, and the spiritual weapons for doing so remained the same, whatever the heresy might be. It is always a cause for joy when we find someone making progress in the faith of Christ (Hilary of Arles, Oecumenius). John's purpose is to show that what he is saying is something that people already know in principle (Bede, Oecumenius). The commandment we have heard from the beginning is that we are to love one another (Augustine, Oecumenius).

4 Rejoicing in the Truth

The Results of Truth. Hilary of Arles: The saints are always overjoyed to see the results of truth at work. Introductory Commentary on 2 John.[1]

Following the Truth. Oecumenius: It is always a cause for the greatest joy when we find someone making progress in the faith of Christ without any drawbacks. The Father's command to which John refers is what Christ said in the Gospel: "Whoever loves me will keep my commandments."[2] Here John calls Christ a father, because he really is the father of all the children who have been given to him by the Father's dispensation, as it is said: "Behold, I and the children whom God has given me."[3] Commentary on 2 John.[4]

5 Love One Another

From the Beginning. Bede: Here John is attacking the heretics who had abandoned the teaching of the apostles and were trying to introduce new doctrines. By doing this they were breaking the bonds of brotherly love. On 2 John.[5]

Not a New Commandment. Oecumenius: Note that this verse closely resembles what is said in 1 John 2:7 and elsewhere in that letter. John's purpose is to show that what he is saying is something which people already know in principle and have even had some past experience of. It is not something strange and unusual which they will find hard to grasp. Commentary on 2 John.[6]

6 This Is Love

Follow Love. Augustine: Meanwhile let us continue in the way we have come along so far, until God reveals it to us if we are otherwise minded. Letters 175.[7]

As You Heard. Oecumenius: John specifies that the commandment which he is talking about is that we should love one another. This was given from the beginning in order to prevent a situation in which we might be honoring God in purely spiritual things but at the same time rebelling against him and denying him in more practical matters. Commentary on 2 John.[8]

---

[1]PL Supp. 3:126. [2]Jn 14:21. [3]Is 8:18; Heb 2:13. [4]PG 119:689. [5]PL 93:121. [6]PG 119:689. [7]FC 32:86. [8]PG 119:689-92.

7-11 KEEPING THE FAITH

[7]For many deceivers have gone out into the world, men who will not acknowledge the coming of Jesus Christ in the flesh; such a one is the deceiver and the antichrist. [8]Look to yourselves, that you may not lose what you[a] have worked for, but may win a full reward. [9]Any one who goes ahead and does not abide in the doctrine of Christ does not have God; he who abides in the doctrine has both the Father and the Son. [10]If any one comes to you and does not bring this doctrine, do not receive him into the house or give him any greeting; [11]for he who greets him shares his wicked work.

a Other ancient authorities read *we*

OVERVIEW: Maintaining a pure confession of faith is of the utmost importance. Many deceivers are causing scandal (POLYCARP, BEDE). Doctrinal errors are a sign of the end of time and must be regarded as the work of the antichrist who is opposed to both the truth and the love that can only be found in Christ. We should not think that if we reject the coming of Christ in the flesh we can receive the full reward that is given to the saints (OECUMENIUS). John refutes those who assert either that the Son is not God or that he is inferior to the Father (BEDE, OECUMENIUS). Anyone who understands that Jesus Christ really did come in the flesh will believe his promise that he is coming again (OECUMENIUS). Right doctrine and clean living are two sides of the same coin, and Christians must stay away from people who lack either or both of them. Association with false teachers is forbidden (TERTULLIAN, AMBROSE, HILARY OF ARLES). Those who make friends of people who speak falsely about God and who even eat with them do not love the Lord who made them and who feeds them (BASIL). You are not to waste time in disputing with them (CLEM-ENT OF ALEXANDRIA) or even greeting them (IRENAEUS, DIDYMUS).

7 Such Is the Deceiver

MANY DECEIVERS. POLYCARP OF SMYRNA: Let us be zealous for that which is good, refraining from occasions of scandal and from false brothers and those who hypocritically bear the name of our Lord, deceiving empty-headed people. LETTER TO THE PHILIPPIANS 6.[1]

DECEIVERS HAVE GONE OUT. BEDE: This verse might apply to a wide range of heretics. It may refer primarily to those who believed that Christ was incarnate but who understood this in the wrong way by denying some aspect of it. Perhaps they rejected the idea that his flesh was real or that his soul was as ours. Or perhaps they refused to accept that he was truly divine, or that his Father was really God or that the Holy Spirit was really Almighty

[1]LCC 1:134.

God. John may even be referring to those Jews who, rejecting any link between Jesus and God, deny that Christ has come in the flesh but are waiting for the antichrist, to their own damnation. ON 2 JOHN.[2]

JESUS CHRIST IN THE FLESH. OECUMENIUS: One ought to add "whoever does not believe this" before the final clause, in order to make the transition from the plural to the singular easier to understand. Here John is speaking in the first instance about the second coming of Christ, not about the first one, though it is clear that whoever denies his second coming has denied his first coming also. Someone who thinks that he really did come in the flesh will certainly believe the promise that he made while he was in the flesh, to the effect that he is coming again. COMMENTARY ON 2 JOHN.[3]

8 Claim Your Full Reward

DO NOT FALL AWAY. HILARY OF ARLES: Here John is warning people not to fall away into heresy or to revert back to the Old Testament law once they have received the New. INTRODUCTORY COMMENTARY ON 2 JOHN.[4]

WIN A FULL REWARD. OECUMENIUS: What if someone were to say: "So what if I do not believe that Christ is coming in the flesh. I have lived a life of good works, so why can I not be rewarded for these insofar as they are in accordance with what is godly and religious?" To this the apostle replies that no one should think that if he rejects the coming of Christ in the flesh he can receive the perfect reward which is given to the saints, or be regarded as a worshiper of God, because someone who does not remain in his teaching does

not have God to begin with. COMMENTARY ON 2 JOHN.[5]

9 Abide in the Doctrine of Christ

HAVING THE FATHER AND THE SON. BEDE: Note how carefully John phrases this. He says that those who do not abide in Christ's teaching do not have God, whereas those who do have both the Father and the Son. By this he demonstrates that the Father and the Son are One and refutes the lie of those who assert either that the Son is not God or that he is inferior to the Father. ON 2 JOHN.[6]

THE DOCTRINE OF CHRIST. OECUMENIUS: How can a person who rejects the divine self-revelation be regarded as a worshiper of God? He is not a worshiper at all but an atheist. However it is important to note that this is his own fault. It is because he has withdrawn himself from the knowledge of God which is common to all creatures that he has fallen into this state. The apostles on the other hand had the right teaching and preached it, so that anyone who accepts them receives it as well and thus possesses both the Father and the Son. COMMENTARY ON 2 JOHN.[7]

10 Do Not Receive a False Teacher

ASSOCIATION FORBIDDEN. TERTULLIAN: Although we ought to be seeking at all times, where ought we to seek? Among the heretics, where all is foreign and opposed to our truth, with whom we are forbidden to associate? ON THE PRESCRIPTION OF HERETICS 14.12.[8]

---

[2]PL 93:121-22. [3]PG 119:692. [4]PL Supp. 3:126. [5]PG 119:693. [6]PL 93:122. [7]PG 119:693-96. [8]APT 462.

AVOID SUCH PEOPLE. AMBROSE OF MILAN: Since it is written that we should avoid such people, how can we not assume that someone who associates with Arians is also an exponent of their heresy? SYNOD LETTERS 40.[9]

TABLE FELLOWSHIP REFUSED. HILARY OF ARLES: Here you see an example of excommunication in the New Testament, both from table fellowship at home and from table fellowship in church. INTRODUCTORY COMMENTARY ON 2 JOHN.[10]

11 Take No Part in Evil

SHARING IN WICKED WORK. IRENAEUS: By wishing that we do not even give them a welcome, John, the Lord's disciple, made their condemnation even stronger. AGAINST HERESIES 1.16.3.[11]

DO NOT WASTE TIME IN DISPUTE. CLEMENT OF ALEXANDRIA: John forbids us to greet such people or to offer them hospitality, which in the circumstances is not at all unkind. But he also warns us not to argue or dispute with people who are unable to handle the things of God, lest we should be taken away from the true doctrine by clever arguments which have the appearance of truth. Furthermore, I think that it is wrong to pray with such people, because during times of prayer there is a moment for greeting and sharing the peace. ADUMBRATIONS.[12]

THOSE WHO SPEAK FALSELY. BASIL THE GREAT: It is obvious that those who make friends of people who speak falsely about God and who even eat with them do not love the Lord who made them and who feeds them. Instead of being content with that food they are led away into blasphemy against the one who feeds them. CATENA.[13]

SEPARATION REQUIRED. DIDYMUS THE BLIND: Anyone who dwells in the doctrine of the gospel and who acts according to its teaching will separate himself from those who think and act differently. COMMENTARY ON 2 JOHN.[14]

---

[9]FC 26:214-15 [10]PL Supp. 3:126. [11]ACW 55:70. [12]FGNK 3:92-93. [13]CEC 148. [14]PG 39:1810.

12-13 FAREWELL GREETINGS

[12]*Though I have much to write to you, I would rather not use paper and ink, but I hope to come to see you and talk with you face to face, so that our joy may be complete.* [13]*The children of your elect sister greet you.*

OVERVIEW: This letter is a provisional instruction written in the expectation that there will soon be a face-to-face meeting, when outstanding problems and divisions can be resolved. The greeting in the final verse seems to confirm that the letter was sent from one church to another, though closer identification of these churches is impossible. When the elder comes, he will be able to talk about things that are difficult to write in a letter (ORIGEN, OECUMENIUS). Meanwhile he greets the churches (BEDE, OECUMENIUS) as sisters in the faith and daughters of God by baptism (HILARY OF ARLES).

12 That Our Joy May Be Complete

PAPER AND INK. ORIGEN: Because of the incapacity of his hearers, John did not think it right to entrust the solutions of secrets of this kind to paper and ink. SERMONS ON EXODUS 4.2.[1]

I HOPE TO COME TO SEE YOU. OECUMENIUS: John explains that the reason this and the following letter are so short is that he hopes to visit them personally before too long. When he comes, he will be able to talk about things which are difficult to write in a letter and to clear up any remaining doubts which his correspondents may have. COMMENTARY ON 2 JOHN.[2]

13 The Children of Your Elect Sister Greet You

UNITED IN BAPTISM. HILARY OF ARLES: John unites the leaders of the churches in peace because they are sisters in the faith of the church and daughters of God by baptism. INTRODUCTORY COMMENTARY ON 2 JOHN.[3]

GREETINGS TO THE FAITHFUL. BEDE: On the one hand John forbids us to greet the enemies of the truth, but on the other he salutes the elect. This is so that unbelievers will be shunned by all good people, unless they happen to repent and change their views, and also so that peace and love between believers will continue to grow forever. ON 2 JOHN.[4]

ADDRESSED TO A CHURCH. OECUMENIUS: This ending proves that John was not writing to a single individual but to a church. COMMENTARY ON 2 JOHN.[5]

---

[1]FC 71:263. [2]PG 119:696. [3]PL Supp. 3:127. [4]PL 93:122. [5]PG 119:696.

THE THIRD EPISTLE OF JOHN

1-8 THE HOSPITABLE GAIUS

¹*The elder to the beloved Gaius, whom I love in the truth.*

²*Beloved, I pray that all may go well with you and that you may be in health; I know that it is well with your soul.* ³*For I greatly rejoiced when some of the brethren arrived and testified to the truth of your life, as indeed you do follow the truth.* ⁴*No greater joy can I have than this, to hear that my children follow the truth.*

⁵*Beloved, it is a loyal thing you do when you render any service to the brethren, especially to strangers,* ⁶*who have testified to your love before the church. You will do well to send them on their journey as befits God's service.* ⁷*For they have set out for his sake and have accepted nothing from the heathen.* ⁸*So we ought to support such men, that we may be fellow workers in the truth.*

OVERVIEW: Gaius was a model church leader and may have been the same person as the Gaius who entertained Paul at Corinth. He set an excellent example of hospitality and encouragement to the church, and those who benefited from his liberality spread his name everywhere they went. Gaius is the only ordinary Christian, apart from Philemon, whom we meet in this way in the New Testament, and therefore his example is particularly important, since anyone with the means to do so could imitate his conduct without needing ordination or any other special spiritual gift. Gaius was a host to the whole church, quite possibly including Paul. He opened his doors to everyone (BEDE). It is John's prayer that Gaius should go on to complete the good works that he intends to do (HILARY OF ARLES, BEDE). There is no greater joy than to know that those who have heard the gospel are now putting it into practice by the way in which they live (BEDE). There are relatively few who are spiritually gifted but many who are rich in the things of this world, and when the latter comfort poor saints with their wealth they gain a share in their spiritual riches (GREGORY THE GREAT). Do not wait for them to come to you, but search them out (ANDREAS).

1 The Elder and Gaius

THE THEME OF THE LETTER. ANDREAS: John writes this letter to encourage some fellow believers. He writes to Gaius and testifies to his great hospitality, which he praises. He says that someone who does such good is from God. He goes on to tell him to expel Diotrephes, who has not learned to do the same thing. He also praises Demetrius for doing the same as Gaius and mentions his faith as a testimony to his virtue. His main purpose for writing is the same as it was in his second letter. CATENA.[1]

TO THE BELOVED GAIUS. BEDE: Who this Gaius was and what he was like becomes apparent in the course of the letter. He was a man who had believed in Christ and as a result of that was living a life of good works. He was not a preacher himself, but he was happy to support the preaching ministry out of his own pocket. He is probably to be identified with the Gaius mentioned by Paul as his host.[2] For Gaius was a host to the whole church, who opened his doors to everyone who came along, whether they were the preachers or the hearers of the Word. ON 3 JOHN.[3]

LOVE IN THE TRUTH. OECUMENIUS: The person who loves God with heartfelt charity loves in the truth, a point which John often makes in his other letters. COMMENTARY ON 3 JOHN.[4]

2 Things Are Going Well

WELL WITH YOUR SOUL. HILARY OF ARLES: Things are going well for Gaius because his soul is carrying on in good works as the will of his mind directs him. INTRODUCTORY COMMENTARY ON 3 JOHN.[5]

COMPLETING GOOD WORK. BEDE: It is John's earnest desire and prayer that Gaius should go on to complete the good works

which he intends to do. His heart is already in the right place, which is the necessary precondition for fulfilling the rest. ON 3 JOHN.[6]

LIVING ACCORDING TO THE TRUTH. OECUMENIUS: Gaius is doing well, says John, because he is living according to the truth of the gospel. COMMENTARY ON 3 JOHN.[7]

3 Following the Truth

THE TRUTH OF YOUR LIFE. HILARY OF ARLES: The truth of Gaius's life was seen in the perfection of his works. He was a man who went about without any guile in thought, word or deed. Instead of that, he followed the commandments of God to the best of his ability. INTRODUCTORY COMMENTARY ON 3 JOHN.[8]

YOU FOLLOW THE TRUTH. OECUMENIUS: Gaius is walking in the truth because he is following the gospel in all its pure simplicity. To walk does not mean to put one foot in front of the other but to make orderly spiritual progress within the limits of what the soul is able to bear. This is something which very few people manage to achieve. COMMENTARY ON 3 JOHN.[9]

4 Hearing That My Children Follow the Truth

NO GREATER JOY. BEDE: There is no greater joy than to know that those who have heard the gospel are now putting it into practice by the way in which they live. ON 3 JOHN.[10]

---

[1]CEC 149. [2]Rom 16:23. [3]PL 93:121. [4]PG 119:700. [5]PL Supp. 3:127. [6]PG 93:122-23. [7]PG 119:700. [8]PL Supp. 3:127. [9]PG 119:700. [10]PL 93:123.

5 Hospitality to Strangers

LOYALTY EVIDENCES FAITH. BEDE: Gaius's loyalty is the result of his faith. What John means is that Gaius is doing all these things because he is a believer and wants to show his faith in the things that he does. ON 3 JOHN.[11]

6 Your Love for the Church

AS BEFITS GOD'S SERVICE. HILARY OF ARLES: Visitors praised Gaius to the rest of the church because of his generous hospitality to those who were in God's service. INTRODUCTORY COMMENTARY ON 3 JOHN.[12]

7 Serving Christ

ACCEPTING NOTHING FROM UNBELIEVERS. HILARY OF ARLES: This means that the servants of God have accepted no assistance from those who are not believers. INTRODUCTORY COMMENTARY ON 3 JOHN.[13]

FOR GOD'S SAKE. BEDE: There are two possible reasons why these people have set out for the sake of Christ. One is that they had gone of their own free will to preach the name of Christ. The other is that they had been expelled from their homes because of their faith in his holy name. ON 3 JOHN.[14]

8 We Ought to Support Such Persons

FELLOW WORKERS IN THE TRUTH. GREGORY THE GREAT: Whoever gives practical assistance to those who have spiritual gifts becomes a coworker with those people in their spiritual work. There are relatively few people who are spiritually gifted but many who are rich in the things of this world, and when the latter comfort poor saints with their wealth they gain a share in their spiritual riches. HOMILIES ON THE GOSPELS 20.12.[15]

LOOK FOR NEEDS. ANDREAS: John teaches us that we should not wait for such needy people to come to us but should rather go out and look for them, for that is what Lot and Abraham did. CATENA.[16]

---

[11]PL 93:123. [12]PL Supp. 3:127. [13]PL Supp. 3:127. [14]PL 93:123. [15]PL 79:1107. [16]CEC 150.

9-12 GOOD AND BAD IN THE CHURCH

[9]*I have written something to the church; but Diotrephes, who likes to put himself first, does not acknowledge my authority. [10]So if I come, I will bring up what he is doing, prating against me with evil words. And not content with that, he refuses himself to welcome the brethren, and also stops those who want to welcome them and puts them out of the church.*

[11]Beloved, do not imitate evil but imitate good. He who does good is of God; he who does evil has not seen God. [12]Demetrius has testimony from every one, and from the truth itself; I testify to him too, and you know my testimony is true.

OVERVIEW: Diotrephes was the opposite of Gaius. He was causing trouble in the church by rejecting the elder's authority and by expelling visitors. To the Fathers his conduct smacked of heresy (BEDE), and they were particularly impressed by the firm way in which the elder dealt with him. Diotrephes preferred to gain control of the church by preaching something new and different rather than by following humbly the apostolic teaching (BEDE). If we do not correct abuses, the abusers will corrupt the minds of others (HILARY OF ARLES, BEDE). We are not to return evil for evil when the injury has been done to us personally, but when it affects others we must correct it (OECUMENIUS). One who does evil has not seen God (DIDYMUS). One who beholds God and understands what he beheld has not seen God himself but rather some refraction of God that is knowable (PSEUDO-DIONYSIUS). A complete contrast to Diotrephes was Demetrius, who seems to have been rather similar to Gaius and who was praised accordingly (HILARY OF ARLES, ANDREAS, OECUMENIUS).

9 *Diotrephes Likes to Put Himself First*

THE LIMIT TO PATIENCE. HILARY OF ARLES: This verse teaches us that we ought to bear the abuse of those who insult us with equanimity, but sometimes we have to protest it because if we do not do so, these people will corrupt the minds of those who might otherwise have heard something good about us. INTRODUCTORY COMMENTARY ON 3 JOHN.[1]

HE DOES NOT ACKNOWLEDGE AUTHORITY. BEDE: It seems that Diotrephes was a leading heretic of those times. He was proud and insolent, preferring to gain control of the church by preaching something new and different rather than by following humbly the old commandments which John had already given them. ON 3 JOHN.[2]

10 *What Diotrephes Is Doing*

CORRUPTING OTHERS. BEDE: It is true that we must do nothing to stir up the tongues of accusers, lest they should perish on our account. Likewise we must patiently endure those who attack us because of their own wickedness, so that we may become better people. Nevertheless there are times when we have to protest, because those who spread evil stories about us may corrupt the minds of innocent people who otherwise would have heard nothing but good about us. This is why John objects to his accuser. ON 3 JOHN.[3]

REFUSING TO WELCOME THE BROTHERS. OECUMENIUS: If the principle of the gospel is that we should not return evil for evil, what is the meaning of this warning? I think that the answer is that we are not to return evil for evil when the injury has been done to us personally and to no one else. But when it affects others, we must heed what Paul says to Elymas, who was corrupting the ways of the

---

[1]PL Supp. 3:128. [2]PL 93:124. [3]PL 93:124.

242

Lord: "You son of the devil."[4] COMMENTARY ON 3 JOHN.[5]

11 *Imitate Good*

ONE WHO DOES GOOD. DIDYMUS THE BLIND: Light has nothing in common with darkness, and there is no agreement between Christ and Belial. The person who does good has Christ, the true light, and not darkness or Belial. But the person who does evil is from Belial and darkness and has not seen God or had any knowledge of him. CATENA.[6]

ONE WHO DOES EVIL. PSEUDO-DIONYSIUS: Someone beholding God and understanding what he saw has not actually seen God himself but rather something of his which has being and is knowable. For in himself, God transcends mind and being; he is completely unknown and nonbeing. He exists beyond being and is known beyond the mind. LETTERS I.[7]

12 *Demetrius Has Good Testimony*

DOING WHAT IS GOOD. HILARY OF ARLES:

Demetrius was highly regarded by everybody because of his virtue. Some people take this verse to mean that he was criticized by everyone, but I cannot see how such an interpretation is possible. INTRODUCTORY COMMENTARY ON 3 JOHN.[8]

WHICH DEMETRIUS? ANDREAS: In my opinion this Demetrius is the same man who made silver idols of Artemis and who once led a riot against the apostle Paul.[9] CATENA.[10]

TESTIMONY FROM EVERYONE. OECUMENIUS: By "all" John means primarily all those who respect the truth, though it is possible that the term should be extended to cover unbelievers as well, since Paul tried to please both Jews and Gentiles.[11] By "the truth itself" he means the fact that Demetrius practices what he preaches. For there are some who sound good when they talk, but their subsequent actions do not live up to what they claim. COMMENTARY ON 3 JOHN.[12]

---

[4]Acts 13:8. [5]PG 119:701. [6]CEC 151. [7]CWS 263. [8]PL Supp. 3:128. [9]Acts 19:24. [10]CEC 152. [11]1 Cor 10:35. [12]PG 119:701-4.

13-15 FAREWELL GREETINGS

[13]*I had much to write to you, but I would rather not write with pen and ink;* [14]*I hope to see you soon, and we will talk together face to face.*
[15]*Peace be to you. The friends greet you. Greet the friends, every one of them.*

OVERVIEW: The letter ends in exactly the same way as does 2 John (HILARY OF ARLES) and provides strong evidence not only that they were written by the same person (OECUmenius) but that they were sent to the same church at the same time. Do not let quarrelsomeness with its love of empty victory creep into our midst, for our aim is the elimination of all discord (CLEMENT OF ALEXANDRIA).

14 *Talking Face to Face*

MUCH TO WRITE. HILARY OF ARLES: John means by this that he still has many commands to give them. INTRODUCTORY COMMENTARY ON 3 JOHN.[1]

THE SAME GREETING. OECUMENIUS: This is just the same as what John said at the end of his previous letter, and there is no point repeating the remarks which I made there. COMMENTARY ON 3 JOHN.[2]

15 *Greet the Friends*

PEACE TO ALL. CLEMENT OF ALEXANDRIA: Do not let quarrelsomeness with its love of empty victory creep into our midst, for our aim is the elimination of all discord. Surely this is the meaning of the expression "Peace be to you." THE TEACHER 2.7.58.[3]

THE FRIENDS GREET YOU. BEDE: John sends the grace of peace and salvation to his friends in order to demonstrate that Diotrephes and other enemies of the truth have no part in their peace or salvation. ON 3 JOHN.[4]

---

[1]PL Supp. 3:128. [2]PG 119:704. [3]FC 23:144. [4]PL 93:124.

THE EPISTLE
OF JUDE

1-2 JUDE GREETS THE CHURCH

¹Jude, a servant of Jesus Christ and brother of James,
To those who are called, beloved in God the Father and kept for Jesus Christ:
²May mercy, peace, and love be multiplied to you.

OVERVIEW: Jude was generally regarded as the brother of James the brother of Jesus, and his apparent unwillingness to say so explicitly is put down to his modesty (EUSEBIUS OF CAESAREA, OECUMENIUS). He is distinguished from Iscariot (HILARY OF ARLES) and may be identified with Thaddeus in Matthew and Mark (BEDE). There was independent testimony to the fact that he was of David's line, and it seems to have been assumed by some that he was a son of Joseph by an earlier marriage. The grandchildren of Jude were still being accused of being related to Christ in the days of Domitian, according to Hegesippus (EUSEBIUS OF CAESAREA). It is in mercy, peace and love (HILARY OF ARLES, OECUMENIUS) that we are kept in Christ (THEOPHYLACT).

1 Servant of Christ and Brother of James

JUDE THE SERVANT. CLEMENT OF ALEXANDRIA: Jude was the brother of the sons of Joseph, but despite his relationship to the Lord, he did not say that he was Jesus' brother. What did he say? He called himself Jude, the servant of Jesus Christ, that is, of the Lord, and the brother of James, who was the Lord's brother. ADUMBRATIONS.[1]

THE DESCENDANTS OF JUDE. EUSEBIUS OF CAESAREA: When Domitian ordered that those of the race of David be slain, an ancient story holds that some of the heretics accused the grandchildren of Jude (the brother of the Savior, according to the flesh), on the ground that they really were of the family of David and were related to Christ himself. Hegesippus makes this quite clear. HISTORY OF THE CHURCH 3.19.[2]

EUSEBIUS OF CAESAREA: Hegesippus says that other descendants of one of the so-called brothers of the Lord, Jude by name, lived until the reign of Trajan [98-117], after giving testimony of their faith in Christ in the time of Domitian [81-96]. HISTORY OF THE CHURCH 3.32.[3]

---

[1]FGNK 3:83. [2]FC 19:166. [3]FC 19:191-92.

NOT ISCARIOT. HILARY OF ARLES: Jude does his utmost to make sure that nobody confuses him with Judas Iscariot, which is why he confesses that he is Christ's servant and James's brother. Note how he also says that the Father chooses us, Jesus keeps us and the Holy Spirit calls us. INTRODUCTORY COMMENTARY ON JUDE.[4]

JUDE CALLED THADDEUS. BEDE: The apostle Jude, whom Matthew and Mark call Thaddeus in their Gospels, is writing against the same corrupters of the faith as Peter and John condemn in their letters. ON JUDE.[5]

THE BROTHER OF JAMES. OECUMENIUS: This apostle, after calling himself the servant of Jesus Christ, went on to add that he was the brother of James because James was so highly regarded in the church that Jude was bound to benefit from so close an association with him. Note that he refers to his correspondents as those who have been "called," because it was not they who decided to follow Jesus, but God who reached out to call them to his service. COMMENTARY ON JUDE.[6]

KEPT IN JESUS CHRIST. THEOPHYLACT: Christ the Lord said: "No one can come to me unless the Father draws him."[7] Jude affirms the truth of this here when he says that those whom the Father has loved are preserved by the Son. COMMENTARY ON JUDE.[8]

2 Mercy, Peace and Love

LOVE MULTIPLIED. HILARY OF ARLES: Jude includes a reference to love here because he has noticed that there is a lack of it among his people. INTRODUCTORY COMMENTARY ON JUDE.[9]

MERCY AND PEACE. OECUMENIUS: Jude prays for greater mercy because it is by the bowels of God's mercy that we have been called back to him and enrolled as his servants. He asks for increased peace because this is God's gift to us, by which he leads us who have sinned back to friendship with him through his Son Jesus Christ. He also desires greater love, since it is because of the love which he has shown toward us that the only-begotten Son sacrificed himself for us by dying on the cross. In praying for these things, Jude is doing no more than imitate David, who said: "O continue thy steadfast love to those who know thee."[10] COMMENTARY ON JUDE.[11]

---

[4]PL Supp. 3:128. [5]PL 93:123. [6]PG 119:705. [7]Jn 6:44. [8]PG 126:88. [9]PL Supp. 3:128. [10]Ps 36:10. [11]PG 119:705-8.

3-16 WICKEDNESS IN THE CHURCH

[3]*Beloved, being very eager to write to you of our common salvation, I found it necessary to write appealing to you to contend for the faith which was once for all delivered to the*

saints. [4]*For admission has been secretly gained by some who long ago were designated for this condemnation, ungodly persons who pervert the grace of our God into licentiousness and deny our only Master and Lord, Jesus Christ.*[a]

[5]*Now I desire to remind you, though you were once for all fully informed, that he*[b] *who saved a people out of the land of Egypt, afterward destroyed those who did not believe.* [6]*And the angels that did not keep their own position but left their proper dwelling have been kept by him in eternal chains in the nether gloom until the judgment of the great day;* [7]*just as Sodom and Gomorrah and the surrounding cities, which likewise acted immorally and indulged in unnatural lust, serve as an example by undergoing a punishment of eternal fire.*

[8]*Yet in like manner these men in their dreamings defile the flesh, reject authority, and revile the glorious ones.*[c] [9]*But when the archangel Michael, contending with the devil, disputed about the body of Moses, he did not presume to pronounce a reviling judgment upon him, but said, "The Lord rebuke you."* [10]*But these men revile whatever they do not understand, and by those things that they know by instinct as irrational animals do, they are destroyed.* [11]*Woe to them! For they walk in the way of Cain, and abandon themselves for the sake of gain to Balaam's error, and perish in Korah's rebellion.* [12]*These are blemishes*[d] *on your love feasts, as they boldly carouse together, looking after themselves; waterless clouds, carried along by winds; fruitless trees in late autumn, twice dead, uprooted;* [13]*wild waves of the sea, casting up the foam of their own shame; wandering stars for whom the nether gloom of darkness has been reserved for ever.*

[14]*It was of these also that Enoch in the seventh generation from Adam prophesied, saying, "Behold, the Lord came with his holy myriads,* [15]*to execute judgment on all, and to convict all the ungodly of all their deeds of ungodliness which they have committed in such an ungodly way, and of all the harsh things which ungodly sinners have spoken against him."* [16]*These are grumblers, malcontents, following their own passions, loud-mouthed boasters, flattering people to gain advantage.*

a Or *the only Master and our Lord Jesus Christ*   **b** Ancient authorities read *Jesus* or *the Lord* or *God*   **c** Greek *glories*   **d** Or *reefs*

OVERVIEW: Jude's main purpose in writing was to combat false teaching in the church, and it is in this section that the parallels with 2 Peter are most obvious. No other foundation is laid than the common faith (BEDE) once for all delivered to the saints (HILARY OF ARLES), which must be contended for against determined opposition (OECUMENIUS, THEO-PHYLACT). This comes from godless persons who twist Scripture wickedly, who have secretly come into the church (CYRIL OF ALEXANDRIA) pretending to preach the gospel (DIDYMUS). Their judgment was decreed long ago (ANDREAS), and they have condemned themselves by their actions (BEDE). They pervert grace into licentiousness (BEDE) and deny the one Lord (OECUMENIUS). Jude writes to remind those who have already been fully informed (BEDE). Those who sin nowadays cannot expect anything better than the fate that befell those who sinned long ago (OECUMENIUS). Those whom God delivered from Egypt he afterward destroyed if they did not believe (CLEMENT OF ALEXANDRIA, DIDYMUS, ANDREAS).

The fallen angels are evil not in their origin but in their failure to hold to their origin (PSEUDO-DIONYSIUS, HESYCHIUS). They are being kept until they are thrown into the ultimate fire and bound in those chains (CLEMENT OF ALEXANDRIA, BEDE) that cannot be seen because of the darkness (ANDREAS). The unnatural lust in which the Sodomites indulged was homosexuality, wrong because it cannot lead to procreation. If God destroyed them, regardless of their earlier state of blessedness, how will he spare us if we act in an ungodly and lustful way (OECUMENIUS)?

The collectors of these catenae were aware that Marcion and Arius and Nestorius were not the direct object of Jude's admonitions. Rather the premise is that Jude was already aware of the tendency to certain heresies that would have correspondences with those that would emerge later (ANDREAS, OECUMENIUS, THEOPHYLACT).

The Fathers did not hesitate to expand as much as they were able on the various enemies of God's truth who appear in the Old Testament and whom Jude mentions here. They were particularly fascinated by the story of Michael and also by the prophecy of Enoch. Jude's allusion to Michael's contention with the devil for the body of Moses (CLEMENT OF ALEXANDRIA, PETER CHRYSOLOGUS) may have had its source in Zechariah (BEDE). Anthony's vision of this incident is recollected (ANDREAS).

The usual connection between false teaching and immoral living is brought out clearly throughout this section. The Fathers lost no opportunity to rub this correlation in with respect to the heretics of their own time. These deluded people imagine that their lusts and terrible desires are good (CLEMENT OF ALEXANDRIA). They defile the flesh (ANDREAS) and like sleepwalkers stumble from one thing to another (OECUMENIUS). Jude is not content to compare them with the sin of Adam (CLEMENT OF ALEXANDRIA) and the fratricide of Cain but adds Balaam, who went out to curse God's people for the sake of money. Korah is mentioned because he seized a teaching authority that God had not granted to him (ANDREAS). Grumblers are people who mutter against others under their breath, whereas malcontents are those who are always looking for ways in which they can attack and disparage everything and everybody (OECUMENIUS). Jude's metaphors of stars, clouds, trees and waves point toward the animal-like behavior of people, their wickedness and corruption (CLEMENT OF ALEXANDRIA, DIDYMUS, ANDREAS). Despite objections (AUGUSTINE), Enoch deserves to be included in the canon because of its author, its antiquity and the way in which it has been used (BEDE), and particularly because of this passage that Jude takes from Enoch (TERTULLIAN).

3 Contend for the Faith Delivered to the Saints

PRESERVE THE HARMONY OF SCRIPTURE. ORIGEN: If we wish woodenly to preserve unchanged the good things once given to the saints and will not adapt the events of the historical account, we will by such action appear to do something like what the heretics do, by not preserving the harmony of the narrative of the Scriptures from beginning to end. COMMENTARY ON JOHN 10.290.[1]

THE FAITH ONCE FOR ALL DELIVERED. HILARY OF ARLES: The faith was first delivered to these people by the apostle Paul, who said: "No other foundation can anyone lay, than the one which is already laid."[2] INTRODUCTORY COMMENTARY ON JUDE.[3]

OF OUR COMMON SALVATION. BEDE: All God's chosen people share one common salvation, one faith and one love of Christ. ON JUDE.[4]

CONTEND FOR THE FAITH. OECUMENIUS: Jude exhorts those who have accepted Christ as their Savior and believed in him to go on struggling. They must not be corrupted by an ungodly mind, but rather they must discipline themselves and show greater dedication to this task. COMMENTARY ON JUDE.[5]

THE PURPOSE OF THE LETTER. THEOPHYLACT: Here Jude reveals what the purpose of his letter is. He is concerned for the salvation of those to whom he is writing and is afraid that in their naiveté they might be seduced by false teachers. In order to combat them, Jude will go on to expose their teachings. Peter had already done the same, but now Jude would give them a fuller exposition. Both Peter and Paul had predicted that such people would appear in the church, and even Christ himself had said: "Many will come in my name and will lead many astray."[6] COMMENTARY ON JUDE.[7]

4 Ungodly Persons Pervert Grace into License

THOSE WHO TWIST SCRIPTURE. DIDYMUS THE BLIND: There are some godless men who twist Scripture wickedly and who have come into the church, pretending to preach the gospel. Their judgment was decreed long ago, and they have condemned themselves by their actions. As a result, they have been handed over to their impure lusts. By their great ungodliness they have turned the grace of our Lord Jesus Christ into wantonness, and by their wickedness even people who have been called by the gospel have denied the one Lord Jesus Christ. It is in order to win them back that Jude goes on to talk of what God did in the past to people who behaved in that way. COMMENTARY ON JUDE.[8]

ADMISSION SECRETLY GAINED. CYRIL OF ALEXANDRIA: These words were written about those who, after attributing the glory of sonship only to the Word begotten of God the Father, say that another son of the seed of David and Jesse has been united with him and been given a share in the sonship and in the glory proper to God. LETTERS 55.41.[9]

DESIGNATED FOR THIS CONDEMNATION. ANDREAS: Jude means that their condemnation was predestined, for even the betrayal of Judas had been foretold. Here he is talking about the Simonians, for they are gluttonous and intemperate, pretending to teach godli-

---

[1]FC 80:319. By too rigidly holding to the plain sense, so as to ignore the spiritual sense of a text, we may offend against Scripture by missing its larger meaning within the whole scriptural narrative. [2]1 Cor 3:11. [3]PL Supp. 3:129. [4]PL 93:123. [5]PG 119:708. [6]Mk 13:6. [7]PG 126:89. [8]PG 39:1812-13. [9]FC 77:34. Cyril thought that Peter's letter was an anticipatory warning about christological heresies that would come into fuller assertion with the Nestorians much later. Whether earlier or later, they were denying the one Lord and Master, Jesus Christ.

ness so that they can worm their way into people's houses. CATENA.[10]

THEY PERVERT THE GRACE OF OUR GOD.
BEDE: The grace of our Lord has softened the hard edges of the law, which prescribed such things as stoning and burning for various infractions. Our Lord, however, relaxed these rules and made it possible to purge sins by making reparations and by giving alms. But now, says Jude, these men have taken this relaxation to the point of license and sin all the more boldly when they think that they are not going to be punished for doing so. ON JUDE.[11]

THEY DENY OUR ONLY MASTER AND LORD.
OECUMENIUS: If those of us who have received the incarnate Word say that he is someone other than the one who was with the Father from all eternity and in the last days was born of Mary, are we not denying that he is our one Lord and master? For there is but one Lord Jesus according to the union of divinity and humanity. He was the Word of God and God before all ages, and from the beginning of his conception in the womb of the holy virgin he added human flesh to the glory of his divinity. COMMENTARY ON JUDE.[12]

5 He Who Saved, Afterward Destroyed

PUNISHMENT FOR THE SAKE OF CONVERSION.
CLEMENT OF ALEXANDRIA: God wanted to teach these people by punishing them. Therefore in the present age they are punished and perish for the sake of those who are being saved until the time when they too are converted. ADUMBRATIONS.[13]

THOSE WHO DID NOT BELIEVE. DIDYMUS THE BLIND: When Moses delivered the people from Egypt, all those who did not believe perished. COMMENTARY ON JUDE.[14]

AFTERWARD DESTROYED. ANDREAS: Jude shows that although God led his people out of Egypt, they turned away from him, and for that reason he gave them over to destruction if they would not repent. CATENA.[15]

ONCE FULLY INFORMED. BEDE: The people to whom Jude is writing have already heard all the hidden mysteries of the faith and have no need to hear anything further from subsequent teachers, as if what they might teach is somehow holier than what they have already learned. ON JUDE.[16]

DISOBEDIENCE PUNISHED. OECUMENIUS: Jude writes this in order to counter the heresies of the Nicolaitans, the Valentinians and the Marcionites.[17] He shows that the author of the Old and of the New Testaments is one and the same God. It is not, as those heretics claimed, that there was one God of the Old Testament, who was cruel and vindictive, and another God of the New Testament, who is mild and forgiving. At the same time he reminds us that those who sin nowadays cannot expect anything better than the fate which befell those who fled Egypt so long ago. For at that time God, in his great power and because of the oath which he had sworn to their ancestors, delivered Israel from slavery in Egypt. But those among them who disobeyed did not go unpunished. The fact that God had blessed

---

[10]CEC 154. Simonians were alleged to be followers of Simon Magus. [11]PL 93:124. [12]PG 119:708-9. [13]FGNK 3:83. [14]PG 39:1812. [15]CEC 155. [16]PL 93:125. [17]That is, Jude was writing in the first century in such a way as to anticipate later heretical developments.

their ancestors was of no benefit to them at that point. COMMENTARY ON JUDE.[18]

6 The Fallen Angels Left Their Proper Dwelling

KEPT IN ETERNAL CHAINS. CLEMENT OF ALEXANDRIA: Jude gives the name *chains* to the loss of that honor in which the angels had stood and the lust for worldly things which had overcome them and taken away any desire to be converted. ADUMBRATIONS.[19]

THEIR ORIGINAL SOURCE. PSEUDO-DIONYSIUS: If devils are called evil, it is not in respect of their created being, since they owe their origin to the Good and were recipients of a good being. Rather it is because being is lacking to them by virtue of their inability, as Scripture puts it, to hold on to their original source. ON THE DIVINE NAMES 4.23.[20]

IRONIC DESTINY. HESYCHIUS: Who can understand God's love for his people or figure out the truth just by his own reasoning? For because of the truth he did not spare the angels who sinned, but on account of his kindness toward us he has allowed harlots and publicans into his kingdom. CATENA.[21]

FALLEN ANGELS KEPT IN CHAINS. ANDREAS: They are being kept until they are thrown into the ultimate fire and bound in those chains which cannot be seen because of the darkness. That he has kept them for the coming judgment can be seen from what Peter has written.[22] CATENA.[23]

UNTIL THE JUDGMENT. BEDE: The Holy Spirit convicts the world of the judgment by which the ruler of this world has been judged,

in these words of the apostle Jude. HOMILIES ON THE GOSPELS 2.11.[24]

7 Sodom and Gomorrah

UNNATURAL LUST. OECUMENIUS: The unnatural lust in which the Sodomites indulged was homosexuality, which is wrong because it cannot lead to procreation. Jude mentions them in order to point out that if God destroyed them, regardless of their earlier state of blessedness, how will he spare us if we act in an ungodly and lustful way? However well-disposed and kind he may be toward us, he is still the righteous God, and because of his righteousness he does not spare those who have sinned against him. COMMENTARY ON JUDE.[25]

8 Defiling the Flesh

IN THEIR DREAMINGS. CLEMENT OF ALEXANDRIA: These deluded people imagine that their lusts and terrible desires are good and pay no attention to what is truly good and beyond all good. ADUMBRATIONS.[26]

NOXIOUS TEACHINGS. ANDREAS: Jude calls them "dreamers" because they have no idea of the truth but fantasize as if they were dreaming and concoct doctrines full of impiety. They say that our flesh, that is to say, our body, is the work of the devil and blaspheme the lordship and glory of the Holy Trinity, accepting the Father as the eternal and uncreated One but reducing the Son and the Holy Spirit to the status of creatures made in time.

---

[18]PG 119:709. [19]FGNK 3:84. [20]CWS 90. [21]CEC 156. [22]2 Pet 3:7-10. [23]CEC 155. [24]HOG 2:102. [25]PG 119:712. [26]FGNK 3:84.

These are the noxious teachings of Marcion and Arius, which explains why the apostle expresses himself so sharply against them.[27] They do not confess that there is one God, Maker of both the visible and the invisible worlds, but they deify matter and darkness and detest the flesh. Jude condemns these people, even to the point of saying that they have polluted their mind and their entire being. CATENA.[28]

LIKE SLEEPWALKERS. OECUMENIUS: It is worth noting here that Jude does not spare us the details of these people's sin, which he attributes to the fact that they are deluded by a kind of dreaming. Those who do such things have lost their powers of reason and act as if they were sleepwalkers, stumbling from one thing to another. COMMENTARY ON JUDE.[29]

9 Michael and the Body of Moses

MICHAEL CONTENDED WITH THE DEVIL. CLEMENT OF ALEXANDRIA: This proves that Moses was taken up into heaven. The one who fought with the devil as our guardian angel is here called Michael. ADUMBRATIONS.[30]

THE BURIAL OF MOSES. PETER CHRYSOLOGUS: The angels were present at the death of Moses, and God himself took care of his burial. SERMONS 83.[31]

ANTHONY'S VISION. ANDREAS: Here Jude shows that the Old Testament agrees with the New and that they were both given by the same God. For the devil objected, claiming that the body was his because he is the lord of matter. . . . But Michael would not accept this and brought on the devil a punishment wor-thy of his blasphemy, though he abandoned him to the discretion of his own master. For when God brought Moses to the mount of transfiguration, the devil said to Michael that God had broken his promise, because he had sworn not to do such a thing. Michael is said to have taken care of the burial of Moses, and the devil is supposed to have objected to this. God then came to the rescue and wanted to show those who at that time saw only a very little that eventually our souls would be changed and we would all ascend into heaven. But the devil and the evil spirits with him wanted to cut off the way to heaven and tried both to do their evil deeds and at the same time weaken the righteous by this angelic warfare. This is what the blessed Antony saw in his vision. CATENA.[32]

SEARCHING FOR JUDE'S SOURCES. BEDE: It is not easy to see what part of Scripture Jude got this tale from, though we do find something like it in Zechariah, who says: "Then he showed me Joshua the high priest standing before the angel of the Lord, and Satan standing at his right hand to accuse him."[33] However, it is easy enough to see that in the Zechariah passage, Joshua wanted the people of Israel to be set free from their captivity in Babylon, and Satan resisted this. But when it was that Michael fought with the devil over the body of Moses is unknown. There are, however, some people who say that God's people were called the "body of Moses,"

---

[27]The collector of this catena, Andreas, was aware that Marcion and Arius were not the direct objects of Jude's admonitions. Rather the premise is that Jude was aware of the tendency to certain heresies that would later have correspondences with those of Marcion and Arius. [28]CEC 158. [29]PG 119:712. [30]FGNK 3:84. [31]FC 17:133. [32]CEC 160-61. [33]Zech 3:1.

because Moses was a part of that people, and if this is the case, it may be that in saying this Jude is referring to the whole nation. But whatever the case may be, here is what we have to learn from this incident: if the archangel Michael refrained from cursing the devil and dealt gently with him, how much more should we mere mortals avoid blaspheming, especially as we might offend the majesty of the Creator by an incautious word. ON JUDE.[34]

10 People Who Behave Like Animals

THEY ACT BY INSTINCT. CLEMENT OF ALEXANDRIA: Jude here refers to those who eat, drink, indulge in sexual activity and do other things which are common to animals who lack the faculty of reason. ADUMBRATIONS.[35]

CONCOCTING BLASPHEMIES. ANDREAS: Not knowing the true doctrine, these people concoct blasphemies for themselves. They are so caught up in lust that they are no different from dumb animals. CATENA.[36]

11 Walking in the Way of Cain

THEY ABANDON THEMSELVES. CLEMENT OF ALEXANDRIA: Because we have sinned according to the likeness of Adam, we share in the burden of Adam's sin. ADUMBRATIONS.[37]

THEY DESERTED THE TRUTH. DIDYMUS THE BLIND: Since it has been declared that heretics have completely deserted the word of truth, Jude shows how they are subjected to different kinds of evil.[38] COMMENTARY ON JUDE.[39]

OUTRAGEOUS UNGODLINESS. ANDREAS: These people are even fratricides, because what they teach kills the souls of those who are deceived by them. Look how he describes their outrageous ungodliness. He is not content to compare them with Cain but adds Balaam and Korah as well. Cain we understand from the above. Balaam he adds because Balaam went out to curse God's people for the sake of money, even if God later turned his tongue around to the point where he blessed them instead. Korah is mentioned because he seized a teaching authority which God had not granted to him. CATENA.[40]

12 Fruitless Trees in Late Autumn

WATERLESS CLOUDS, TWICE DEAD. CLEMENT OF ALEXANDRIA: "Clouds without water" are those who do not have the divine and fruit-bearing Word in them. They are twice dead: Once, because they sinned by transgressing, and again when they were handed over to the punishments foreordained by God for them. A person may be said to be dead even when he is alive but not enjoying his inheritance. ADUMBRATIONS.[41]

FRUITLESS TREES. DIDYMUS THE BLIND: These people may say that they will bear fruit, but they are lying because they are incapable of doing that. The reason is that they are thorns and weeds, and trees without any fruit at all. They are fit for nothing except to be thrown into the fire. COMMENTARY ON JUDE.[42]

THE METAPHORS OF STARS, CLOUDS, WAVES AND TREES. ANDREAS: The apostle's

---

[34]PL 93:126. [35]FGNK 3:84. [36]CEC 163. [37]FGNK 3:84. [38]Cf. Rom 1:28-32. [39]PG 39:1815. [40]CEC 164. [41]FGNK 3:84-85. [42]PG 39:1817.

words about these men who will not be pardoned have to be understood metaphorically. For he is not talking about stars and clouds, waves and trees, though he uses them as examples, because what they have they have by nature, whereas these men have the same things by deliberate choice. For waterless clouds which are blown about by the winds are not punished, nor are fruitless trees which just die. Wild waves have nothing to be ashamed of either, because they are mindless and devoid of sense. Likewise, the stars we call planets do not inherit the darkness—sinful people do! The ones whom Jude is talking about are like wandering planets which are going along the pathway which is diametrically opposed to virtue. The darkness is reserved for them, not as stars but as men. For Jude's point has nothing to do with stars or clouds or waves, but rather it is concerned with the animal-like behavior of men, their wickedness and corruption. CATENA.[43]

BLEMISHES ON YOUR LOVE FEASTS. BEDE: Those who sin are blemished, because the crime itself is the blemish which contaminates the one who commits it. Likewise Jude calls heretics blemishes because not only do they eat and drink their way to damnation but they also lead others along the same path. ON JUDE.[44]

13 Wild Waves of the Sea

A MISERABLE LIFE. CLEMENT OF ALEXANDRIA: In these words Jude describes the life of worldly people, who will come to an unhappy end. ADUMBRATIONS.[45]

WANDERING STARS. HILARY OF ARLES: These people are called wandering stars

because they do not follow the sun of truth. INTRODUCTORY COMMENTARY ON JUDE.[46]

KILLING THEMSELVES A SECOND TIME. ANDREAS: These are people who by their wicked life and ungodliness have killed their souls with false doctrines. Before they believed, they were dead in their ungodliness, but when they turned to the gospel they found life. However, they gave themselves up again to ungodliness and lust, thereby killing themselves a second time. How can someone who is this guilty, doing evil and living in ungodliness and lust, ever find stability or roots in such a topsyturvy life? CATENA.[47]

14 Enoch's Prophecy

THE STATUS OF ENOCH'S WRITINGS. TERTULLIAN: Since Enoch in the same book tells us of our Lord, we must not reject anything at all which genuinely pertains to us. Do we not read that every word of Scripture useful for edification is divinely inspired[48]? As you very well know, Enoch was later rejected by the Jews for the same reason that prompted them to reject almost everything which prophesied about Christ. It is not at all surprising that they rejected certain Scriptures which spoke of him, considering that they were destined not to receive him when he spoke to them himself.[49] But we have a witness to Enoch in the epistle of Jude the apostle. ON THE DRESS OF WOMEN 3.3.[50]

WHETHER ENOCH IS A PROPHET. AUGUSTINE: Does not the canonical epistle of Jude

---

[43]CEC 165. [44]PL 93:127. [45]FGNK 3:85. [46]PL Supp. 3:130. [47]CEC 166-67. [48]2 Tim 3:16. [49]Jn 1:11. [50]FC 40:122.

the apostle openly declare that Enoch spoke as a prophet? It is true that his alleged writings have never been accepted as authoritative, either by Jews or Christians, but that is because their extreme antiquity makes us afraid of handing out as authentic works those which may be forgeries. THE CITY OF GOD 18.38.[51]

WHETHER ENOCH IS APOCRYPHAL. BEDE: The book of Enoch, from which this quotation is taken, belongs to the Apocrypha, not because the sayings of that prophet are of no value or because they are false but because the book which circulates under his name was not really written by him but was put out by someone else who used his name. For if it were genuine, it would not contain anything contrary to sound doctrine. But as a matter of fact it contains any number of incredible things about giants, who had angels instead of men as fathers, and which are clearly lies. Indeed, it was precisely because Jude quotes him that for a long time his letter was rejected by many as being uncanonical. Nevertheless it deserves to be included in the canon because of its author, its antiquity and the way in which it has been used, and particularly because this passage which Jude takes from Enoch is not in itself apocryphal or dubious but is rather notable for the clarity with which

it testifies to the true light. ON JUDE.[52]

15 Convicting the Ungodly

UNGODLY DEEDS, AN UNGODLY WAY. OECUMENIUS: The ungodly differ from sinners in that an ungodly person is someone who has sinned against God, whereas a sinner is someone who departs from the path of righteousness in matters to do with his behavior in this life. COMMENTARY ON JUDE.[53]

16 Flattering to Gain Advantage

LOUD BOASTERS. ANDREAS: These people have no confidence in their own teaching. For how can it not be dangerous to spread it with such wickedness and blasphemy? CATENA.[54]

GRUMBLERS AND MALCONTENTS. OECUMENIUS: Grumblers are people who mutter against others under their breath, whereas malcontents are those who are always looking for ways in which they can attack and disparage everything and everybody. COMMENTARY ON JUDE.[55]

---

[51]FC 24:145. [52]PL 93:129. [53]PG 119:717. [54]CEC 167-68. [55]PG 119:717.

17-23 THE CHRISTIAN COUNTERATTACK

[17]*But you must remember, beloved, the predictions of the apostles of our Lord Jesus Christ;* [18]*they said to you, "In the last time there will be scoffers, following their own ungodly pas-*

sions." [19]It is these who set up divisions, worldly people, devoid of the Spirit. [20]But you, beloved, build yourselves up on your most holy faith; pray in the Holy Spirit; [21]keep yourselves in the love of God; wait for the mercy of our Lord Jesus Christ unto eternal life. [22]And convince some, who doubt; [23]save some, by snatching them out of the fire; on some have mercy with fear, hating even the garment spotted by the flesh.[e]

e The Greek text in this sentence is uncertain at several points

OVERVIEW: It was not enough merely to identify and condemn the heretics. Christians had to provide a credible alternative, and Jude devotes the closing section of his letter to outlining what that was. Christians were not to be surprised by the presence of error in the church or to regard it as anything unusual, because the apostles had predicted this situation. The only way to deal with it was to maintain an orthodox faith, live a pure life and evangelize others as thoroughly as possible. The faithful are called to remember the predictions of the prophets (HILARY OF ARLES) and to avoid divisions caused by scoffers and those devoid of the Spirit (AUGUSTINE, CYRIL OF ALEXANDRIA, ANDREAS, OECUMENIUS), ever reforming themselves according to the Spirit's guidance (OECUMENIUS). He alludes to the Christian life as a cloak that may be soiled (CLEMENT OF ALEXANDRIA, MAXIMUS THE CONFESSOR). The cleansing of this garment cannot be done in our own strength but only by the power of God (BEDE).

17 Remember the Predictions of the Apostles

WHICH APOSTLES? HILARY OF ARLES: Jude does not specify which apostles he is referring to, but many people assume he means Peter, James and John. INTRODUCTORY COMMENTARY ON JUDE.[1]

A LATE WRITING. OECUMENIUS: The predictions of the apostles can be found in 2 Peter and in most of Paul's letters. From this statement it is clear that Jude was writing toward the end of his life, when his and the other apostles' ministry was coming to an end. COMMENTARY ON JUDE.[2]

18 Scoffers at the End of Time

FOLLOWING UNGODLY PASSIONS. ANDREAS: Jude got this from Peter's second letter, where he talks about Paul's writings,[3] for Paul has a lot to say about this. CATENA.[4]

19 Worldly People Devoid of the Spirit

DIVISIONS AMONG BELIEVERS. CLEMENT OF ALEXANDRIA: These are people who separate believers from one another, under the influence of their own unbelief. They cannot distinguish between holy things on the one hand and dogs on the other. ADUMBRATIONS.[5]

DEVOID OF THE SPIRIT. AUGUSTINE: The enemy of unity has no share in God's love. Those who are outside the church do not have the Holy Spirit, and this verse is written of them. LETTERS 185.50.[6]

---

[1]PL Supp. 3:131. [2]PG 119:720. [3]2 Pet 3:15-16. [4]CEC 168. [5]FGNK 3:85. [6]FC 30:189.

DIVIDING EVEN CHRIST HIMSELF. CYRIL OF ALEXANDRIA: The Nestorians are sensual men, not having the Spirit, because they divide the one Christ and Son and Lord into two sons. . . . For they pretend to confess one Christ and Son and say that his person is one, but by dividing him into two separate *hypostases* they completely sweep away the doctrine of the mystery. LETTERS 50.20.[7]

THIEVERY. OECUMENIUS: Here we see yet another crime which these awful heretics have committed. Not only are they perishing themselves; they have raided the church and taken people away from it, which means that they have taken them outside the faith into their own assemblies, which are dens of thieves. Such people behave as if they were animals, living according to the pattern of the world and the demands of their instincts. COMMENTARY ON JUDE.[8]

20 Build Yourselves Up in Faith

PRAY IN THE SPIRIT. BEDE: We pray in the Holy Spirit when we are moved by divine inspiration to ask for heavenly help, so that we may receive the good things which we cannot obtain on our own. ON JUDE.[9]

BUILD YOURSELVES UP. OECUMENIUS: Jude says that his beloved people must continue to build themselves up in their most holy faith, forever reforming themselves according to the Holy Spirit's guidance; in other words, by building congregations up, by their preaching, in the teaching of the Holy Spirit. COMMENTARY ON JUDE.[10]

21 Keep Yourselves in the Love of God

WAIT FOR MERCY. OECUMENIUS: Jude tells his people to look after themselves in the mercy which they have received from God in preparation for the last judgment. COMMENTARY ON JUDE.[11]

22 Convince the Doubters

DOUBTING. ANDREAS: Jude is recommending mercy for those who doubt the truth of the words of false teaching. As for other kinds of doubters, James condemns them in his letter.[12] CATENA.[13]

23 The Garment Spotted

THE SPOTTED TUNIC. CLEMENT OF ALEXANDRIA: The spotted tunic of the soul is a spirit which has been corrupted by worldly lusts. ADUMBRATIONS.[14]

THE GARMENT STAINED AND CLEANED. MAXIMUS THE CONFESSOR: What is meant by "a cloak stained by corrupted flesh"? This is said of those who have a life stained by the lusts of the flesh. We all have clothes which bear the marks of our life, whether we are righteous or not. The person who has a clean cloak is one who leads a pure life, whereas the one who has a soiled one has got mixed up with evil deeds. Or a cloak may be soiled by the flesh if the latter is formed in its conscience by the memory of those evil deeds which spring from the flesh and which still work on the soul. Just as the Spirit can make a cloak for the soul out of the virtues which come from the principle of incorruptibility, so

---

[7]FC 76:222. [8]PG 119:720. [9]PL 93:129. [10]PG 119:721. [11]PG 119:721. [12]Jas 1:6. [13]CEC 168-69. [14]FGNK 3:85.

by analogy the flesh can produce an unclean and soiled cloak from the lusts which belong to it. Catena.[15]

Save Some. Andreas: If someone can use the word of God to rescue those who have already fallen into the all-embracing fire set alight by the flaming arrows of the devil, he will snatch the most promising ones from the fire. For this person is not called to snatch back those who have been condemned by God. Catena.[16]

The Stained Cloak. Bede: The stained cloak is our flesh. However, we are not called to hate our own flesh as such but only the fact that it has been stained by sin, and we are called to work for its cleansing, so that what is carnal may become spiritual. However, this cannot be done in our own strength but only by the power of God, as Jude goes on to say in his closing blessing. On Jude.[17]

---

[15]CEC 169. [16]CEC 169. [17]PL 93:130.

24-25 FAREWELL BLESSING

24Now to him who is able to keep you from falling and to present you without blemish before the presence of his glory with rejoicing, 25to the only God, our Savior through Jesus Christ our Lord, be glory, majesty, dominion, and authority, before all time and now and for ever. Amen.

Overview: Jude's farewell strikes a note of triumph by reminding the hard-pressed believers that God is still on the throne and that his glory, power and majesty will be fully revealed at the right time. For Christians the most important thing is to be ready to enter into his presence without blemish, so that we may join the heavenly chorus of praise to his eternal power and dominion. Being in the presence of God's glory does not mean that we shall see him in the physical sense, since that is impossible. Rather it means that everything we do will be seen by him (Clement of Alexandria). Praise is given to God alone, for he is the only one who deserves our worship (Hilary of Arles). The Son does not have a beginning at some point in time but has been there from all ages, is there now and will be there forever (Bede).

24 Without Blemish in God's Presence

The Presence of His Glory. Clement of Alexandria: Being in the presence of God's glory does not mean that we shall see him in the physical sense, since that is impossible. Rather it means that everything we do will be seen by him. Adumbrations.[1]

---

[1]FGNK 3:85-86.

PERSEVERANCE. AUGUSTINE: When Jude says this, does he not show that perseverance in good to the end is a gift of God? ADMONITION AND GRACE 6.10.[2]

ABLE TO KEEP YOU FROM FALLING. BEDE: Jude is right to say this because the more careful we are in what we do here on earth, the more fully we shall rejoice in the blessing which we shall receive in the future. ON JUDE.[3]

25 Glory, Majesty, Dominion and Authority

TO THE ONLY GOD. HILARY OF ARLES: Praise is given to God alone, for he is the only one who deserves our worship. He is our Savior, because "he has saved his people from their sins."[4] Glory is ascribed to him because he is the victor in every battle; majesty, because the praise of the heavenly virtues is so great;

dominion, because he rules over all he has made; and authority, because he has the power to destroy or to set free everything in creation. He exists from the beginning, in the present and forever. INTRODUCTORY COMMENTARY ON JUDE.[5]

TO OUR SAVIOR. BEDE: This verse gives equal glory to the Father and the Son in all things and for all time and eternity. By saying that glory, majesty, dominion and power should be attributed to God the Father through our Lord Jesus Christ, Jude is refuting those who believe that the Son is inferior to the Father. As he goes on to say in conclusion, the Son does not have his beginning at some point in time but has been there from all ages, is there now and will be there forever. Amen. ON JUDE.[6]

---

[2]FC 2:257. [3]PL 93:130. [4]Mt 1:21. [5]PL Supp. 3:131. [6]PL 93:130.

Early Christian Writers and the Documents Cited

The following table lists all the early Christian documents cited in this volume by author. Where available, Cetedoc and TLG digital references are listed.

Ambrose

"Letters to Laymen" (*Epistulae*)	Cetedoc 0160
"Letters to Priests" (*Epistulae*)	Cetedoc 0160
"On Jacob and the Happy Life" (*De Jacob et vita beata*)	Cetedoc 0130
"On Joseph" (*De Joseph patriarcha*)	Cetedoc 0131
"The Prayer of Job and David" (*De interpellatione Job et David*)	Cetedoc 0134
"Synod Letters" (*Epistulae*)	Cetedoc 0160

Ammonius

"Catena"

Andreas

"Catena"

Apollinarius

"Catena"

Athanasius

"Festal Letters" (*Epistulae festales*)	TLG 2035.014

Augustine

"Admonition and Grace" (*De corruptione et gratia*)	Cetedoc 0353
"Adulterous Marriages" (*De adulterinis coniugiis*)	Cetedoc 0302
"Against Julian" (*Contra Julianum*)	Cetedoc 0351
"Against Lying" (*Contra mendacium*)	Cetedoc 0304
"The City of God" (*De civitate Dei*)	Cetedoc 0313
"Commentary on the Sermon on the Mount" (*De sermone Domini in monte*)	Cetedoc 0274
"Confessions" (*Confessionum libri tredecim*)	Cetedoc 0251

"Eight Questions of Dulcitius" (*De octo Dulcitii quaestionibus*)	Cetedoc 0291
"Holy Virginity" (*De sancta virginitate*)	Cetedoc 0300
"Letters" (*Epistulae*)	Cetedoc 0262
"On Christian Doctrine" (*De doctrina christiana*)	Cetedoc 0263
"On Continence" (*De continentia*)	Cetedoc 0298
"On Faith and Works" (*De fide et operibus*)	Cetedoc 0294
"On Grace and Free Will" (*De gratia et libero arbitrio*)	Cetedoc 0352
"On Nature and Grace" (*De natura et gratia*)	Cetedoc 0344
"On Patience" (*De patientia*)	Cetedoc 0308
"On the Christian Life" (*De disciplina christiana*)	Cetedoc 0310
"On the Gift of Perseverance" (*De dono perseverantiae*)	Cetedoc 0355
"On the Good of Marriage" (*De bono coniugali*)	Cetedoc 0299
"On the Predestination of the Saints" (*De praedestinatione sanctorum*)	Cetedoc 0354
"On the Spirit and Letter" (*De spiritu et littera*)	Cetedoc 0343
"On the Trinity" (*De Trinitate*)	Cetedoc 0329
"Retractations" (*Retractionum libri duo*)	Cetedoc 0250
"Sermons" (*Sermones*)	Cetedoc 0284
"Ten Homilies on 1 John" (*In Johannis epistulam ad Parthos tractatus*)	Cetedoc 0279
"Tractates on the Gospel of John" (*In Johannis evangelium tractatus*)	Cetedoc 0278

Basil of the Great of Caesarea

"Ascetical Discourses" (*Prologus 5 [sermo asceticus]*)	TLG 2040.046
"On Baptism" (*De baptismo*)	TLG 2040.052
"On Renunciation of the World" (*Sermo 11 [sermo asceticus et exhortatio*	
de renuntiatione mundi])	TLG 2040.041
"On the Judgment of God" (*Prologus 7 [de judicio dei]*)	TLG 2040.043
"Sermons"	
10 "Against Those Who Are Prone to Anger" (*Homilia adversus eos qui irascuntur*)	TLG 2040.026
13 "A Psalm of David at the Finishing of the Tabernacle"	
(*In Psalmum 28*)	TLG 2040.053

Bede

"Concerning the Epistle of St. James" (*In epistulas septem catholicas*)	Cetedoc 1362
"Homilies on the Gospels" (*Homiliarum evangelii libri ii*)	Cetedoc 1367
"On Acts" (*Expositio actuum apostolorum*)	Cetedoc 1357
"On 1 John" (*In epistulas septem catholicas*)	Cetedoc 1362
"On 2 John" (*In epistulas septem catholicas*)	Cetedoc 1362
"On 3 John" (*In epistulas septem catholicas*)	Cetedoc 1362
"On Jude" (*In epistulas septem catholicas*)	Cetedoc 1362
"On 1 Peter" (*In epistulas septem catholicas*)	Cetedoc 1362
"On 2 Peter" (*In epistulas septem catholicas*)	Cetedoc 1362

"On the Tabernacle and Its Vessels" (*De tabernaculo et vasis eius ac vestibus sacerdotum librii iii*)   Cetedoc 1345

Braulio of Saragossa
"Letters" (*Epistulae 15*)

Caesarius of Arles
"Sermons" (*Sermones ex integro a Caesario compositi vel ex aliis frontibus hausti*)   Cetedoc 1008

Cassiodorus
"Summary of James" (*Complexiones in epistulas apostolorum, actus apostolorum et apocalypsim Johannis*)   Cetedoc 0903
"Summary of 1 Peter" (*Complexiones in epistulas apostolorum, actus apostolorum et apocalypsim Johannis*)   Cetedoc 0903

Clement of Alexandria
"Adumbrations" (*Adumbrationes*)
"The Teacher" (*Paedagogus*)   TLG 0555.002
"Stromateis" (*Stromata*)   TLG 0555.004

Clement of Rome
"Letter to the Corinthians" (*Epistula i ad Corinthios*)   TLG 1271.001

Cyprian
"On the Unity of the Catholic Church" (*De catholicae ecclesiae unitate*)   Cetedoc 0041
"Letters"
   "To Pompey"
   "To Magnus"
"The Lord's Prayer" (*De dominica oratione*)   Cetedoc 0043
"Works and Almsgiving" (*De opere et eleemosynis*)   Cetedoc 0047

Cyril of Alexandria
"Catena"
"Sermons" (*Homiliae ad Successum episcopum Diocaesareae*)   TLG 4090.x50
"Letters"
   1 (*Ad monachos Aegypti*)   TLG 4090.x01
   39 (*Ad Joannem Antiochenum*)   TLG 4090.x33
   40 (*Ad Acacium Melitenum*)   TLG 4090.x34
   50 (*Ad Valerianum episcopum Iconii*)   TLG 4090.x31
   55 (*Ad Anastasium, Alexandrum, Martinianum, Joannem, Paregorium presbyteros et Maximum diaconum ceterosque monachos orientales*)   TLG 4090.x40

Cyril of Jerusalem
"Catechetical Lectures" (*Catecheses ad illuminandos*)   TLG 2110.003
"Sermon on the Paralytic" (*Homilia in paralyticum juxta piscinam jacentem*)   TLG 2110.006

Didache
"Didache" (*Didache*)   TLG 1311.001

Didymus the Blind
"Catena"
"Commentary on James" (*In epistulas catholicas brevis enarratio*)   TLG 2102.030
"Commentary on Jude" (*In epistulas catholicas brevis enarratio*)   TLG 2102.030
"Commentary on 1 John" (*In epistulas catholicas brevis enarratio*)   TLG 2102.030
"Commentary on 2 John" (*In epistulas catholicas brevis enarratio*)   TLG 2102.030
"Commentary on 1 Peter" (*In epistulas catholicas brevis enarratio*)   TLG 2102.030
"Commentary on 2 Peter" (*In epistulas catholicas brevis enarratio*)   TLG 2102.030

Dionysius
"Catena"

Eucherius of Lyons
"Exhortation to His Kinsman Valerian"

Eusebius of Caesarea
"Catena"
"History of the Church" (*Historia ecclesiastica*)   TLG 2018.002

Fastidius
"On the Christian Life" (*De vita christiana*)

Gregory of Nazianzus
"Theological Orations" (*De filio [orat. 30]*)   TLG 2022.018

Gregory of Nyssa
"On Virginity" (*De virginitate*)   TLG 2017.043

Gregory the Great
"Sermons on Ezekiel" (*Homiliae in Hiezechihelem prophetam*)   Cetedoc 1710
"Commentary on 2 Peter" (*Expositio super epistolam ii b. Petri apostoli*)
"Homilies on the Gospels" (*Homiliarum xl in evangelia libri duo*)   Cetedoc 1711
"Lessons in Job" (*Moralia in Job*)   Cetedoc 1708

Hermas
"Shepherd" *(Pastor)*   TLG 1419.001

Hesychius
"Catena"

Hilary of Arles
"Introductory Commentary on 1 John" *(Tractatus in septem epistulas catholicas)*   Cetedoc 0508
"Introductory Commentary on 2 John" *(Tractatus in septem epistulas catholicas)*   Cetedoc 0508
"Introductory Commentary on 3 John" *(Tractatus in septem epistulas catholicas)*   Cetedoc 0508
"Introductory Commentary on Jude" *(Tractatus in septem epistulas catholicas)*   Cetedoc 0508
"Introductory Commentary on 1 Peter" *(Tractatus in septem epistulas catholicas)*   Cetedoc 0508
"Introductory Commentary on 2 Peter" *(Tractatus in septem epistulas catholicas)*   Cetedoc 0508
"Introductory Tractate on the Letter of James" *(Tractatus in septem epistulas catholicas)*   Cetedoc 0508

Hilary of Poitiers
"On the Trinity" *(De Trinitate)*   Cetedoc 0433

Irenaeus
"Against Heresies" *(Adversus haereses libri 1-2)*   TLG 1447.001
    (Adversus haereses liber 3)   TLG 1447.002
    (Adversus haereses liber 5)   TLG 1447.008

Isaac the Syrian
"Ascetical Homilies"

Isho'dad of Merv
"Commentaries"

Jerome
"Against the Pelagians" *(Contra Pelagianos)*   Cetedoc 0615
"Letters" *(Epistulae)*   Cetedoc 0620
"Sermons"
    15 "On Psalm 82 (83)"
    41 "On Psalm 119 (120)"
    86 "The Rich Man and Lazarus"
    91 "On the Exodus: The Vigil of Easter"

John Cassian
"Conferences" *(Collationes)*   Cetedoc 0512

John Chrysostom
"Catena"
"Commentary on John" (*In Joannem*) TLG 2062.153
"On the Incomprehensible Nature of God" (*De incomprehensibili dei natura*) TLG 2062.012
"Sermons on Genesis" (*In Genesim*) TLG 2062.112

John of Damascus
"Barlaam and Iosaph" (*Vita Barlaam et Joasaph*) TLG 2934.066

Josephus
"Jewish Antiquities" (*Antiquitates Judaicae*) TLG 0526.001

Leander of Seville
"The Training of Nuns"

Leo the Great
"Letters"
"Sermons" (*Tractatus septem et nonaginta*) Cetedoc 1657

Macarius of Egypt
"First Syriac Epistle"

Maximus of Turin
"Sermons" (*Homiliae*) Cetedoc 0219a

Maximus the Confessor
"Catena"

Niceta of Remesiana
"Explanation of the Creed"
"The Power of the Holy Spirit"

Novatian
"On the Trinity" (*De Trinitate*) Cetedoc 0071

Oecumenius
"Commentary on James"
"Commentary on 1 John"
"Commentary on 2 John"
"Commentary on 3 John"
"Commentary on Jude"

"Commentary on 1 Peter"
"Commentary on 2 Peter"

Origen
"Against Celsus" (*Contra Celsum*)   TLG 2042.001
"Commentary on John" (*Commentarii in evangelium Joannis [lib. 1, 2, 4, 5, 6, 10, 13]*)   TLG 2042.005
    (*Commentarii in evangelium Joannis [lib. 19, 20, 28, 32]*)   TLG 2042.079
"Exhortation to Martyrdom" (*Exhortatio ad martyrium*)   TLG 2042.007
"Homily 27 on Numbers"
"On First Principles" (*De principiis*)   TLG 2042.002
"Sermons on Exodus" (*Homiliae in Exodum*)   TLG 2042.023
"Sermons on Genesis" (*Homiliae in Genesim*)   TLG 2042.022
"Sermons on Leviticus" (*Homiliae in Leviticum*)   TLG 2042.024

Pachomius
"Book of Our Father Horsiesios"
"Communion"

Paschasius of Dumium
"Questions and Answers of the Greek Fathers"

Peter Chrysologus
"Sermons" (*Homiliae*)   Cetedoc 0227

Polycarp of Smyrna
"Letter to the Philippians" (*Epistula ad Philippenses*)   TLG 1622.001

Prudentius
"Hymns" (*Liber Cathemerinon*)   Cetedoc 1438

Pseudo-Dionysius
"Letters" (*Ad Gaium monachum*)   TLG 2798.006
"On the Celestial Hierarchy" (*De caelesti hierarchia*)   TLG 2798.001
"On the Divine Names" (*De divinis nominibus*)   TLG 2798.004
"On the Ecclesiastical Hierarchy" (*De ecclesiastica hierarchia*)   TLG 2798.002

Salvian the Presbyter
"On the Governance of God" (*De gubernationes Dei*)   Cetedoc 0485

Severian of Gabala
"Catena"

Severus of Antioch
"Catena"

Sulpicius Severus
"Letter to Eusebius"

Symeon the New Theologian
"Discourses"

Tertullian

"Apology" (*Apologeticum*)	Cetedoc 0003
"On the Soul" (*De anima*)	Cetedoc 0017
"On the Crown" (*De corona militis*)	Cetedoc 0021
"On Prayer" (*De oratione*)	Cetedoc 0007
"On Flight in Time of Persecution" (*De fuga in persecutione*)	Cetedoc 0025
"On the Dress of Women" (*De cultu feminarum*)	Cetedoc 0011
"Prescriptions Against Heretics" (*De praescriptione haereticorum*)	Cetedoc 0005

Theodoret of Cyr

"Catena"	
"On Divine Providence" (*De providentia orationes decem*)	TLG 4089.032

Theophylact
"Commentary on James"
"Commentary on 1 John"
"Commentary on 2 John"
"Commentary on Jude"
"Commentary on 1 Peter"
"Commentary on 2 Peter"

Valerian of Cimiez
"Sermons"

See the volume *Commentary Index and Resources* for a collection of supplemental ACCS material, including a comprehensive Scripture index and authors/writings index.

Subject Index

Abel, 201
Abraham, 31-33, 221, 241
Adam, 253
adoption, 78, 195, 216
adultery, 25
adversity, 9
afflictions, 6, 110, 118-19. *See also* suffering
almsgiving, 203
ambition, 42-43
Ammonius of Alexandria, xxvi
Andreas, xxvii
angels, 75
    cast into hell, 146
    evil spirits, 149
    fallen, 248, 251
    guardian, 149
    hierarchy, 110
    judgment of, 147, 251
    sin of, 146
anger, 17-20
anointing, 60, 188, 191
Anthony's vision, 252
antichrist, xxii, 189, 210, 211, 236
antichrists, 186-88, 211
apostles, 256
apostleship, 2, 3
apostolic doctrine, 190, 236
Arians, xxii, 237
Arius, 248, 252
arrogance, 50. *See also* pride
assurance, 206, 216-18
atheist, 236
atonement, 96
Augustine, xxvii
authorities, 94
authority, 242
Babylon, 126-27
Balaam, 140-41, 150-51, 253
baptism, 145, 188, 211, 223-34
    of Christ, 223
    consecrated by blood, 223
    grace of, 130
    in name of Trinity, 206
    and redemption, 81
    salvation and, 109
    and Satan, 52

sin after, 228
    unity through, 238
Bede, xxviii
Belial, 243
bishop, 121, 231-32
blessings, 72, 259
blood, 223
boasting, 40, 52. *See also* pride
body, 28-29, 138, 159
born again, 223, 228. *See also* regeneration
born of God, 200
brotherhood, 203
Cain, 201
catena, xxvi-xxviii
Catholic Epistles, xviii, xx-xxiii, xxv
Cerinthus, 233
charity, 85, 134
children of God, 83
children of light, 16
chosen race, 88
Christian life
    Christ-bearers, 132
    conduct of, 91, 105
    dignity as body of Christ, 133
    freedom, 93-94
    heavenly and earthly delights, 91
    a holy people, 88
    obedience, 212
    perfection, 78
    perseverance in, 112
    in perspective, 52
    process of maturity, 133, 240
    respecting earthly authorities, 92-93
    returning good for evil, 102
    self-centered, 134
    self-control, 133-34
    and simple faith, 134
    suffering, 118-19, 125
    world, not of the, 88
Christianity, 48
church
    accusations in the, 242
    born of blood and water, 223
    catholic, 232
    external signs of, 206
    house of God, 85
    unity of, 91, 109-10
    universal, 85
church discipline, 237
circumcision, 88
citizenship, 93-94
Clement of Alexandria, xxv-xxvi
commandment, 179-80, 229, 234

commandments, 29, 178, 218, 222, 244
comparison, 45
compassion, 29, 203
conceit, 48
confession, 49, 210, 215
confidence, 205
conscience, 105, 204-5
conversion, 91, 216
correction, 62
creation, 157-60
cross, 95
darkness, 170, 180-82
day of judgment, 148-49, 158, 216. *See also* day of the Lord; judgment; last judgment
day of the Lord, 159. *See also* day of judgment; judgment; last judgment
day of visitation, 92
dead, the, 112-14
death, 202-3, 253-54
Demetrius, 240, 243
desire, 12, 45, 90-91, 184. *See also* passion; lust
destruction, 157
devil
    and hatred, 215
    in Job, 124-25
    judgment of, 146
    prince of darkness, 170
    and sin, 198-201
    traps of, 152
devils, 251
Didymus the Blind, xxvi-xxvii
Diotrephes, 240, 242, 244
discrimination, 22-24
disobedience, 86-87
divinity, 214
division, 237, 244, 256
doctrine, 84, 91, 229
Donatists, 178
double-mindedness, 49
doubt, 8, 257
dualism, 228, 252
elders, 121
elect, 80, 109, 150
elect lady, 231
election, 85-86, 135, 246
Elymas, 242
end of time, 115, 160, 187
endurance, 71. *See also* perseverance
enemies, 180
Enoch, 248, 254-55
envy, 47

tongue
- control of, 19-20, 37-41, 102
- discipline of the, 17
- a fire, 39
- a great evil, 40
- power of, 35, 40
- and Satan, 102
- sins of, 38-39
- worthy speech, 37

tongues, 206

transfiguration, 140

trees, 253

trials
- and joy, 6
- overcoming of, 10
- and patience, 6-7
- refinement through, 71
- unwanted, 6
- *See also* afflictions; suffering

Trinity, 189-90, 211, 235-36, 251
- name of, 206
- relationship of, 216

truth, 234, 240
- hearing the, 17
- knowledge of, 189, 221
- and light, 170
- practice of the, 17

way of, 145

unbelief, 250

unbelievers, 238

ungodly, 255

unity, 22, 85
- of church, 91
- in doctrine, 87
- enemy of, 256
- and fellowship, 168
- in heart and mind, 102
- through love, 93
- of one mind, 215
- spiritual, 101

Valentinians, 250

Valentinus, 189

victory, 222

virtue, 11, 46, 135, 136

wages, 55

water, 223

weak, 22

wealth, 9-10, 21-22, 54. *See also* money; rich; riches; wealthy

wealthy, 54

wickedness, 18, 184

widows, 20

wisdom, 42-43, 98
- and faith, 8

from God, 161-62

God's gift of, 7

right use of, 47

source of, 7

spiritual, 7

and temptation, 7

witness, 112, 168, 215, 223-24

wives, 94, 99-100

women, 98-99

Word, 18-19, 81, 167. *See also* Jesus Christ

works. *See* faith, and works

world, 194
- end of, 184-85
- friend of the, 47
- against godliness, 202
- identification of, 20
- overcoming of, 222
- rejects Christians, 211-12
- renunciation of, 183-85
- right use of, 184
- speaks against love, 211
- subjected to evil, 228

worldliness, 77, 254

zeal, 62

Zion, 31